The Failure of Elites

*A joint study of the
Center for International Studies,
Massachusetts Institute of Technology,
and the
Centro de Estudios del Desarrollo,
Universidad Central de Venezuela*

The Failure of Elites

Frank Bonilla

THE MIT PRESS
Cambridge, Massachusetts, and London, England

For Tamara

CONTENTS

LIST OF FIGURES

LIST OF TABLES

Foreword

During the life of this research, the most fundamental propositions that support work of this kind — moral, scientific, technical, and ideological — have been justifiably brought profoundly into question. A principal impulse behind this crisis of conscience in the field of social research has been the evidence accumulated over recent years of a substantial appropriation by the United States defense and intelligence establishments of the institutions, personnel, and methods of the social sciences. Coming as it does at a time when few at home or abroad find evidence of increased wisdom or humaneness in the operations of these agencies, the growing awareness of the dimensions and possible significance of this fusion of imperfect knowledge and great power continues to provoke apprehension and dismay. This is all the more so since practically all of the research in question about which information exists is explicitly aimed at closing off particular lines of action and social experimentation to young nations whose future now hangs in the balance.

It will take social science and the institutions and individuals involved a long time to assess the consequences of the complex relationships with certain areas of government into which a part of the academic community drifted in the last two decades. Many presumed gains of that association will prove to have been hollow; others will collapse under the wave of reaction already affecting the field. Among the more visible outcomes has been a serious spoiling of the research environment in many countries, not only for U.S. scholars but for all who continue to look to social science methods as a partial guide to informed collective decisions on human problems.

The present series of studies set out to test the limits of the possible usefulness of social science approaches to the elucidation of such problems in a country gripped in political struggle and with widely divergent groups in contention. It therefore stands perhaps as a unique instance of research on a national political system actually executed on a scale that makes real many of the hypothetical dangers associated with research of this kind. The study group was from the start deeply conscious of the considerable risks and heavy responsibilities involved in an enterprise bringing together such diverse actors for the performance of such a sensitive task. The research itself has further heightened our awareness of the difficulties involved. Some of the affirmations concerning the building of institutions for the production and dissemination of social knowledge that are sprinkled throughout the first volume now seem ingenuously optimistic. Contrary to our expectations, the years since then have seen a progressive cutting back by leadership of the aggressively articulated development and social reform goals of the 1950s and early 60s. With this cutback has gone a hardening of resistance at the top, both internationally and within nations, to the multiple pressures urging more decisive action in behalf of the presently disadvantaged. This context of hardening conflict provides the essential background to the further demoralization over this period of intellectual institutions and the propagation of profound self-doubts and feelings of impotence among social scientists.

No single piece of work or institution can begin to turn the tide of a process that seems so profoundly rooted and widespread. Many of the ideas stated early in the research concerning the systematic feedback of research-produced knowledge into the political process as a way of giving realistic content and vitality to political activity seem less practicable today than seven years ago. But these difficulties and the sacrificed potential that lies behind them might not have been perceived without the extended probing into Venezuelan political reality encompassed by these three volumes. The group has neither found nor created very favorable conditions for the generation and sharing of social knowledge in Venezuela. Still it has opened up an extraordinary range of new information, lines of inquiry, and possible modes of action.

It needs to be fairly said here again that this project represents a highly productive collaboration among individuals and institutions. It is also a collaboration that has fallen short of its most ambitious objectives. Study shortcomings do not lie in carelessness about the possible misuse of these results by hidden actors but in the inadequacy of the steps taken to bring these results before a large Venezuelan public in a timely and usable form. Research performed on this scale and with this degree of communication to the diverse publics concerned — scholars, students, politicians, planners, citizens of every persuasion and condition. Social scientists have only begun to perceive and tentatively test fresh approaches to these needs.

Acknowledgments

The essential team nature of this research has been emphasized in the introduction to Volume I. The extensive acknowledgment of institutional and individual contributions made there is fully applicable to the present work. In addition brief mention is gratefully made here of those persons who contributed most directly to the VENELITE study in its several phases.

The elite informants themselves stand most properly at the head of such a list. Their identities have not been individually recorded in this volume, but such a roster, without indication of the interview number, is available at CENDES.

During the first two years of work, covering the period of interviewing and the elaboration of codes for the biographies and extensive interview texts, Julio Cotler was a constant and generous collaborator. Gabriela Bronfenmajer, Ramón Pugh, and Graciela Sosa were the principal research assistants during that time. The interviewing team, in addition to all of the above, included Betzaida Balbas, Hildebrando Barrios, Dulce Arnao Machado, Elvia Nuñez, Betty Nussenbaum, Lucia Pinedo, Julieta Pardo de Rodriguez, Elsa Romero, and Elsa Torres. Paula Lawton Bevington and Tamara Z. Bonilla interviewed American businessmen active in Venezuela. The difficult interview text-coding operation was carried out by Mrs. Bronfenmajer along with Karen Stenbo Sapolsky, Lisa Hinaker, Mary Louise Nunes, Laura Solomon, and Celia Silva. Philip Raup, Jr., Nancy Smith Naro, and Margherita Ciacci helped importantly with the preparation of data for several chapters. Stuart McIntosh, David Griffel, and Allen Kessler gave irreplaceable and patient counsel with respect to computer solutions for difficult data manipulations. Peter Bos, Robert Wallace, and Jeremy Pool all contributed to the design and implementation of the list-processing approach to the interview texts. A Spanish version for simultaneous publication of this volume in Caracas has been prepared with the aid of Marilu Mehler, Ilda Moreyra Basso, Ruth Hurtado, and Ludovico Silva. Throughout a great part of this period, Rosa Peña acted as secretary and quiet factotum helping in the coordination of these and many other activities. Martha Gillmor quixotically accepted major responsibility for the editorial supervision of all three volumes. Daniel Lerner gave an especially attentive and encouraging reading to this manuscript.

Throughout this time unfailing support was provided by the administrative staff of the Center for International Studies.

The companionship and intellectual stimulation of the several years of joint effort with José A. Silva Michelena constitute a uniquely rewarding feature of this experience. During his year in Cambridge and thereafter, the opportunity to accompany at close range the work of Carlos Domingo has been similarly enriching. My various sojourns in the CENDES community and the association with its directors during this time, the late Jorge Ahumada and Luis Lander, are valued spaces in my professional life. To Jorge goes my gratitude for convincing me that it was all worthwhile and perhaps possible in the first place.

                                                              FRANK BONILLA

Belo Horizonte, Brazil
July 1970

The Failure of Elites

1 THE DIAGNOSTIC STUDY OF ELITES

In Volume 1 of this series mention was made of the gradual crystallization in the course of this research of a "diagnostic" approach or generalized scheme for analyzing political systems. The diagnostic features derived primarily from an essay by Jorge Ahumada outlining a set of hypotheses for exploring social change in Venezuela.[1] In the ensuing years there has been a progressive elaboration of ideas contained in that essay. In this enterprise not the smallest of dangers was the possibility of foundering indefinitely in the sea of empirical materials collected. The richness of the diagnostic approach as a steadying point of theoretical reference in these circumstances became increasingly evident. When a group works together as intensively as have those involved in these studies, and the time between initial formulation of research design and the drafting of research reports extends over such a long period, the difficulties of unraveling the process of the accretion of ideas and their sources become practically insurmountable. However, the passage of time brings fresh insight and awareness of the significance of early choices. For these reasons it seems of some importance to recapitulate here several of the ideas with which the research began and to suggest both the ways in which they lent themselves to later elaboration and the general direction in which that elaboration moved.

Apart from the closely reasoned synthesis of recent economic, political, and sociocultural change in Venezuela, the most decisive element of that early diagnosis was the primacy assigned to what Ahumada designated as

---

[1] Volume 1 of *Politics of Change in Venezuela*, Frank Bonilla and José A. Silva Michelena, eds., *A Strategy for Research on Social Policy* (Cambridge, Mass.: The M.I.T. Press, 1967), pp. 3–23, also p. 36. The original diagnosis was a collective product by Ahumada and Messrs. Julio Cotler, Luis Lander, and José A. Silva Michelena. Hereafter, Volume 1 will be referred to as *SRSP*.

3

"the evaluative function." In this view, evaluation — the formulation of judgments concerning a variety of aspects of the society and their significance for the evaluating individuals and groups — is a continuous, primary activity. Without positing this, it is impossible to conceive any meaning for a term like consensus. The most obvious feature of such evaluations in any but the simplest of societies is the variety, selectivity, and particularity they manifest when examined with reference to individuals or population subsets with different social locations and different experiences of change. In this sense one can only hope to find *degrees* of consensus in a society undergoing change. A first source of such variation in evaluations emphasized in the opening diagnosis was sociocultural dualism (defined as the coexistence of traditional and modern structures and/or the functioning of modern organizations according to traditional norms). As the diversity of evaluative configurations came to the surface in early explorations, this soon came to be treated as sociocultural heterogeneity.

A second dimension that was expected to affect evaluative styles and "efficiency" was power, taken here to mean political capacity in a broad sense. Ahumada hypothesized impediments to rational evaluation at the very top of the power pyramid (defensive rationalization) and at the very bottom (low information and stereotyped thinking). The most efficient evaluators would thus be found among those very close to, but just short of, the top positions. Evaluations in this scheme are affected not only by the relative power position of the evaluator but by the nature of the general distribution of power, an effect especially intense under conditions of power dispersion with dissociation (compartmentalization) and low issue consensus. All of these conditions were significantly present in the Venezuelan case according to the diagnosis. The theoretical substructure of the diagnosis thus rested primarily on ideas about evaluations, political capacity, and social change. Ahumada sought a framework in which the complex array of meanings attributed by diverse social groups to their situation within a given sociopolitical structure could be linked to capacities for action in order to test the feasibility of desired social changes. Social innovation was expected to flow from shifts in evaluative orientations backed by politically effective force.

The first research proposals flowing from the diagnosis (authored by Arthur Vidich) further specified and clarified these basic orientations.[2]

[2] See CENDES, Universidad Central de Venezuela, "Subproject A: On Leadership and Power Relationships in Venezuela," and "Subproject B: A Study of Class Dynamics," both dated June 1962.

They sought explicitly to link the facts of psychocultural heterogeneity to class and especially to variants in the concrete experience of mobility. By emphasizing the multiplicity of social perspectives and real life situations of individuals of very similar social origins and conditions, Vidich called attention to the idiosyncratic and the unexpected in political commitments and antagonisms, rejecting simple associations between class positions or interests and political behavior. This focus on the particularity of individual and group experiences brought clearly into the picture the history of interaction among individuals and groups as a significant factor in judging the political consequences of diversity or congruence in group evaluations. Vidich also insisted on maintaining perspective on the thrust of the total system under study, on the nation's capacity to guide and adjust to change. Though there were many explicit and implicit hypotheses concerning the multiple factors in play, the study's aims were not articulated in terms of tracing the relationships among a handful of variables. The concern was with indicators of total system political states and capabilities.

> Depending then on the issue up for consideration, alternative policy proposals or the direction of movement of the society due to uncontrollable factors, we could hope to be able to state the potential responses of different leaders and the probable constellations of alliances which might be formed.[3]

This tension between macrostates and especially macro*guidance* and self-steering capabilities as against detailed attention to the experiential and interactional sources of political orientations was to dominate the entire research endeavor.

A final research paper completed just before the field work began in earnest in mid-1963 sought to pull together these several strands into an operational working design for the study of elites.[4] In addition to the considerations already stated, this document sought to make six basic points:

1. An effort was made to trace historically the principal transitions in political leadership from the time of Independence and to establish the historical roots of certain features of elite behavior and particularly political styles.[5]

---

[3] Ibid., "Subproject A," p. 7.
[4] Frank Bonilla and Julio Cotler, "Los hombres de poder en Venezuela: Un plan de estudio," mimeo (CENDES, Universidad Central de Venezuela, July 1963). Some of the commentary here is also repeated in the Introduction to *SRSP*.
[5] The primary initial effort in this respect was carried out by Julio Cotler. Chapter 2 in this volume is a much extended version of that first historical synthesis.

2. Given the diagnosis that power at its highest reaches in Venezuela was diffuse, precariously held, compartmentalized, and in conflicting concentrations, it was affirmed (as it was by Vidich earlier) that there was not much to be gained by appealing to theories linking power or elitehood directly to class or interests. The possibility of the existence of a coherent, tightly knit ruling clique, elite, oligarchy, or class was not entirely discounted; but the way was opened for a more complex and detailed view of the actual relations between power and group or class interests in Venezuela. There was as much concern with the apparent fluidity, dispersion, and difficulty of coordinating leadership and command as with rigidities and inequalities of power.

3. The principal dimensions of intraelite differentiation were thus, in line with the diagnosis, not class but institutional area (main sphere of action) and power (the rationalizers of the status quo at the very top and the more efficient evaluators just below).

4. In view of points 2 and 3, the research task was not so much to devise a means of observing a well-structured, entrenched power group but to discover how men new to power and influence, new to concerns of national policy, working through emergent institutions and organizations, guided by newly evolving canons of leadership and collective responsibility, could be expected to perform the task of leading the country through a critical phase of development.

5. Taking all these factors into account it made as little sense to talk of a unitary counterelite as it did to talk of a single dominant elite. In fact, as the study began, individuals and factions representing all the contending versions of what the nation should be were operating visibly at the highest levels of power in Venezuela. There was no a priori justification for assuming consensus among men in power or presuming that viewpoints outside the mainstream were without political resources or representation at the top. Whatever the scope of the group reached, then, or the canons applied in its selection, obtaining a list of the notable elite, powerful or influential, would be a bare beginning toward getting a picture of political operations at this level.[6]

---

[6] Early study documents deliberately avoided the word "elite" in view of the heterogeneity, instability, and dubious political effectiveness of individuals at the top and the consequent disunity and apparent near-impotence of this subset of influentials as a group with respect to the realization of some commonly identified national needs. Designating our subjects as men of power, influentials, decision makers, or incumbents of key or authoritative positions also proved unsatisfactory (though we do so occasionally when it seems appropriate or merely to break the tedium). We reverted to the term elites after performing the sociometric analysis (refer to *SRSP,* Chapter 7)

6. A number of exogenous factors ranging from the obvious international extensions of the economy to the equally obvious United States concern with events in the Caribbean as well as the diverse ties abroad of political groups (for example, AD links to San Juan, San José, and Washington; COPEI, the Christian Democratic Party, links to Santiago and Bonn; MIR-PCV links to Havana) seemed to represent influences and constraints on policy options that required some investigation.

This emphasis on factors of diversity, fragmentation, newness, and dependency within the elite did not represent an ingenuous disregard of the structural underpinnings of power and privilege. In particular there was no intention of losing sight of the economic and international dimensions undergirding and guaranteeing the favored position of many within the elite nor of confounding political ineffectiveness or inaction with weak defensive capacity within this group. But enhanced system capacity and autonomy, and how these might emerge from the existing framework, remained a principal reference point.

> In its broadest sense, the goal of the research program is to identify those elements in Venezuelan society that can expand the nation's capacity to satisfy human needs on a large scale and at the same time diminish the repressive and deprivational features of the present system or any alternative that may evolve in the near future.[7]

These implicit commitments to a systems analysis approach to our data were further crystallized and in part implemented during the many months spent searching for analytical instruments that could even partially meet these aspirations and adequately manage the massive amount of information on Venezuelan politics that was generated under these directives. The "integrated analytical scheme" presented in *SRSP* was a fresh attempt at a formalization of these ideas. It advanced clarification in three ways.

1. In Figure 1.1 (representation of CONVEN samples in a social space) it attempted to locate the groups being surveyed in a grid whose main dimensions indicated socioeconomic status and experience of (exposure to) modernizing change (including urban residence). The range and mix of possible political consequences were suggested in the chart by showing rates of political participation as established in the surveys.

---

which, in addition to generally confirming the relative power or influence ratings made by judges, demonstrated that our subjects constitute a mutually self-aware circle of notables, whatever the degree to which they in fact exercise power, authority, influence, or act as leaders or decision makers with reference to issues of national import.

[7] Bonilla and Cotler, "Los hombres de poder en Venezuela," p. 1.

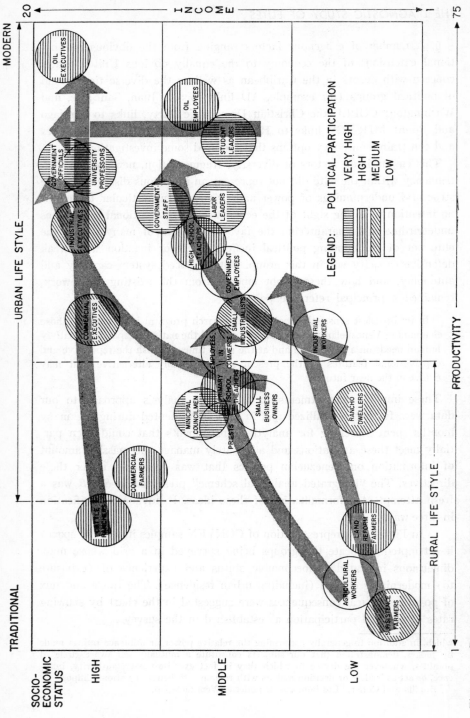

Figure 1.1   Representation of CONVEN Samples in a Social Space

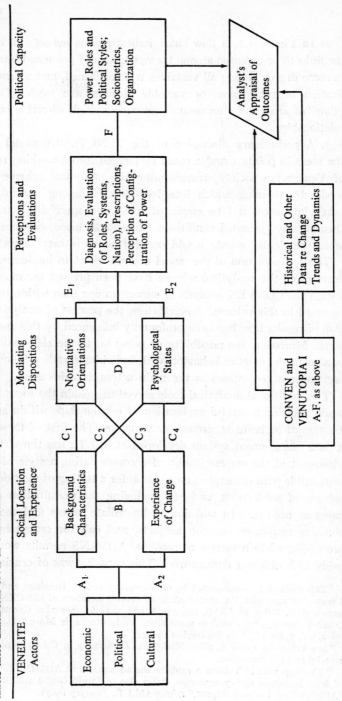

Note to Figure 1.1 Figure 1.1 seeks to represent the initial, intuitive judgments of the research team regarding the location of the sample groups in a space defined primarily by the dimensions of socioeconomic status and traditionalism-modernism. The research itself includes numerous alternative concepts linked to appropriate empirical indicators of these dimensions. The two ratios shown here — 20:1 for income and 75:1 for productivity — are noted to convey a sense of the sizable social distances these dimensions cover in Venezuela. In developed countries these ratios are both closer to 4:1. The overlap of rural and urban on the chart is meant to portray the interpenetration of rural and urban life styles both in the largest cities and the small towns. The arrows suggest a variety of paths and stages in upward movement through this social space for groups and individuals. The values for the categories of political participation are: very high, 40 per cent or more; high, between 25 and 40 per cent; medium, between 15 and 25 per cent; low, less than 15 per cent.

Figure 1.2 Integrated Analytical Scheme for CONVEN, VENELITE, and VENUTOPIA I. Letters indicate families of propositions or conventional laws; boxes are families of concepts.

2. In Figure 1.2, a flow chart indicating the subsets of variables and the links to be explored among them, the idea of presumed interdependence in some degree among all variables was reaffirmed, and a tentative identification of subsystems or variable clusters was made. The suggested "flow" of analysis by no means presumed a single direction or sequence of relationships.

3. A preliminary discussion of the VENUTOPIA model showed how the ideas in points 1 and 2 could be merged into a working representation of Venezuelan society, transforming the analytical scheme into a true model by defining which interdependencies among variables would be taken into account (the empirical laws) and specifying some additional, theoretically grounded conditions (thresholds, loops, contingencies) under which particular events would occur (the "arbitrary" laws).[8]

The formalization of the model and the effort to implement the system features of the analytical scheme have been pressed far more extensively within the CONVEN analysis of survey groups than within the elite study reported in this volume.[9] Nevertheless, the process of analysis and exposition of results here has been profoundly influenced by this common framework. Moreover, the possibility of going on to the elaboration of a companion model of elite behavior, with individuals rather than occupational sectors or organizations as the main actors, remains open.

Two additional analytical tools served to sustain the focus on the whole while allowing a careful exploration of relationships within subsystems or clusters of individuals, groups, or variables. The first of these, ADMINS, a data management system developed at M.I.T., has the virtue, from the viewpoint of the present study, of accommodating a style of work highly compatible with the exploratory search for a testing of relationships among subsets of subjects or variables including the examination of individual cases as needed.[10] In addition to immediate access and the capacity to combine responses, regroup subjects, and call for cross-tabulations that are displayed in a matter of seconds, ADMINS permits work simultaneously with different data sources. This capacity was of crucial importance

[8] This method was elaborated by O. Varsavsky and C. Domingo and applied to the Venezuelan case with the participation of several members of the CENDES social research staff. Refer to *SRSP*, pp. 34–36 and 333–367. See also Carlos Domingo and Oscar Varsavsky, "Un modelo matemático de la utopía de Moro," *Desarrollo Económico*, vol. 7, no. 26 (July–September 1967).

[9] See Volume 3 (José A. Silva Michelena, *Democracy in Crisis*), especially Chapters 1 and 9 and the Appendix.

[10] The Appendix in Volume 3 explains the advantages of ADMINS for the treatment of large bodies of survey responses. Refer also to David Griffel and Stuart McIntosh, "ADMINS—A Progress Report," mimeo (M.I.T., January 1967).

to this study for there were several kinds of information about each subject, with each type of information having quite different formats (for example, biographical data, career changes, sociometric choices, textual responses) and with varying gaps in the information available for each subject. Chapters 3, 4, and 6 in the present volume relied heavily on ADMINS and the interfacing of diverse data sets.

The application of a list-processing approach to the reduction and processing of the extensive textual materials accumulated in the open interviews maintained a similar perspective on internal structures and wholes with respect to this part of the data.[11] The principal objective of this method was to reduce the volume of these data and formalize the counting aspects of the qualitative analysis (that is, to do some coding) without dismemberment or fragmentation of responses. This was achieved by in effect reducing the texts to lists of connected symbols in which the natural sequence and some of the explicit links of symbols to each other were retained. These reduced texts or lists constituted a middle ground for qualitative work between the abstract codes and the massive raw data. Because these lists were also computer manipulatable, they permitted rapid machine testing for the presence of complex patterns and the location of subjects in whose discourse particular sequences of symbols could be found. This opened the way to thinking in more differentiated detail than is ordinarily possible about the nature of cognitive structures (for example, the ideological patterns treated in Chapter 8 of the present volume).

The techniques applied to the sociometric materials (a unique resource within a study of an operative national elite) attempted to provide yet another perspective on internal structures. An adaptation of HIDECS elaborated by Carlos Domingo allowed a tentative identification of cliques among the subjects reached and a set of routines prepared by Allan Kessler permitted measures of the rates and concentrations of interaction within and across subsets defined both analytically and "naturally" through clustering.[12]

[11] Details of the method are given in *SRSP*, Chapter 6. Chapter 7 in that volume, as well as Chapters 7 and 8 in the present one, are products of that approach to qualitative analysis. Peter Bos performed the major task of making the system operative on M.I.T.'s time-sharing system. Jeremy D. Pool contributed importantly to the early formalization of the coding language, and Robert Walker assisted in the final phase of "debugging" and documenting the complex set of programs composing the system.

[12] Refer to *SRSP*, Chapter 9, and to Chapter 6 in this volume. HIDECS stands for the "hierarchical decomposition of a set with an associated linear graph." See Christopher Alexander, *Notes on the Synthesis of Form* (Cambridge, Mass.: Harvard University Press, 1964).

All of us involved in this research venture are keenly aware of the limited degree to which the potential of these ideas and this array of research tools has been realized in our work. Nevertheless, we are convinced that together they represent a major opportunity for advancing social science knowledge and for bringing research operations more genuinely in line with both the needs of planners concerned with guided change and the desire of many, whether imaginative utopians or revolutionaries, to speculate more freely about conditions under which a radical emancipation from present constraints on individual and collective fulfillment may be achieved.

An outflow of recent work on related themes (social accounting, modes of assessing the value and institutional consequences of gains in technology, the nature of institutions in highly participant societies with a strongly developed capacity for self-steering) has served to reinforce our belief that such attempts to grapple with social phenomena with a realistic sense of their complexity, immediacy, and fluidity but without losing sight of the potential for human control and responsibility can now be pressed with advantage.[13] Recent and still cautious appraisals of the possible contribution of modern systems theory to the solution of stubborn problems of theory and conceptualization regarding social processes tend to emphasize those aspects that are given prominence in the "diagnostic" approach: techniques for handling variety, the changing, the new; capacity for synthesis; information and communication as the essence of the sociocultural; interactions as the matrix for the elaboration and testing of meanings; collective purpose; events rather than continuous relations within a system.[14]

As shall be seen, neither the language nor the forms of representation of systems analysis are particularly obtrusive in the main body of this book. Although this remains basically a qualitative study of elites in action, it is inserted within a larger research framework that at some points permits a more rigorous pursuit and application of these ideas. In addition, where appropriate, we have sought to enlarge and shore up confidence in the present findings by putting them to the test of formal methods devised to

[13] To cite just a few items, see particularly Bertram R. Gross, "The Coming General Systems Models of Social Systems," *Human Relations*, vol. 20, no. 4 (November 1967), as well as his chapters in Raymond A. Bauer, ed., *Social Indicators* (Cambridge, Mass.: The M.I.T. Press, 1966). Refer also to Olaf Helmer, "A Use of Simulation for the Study of Future Values," RAND, 1966, and Amitai Etzioni, *The Active Society* (New York: Free Press, 1968).

[14] Walter Buckley, *Sociology and Modern Systems Theory* (Englewood Cliffs, N.J.: Prentice-Hall, 1967).

search for relational structures within systems of interconnected elements. Some obvious liberties and possible pitfalls are involved in attempting such partial appraisals of structure when one knows the elements involved ("members" of the elite) are not all present in the calculations. Cues taken from the larger analysis, which includes several groups that are often treated as "elites" (for example, labor leaders, student leaders, university professors, business executives, government officials), have also guided the necessarily more tentative but often richer search for patterns in elite experience and action.

To simplify considerably, this is a study of elites in action that is more concerned with questions of "whether" and "how" collective goals are, or may be, realized rather than with issues of exactly who rules or to what precise degree advantaged individuals are able to impose their will on others, advance private interests, or define collective goals to their taste. Questions of the latter type have not been sidestepped, but they have not been allowed to dominate the research. At the same time, although we have increasingly gravitated toward a systems representation of our field of observation and sought to organize our information in a compatible form, the intent has not been merely to substitute an idealized model of group goal-seeking for the conventional imagery of traditional oligarchic or neocolonial domination.[15]

A simple, cybernetic feedback model of explicit group goal-seeking does not fit most societies of the past and present because of a lack in those societies of informed, centralized direction and widespread, promotively independent group behaviors of individuals and subgroups. In some cases in history, large-scale, planned social development or change fitting this model has occurred, based on a strong centralized leadership and an efficient administrative apparatus; but the goals attained were not salient for large segments of the population, and problems of internal consensus and cohesion have usually arisen sooner or later to halt the process. Extensive, conscious attempts to direct a complex society in a viable, adaptive manner have only just begun in modern history, and much remains to be learned to avoid the mistakes of the past. An intimate understanding of the workings of the sociocultural level of complex adaptive systems is essential.

[15] A timely plea for more precision in spelling out the political operations behind these commonplace labels is James L. Payne's "The Oligarchy Muddle," *World Politics*, April 1968. The citation that follows is from Buckley, *Sociology and Modern Systems Theory*, p. 206.

VENELITE: The Choice of Subjects[16]

To our best knowledge the VENELITE research has managed to collect more information about more of the very top people in an actively operative national power system than has ever been obtained before. Nevertheless, results fall well short of a total census or a controlled sampling of influentials, and it is important to weigh the meaning of the various ways in which such standards are not met. As work of this nature seems likely to have to face the same type of problem wherever it is done, it also may be useful to provide a fair amount of detail regarding our experience.

No satisfactory way of unequivocally identifying the most powerful or influential individuals in a complex social system has been elaborated. When the social system in question is a national state in the process of profound and rapid political change, even minimally plausible theoretical approaches prove difficult to implement. As has been noted, the preliminary diagnosis emphasized newness, fluidity, dependency, and fragmentation within the elite. All of these conditions would tend to aggravate the normal uncertainties of identifying subjects for a study of this kind.

At any given moment in any country a large number of individuals acting on their own, or on behalf of various types of organizations and other collectivities, will be consciously engaged in attempts to formulate or influence national decisions. Some of these individuals will be more visibly located than others. Some will be established hands at the game, others relative newcomers. Some will be successful, others totally ineffectual. Some men of power will be in periods of inactivity, some may be newly and only momentarily engaged in efforts to shape policy in areas far afield from their ordinary concerns. If our early hypotheses about the significance of past patterns of power organization in Venezuela had any validity, abrupt and fairly extensive changes could be expected in the principal figures shaping high-level policy as well as in the relative power of such individuals. The option of placing major emphasis on getting a reasonably comprehensive and detailed picture of how Venezuela is run rather than on locating and ranking in some absolute and exhaustive way the specific individuals running the nation at a given moment was thus a preferred strategy consonant with the diagnostic view of the political process that has been outlined. Still, a considerable effort was made to systematize the procedure for selecting the subjects.

[16] This is a substantially expanded version of pp. xiv–xvii in *SRSP*.

The basic methods for identifying influentials that have been used in studies of community and national power structures are the reputational, positional, and the decision participation approaches. The first method relies on the judgments of well-informed individuals regarding who is powerful and the relative status of those within the power group. The second identifies power with formal positions, working on the supposition that the ultimate basis of power, particularly power that is national in scope, involves the command of major institutions and organizations. The last method attempts to reconstruct how past decisions were made or to follow through a number of major current decisions and to weigh the relative importance of the role played by the principal actors in determining outcomes. Each of these methods has some well-recognized inadequacies; none forecloses the probability that some people of tangential importance will be included in the final roster of notables or that some key figures will be omitted.[17] The import of our comment here is that in actual operation these methods tend to overlap and that none lends itself to unequivocal and easily reproducible selection procedures, and even less to clear-cut rankings of individuals. Although the identification of *positions* according to tables of organizations seems on the surface more readily performed according to objective criteria, it is not hard to show that beyond a handful of top positions the actual operation quickly reduces to a choice of positions according *to their reputation*. Similarly, the examination of any list of individuals to whom judges attribute power quickly reveals that the positions occupied by subjects clearly weigh in the rankings made. Again, even in the most careful studies of decisions with a view to locating influential individuals, the opportunities for making the full range of observations necessary seem plainly absent. Here also inferences on the basis of formal positions occupied and personal reputation inevitably color the evaluations of the meaning of the behavior of participants.

When the writer entered into the VENELITE project, a very substantial amount of work toward the identification of candidates for interview already had been done. An extensive list of influentials had been put together through all of the methods that have been mentioned here. The core of the listings came from a canvassing of positions, but this was amplified

---

[17] The main arguments on the various sides of this particular methodological controversy are well summarized in the *American Sociological Review*, vol. 27, no. 6 (December 1962), pp. 838–854. A recent compact and comprehensive review of the issues involved in the identification of elites from the perspective of cross-national research is Richard L. Merritt's *Systematic Approaches to Comparative Politics* (forthcoming).

by scanning newspaper files of over more than two decades (1940–1963) as a further means of identifying individuals who had figured prominently in national affairs within four main sectors of activity — economic, political, cultural, and military. Though principally anchored in the occupancy of institutional positions, inclusion in this first listing was thus influenced by an individual's reputation and general visibility in decisions and other activities of national concern.

For the economic sphere the initial listing included principal proprietors or directors of companies with more than one million bolivares capitalization, covering banks, insurance firms, import firms, distributors, and industrial establishments. Included as well were directors of associations of businessmen, chambers of commerce, trade associations, and similar groups. The more formal sources for such listings were the files of the Central Bank of Venezuela and an economic geography of Venezuela published in 1959, which listed a large number of Venezuelan firms and the individuals connected with them. Listed here as well were directors of the national labor confederations and important national federations (transport, petroleum, and construction). Although many of the businessmen listed had important connections with foreign-controlled firms, only Venezuelans figured in this compilation. The study of the activities of foreign investors and firms from the start had been thought of as a separate subproject.

In the political sphere the list covered cabinet ministers, members of the Congress, executive officers and national committee members of the political parties, members of certain key committees within the parties, and prominent politicians no longer formally active in party life but generally recognized as influential.

University rectors and deans of faculties (schools) within the universities made up one important sector within the cultural sphere. Also included were the officers of the professional associations of professors and school teachers, the directors and editors in chief of newspapers and magazines with national circulation, the directors of radio and television stations, a number of outstanding writers, and prominent members of the prelacy.

The military sphere presented difficulties from the start. A few names were gathered through newspaper references to individual officers in key command posts, but it was not possible to get a complete military table of organization or a listing of officers for any of the services. Later in the research some advances were made both in getting access to official sources and in obtaining impressionistic rankings of influentials in the military. However, because no interviews were obtained within this sphere, the accuracy of listings and the judges' ratings of military men remains uncertain and unverifiable.[18]

In this fashion, a list of 1,088 names was put together. The list was then submitted to a panel of nine judges who were asked to perform two basic tasks:

1. To rank on a three-point scale (A, B, C) the individuals listed in terms of their power to propose, intervene in, or influence decisions of national import.

2. To add to the list the names of individuals they felt should be included and to rank these also.

Although the judges were known to have special knowledge of specific spheres (economic, political, or cultural), they were chosen primarily because of their presumed broad perspective and intimate and extensive acquaintance with the leading groups in all sectors of national activity. Among the judges were two prominent members of the governing coalition (Acción Democrática and COPEI parties), a Communist Party leader, and a member of the platform committee of Unión Republicana Democrática (the major party in what was then referred to as the democratic, that is, nonviolent, opposition). The judges also included the director of a major brewery, a board member of a leading oil company, and an influential financier. Judges with a special interest in the cultural sphere were members of the national academy of historians, the manager of one of the principal magazines with national circulation, and the secretary-general of a university. Interestingly enough, these judges added only eighteen new names to the list. None of the new names, however, was brought forward by more than one judge.

The first step in pruning this list was to eliminate all those who had not been attributed some degree of power by at least five of the nine judges. This reduced the list to 375 names. A factor analysis of the judges' ratings was then carried out to determine the degree of consistency among the various judges. This analysis showed a clustering of judges into two groups. Three judges seemed to give consistently higher ratings than the other six. No simple factor seemed to account for this difference (that is, the three judges did not come from a particular sphere or identifiable group and did not seem to favor any particular group in their judgments). However, if a cutting point were set at a score of 2.0, the two groups of judges agreed in the placement of 82 percent of the 1,088 cases above or below this line. Taking only the 375 cases who had been attributed some degree of power

[18] A note on the military and other "invisible" elites is provided in Chapter 9.

by at least five judges, agreement among the two sets of judges as to whether an individual was above or below the 2.0 line was evident in 85 percent of the cases. The target group was thus first set at those 346 cases with a minimum *over-all* score of 2.0.[19] In this way the prime task of identifying a group that had a high probability of including the very top power wielders was performed. By pushing the criterion for acceptance upward, the gray area of ambiguity among the judges was largely excluded from central attention in the research. It should be remembered that the CONVEN samples ranged quite high in the status hierarchy — some of those dropped from the master list of 1,088 names fell within the populations to be sampled in the surveys.

After some ten weeks of field operation, it became clear that the group of interviewers was not likely to achieve the level of productivity on which time and costs estimates had been established. Two measures were taken in February 1964 to reduce field objectives to more manageable proportions in terms of the time and resources then still available to the project for the interviewing effort. One was to reduce the number of interviews by raising the criterion for inclusion in the target group; the minimum power score required for qualification was shifted from 2.0 to 2.4. The second step was a decision to omit, with most remaining respondents, certain sections of the interview for which it seemed to be of secondary importance to have quantifiable results for all informants. Two premises lay behind the second of these measures: (1) that part of the latent resistance presumably at work (there had been few formal refusals) stemmed from a reluctance by busy leaders to submit to such a time-consuming interrogation (the average interview time was running at seven to eight hours), and (2) that we were already amassing an unnecessarily broad and possibly indigestible volume of detail about the individuals being interviewed. The drain on project resources in the field phase foreshadowed a need for economies in the data-processing and analysis that in turn counseled a curtailment of the substantive scope of the inquiry along with the reduction in the number of informants.

In addition to the permanent pressure from interviewers, a variety of individual and group efforts at persuasion were periodically mounted. Letters and telegrams signed by top CENDES staff members, influential

[19] These 346 might be thought of as Venezuela's "400." The recurrence of this number in efforts to identify the notables in social systems of quite different magnitudes suggests that there may be some natural limit on the number of persons mutually aware of being involved at the upper reaches of power or status systems of a given complexity.

friends, government officials, and even by the Office of the Presidency were used. All this activity proved highly time-consuming and relatively unproductive against the hard core of difficult cases. Conversations with the government in efforts to reach military leaders and detained members of proscribed parties, for example, extended over several months and involved even the President of the Republic and several cabinet members. These contacts were always cordial and highly promising up to the acid moment of actually scheduling interviews. In regard to the leftist and military leaders, as in the case of those individuals not reached who are not part of any specific group, it can be said that every resource available to CENDES and the interviewers personally was applied in efforts to penetrate the protective shield that seals off important Venezuelans from unwanted invasions of privacy.

In February 1964, then, the minimum score for inclusion in the main target group was raised to 2.4. The 230 respondents in this group were further subdivided into a group designated for the full interview and a smaller group earmarked for abbreviated interrogation. In addition, a sampling of 59 of the 111 respondents with scores between 2.0 and 2.3 was set as a second goal. Actual results for the two main groups are shown in Tables 1.1 and 1.2.

TABLE 1.1 Subjects with Ratings of 2.4 and Higher

		Designated for Full Interview		Designated for Abbreviated Interview	
	Total	Completed	Not Reached	Completed	Not Reached
Economic	70	27	6	14	23
Political	113	42	19	26	26
Cultural	39	26	13	–	–
Total	222	95	38	40	49

NOTE: The table does not show eight military men with the required scores who were not reached for reasons explained in the text.

With respect to Table 1.2 it should be noted that four of the five politicians not reached were officers of proscribed parties in prison. Five military men within the group and also not reached do not appear on the table. The selection from among the total of 116 notables with power scores between 2.0 and 2.3 shown in this table is not a random sampling. However,

TABLE 1.2 Subjects with Ratings of Less than 2.4

	Total	Completed	Not Reached
Economic	19	18	1
Political	23	18	5
Cultural	12	12	—
Total	54	48	6

the 54 interviews obtained represent about half of the total cases in this group as a whole and for each functional sector; they show almost identical average power scores over-all and by sector when compared with those who were excluded; and they distribute quite evenly over the main special activities within sectors in a way that also parallels the residual group not interviewed.

Table 1.1 requires more extended comment. On deciding that a certain number of the high scorers could be interviewed in abbreviated form, we could not make a random assignment of cases because we already had 71 completed interviews and another 30 or so under way. In the economic and cultural sectors the interviews that had already been completed or were well under way were approximately half of the total to be obtained, had average scores that differed by only 0.1 from those of the interviews remaining to be done, and were distributed over a range of activities within their sectors that closely matched the specialties of those still unreached. In the political sector the interviews completed at that time did not include any of the Communist and MIR leaders on the list, were missing a good number of important figures who were inaccessible during the campaign (presidential candidates, some party and governmental officials), and did not cover certain important factions within parties. This was the only sector in which a fair number of interviews was designated for completion in full on some basis other than the fact that they had already been done or were under way. The small number of cases in the cultural sphere also inclined us to attempt all those interviews in complete form.

Nearly 4 in 10 (87 cases) among the high scorers were not reached. Nine of these were in prison; 17 were abroad. Ten refused outright to grant interviews. The greater number (51) adopted a variety of evasive tactics. No great hostility or rejection of the study was in evidence or needs to be assumed with regard to these elusive individuals. Sheer inertia in the face of a new and not particularly compelling demand on time and effort explains much of the delaying, evasive behavior of these men. Those in the group who were not reached, for what we have called "indeterminate" reasons, are very similar in power scores and positions to those who granted interviews. Although some kinds of failure have systematic adverse effects (for example, the failure to interview people abroad materially reduces our take among high-level diplomats), no similar systematic bias has yet been uncovered among these 51 cases. Many are in the same or parallel organizations as are our most valuable informants; many are in fact intimate associates of people who have been interviewed. As the roster of those who gave interviews demonstrates, rarely, if ever, has such a select and broad-ranging group of manifestly key figures within a national power structure been persuaded to give such extensive testimony about themselves. The study was from the start conceived as essentially qualitative, and results cannot be appraised without considering *who* the people reached are. Nevertheless, some range of quantification was also to be essayed. The basic restrictions on such efforts are roughly defined in the facts on field performance that have been noted.

Some form of replicated sampling is the main defense against these sources of error in field situations where sudden interruptions of work or high loss rates may be anticipated. By dividing a total sample into two or more equivalent parts, each of which is attacked in succession, any unexpected suspension of interviewing leaves the researcher closer to an acceptable sample of his total target group. More important with respect to the present case, replication allows early estimates of over-all sample performance. The method can also lead to the early identification of the universe of difficult cases, permitting a concentrated effort among a sample of those who prove difficult to locate or persuade to cooperate. Where sufficiently successful, a reasonable basis for estimating bias through interview loss is established in this way.

For a variety of reasons these precautions could not be efficiently introduced in the early field work phase of this particular study. To begin with, the main problem in the early stages was one of keeping an expensive corps of interviewers as fully occupied as possible in *interviewing*, for there were then no other study tasks to fill their time. This meant that each interviewer had to have a fairly large number of cases to work on simultaneously; it would have been uneconomical to ration assignments on the basis of a random selection among all the cases beyond the first three or four weeks of effort. Because each interview once begun extended over several sessions that might take several weeks to schedule, and the negotiations to initiate an interview might be similarly prolonged, it was difficult to identify early which cases were going to be problematic. Moreover, early efforts to enlist cooperation were organized on a group basis. That is, major *organizations* rather than individuals were approached. The work thus began with a heavy concentration of informants from one political sector and one business organization. On the other hand, there were groups that could not be approached at once. These groups and others naturally crosscut any random sampling. Once embarked on the mobilization of group support, which seemed indispensable, we could not refuse interviews in order to adhere to a rigid random scheduling of individual cases. Moreover, no particular gain in terms of total take could have been expected from a replicative design for every case among the 276 in the two main target groups finally defined who was in Venezuela was the object of an all-out effort within the ten months of field work.

These practical impediments foreclosed the use of these protective devices in the field phase but did not preclude the use of similar devices to analyze and correct for bias in the data obtained. The practicability and usefulness of such stratagems remain uncertain, and not very much was done in a formal way in this connection during the present analysis. Nevertheless, the need to explore seriously such devices as post-hoc replications and other measures for nonresponse error or even to "simulate" unobtained responses is pressed home by this experience. In all such efforts the main consideration is that the task of data reconstruction is not merely directed at patching up a particular piece of imperfectly realized research. Studies of elites or any other group difficult of access and difficult to control in the interview situation will always face the variety of nonresponse problems discussed here. The concern for elaborating adequate methods of dealing with these limitations in interview data thus goes beyond the immediate interest of putting any single piece of analysis and interpretation on as secure a footing as possible. The matter cannot be pursued at any length here. The important factors are (1) to suggest a particular attitude toward data on the part of the investigator, and (2) to bring home the idea that when there is a large body of information present, the justification for taking considerable liberties in filling in (inventing) missing fragments may be substantial.

The Interviews

The scope of the information obtained on elite respondents and its place within the analytical framework common to the elite study and the larger surveys has been suggested in Figure 1.2.[20] Table 1.3 is an earlier mapping of the elite interview data intended to clarify the principal ways in which this set of observations sought to go beyond the conventional survey. Three basic types of information were gathered through interviews:

1. *Social backgrounds data:* fact sheets constituting detailed educational, residential, occupational, and organizational histories. Partial information on wives, siblings, wives' siblings, parents, and grandparents was also obtained as well as a record of travel, publications, public appearances, and attendance at professional and other conferences.

2. *Sociometric data:* another simple form listing all persons within the elite group designated for study and providing space in which each respondent could indicate for every other prospective subject: (a) degree of friendship, (b) frequency of communication, (c) activities in common, and (d) degree of kinship.

3. *Open-ended interviews:* ranged over four core topics: (a) decisive changes in the individual career, (b) perspectives on national issues, (c) activity in power roles, and (d) personal attitudes.

The content and intent of the probing with respect to the various themes of the open interview can perhaps best be conveyed by citing at some length from the interview guide.[21]

I. *Decisive changes in the individual's life.* Even though the principal features of each individual's life trajectory are clearly detailed in the social backgrounds data, some additional detail is required to understand the movement from one position to another of persons in the various spheres of power and influence. Four aspects of these personal changes are of special interest: changes in the several occupational spheres, participation in organizations and parties, intellectual development, and finally relations with influential individuals, groups, and organizations. Our primary interest is to identify decisive changes along these dimensions and to determine the extent to which these movements present regularities.

II. *National perspectives.* To the extent that respondents try to act rationally, it may be supposed that conflict among them stems principally from disagreement with respect to (1) the nature of the problems confronting Venezuela, (2) the objectives the country should pursue, (3) the relative efficacy of instruments for attaining those objectives. This section attempts to throw into relief these sources of dissensus and conflict and also the configurations

---

[20] *SRSP,* Appendix 2B, pp. 43–44, specifies much of the content within each data category for the surveys.

[21] "Guía del entrevistador, Estudio de liderazgo," mimeo (CENDES, Universidad Central de Venezuela, September 1963). The material cited is from the section headings which, in the guide, are followed in each case with the set of questions that serve as a checklist of points to be covered.

TABLE 1.3   VENELITE Interview Data

Type of Data	Theoretical or Structural Relevance	Relevance to Study Aims
Social Characteristics	Social bases of common interest, selection, and mutual identification of powerful individuals as a group or congeries of groups.	Determine extent to which common or divergent social origins unite or divide leaders; the social nature of the group in power.
Biography-Career Lines	Institutionalized patterns for recruitment and socialization to leadership or for penetration into positions of power.	Identify patterns of career advancement and channels of entry to power circles.
Power-Role Activities Resources Scope Stability Links with individuals and organizations Information processing Communication Coordination Control (motivation and compliance) Collaboration	Structure and processes of decision making at various levels and in various spheres of national activity.	Define the scope of decisions actually subject to conscious structuring by individuals designated as powerful and the actual mechanics of the operations by which leaders try to direct and control national life.
Personal Qualities Cognitions (analysis of national situation)	Nature and degree of conflict and consensus on policy.	Consciously perceived policy problems and distribution of preferences and priorities.
Motivation	Personality needs linked to exercise of leadership.	Latent stimuli to power striving.
Values	Internalized social orientations.	Effective socialization of leaders.
Ideology	Systematic justifications of power inequalities.	Current rationalization for style of leadership exercised and privileges or rewards demanded.
Sociometric Data	Friendship and communication links among subjects.	Nature of intra- and cross-institutional clique structures.

of power and influence produced around each issue. We are interested in the content of opinion with respect to certain national issues and the distribution of these opinions among leaders as well as with the ways in which power and influence are mobilized with a view to producing determinate effects with respect to issues.

III. *Activity in power roles*. This section of the guide is designed to elicit (1) a description of the behavior of individuals in positions of power, (2) some clues that may reveal the principal attitudes being expressed in that behavior, and (3) a vision of how some key national organizations operate. It is necessary again to stress that we are not interested in investigating *all* power relations in which the respondent figures, but rather those which seem to have some relevance for national decisions.

IV. *Personal attitudes*. This section contains a diverse set of questions designed to amplify and provide greater depth to the information on attitudes, values, and aspects of personality that may have been revealed in the sections touching on decisive life changes and attitudes toward power roles.[22]

The interviews constitute only a fraction of the data gathering effort. A substantial amount of biographical material had already been gathered about prospective subjects, and every effort was made to build up a fund of information about every respondent and his main institutional connections before interview. This material not only helped to apportion interview time more economically but also oriented the development of each particular interview. Concretely, there was a group session *before* each interview during which all of the available material on an individual was analyzed and a specific strategy formulated for the interview in question. The interview schedule thus genuinely served as a basic guide — a point of reference indicating the range of topics to be covered and suggested lines of questioning. In a similar way, an effort was made to assign interviews to team members or others on the CENDES staff in a way that capitalized on the knowledge, acquaintanceship, and skill of interviewers in terms of what was known beforehand about respondents.

Apart from the few interviews carried out by the writer and Julio Cotler, all of the material was gathered by Venezuelan members of the CENDES staff and a team of interviewers made up largely of recent graduates in sociology from the Universidad Central de Venezuela. As is the case with that school in general, the study team had a majority representation of women. No formal effort has been made to assess the possible effects of that imbalance on the interviews. The study can claim no special virtues as regards attempts systematically to control for or seriously examine in-

[22] These questions ranged over such topics as religiosity, family life (in childhood and maturity), friendship, and vocation. This was one of the principal sections suppressed as an economy in the course of field work. The results are treated in Chapter 5.

terviewer or other effects on the body of data finally accumulated. In some cases more than one interviewer dealt with the same respondent, and throughout, as has been made clear, the team sought to bring resources to bear in such a way as to get the most out of each interview, as each case was so valuable individually. In these circumstances, which we have elsewhere referred to as a kind of sociological guerrilla operation, the opportunities to maintain sophisticated controls or pursue certain kinds of methodological issues are understandably limited.[23]

The Present Volume

This elite study, then, identifies a set of individuals who, by and large, are self-consciously involved, and perceived to be so by elite peers, in the consideration of issues and the making of decisions that affect national development. With respect to such national development goals, the study takes as a reference point the objectives articulated in national plans, party programs, and in the discourse of elite individuals themselves, rather than more abstract system functions, requisites, or crises. As has been shown in earlier analyses, there is in fact substantial consensus regarding the substance of major development problems.[24] This elite set of actors is visualized as a network with overlapping and cross-cutting connections deriving from actual interactions as well as relations of kinship and perceived sympathies grounded in common interests, shared values, or ideologies. A similar set of links and cleavages is taken to exist between this elite set and other groups within the nation as well as external actors who constitute additional constraints on elite action. Interest lies on the one hand in adaptive capabilities (particularly informed modalities of self-control) and on the other in the attendant social costs of achievement, failure, or inaction.

Obviously, no single study group is likely to be in a position either to make the full range of observations necessary or to organize its data in a way that genuinely meets the requirements of a full-scale analysis of such a system. An effort has been made to be explicit at every point regarding the ways in which the partial perspectives on this complex system provided by the study fall short of such a comprehensive view.

Each of the nine chapters that follow takes up a specific aspect of this total system and its context, seeking to delineate the major internal rela-

[23] For additional comment, see "A Note on the Interviews" at the end of Chapter 5.
[24] *SRSP,* Chapter 7.

tionships of each such subsystem and its principal projections into the larger whole. The diagnosis and other commentary in *SRSP* and in the opening pages of this chapter foreshadow much of the historical treatment in Chapter 2. It traces major historical shifts in the composition of elites and the emergence of particular configurations of relations both among elite individuals and between elite and mass. The decisive features of this experience in our view include the successive extreme concentrations of individualized power, the persistence of marked social stratification (the disconnection of elite and mass), and the internal and external limits on the action of those social groups who, through family lineage, control of property, education, or other advantage, might have been expected to dominate national life. These restrictions are seen as, in part, a result of the late consolidation of the nation as a political and economic unit. The fact that the first of these was primarily military and the second stimulated principally by foreign investment served to divide and restrict the range of action of elites outside these sectors and continues to do so. This historically established cleavage between the economic and military sectors on the one hand and the political and cultural sectors on the other remains visible, though considerably complicated by developments over the last three decades. The emphasis here is on the continuity of these system characteristics despite the discontinuity of actors. This discontinuity lends a deceiving appearance of openness to elite structures. Nevertheless, it also impeded the formation of a well-entrenched, traditional oligarchy. In fact, it may be said that the factors that blocked the emergence of such a ruling class in Venezuela now stand in the way of the consolidation of a more genuinely democratic, autonomous, and nationally oriented leadership.

Chapter 3 sets out to test the basic propositions concerning intraelite differentiation that were formulated in the diagnosis. It attempts to establish the principal correlates of relative power standing and specialization by sphere within the elite and to link these to class and mobility. Together with Chapter 4, which treats in a somewhat more qualitative fashion the actual paths through which individuals in the several spheres arrive at elite positions, an effort is made to document and specify the process leading to the appearance of what may be regarded as Venezuela's first national elite with defensible claims to competence and representativeness. As is later shown, these claims are seriously compromised by the actual behavior and orientation of these elite individuals as a group. Still, such claims have been brought forward and supported largely by the kind of evidence discussed in these chapters. Fortunately, in the present case, this social backgrounds analysis is the point of departure for the exploration of other data and not merely a jumping off point for tenuous inference.

The chapters on social backgrounds establish clearly that present elites, except for a few in the economic sector, are the vanguard of middle-class groups on the rise. The political sector especially is heavily weighted with men of modest origins whose private lives are still rooted in a world peopled by persons of circumscribed perspectives and achievements. Chapter 5, which presents the materials on the private sentiments of elite informants, is not so much a treatment in depth of personality and politics as it is a depiction of the class-marked private milieu of shallow conventionality and conformity which these men occupy. To whatever degree these men may be playing modernizing or rationalizing roles in public life, the values reigning in the private world of family, friendship, and personal aspirations center on status, job success, propriety, social decorum, and idealized affect.

Chapters 6 and 7 turn to the structure of intraelite relations. The first takes the perspective of the sociometric data, showing interaction rates within and across various types of groupings and illustrating types of cliques within and across institutional spheres. The second takes off from the mass of accumulated descriptions of power interactions to build up an image of intraelite relations that holds some surprises, revealing as it does the inadequacy of models of power relations that stress the determinateness of outcomes (ideas of command, enforcement, coercion) when dealing with patterns of action between persons within or close to the circle of power. Some of the complexity of the connections between the effectiveness of individual elite actors or subgroups and capacity of the over-all system are brought out as are some of the internal, subjective constraints on action. Along with combativeness and aggressiveness (especially among factions of current or former associates), there is considerable caution, timidity, and a disposition to accommodation.

Two additional themes are explored (Chapters 8 and 9) before the final essay at synthesis in Chapter 10. First, the issue of elite-mass relations is approached through an examination in depth of elite ideologies of the mass. The principal point stressed is the remaining disconnection of elite and mass, and the fact that those groups most sympathetic to mass revindications and most committed to structural change are no more disposed than others to conceive an active, autonomous role for the mass in its own liberation. Chapter 9, a highly impressionistic note on the main groups not reached in the survey — the military, the foreign top management of the oil companies, and the leadership of proscribed parties — seeks not to leave entirely without an answer the nagging question of dependency and the nature of the relations between those visibly in command and responsibility and those who prefer to remain in the background or are reduced to clandestine action. Again, the emphasis has been on penetrating beyond the surface "hard" estimates of power (which tend to assign overwhelming capability to two of these groups and dismiss the third as not viable), and getting at the subjective experience and appraisal of expressions of power from these sectors by elite informants.

This schematic overview of the chapters that follow is intended to suggest the concrete way in which the "systems" or "diagnostic" commitment has structured the present analysis. The book shows "groupings of individuals seeking material and social goals in a physical and sociocultural environment [who] generate meanings, interaction patterns, and ecological arrangements that are more or less temporary adjustments always open to redefinition and rearrangement. These social and cultural patterns involve, in varying degrees, an internal component of voluntary, informed self-control and an external component of direct or indirect constraint." [25] In the specific system under observation the subjective awareness of constraints seems to dominate easily over the awareness of or confidence in the "internal components of voluntary, informed self-control."

In short, we are studying the apex of the power system in a nation undergoing rapid change. Simple models of oligarchic or colonial domination are no longer appropriate to the Venezuelan case. The takeover of the publicly visible reins of power by middle-class individuals has been substantially achieved except in the economic sector. In addition, substantial state controls over the economy, including the foreign-dominated petroleum sector, have been imposed under the leadership of this reformist, moralizing, middle-class political vanguard. An external framework of popular competition for office based on universal suffrage and multiple party organizations has proved its viability under severe tests. The beginnings of an ambitious planning apparatus have been laid.

Yet these political gains are shadowed by the permanent fear of regression to earlier forms of open military domination, fears that have increased as the region's military regimes have multiplied. In less than a decade the country has witnessed the progressive fragmentation of this middle-class political leadership and its mass following. That the reformist drive which took its original activating impulse from the political sector has been so rapidly exhausted has brought bafflement, disillusion, and cynicism. It

[25] Buckley, *Sociology and Modern Systems Theory*, p. 206.

has been possible convincingly to revive outworn imagery of traditional political domination in Venezuela because many features of more simple, former authoritarian regimes have survived or re-entered the present framework. Intense intraelite conflict, status quo politics, fear of mobilization, treatment of the mass as object, deference to and suppression of opposition — all features often ascribed to regimes dominated by authoritarian elites — are part and parcel of the elite system brought into view by this research.[26] But the prime objective of this effort is not to find a proper name for the system under observation nor merely to catalogue its good and bad characteristics. The hope remains that the insistent rationality and hard calculus of the planner plus the technique and sensibility of the social scientist may be harnessed in the service of those "efficient evaluators" that Ahumada dreamed of (wherever they may be) to make this system not only more adaptive but more humane and more authentically its own.

[26] Carl Beck identifies these as characteristic of authoritarian elite regimes on the basis of an extensive review of elite studies in *A Survey of Elite Studies* (Washington, D.C.: Special Operations Research Office, American University, 1965). See also Juan Linz, "An Authoritarian Regime: Spain," in Allardt and Y. Littuaen, eds., *Cleavages, Ideologies, and Party Systems* (Helsinki: Transactions of the Westermarck Society, 1964).

2   THE PAST AS MODEL AND IMPULSE

Historical interpretation in Venezuela inevitably gravitates toward great man theories. Even the most studiously counterposed approaches to the country's past must acknowledge the steady sequence of powerful individuals who have successively dominated the political scene. The popular imagery surrounding these figures has turned persistently to feral symbolism — condors, bulls, lions, jaguars, crocodiles, centaurs. A ferocious menagerie roams the political landscape of the past. Yet this imagery denotes more than a people's enduring appetite for strong leadership; expressed as well is the dogged desire for a decisive break with a past that refuses to be easily shaken. In looking to history for clues to the workings of power in contemporary Venezuela, one must thus be attentive to the full range of elements that recurrently make possible and attractive such individualistically centered concentrations of power, including the degree to which such patterns represent a repeatedly frustrated quest for new alternatives.

This exercise, then, seeks to go beyond biography and conventional political chronologies by attempting to specify features of Venezuela's history relevant to the issues concerning elite functioning raised in the Ahumada diagnosis and in the first chapter of the present volume. Four themes are highlighted: (1) the sequence of major successions to power and the composition of the ruling coterie in each period; (2) patterns of interaction among high status peers, that is, among those potentially eligible for entry into the inner circle of power at a given time; (3) leader-follower relations, where the implications of the political zoology already alluded to will be further explored; and (4) the shifting nature of the historical challenge confronted by ruling groups. Each of these themes will subse-

quently be treated in depth in separate chapters on contemporary men of
power.

Successions to Power

Venezuelans have never allowed the bleak experience of the past to dim
for long an unbounded optimism concerning future greatness. The weight
of past disasters, the sharp sense that history provided little foundation
on which to anchor and enlarge individual and institutional capacity, have
always been offset by an easy confidence that a fresh start could be made.
The very poverty and precariousness of institutional life have sustained
the feeling that at any moment the slate could be wiped clean and a firm
march toward utopia undertaken.

Writing from Jamaica in 1815, at a low point in the long wars of independence, Bolívar gives a portrayal of Venezuela that could have been
repeated with only minor emendation well into the present century.

> With regard to the heroic and unfortunate Venezuela, events there have
> been so rapid and devastation such that the country has been reduced to an
> almost absolute indigence and a frightful loneliness, even though it had been
> one of the most beautiful of the nations that were the pride of America. Her
> tyrants govern a desert, oppressing only the miserable few, who having es-
> caped death, nourish a precarious existence. . . . There were close to a million
> inhabitants in Venezuela and without exaggeration it may be affirmed that a
> fourth of these have been sacrificed by the earth, the sword, hunger, pestilence,
> wanderings — all of these, except for the earthquake, the consequence of the
> war.[1]

Bolívar's assessment of the colonial contribution to local capacity for
self-rule is probably somewhat overdrawn but again points to a chronic
deficiency and a perennial embarrassment to brave political causes since
his time.

> We were insulted by conduct that, in addition to denying us rights to
> which we were entitled, left us in a kind of permanent infancy with respect
> to public transactions. . . . We were, as I have explained, withdrawn and,
> let us say rather, absent from the universe with respect to the science of the
> government and administration of the state. We were never viceroys nor gov-
> ernors except by very extraordinary circumstances, archbishops and bishops
> hardly ever, diplomats never, military men only as subordinates, nobles with-

[1] From the "Carta de Jamaica," reproduced in Arturo Uslar Pietri, *Las mejores
páginas de Simón Bolívar* (Lima: Ed. Latinoamericana, n.d.), p. 29.

out genuine privileges. We were, in short, neither magistrates nor financiers and almost not even merchants. . . .[2]

After an incisive and dispirited analysis of the prospects for democratic self-government in the Americas, including some prophetic judgments regarding the destiny of the major nations in the region then approaching independence, Bolívar nevertheless concluded on this bouyant note:

> When events are not assured, when the state is weak, and when undertakings are remote, all men hesitate, opinions are divided, passions are aroused, and the enemy further excites them in order to triumph by these easy means. When we become strong, under the auspices of a liberal nation that will lend us its protections, we shall be seen to cultivate the virtues and talents that lead to glory. Then we shall continue the majestic march to the great prosperity that is destined for southern America. Then the sciences and arts that were born in the East and have enlightened Europe will fly to the free Columbia, where they will be invited to take refuge.[3]

Bolívar was never to govern a free and united Venezuela, nor did those in his most intimate circle fare well politically once independence was secured. Until midcentury *bolivarianos* were to figure as malcontents and conspirators against the postindependence conservative oligarchy and its major caudillo, Páez.[4] Yet Bolívar remains the central architect and artificer of the major transfer of power that came with independence. It was an experience that was to be relived many times with all the tragedy, destruction, and vain heroism that attended the first drive for autonomy.

Little in Venezuela's early history augured so decisive a role for the fledgling nation in the winning of South American independence. Until mid-eighteenth century it remained a colonial backwater to which Spain gave scant recognition, managing its affairs through intermediary Crown officials in New Granada, Santo Domingo, and even as far away as Mexico.[5] The numerous Indian tribes of the region, though representing a broad array of indigenous cultures, nowhere manifested the high levels of civilization encountered in other regions by the Spaniards. Several of the major Indian groups were, however, enough advanced socially to practice

---

[2] Ibid., pp. 33–34.

[3] Ibid., p. 44.

[4] The political intrigue in Caracas directed against Bolívar and his supporters is vividly described in Ramón Díaz Sanchez, *Guzmán, Elipse de una ambición de poder* (Caracas: Hortus, 1953).

[5] Between 1705 and 1721 no merchant ship from Spain touched at the main ports of La Güaira, Puerto Cabello, or Maracaibo according to José Gil Fortoul, *Historia constitucional de Venezuela,* vol. 1, 5th ed. (Caracas: Ediciones Sales, 1964), p. 131.

organized warfare, slavery, and ritual cannibalism.[6] The first two of these activities were to occupy both Spaniards and Indians for more than two hundred years. By the middle of the sixteenth century Caribs were vying with Spanish raiders as commercial slave hunters and extractors of other forms of tribute from more pacific tribes. This trade supplied not only local but also Spanish off-shore island needs (including the major islands of the Antilles) as well as the requirements of the Dutch, French, and British slavers operating from the Guianas.

Those Indians who did not die in combat with Spaniards, other Europeans, or each other were in large part decimated by disease, enslavement, and other abuses committed by or with the consent of both soldiers and clerics. Their number at the turn of the nineteenth century has been put at some 120,000, all living in some form of marginal dependency or serfdom.[7] Those still in religious "reductions" (protected settlements closed to anyone except those permitted entrance by the missions) were soon to be armed against the rebels fighting for independence. Despite elaborate prescriptions for the humane treatment, religious instruction, education, and sheltering of the Indian from the corrosive vices of their European conquerors, not a single Indian was permitted to rise above the crushing weight of social oppression and backwardness into which they were locked by the colonial system. Beyond the handful of notable warriors in the early conquest, the Indian moves through the colonial cosmos in silent anonymity.

Nevertheless, the permanent restiveness of Indians, Negroes, and pardos (mixed bloods) was a chronic source of turbulence, keeping the menace of public violence ever-present and making it impossible to mask the harshly repressive features of the colonial regime. Official importation of slaves is first recorded in 1525, but the first sizable concentration of Negro workers came to the gold mines at Buria at mid-century.[8] The first uprising followed almost immediately. Fugitives from the mining camp organized mass desertions of both Negroes and Indians, mounted a small army, and marched on Barquisimeto.[9]

As the slave traffic and miscegenation flourished the class composed of

[6] Miguel Acosta Saignes, *Estudios de etnología antigua de Venezuela,* 2d ed. (Caracas: Universidad Central de Venezuela, 1961), especially pp. 69 ff. and 148 ff.

[7] Fortoul, *Historia constitucional de Venezuela,* pp. 86 ff.

[8] Federico Brito Figueroa, in *Ensayos de historia social venezolana* (Caracas: Universidad Central de Venezuela, 1960), attempts to reconstruct the figures on the entry of slaves via both legal traffic and contraband up to 1800. He estimates that a total of some 100,000 entered Venezuela, about half under royal license. Refer to pp. 101 ff.

[9] Fortoul, *Historia constitucional de Venezuela,* pp. 98 ff.

mixed-bloods, as well as Negroes and Indians who were technically free men but bound in various forms of servitude and legally prescribed social inferiority, became the largest group in the society. The many slaves who bought, were granted, or simply appropriated freedom remained hemmed in by restrictions governing their occupations, dress, associations, and movement within the cities or from one place to another. Countermeasures against the rebellious rose in severity as the climate of dissidence and conspiracy made itself felt.

Rumors of a threatened Negro uprising in 1749, for example, led to brutal reprisals. The Negro conspiracy was allegedly intending to force publication of a royal decree freeing slaves, which blacks had been made to believe was being suppressed by criollos. The fact that no such decree existed and that the rumored insurrection was certainly abortive and perhaps a false alarm did not deter criollos from a signal vengeance. The sentence of the accused leader included two hundred lashes in public, the mutilation of his left ear, five years hard labor on short rations, and a permanent proscription on returning to Caracas. The punishment of numerous lesser figures was only slightly less savage.[10] A more famous black revolt, led by José Chirinos in Coro in 1795, was put down with equal bloodthirstiness. Chirinos himself was hanged, beheaded, drawn and quartered, and his head and hands carried back to Coro, where they were displayed on pikes. A few years later the leaders of the first republican conspiracy, whites and mixed-bloods, were to meet the same fate.[11]

This background of racial exploitation and class strife, in which both creole and peninsular (Spanish-born) whites were deeply implicated, is essential to an understanding of both the process and outcome of the power shift that was in the making. Although some rude, naturalistic, democratizing impulse may have been germinating on the frontiers or in the cattle areas where men of every social condition were thrown together in a rough-and-ready mix, only a few luminaries among the independence-minded can be said to have been seriously motivated by populist convictions. On the contrary, criollos seemed obsessed by the determination to

[10] Héctor García Chuecos, *Relatos y comentarios sobre temas de historia colonial venezolana* (Caracas: Imprenta Nacional, 1957), pp. 75 ff.

[11] Fortoul, *Historia constitucional de Venezuela*, pp. 155 ff. About this time the executioner in Caracas, an aging slave who had been impressed into service while under death sentence, pleaded to be exempted from further duty on the basis of failing strength and the horror his duties caused him. Especially harrowing to him was the butchery of his victims, which he was forced to carry out in public view at the foot of the gallows. See García Chuecos, *Estudios de historia colonial venezolana*, vol. 2 (Caracas: Tipografía Americana, 1937), p. 188.

set themselves apart from the racially impure "castes" and to block moves
from the metropolis opening the way to new social advantages to the
pardos even while conspiring against the Crown themselves. To some, the
fact that this royal liberality toward the pardos was a political move to
separate the bourgeois from the masses must have been plain, but the
deep roots of class feeling are manifest in the intense outrage of the protests and attendant litigation. At issue were the pretensions of pardos to
social distinctions of address and attire, rights to free intermarriage with
whites, and access to religious orders, officer ranks in the militia, and public
office.[12] Whites threatened to withdraw from all the latter activities should
they be opened to persons of low condition. At the same time less-favored
whites were protesting that their births were being registered among those
of mixed-bloods merely because they were not in occupations of the first
rank.[13] White notables, native and peninsular, closed ranks in endorsing
energetic measures against the 1797 republican insurrection mentioned
earlier, which had as its main actors Spanish emigré revolutionaries and
pardos. The successful black revolt in nearby Haiti further fed the anxieties raised by the specter of a pardo-led uprising of Negroes and Indians.
Bourgeois criollo conspirators could by no means count on mass loyalty
and support in any move against the Crown.

What passed for an aristocracy in the late colonial period in Venezuela
was a group of recent formation with more ambition than experience.
Immigration from the homeland during the first two centuries had been
slow and by all accounts was composed of socially undistinguished persons. The dispersal of this meager number of whites over the sizable ter-
ritory, the relative poverty of the colony, and the rustic pursuits to which
the settlers gave themselves apparently lent a roughly equalitarian quality
to social relations, at times even to those between master and slave. This
primary fact constitutes one of the feeble underpinnings of an enduring
myth about social democracy in Venezuela.[14] Land, *encomiendas* (rights
over Indian labor), smuggling, and military exploits were the main paths
to wealth and social distinction. The eighteenth-century surge of cacao

[12] Fortoul, *Historia constitucional de Venezuela*, pp. 102 ff.
[13] García Chuecos, *Estudios de historia colonial venezolana*, pp. 294 ff. Brito
Figueroa, *Ensayos de historia social venezolana*, pp. 171–210, discusses the role of class
as against ideological factors in the independence movement at some length.
[14] Laureano Vallenilla Lanz, *Cesarismo democrático* (Caracas: Tipografía Garrido,
1961), p. 207, makes one of the more extreme claims in this connection: "Our absolutely equalitarian instincts, our individualism, still undisciplined, adventuresome, ir-
reducible, and heroic, have made impossible the predominance of any single caste, class,
or oligarchy, whatever its origin. . . ."

production and exportation brought into a momentarily satisfying mutuality a Crown chronically short of pocket and a criollo class new to wealth and eager to establish social equality with or superiority to the king's envoys, who themselves now more often bore distinguished titles.

The cacao bonanza brought far more than the purchased dignity of courtly titles and privileges to the proto-gentry of the colony. It gave the criollo class a basis and context for self-definition, it provided the means and set the stage for internal differentiation and division within the circle of criollo notables, and it came to pit an important sector of that native elite against the metropolis.

The steady ascent of the volume of cacao exports throughout the eighteenth century up to about 1770 and its abrupt decline thereafter is shown in Figure 2.1. The chart further demonstrates that all subsequent major transfers of power in Venezuela similarly occurred after sudden reversals in economic growth and at moments when decisive shifts in basic economic structure were imminent. Throughout that first century of vigorous expansion (from about 1660 to 1760) criollos had in fact defended their interests with some success against the monopolistic practices of the metropolis. A brisk clandestine trade with the Dutch, English, and French was one main line of defense. Criollos also demanded and won participation as shareholders in the Compañía Guipuzcoana (the cacao monopoly) and others controlling trade in slaves, spices, and shipping. The clash between producers and traders was therefore not, as it has often been depicted, unequivocally a conflict between criollos and *peninsulares*.[15] The more galling constraints were those that attempted to shut off alternative economic activities at a time when the world market for the colony's major export was in crisis.

> Within the Spanish system, today more effective than ever, we are allowed only to labor as servitors or to be simply consumers, but with shocking restrictions such as: the prohibition of cultivating European fruits, the monopolies on many products that must be reserved for the King, the interdiction on establishing factories, even those that do not exist in the metropolis,

[15] The Royal Consulate established in 1793 brought together all these groups in a single organism intended to promote production and trade. "The Consulate composed, as is the rule, by owners of haciendas and merchants, European and American, brings together each and every group, and in addition to identifying the interests of all in the objectives of a single body, whose aim is to foment agriculture and trade, provides the means for one and all to strive for, promote, and influence their own good fortune, which up to this time they have regarded as dependent wholly on the caprice or perhaps the despotism of the heads of the province." (Letter cited in Brito Figueroa, *Ensayos de historia social venezolana*, p. 147.) Almost all of the economically powerful families seem to have been represented in the Consulate.

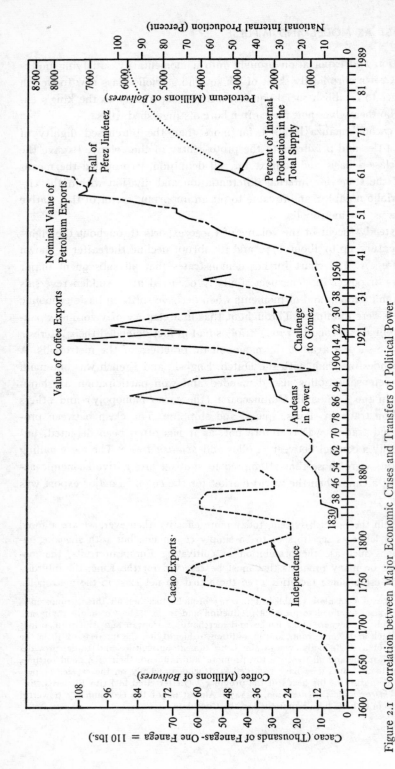

Figure 2.1 Correlation between Major Economic Crises and Transfers of Political Power

NOTE: This chart is taken from Volume 3, Chapter 3, which reviews these same events from the perspective of broader changes in social structure rather than the shifts in elite composition under examination here.

excessive taxation on merchandise and even on articles of prime necessity, barriers of all kinds to impede mutually helpful arrangements among the American provinces.[16]

Although the definition of a local economic interest opposed to that of the Crown was often clothed in the moralistic rhetoric of the rural, primary producer defending himself against the avarice of the urban trader, the political impetus behind economic protest and the drive for independence was primarily urban. It was, of course, the cacao wealth that had brought urbanity — local politics, universities, well-traveled and literate residents — to the colony's few cities. The population of Caracas tripled between 1650 and 1750 and doubled again by 1810, when it approached 33,000.[17] The university, established in 1725, had in 1803 thirteen chairs in five major fields (philosophy, theology, civil law, canon law, and medicine). There were forty-five law students that year and fifteen in medicine.[18] The noble professions — law, the priesthood, the military — constituted influential corporate bodies within the larger framework of colonial power and eliteship. A lawyer's college (guild) dating from about 1788 held a privileged and honorific position in a society greatly given to litigation and governed by a massive corpus of regulations overlaid by a web of dispensations, exemptions, and special rights, corporate and individual.

The university was not then a seedbed of sedition or any challenge to the established order. As late as 1811, when the impact of libertarian ideas among intellectuals was presumably approaching a climax, the governing council of the university was unanimously expounding a primitive version of the divine right of monarchs:

> The authority of kings is derived from heaven. The persons of kings, even if they be tyrants, are inviolable, and though their will is not always to be taken as the will of God, they should always be respected and obeyed. The Inquisition is a legitimate and necessary tribunal. There is no other recourse against the general corruption than religious and political intolerance.[19]

Perhaps because of this surface climate of orthodoxy, the Inquisition found little to alarm it in Venezuela. Agents of the tribunal are in fact said to

[16] Ibid., p. 217. The quotation is from Simón Bolívar.

[17] Fortoul, *Historia constitucional de Venezuela*, p. 144.

[18] A report from the holder of the chair of medicine at the time announces a major pedagogical reform: he had instituted a system whereby his students were to learn one disease and one part of the anatomy each day. As the process was to be repeated three times (it was a three-year course), he felt the new graduates would go into the world with a firm command of the known diseases of mankind. García Chuecos, *Estudios de historia colonial venezolana*, p. 61.

[19] Fortoul, *Historia constitucional de Venezuela*, p. 147.

have closed their eyes on the few occasions when they uncovered some heretical or politically dangerous text.[20] The Church itself gave no leader of note to the cause of independence or republican ideas as it did in other countries.

The political primacy of Caracas had been progressively buttressed by the centralization there of numerous government services covering the several provinces that today constitute Venezuela. These began characteristically with a military and tax-collecting organism (the Intendencia del Ejercito y Real Hacienda, 1776), the designation of Venezuela as an administrative entity (Capitania General, 1777), the establishment of a superior court (Real Audiencia, 1786), and finally the creation of a commercial tribunal and economic development agency (Real Consulado, 1793). Higher offices in all these arms of government were reserved for *peninsulares;* the competing power of criollos continued to find its voice and arena of action in the municipal councils. Positions in these councils, though theoretically elective, early became hereditary and negotiable. The municipal legislative bodies (*ayuntamientos* and *cabildos*), though occasionally defiant of royal power or at least willing to challenge Crown functionaries from time to time, were by no means redoubts of popular democracy. Right up to the independence crisis, they remained conservative bastions of the locally economically powerful.[21] The unwillingness of several provinces to follow the Caracas *cabildo* in its affirmation of national autonomy reflects the reluctance of these groups to venture such a profound change in a social order in which the root principles of authority already seemed to them to have been dangerously undermined. The refusal also heralded the crystallization of regional rivalries that were to plague the nation well into the twentieth century.

The genuine countervision to the colonial order came from abroad and was personified in a handful of individuals who, though drawn from the criollo class, came to a sense of identity and purpose as national revolutionaries not by transforming a narrow class interest into an appealing ideology but by assiduously exploiting class concerns in behalf of political goals and ideals that their class peers barely perceived and were disinclined to honor. A small number, influenced by education and travel abroad toward cosmopolitanism rather than *criollismo,* provided the essential leadership and organizational drive behind the movement seeking a defini-

[20] García Chuecos, *Relatos y comentarios sobre temas de historia colonial venezolana,* p. 72.
[21] Ramón Escobar Salóm, *Orden político e historia en Venezuela* (Caracas: Italgráfica, 1966), pp. 35 ff.

tive break with Spain. The long sojourns in Europe of many key figures
in the revolutionary vanguard offered them not only the discovery of the
backwardness of the colony and exposure to modern ideological infection
but also opportunities for military adventure and for contact and conspiracy with men at the centers of world power. A man like Francisco de
Miranda, for years in intimate correspondence with British ministers of
state, a friend to United States presidents, having residence in the major
courts of Europe (he was allegedly a favorite of Catherine the Great),
with important experience of military command in the French Revolution
and a network of associations with like-minded men throughout Spanish
America and Brazil, was a figure not readily understood nor accepted in
conservative criollo ranks.[22] Some of these criollo notables no doubt remembered that a scant half century before, the right of Miranda's father
to hold an officer's rank in the militia had been challenged on the ground
that he was no more than a shopkeeper. Yet it was Miranda's tenacity
and that of men of similar scope and vision that kept the revolutionary
purpose alive when plausible reasons and opportunities to accept a compromise short of independence repeatedly presented themselves.

When the Caracas *cabildo* took the first hesitant steps toward setting
up a government under local control but loyal to the deposed Ferdinand
VII, it was a group of officers with this kind of international experience
that led the missions to Washington, London, and Bogotá to sound out the
official mood in these capitals and the availability of arms or other support
in order to encourage the hesitant *cabildo*. Despite discouraging results,
they returned with their determination undimmed and continued to prod
the reluctant criollo councils into more affirmative actions. The Patriotic
Society operated as a paraparliamentary body, exerting every form of
pressure on the first Congress in order to bring it to an unequivocal break
with Spain. By then Bolívar was a prominent figure among the most skilled
agitators.

> To unite in order to rest, to sleep in the arms of apathy was yesterday
> wasteful folly and today is treason. The National Congress is discussing what
> ought to have been already decided. And what do they say? That we should
> begin with a Confederation, as though we were not all confederated against
> foreign tyranny. That we should await political developments in Spain. What
> does it matter to us whether Spain keeps its slaves or sells them to Bonaparte

[22] An invasion attempt in 1806 captained by Miranda with British financing and
manned largely by U.S. mercenaries recruited in New York failed to inspire the general uprising against the Spanish that Miranda had promised his sponsors. Fortoul,
Historia constitucional de Venezuela, pp. 171 ff.

if we are resolved to be free? Are these doubts the sad effects of our ancient bonds? That great enterprises should be prepared with calm? Are not 300 years of calm enough? The Patriotic Society respects, as it should, the Congress of the nation; but the Congress should hear the Patriotic Society, center of light and of all revolutionary interests.[23]

Unfortunately, these men were unable to guarantee the military security of the new regime nor win for it indispensable mass support. Maracaibo, Coro, and Guayana — dissident royalist provinces since 1810 — had not been brought to terms and provided bases for Spanish military operations and recruitment. Token representation in revolutionary councils and in the military high command did not convince the pardos that they would fare better under the republicans; mass support went to the Spaniards. An earthquake, major defections of officers and military units, divided leadership, clashes with the Church, and the general incapacity to raise and hold together an adequate armed force brought defeat to the rebels. Bolívar, himself forced to surrender Puerto Cabello, went into exile, while Miranda, first dictator and commander in chief, under a cloud and perhaps betrayed by his principal lieutenants, went off in chains to Puerto Rico and on to a Spanish prison, where he was to die shortly. The defenseless criollo gentry was left to face the bloody and unforgiving vengeance of the victorious Spaniards.

Bolívar's driving genius was almost singlehandedly to sweep Spanish military power from northern South America over the next decade and a half, but he was never more than momentarily to control mass support at home nor to enjoy the full confidence of the oligarchy from which he sprang. Bolívar returned after this first defeat, determined to match Spanish terror with even greater ruthlessness and to exercise without qualm whatever tyranny was necessary to compel the enslaved masses to fight for their own freedom. He proved the implacability of his first resolve by ordering the decapitation of nearly a thousand Spanish prisoners, including substantial numbers of sick and wounded. He sought to achieve his second resolve less successfully by promising freedom and land to all who would fight for independence. In mid-1814 one of his generals reports,

> The people oppose their own welfare; the American soldier is viewed with horror. There is no man who is not our enemy; they come together voluntarily in the fields to fight against us. Our troops march through the most bountiful regions and find no food. Towns are abandoned as our troops draw near.

[23] Ibid., pp. 240–241.

Their inhabitants flee to the hills; they hide the cattle and all other provisions. The unfortunate soldier who becomes separated from his comrades, perhaps to seek food, meets his death.[24]

Finding himself, at the end of that year, again facing the prospect of defeat and exile, Bolívar forthrightly articulated his dilemma:

> The army of liberation exterminated the enemy bands, but it neither has nor ought it to have been able to exterminate the people for whose good fortune it has contended in hundreds of battles. *It is not just to destroy men who do not wish to be free.*[25]

The answer to Bolívar's dilemma materialized in the person of José Antonio Páez, one among numerous guerrilla leaders sympathetic to the revolutionary cause, who had begun to gain ascendency over the fierce plainsmen (*llaneros*) who earlier, under the Spaniard Boves, had been the scourge of the hastily assembled militias of the criollo rebels. The two men campaigned side by side right up to the decisive victory at Carabobo, where Bolívar appointed Páez, who had begun life as an unschooled cowhand, general and commander in chief of the revolutionary armies in Venezuela. With characteristic insight Bolívar early foresaw that through Páez all of the regressive impulses and the smallness of vision that he perceived in the mass of Venezuelans and the remnants of the criollo oligarchy would find a new fusion. The key to the shape of the postrevolutionary society, he sensed, lay not in grand theories of ideal polities nor within the circle of his most intimate collaborators but in the will and capacity of men like Páez. On the brink of the great victory at Carabobo, Bolívar records his disquieting intuitions in a letter to Gual, Minister of Foreign Relations of the newly constituted government in Bogotá:

> These are not the kind of men you are familiar with there; they are the ones you do not know: men who have fought a long time and regard themselves as highly deserving but humbled and miserable and without hope of winning the full fruit of the conquests of their lances. They are determined *llaneros* who never believe themselves the equals of men who know more or seem better. I, myself, who have always been at their head do not yet know of what they may be capable. I treat them with utmost consideration but even this consideration is not enough to inspire in them the confidence and frankness that should reign among comrades and fellow citizens. Persuade yourself, Gual, that we are suspended over an abyss or better on a volcano about to explode. I fear the peace more than war. . . .[26]

[24] Ibid., p. 357.
[25] Ibid., emphasis added.
[26] Ibid., p. 478.

Nor were Bolívar's aides insensible to the precariousness of the authority
they could exercise over men like Páez in the absence of the controlling
presence of the Liberator himself. As Bolívar left Venezuela to pursue
the war against the Spanish to the south, his vice president, Soublette,
warned,

> You leave me in Venezuela, and you know that I cannot manage this world.
> To lighten my cares there remain with me Páez and Mariño, with great mili-
> tary commands, independent of one another and subject to God alone, be-
> cause you have told me nothing. If they are subject to this Vice Presidency,
> as would be normal, it is easy to conceive the difficulties I will encounter, and
> that anyone but yourself would encounter, to run things smoothly, to collect
> taxes, and to keep the country from becoming one Lower Apure and one
> Maturín.[27]

Events unfolded almost exactly as foreseen and with so compelling a
sense of inevitability that for another century it would be argued in
Venezuela that leaders like Páez were the only possible natural product
of the nation's social condition. Páez was indeed the prototype of a style
and genre of political power around which public life was to gravitate
until twentieth-century intrusions imposed a more complex framework
on national life. The still vigorous campaigner (he was to survive Bolívar
by over forty years though only seven years his junior) soon manifested
an abiding contempt for the incipient civil apparatus of administration,
law-making, and justice that he had been delegated to defend and obey.
His communications to Bolívar and the ministers of the confederation
are classic statements of the pique, impatience, and mistrust of the war-
rior for legal process and the intellectual articulators of principles of law:

> I warn you that it will be a misstep and untimely to reduce the army to the
> state of depression and weakness that your jurists propose. It is not they who
> wage war; they flatter the military when gripped by fear and insult them in
> prosperity and peace.[28]
>
> You would be appalled to see the people who govern your country. They are
> of the kind that in any other place, where there was public morality, would
> occupy prisons for their crimes, but unfortunately it is not so. They manipu-
> late elections at their caprice, designate the first magistrate of the Republic,
> and speak of your reelection, though not in good faith but rather through
> fear, for those who set themselves up as your panegyrists in news sheets
> called *Astronomos* and *Triquitraques* are your greatest enemies and pretend
> to defend you only to indispose others. . . . When I see all these things in

---

[27] Ibid., p. 451. The reference to the Lower Apure and Maturín point to the regional
bases of the two generals.

[28] Ibid., p. 589.

what is called the people, when I see those who call themselves deputies travel
to what they call the Congress, and that the most strident declaimers against
what they call despotism instantly snap up one of those little jobs they call
tyrannous and a thousand other things, then it seems to me one may say that
this country needs something different that will establish order, give due consideration to those who merit it, and impose silence on schemers.[29]

At the first reproof for alleged excesses in recruiting for the still much
needed militias and fearing graver consequences, with Bolívar's approval,
as a result of his defiance of civil authority, Páez is at once ready to
pit his regional following against whatever force may be raised against him.

> The moment has come to enter into action; prepare yourself and put your
> region on guard against any invasion by force or seduction. Firmness, *com-*
> *padre*, that is what will save us. . . . No one has more experience of the
> courage of the men of Apure than I. . . . The base of my operations is
> Apure, with it I mean to prevail, along with my old comrades. Beware, *com-*
> *padre*, do not allow yourselves to be deceived; they are raising gallows and
> execution blocks for us. Let us oppose them with firmness, lances, and swords,
> and we shall destroy their power. He is a siren who thinks to flatter us with
> honeyed words; strong men do not succumb to such feeble weapons. Show
> this letter to all our comrades and tell them I count on them all, all, all, and
> not to trust in the name of Bolívar because through him they mean to sur-
> prise us and carry us back to Bogotá in bonds.[30]

Bolívar's final, embittered fulminations against the America he had
sought to remake politically were clearly aimed at the diabolical alliance
of criollo conservatism and primitive caudillism that he saw rising to take
possession of the nations he had freed.

> These nations will infallibly fall into the hands of uncontrolled multitudes,
> passing then to the hands of trifling, petty tyrants of all colors and races,
> devoured by crimes and scourged by ferociousness. . . . If it were possible
> for a part of the world to revert to primitive chaos, this would be the final
> destiny of America.[31]

In fact, the surviving wing of the criollo oligarchy at odds with Bolívar
bought through Páez a number of coveted conditions. They were assured
an effective pacification of most of Venezuela and they could reassume
unequivocal ascendancy with Páez in a Venezuela unencumbered by con-
federative ties subordinating it to a larger collectivity. They could dis-
engage from a complex array of international commitments and thus

[29] Augusto Mijares, "La evolución politica (1810–1960)," in Mariano Picon Salas et
al., *Venezuela independiente, 1810–1960* (Caracas: Fundación Mendoza, 1962), p. 72.
[30] Fortoul, *Historia constitucional de Venezuela,* p. 604.
[31] Ibid., p. 712.

simplify the diplomatic consolidation of their hard-won independence. The issue was not immediately one of chaos versus stability or reaction versus progressivism; the conservative oligarchy that made itself available to Páez provided him with a desperately needed period of peaceful rule that was more liberal in many respects than Bolívar's final Colombian dictatorship. The crucial point is that an enduring pattern of interdependencies among the various sectors of power-wielders in the society was crystallizing in that first postindependence regime.

The term *caudillismo* brings to the forefront the central role of "individualized, entrepreneurial political violence" as well as the social disorganization, arbitrariness, and turbulence that marks the next hundred years in Venezuela. Though these features of the emergent political system unquestionably marked later political events, from the perspective taken here it is important not to lose sight of the more intricate connections among the several power sectors that were in a position to abet or challenge the caudillo. In this connection two vital points should be noted about the 1830 fusion of caudillism and criollo conservatism: (1) the presence of caudillos in this coalition did not mean the primacy or strengthening of military institutions, and (2) the dominance of conservative values and interests did not lead to a reimposition of Church power or privilege.[32] Precisely this — its emphasis on civilism, secularism, and legal equalitarianism (constitutionalism) — gave the first Páez regime its reputation as a golden period of Venezuelan democracy.

Páez and his oligarchic following were led into their opposition to army and Church by their animosity toward Bolívar as well as by broader considerations of policy and political strategy. In 1831, the nearby island of Curaçao was described as a political council, a military barracks, and an ecclesiastical synod for Bolívar.[33] The small core of professional officers who were largely loyal to Bolívar and might have formed the nucleus of a national army were viewed as enemies of the regime and were only slowly allowed to drift back from exile after Bolívar's death. The occasional soldiers, like Páez, with regional roots, turned back to the land, fortifying the local landholding clans and forming the new and broader circle of *compadres* that gave an underpinning of security to the

---

[32] On the military implications, see the excellent treatment by Robert L. Gilmore, *Caudillism and Militarism in Venezuela, 1810–1910* (Athens, Ohio: Ohio University Press, 1964). A detailed account of the relations between the Church and major nineteenth-century caudillos is given in Mary Watters, *A History of the Church in Venezuela* (Chapel Hill, N.C.: University of North Carolina Press, 1933).

[33] Watters, *History of the Church,* p. 135.

regime. Military organization remained rudimentary despite successive large-scale internal wars and a permanent semimilitarization of rural life. The army as an institution was not to take shape or begin to play a role politically until the 1930's.

Opposition to the Church was similarly linked to the running quarrel with Bolívar and the feeling that in his last days the Liberator had actively sought to reinstate a clerical order in Colombia, intriguing with the Church against the Venezuelan secessionists. Moreover, the organic weakness of the Church in Venezuela at the time made it in fact a weak resource or ally in the task of pulling together the nation faced by the new regime. A letter from Archbishop Méndez to political authorities in Bogotá depicts the weakened condition in which the Church came out of the independence struggle.

> The pitiable state of the Church is what has decreased its ministries, for no one aspires to a position in which he will be the mark of all the malignity of the century, impoverished to the point of being reduced to beggary, and regarded with the utmost scorn. Formerly one parish in this city had more pastors than all of them now. The curacies that I have vacant are infinite. . . . Of the wise and respectable clergy that I knew there barely exists a remnant; a group of barbarians are the pastors here today, except a very few.[34]

What seems to have most aroused conservative ire against the Church was its opposition to immigration and its reluctance fully to acknowledge Venezuelan independence and the legitimacy of the regime by recognizing the nation's right of patronage over local ecclesiastics. The regime's economic policy and diplomatic objectives counted heavily on winning the favor of Britain and the United States; conservatives were especially eager to attract immigrants from northern Europe and North America. None of these ends seemed attainable as long as the Church could effectively block freedom of worship and impose constraints on marriages, burials, education, and cultural life generally that were intolerable to non-Catholics. The Páez regime held to the Law of Patronage established in 1824, which was to remain unchanged through more than a score of constitutions until a new concordat was signed with Rome in 1964.[35] With rare exceptions, the Church until shortly before that concordat played an accessory, opportunistic, or passive role in public affairs.

---

[34] Ibid., p. 109.
[35] The text of the Law of Patronage is given in the appendix to Watters, *History of the Church*.

Public support for curbs on military and clerical privileges was invoked in the name of high principles — the primacy of the state, the desire for technical progress and intellectual freedom, equality before the law. The attack on colonial *fueros* (the individualizing principle of Spanish law) was portrayed as a fight to make all in the nation subject to a single law. In fact the new order replaced an institutionalized, codified system of prescribed and clearly delineated individual powers and privilege with the free-wheeling, personalistic patronage of the caudillo and the favorites within his retinue. It enthroned in politics the only principles in which Páez and his *compadres* genuinely had confidence — friendship and force.[36]

A considerable sense of openness in the society was maintained by the very primitiveness of the system. No aristocracy could take root in such a fluid and intellectually impoverished milieu. Attachment to the following of a promising regional chieftain was a first step on the ladder to influence. Personal power and upward movement hinged on the judicious exercise of the capacity to serve, menace, or victimize others. The caudillo was at the center of the operation, but there was inevitably a division of functions and only momentarily a firm prepotency in his hands. Men, supplies, and leadership for battle as well as guaranteed votes and submissive legislators came from the *compadres*. The academically titled *doctores* and *bachilleres* gave an intellectual patina to government decrees, party manifestos, and the caudillo's correspondence. Businessmen provided capital, international connections, and arms.

The strong reliance on economic power and violence as instruments of control, which at first seemed to compensate for the demolished colonial institutions (army, Church, bureaucracy) and the primary nature of cultural and political skills in the leadership, soon came to stand in the way of any alternative organization of power. Nevertheless, personal rivalries among caudillos, regional ambitions and shifts in economic power, tensions among various sectors of the economic elite, and ideological dissension among the few intellectuals kept the political pot boiling despite the ruthlessness with which each regime pursued its foes. Unpredictability, arbitrariness, sudden ascensions to and precipitous falls from power marked action in every sphere — economic, political, and cultural. Sporadic outbursts of mass violence and guerrilla action became recurrent forms of popular protest not always controlled or manipulated from above.

---

[36] Díaz Sánchez, *Guzmán, Elipse de una ambición,* p. 163. This biography graphically pictures the devious and degrading paths to influence and office followed by politically ambitious intellectuals of the period.

The incidence and permanent menace of popular uprising was exploited, both to incite fear among the bourgeois and attribute irresponsibility and demagoguery to political opponents. Archbishop Guevara's dictum about Páez, "Beyond the supreme chief there is chaos," established the image of the caudillo as peace-giver, a title that no leader thereafter failed to claim.[37]

The secular periodicities in the turnovers of power in this system are, as has been noted, economic and regional (Figure 2.1). Clearly, many other forces and circumstances enter into play and many lesser shifts occur without the visible influence of these factors. Still the pattern is an arresting one. Páez and Soublette (western *llaneros*) take over in 1830 as a second surge in cacao production and the beginning transfer to coffee growing manifest themselves. Easterners (followers of the Monagas clan) succeeded in displacing Páez in 1845. The challenge to Páez comes like others at a moment of incipient economic crisis, but is followed in this case by a prolonged period of economic disorganization and destructive civil war. In this anarchic stretch of time *orientales, llaneros,* and *corianos* (men of the northwest coast under the leadership of Falcón) wrest from each other short periods of hegemony. Guzmán Blanco (a *caraqueño* who had attached himself to Falcón's staff) successfully holds on to power for nearly two decades during the first steep ascent in coffee earnings only to be toppled by the Andeans during the late-century coffee crisis. The Andeans, Castro and Gómez, ride the crest of a second coffee cycle (Castro is squeezed out during a mild recession), and no effective challenge is posed to Gómez until coffee begins to fade out as the dominant product in the economy after a second abrupt decline between 1925 and 1930. The tendency for political power to follow economic power regionally is broken with the appearance of petroleum. Petroleum enthrones the last caudillo and prolongs the ascendancy at the center of the region that was last to make its assault on Caracas.[38] Andeans continue in command until the fall of Pérez Jiménez in 1958 (during yet another setback to the economy). A brief interlude of democratic government in the 1940's foreshadows a new era of participant, social democracy that is to come in the 1960's. In 1964 an elected president for the first time completes his term in office and passes on executive powers to a duly elected successor.

---

[37] Watters, *History of the Church,* p. 188.
[38] See Germán Carrera Damas, *Historia de la historiografía venezolana* (Caracas: Imprenta de la Universidad Central de Venezuela, 1961), p. 188.

Probably not too much should be made of the coincidence of economic mishaps, changes in the structure of the economy, and changes of the presidential guard. Still, one may speculate whether democratic regimes in Venezuela will prove any more capable of surviving economic difficulties than the strong men of the past. More pertinent at this juncture is to try to understand what each of these major changes has meant for the nature of relations among elite sectors, the quality of the ties between national leadership and the mass of citizenry, and the capacity of those who have been given or have taken power to serve national purposes.

Elite-Elite Relations

Not much is gained by labeling the complex and uneasy amalgam of caudillism, constitutionalism, and oligarchic domination that has been described as "traditional," "feudalistic," "caesaristic," or as a "gendarmerie." Plainly the profundity and the destructiveness of the prolonged independence crisis in Venezuela sorely taxed and debilitated the capacity among the survivors to create a society in the image cherished by the most enlightened and idealistic among them. Plainly as well, the country since independence has been governed exploitatively by a succession of strong men, each abetted by central and provincial coteries of landowners, politicians, businessmen, soldiers, intellectuals, and general hangers-on. Most important to the purpose at hand is to understand better the nature of the groups that have clustered around the numerous caudillos, their relations to him and to each other. As has been seen, history in this case reaches very directly into the lives of men at the top in Venezuela today. Almost all of them grew to manhood in the shadow of Gómez, under what is perhaps the most primary tyranny the country has known; all of them lived critical periods of their lives under Pérez Jiménez, a dictator with more resources and far more advanced models of totalitarian control available to him. One of the major motivations of this research was precisely the desire to know what patterns rooted in the past still survive in the relations among men in power in the 1960's.

Since the early days as agitator of Guzmán the elder (Antonio Leocadio Guzmán, father of Guzmán Blanco, dictator from 1870–1888), Venezuelans have been calling for new men to take power. The country has in fact since then rarely had anything other than new men in government or in command of any of its major institutions — a situation that, as will be seen, remains fundamentally true today. It is this continuous turnover of people in high places that has brought many to challenge the appropriateness of speaking about an "oligarchy" or even about "an elite" or "elites" in Venezuela; the short life and the precariousness of the hold on power of any such group, it is affirmed, make it impossible for any organic group sense to develop among them. More critically, the incapacity to hand on power to a new generation drawn from their own ranks effectively makes nonsense of the attribution of any degree of oligarchic control to such groups. Mijares denies the existence not only of an oligarchy (a set of families importantly controlling power over more than one or two generations) but even of a *tradition* of oligarchic rule.[39] That is, he denies not only the social but the cultural reality of the oligarchic principle in Venezuela. The ruling circle at any time, he contends, neither constitutes an oligarchy nor acts like one. Not even personal fortunes are safe from the ups and downs of the relentless scramble for political dominance and favor; not businessmen, but successful politicians who masquerade as businessmen, manipulate politics.[40] The highly touted and all-powerful oligarchy that youthful leftists have always dreamed of toppling, he would have it, has never been more than a fragmented, hapless, and servile claque at the mercy of the public power personified in the caudillo.

In part, Mijares magnifies the power of the caudillo in order to see some hope and basis for the redemption of the bourgeoisie.[41] To have wild men govern the civilized, he implies, is an anomaly that must fall of its own weight. But he at least invites attention to the main issue that can shed some light on the matter: (1) What besides raw ambition, greed, or loyalty to the caudillo has held together the groups in power at any historical moment? (2) What social factors can explain the peculiar inversion of power that allows men of modest origin, education, talent, and morality to make lackeys of others who in every other social hierarchy would be their superiors?

The partial answers to these questions that can be gleaned from his-

---

[39] Augusto Mijares, *La interpretación pesimista de la sociología hispanoamericana* (Madrid: Afrodisio Aguado, 1952), especially pp. 201 ff.

[40] Ibid., p. 248.

[41] The term bourgeoisie is used here to designate those persons who through economic power (landowners, merchants, bankers), education (professionals, journalists, and varied intellectuals), institutional connections (clergymen and some military), or family connections were within the circle of individuals who could aspire to positions within the elite. The active complicity or passive submission of this group was indispensable to the maintenance of the situation of dominance and control by force that characterized political life during this long period.

tory are not especially flattering to the bourgeoisie, for the progressive brutalization of the tyrannies they have endured is in part but the mirror image of their own short-sightedness, deterioration, and corruption. The connections between major economic events and changeovers of power have already been delineated. However, it is worth noting also that the long-term economic trend throughout the period under scrutiny is strongly favorable, implying a steady expansion and strengthening of the bourgeois sector. The political trend, by contrast, is sharply negative; dictatorships grew more absolute, more corrupt, more cynical, more blatantly devoid of any compensating moral or social mission as the nation's economic capacity expanded. The less a dictator did for the nation, the higher the price bourgeois supporters seemed prepared to pay to keep him in power.

The alliance between Páez and surviving criollo notables held the seeds of some of the evils that were to befall the polity, but it was in itself, as has been seen, a decent accommodation of interests, seriously committed to the achievement of vital national goals, responsive to law, and reasonably restrained in the exercise of power. Páez himself is often described as diffident and deferential with those he continued to perceive as his social betters; his greatest violence to oligarchic sensibilities, once installed as chief executive, was to appear in public with a favorite mistress. His genuine services to the cause of independence and the security he provided the republican government were plausible legitimations for the rewards he appropriated or was granted. In fact, it was primarily the ambition and spleen of rival groups within the oligarchic sector itself rather than among the old guerrilla generals that set off and fed the chaos that came on the heels of Páez's displacement. The price of dictatorship took its first sharp rise not with the appearance of some new rustic risen to general but with the first authentically bourgeois caudillo, Guzmán Blanco.

Guzmán Blanco, a man of legendary egomania in a nation whose politicians have not been given to self-effacement, was the first to elicit and systematize the unbridled sycophancy that every strong man to follow was to claim as his due and that was at the same time the most definitive mark of the intellectual and moral capitulation of his bourgeois adulators.[42] Guzmán held the presidency in a variety of guises between 1870

---

[42] A sympathetic biographer, R. A. Rondón Márquez, explores this matter at considerable length in *Guzmán Blanco, El autócrata civilizador*, 2 vols. (Caracas: Tipografía Garrido, 1944).

and 1887. During this time he was simultaneously rector of the university and president of several states. In 1885 he was elected senator from all the states concurrently. He also held the military rank of general in chief (by his own account undefeated in battle) and was several times Serene Grand Master of the Masons. He was widely depicted in heroic portraiture and statuary. The number of his decorations, the acclamations and oratorical tourneys in his praise, the commemorative volumes in his honor are beyond reckoning. One such volume, entitled *Sketches of the Illustrious American, General Guzmán Blanco, in the Multiple Facets of his Privileged Nature for the Album of His Children,* celebrates in high-flown verse the dictator's unmatched qualities of personal beauty and physique as well as his accomplishments as soldier, diplomat, administrator, orator, man of letters, and director of national progress.[43] The facts seem to be that he enriched himself illicitly on an unprecedented scale at the expense of his enemies, the national treasury, and the university; that he was a mediocre and timid officer who claimed for himself the victories of others' courage and military talent; that he was implacably brutal with his enemies and rarely found reason to spare a life or curtail the punishment of any who fell into his hands; that he was high-handed and willful; that his literary talents were not much above the level attained by the hired panegyrists who gratified his self-infatuation. Guzmán is credited with numerous public works that began to give Caracas the physiognomy of a modern city and with a reorganization of the nation's finances (from which he profited); he is in addition credited with consolidating liberal curbs on the Church (he closed seminaries, established civil marriage and secular cemeteries). But here again he seems to have acted more out of personal pique and resentment over any questioning of his authority than out of concern for principle or national policy.[44]

However, the purpose here is not to take the measure of Guzmán as a personality or as a political leader but to evoke the mood, climate, and morality in which he and those to follow, especially Castro and Gómez, enveloped the growing bourgeoisie. No abstraction can mask the raw evil and sense of social atomization that pervades the several memoirs, commentaries, and fictionalized accounts covering the period, whether by

[43] *Bocetos del Ilustre Americano General Guzmán Blanco en las múltiples faces de su privilegiada naturaleza para el album de sus hijos* (Caracas: Imprenta de la Opinión Nacional, 1886)
[44] Watters, *History of the Church,* Chapter 5.

surviving dissidents, apologists, or allegedly dispassionate analysts.[45] The weight of that literature constitutes a crushing indictment of the groups who stood closest to power — who abetted, condoned, and reaped the rewards of their submission — for in the nature of the system, the greater the proximity to power the more individualized the degradation that was imposed. This particular feature of twentieth-century caudillism in Venezuela would seem to be of central importance. What are the consequences for a nation presently committed to democratic, neocapitalist development of having gestated a bourgeoisie in a climate of overweening terror, corruption, and individualized favor-seeking? One consequence is to have it perceived retrospectively as "ornamental and narcissistic," [46] as pretentious, callow, servile, self-serving, hypocritical, and antinational.

> Never did the devil have such excellent aides as the defenders of order. From no one did Venezuela receive greater evils than from its wealthy classes. To defend their privileges they accepted the most notorious outrages.[47]
>
> It was not Juan Vicente Gómez who emasculated Venezuela during twenty-seven years, but rather an emasculated Venezuela that stretched out to slumber under a tree of bounty with the arch representative of all the deforming vices that had come to characterize the nation.[48]

These bitter appraisals are not isolated attacks by intransigent class enemies; nor are they balanced judgments, even though they gain significance by being self-recriminations rather than accusations by outsiders. They are cited here only as evidence that the bourgeoisie from which many of our respondents have sprung has been subjected in the life of our subjects to a searing experience that has left behind it a legacy of guilt, complicity, self-doubt, and lingering enmities.

A sense of the depths to which the country had been carried politically in the first three decades of this century is essential to an understanding of the generation of leaders who are the subject of this volume. The

---

[45] See José Rafael Pocaterra, *Memorias de un Venezolano de la decadencia*, 2 vols. (Caracas: Ed. Elite, 1937); Arturo Uslar Pietri, *Del hacer y deshacer de Venezuela* (Caracas: Ateneo de Caracas, 1962); Mariano Picón Salas, *Los días de Cipriano Castro* (Lima: Ed. Latinoamericana, 1958); Miguel Otero Silva, *Fiebre* (Caracas: Reproducciones Gráficas, n.d.); *Memorias del Doctor Pedro Manuel Arcaya* (Caracas: Talleres del Instituto Geográfico y Catastral, 1963); Mario Briceño Iragorry, *Los Riberas* (Caracas-Madrid: Ediciones Independencia, 1957).

[46] Uslar Pietri, *Del hacer y deshacer*, p. 125.

[47] Quoted in Germán Carrera Damas, *Tres temas de historia* (Caracas: Universidad Central de Venezuela, 1961), p. 86, from Briceño Iragorry, *Los Riberas*, p. 353. Carrera Damas comments interestingly on the methodological problems of reconstructing the historical experience of a social class.

[48] Pocaterra, *Memorias de un Venezolano*, p. 395.

decidedly elliptical treatment of these events here means merely that the story of our respondents begins precisely in this setting and will be taken up at that point in later chapters. The transformations wrought during their lives and in important part by these men may have obliterated the conditions under which a primitive autocracy such as that of Gómez was possible. Yet many of the essential features of that dark time were reproduced in the later military regime captained by Pérez Jiménez (1948–1958), and the threat of fresh, regressive reconcentrations of power remains present.

The bourgeoisie that has been so one-sidedly characterized here was, at the turn of the century, a fluid, incipient class in constant agitation and peril. It was both united and riven by a sense of distance from the anonymous mass, from which not a few among its members had only recently escaped, and by the paradoxical and galling circumstance that the security and order they craved could apparently be had only by subjecting themselves to the whim of pitiless and unpredictable men. They sought to build small islands of safety around themselves by carefully cultivating alternative bases for favor and support — familial, regional, in ritual friendships, on party lines, and later by links to the foreigner (the "m'sieu"). Schooled in the assertion of high ideals, they lived in a network of distrust, duplicity, and capricious violence or unexpected largesse. Although the politician was most exposed in this deadly game, no field of activity was entirely shielded from it. The only secure refuge was to sink back into namelessness. A few escaped abroad and gained a wider perspective on their own affairs and those of the nation. The more discreet among these on their return often dissembled such knowledge, displaying only those facets of it that certified their own cultural accomplishments. It is this ulcerous reality and not a stately tradition of seignorial rule that is the critical reference point in the past for the study of contemporary elites in Venezuela.

Elite and Mass

Juán Vicente Gómez has been described as "a man who carved a serpent out of wood and then slew his mother, his wife, and his children so they would not be bitten by the serpent." [49] The same could be said of those who might logically have been expected to govern Venezuela and guide its growth according to their professed ideals but who instead threw

[49] Pocaterra, *Memorias de un Venezolano,* p. 394.

themselves and the nation on the mercy of men whose savagery they thought would shield them against an even greater evil, the wooden serpent they had fashioned — the mass. By bringing themselves to believe that in Venezuela the alternatives have always been between despotism and anarchy, it was easy for the defenders of civil order to choose the despot, especially if he happened to personify dramatically the fascination of the very evils from which he was to protect society. But opting to embrace the despot was also a revelation of fear, impotence, distance, and disconnection vis-à-vis the mass.

Viewed in this light, the copious national literature on the psychology of the mass and the natural leader or caudillo is far more revealing of the mental states of its bourgeois authors than of its ostensible subjects. Even Marxist revisions of the past, by seeking to identify the beginnings of class struggle as far back in time as possible, have in part served to accentuate this vision of the nation as a small, sensate nucleus ringed by a mutinous horde. But this counterinterpretation has at least the virtue of portraying the mass as responsive to a sense of its own interests and a reasoned perception of its social condition. The more traditional analyses, frankly rooted in comfortably simplified notions culled from Darwin, Comte, Taine, and Lombroso, conjure up terrifying specters of immutable primeval forces ever ready to devastate the small enclaves of civilization that had been thrown up in the sea of barbarism that was America. The caudillo was the quintessence of the inchoate forces he represented and therefore could exercise direct, empathic control and communication over them. The feral imagery noted in the opening of this chapter squares with this vision of a politics in which only the savage predator can dominate the anarchic impulses loose in the nation. The theory seems to have been that if the irrationality of the many could be condensed into the person of a single man, some way of containing it might be discovered. But in general, force and instinct were taken to prevail over reason.

> [The caudillo] is the impetus of biological forces taking concrete form in a human synthesis capable of channeling the heterogeneous will of a people in moments of collective confusion.[50]
>
> The dialectic of national history is that caudillos flourish and *doctores* are soon destroyed.[51]

The people are anarchic by nature, driven by racial atavisms to war and nomadism (deep in their hearts all Venezuelans are grandees or

---

[50] Díaz Sánchez, *Guzmán, Elipse de una ambición*, p. 431.

[51] M. Picón Salas, "La aventura Venezolana," *150 años de vida republicana (1811–1961)* (Caracas: Ediciones de la Presidencia de la República, 1963), p. 232.

bedouins). Therefore, those who are not themselves Caesars or the Great Gendarme welcome these when they rise into sight. The marauding band tied by fear and love to its chieftain is the most natural and elevated form of human association. Wars are purifying blood baths that rain "torrents of civilization" on nations fortunate enough to be gifted with fierceness of spirit.[52]

Whatever threads of plausibility this vision of the world may have had or may yet retain in Venezuela, it would seem clearly to have blocked the way to any rational and confident approach to power by anyone who did not stand at the head of an army of personal followers. By looking for the reasons behind the permanence of caudillism in the irrepressible qualities of leaders, the needs or psychic debilities of the mass, or the historic weakness of social institutions, the bourgeoisie comfortably left itself out of the problem. At the same time it helped to fashion the instruments for its own progressive demoralization and near-destruction.

By turning over the mass to the caudillos the bourgeoisie was in effect abdicating any meaningful political responsibility for the fate of most in the nation and positively promoting the state of barbarism in the mass that it pretended to lament. An acceptable condition of peace and order was one in which the faceless followers of the caudillos and local chieftains (*gamonales*) killed only each other or only in the service of the group in power. The bloodlust of the hired killer (*machetero*) was cultivated and rewarded. By happenstance this crudely organized brutality and all its offshoots not infrequently came home to lodge, particularly on the dissident sons of the class that encouraged its creation and who shrugged fatalistically when it struck others. A tragically blind and one-sided form of class warfare has been in progress for decades in the torture chambers of Venezuela's political prisons, for it is there that the bourgeoisie and its offspring have paid the price in blood for the inversion of power and command to which they acquiesced in the name of order, work, and domestic peace.

As should be apparent, not only the psychology but the social structural aspects of the mutual perceptions and relationships between the mass of low-status individuals and the reduced circle from which elites tend to be drawn have historically been too complex to be subsumed by conventional notions of the personalized links between benevolent but stern masters and submissive but impulsive bondsmen. Portrayals of the

---

[52] The foregoing are recurrent themes in the writings of Laureano Vallenilla Lanz and Pedra Arcaya, the most devoted sociologists of Venezuelan caudillism.

country as a permanent armed camp or barracks in which general and private learn the ways of democracy in the easygoing camaraderie of the simple soldier's life also cast little light on the range and quality of these ties. The number of freed and runaway slaves, Negroes, Indians, and mixed-bloods — many of them outlaws fleeing the constraints of the main centers of population where white dominance could make itself felt — was in 1810 already larger than those counted as effectively bound.[53]

The main inducements that drew this mass into the bloody clash between royalists and *independentistas* were the opportunity to avenge themselves on whites, especially criollos, and the promise of impunity for crimes, subsequent freedom, and land. The only one of these promises that was generally honored was that of impunity for crime; for nearly a hundred years the main avenue of social ascent open to the largely rural mass was to attain distinction as killers in the service of some local *gamonal* and eventually to carve out a place for themselves equal to that of the *gamonal*. Pacification and consolidation of national power by Gómez did in fact bring all these chieftains under one command; it also transformed local guerrillas into irregular police forces — into protected assassins, jailers, and torturers of the politically suspect. Police organization in Venezuela has yet to recover from this legacy.

With this background it is easier to understand the magnitude of the threat to the established order represented by the efforts of young men in the generation of leaders we are studying here to reach out to and speak for the mass of Venezuelans, to mobilize them politically in behalf of objectives of their own and via organizations more complex than marauding bands. The last thirty-five years have seen the growth of mass parties, a mass labor movement, the universalization of the franchise, and the incorporation of the mass of Venezuelans into the cities and into an operative national network of education and communication. How much of the past subsists in the relations between leader and led within the external framework of purposive organization, procedural equality, and mass participation that Venezuela now presents to the world?

The Historical Challenge

If the tracing of recurrences, persistences, and major shifts in elite composition, intraelite interaction, and the ties between elite and non-

---

[53] Population estimates according to the social categories current at the time are given in Federico Brito Figueroa, *Historia económica y social de Venezuela,* vol. 1 (Caracas: Universidad Central de Venezuela, 1966), p. 160.

elite are crucial to an understanding of contemporary politics in Venezuela, it seems equally plain that the significance of such patterns is not the same for all moments in history. At the same time to attribute to each historical elite a style, outlook, and mission particular to its time and social context is to ignore the obvious fluidity in time and space of the organizing principles and ideologies around which elite action has centered. The intention here is thus not to conjure up a set of historical imperatives or canons by which elite performance at specific points in time must be uniquely judged but to point again, in closing these remarks on the relevance of the past, to (1) the critical factor of elite perceptions of past achievement as a weight on the present and (2) the specific array of goals and national aspirations by which elite performance in the 1960's is likely to be assessed.

In certain cultural contexts, it has been affirmed, the effective thrust of felt identifications rooted in the past is potent enough to provoke physiological reactions. "Incredible as it may be to a Westerner, in Asia it is possible for a person to blush because of a decision his ancestors made two thousand years ago." [54] There is little ground for supposing that the subjective involvement of contemporary Venezuelan leadership with historical actors in the nation has such a profoundly visceral quality. It is enough to emphasize here that after the towering figure of Bolívar the next century and a half is almost entirely barren of symbolic heros whose vision, acumen, and decisiveness in action seem relevant to present national tasks. Still, there is little evidence that the record of historical opportunities missed or the manifest absence of inspiring models in the past has generated any crippling sense of failure or self-doubt. On the contrary, a stubborn and almost careless optimism seemed to prevail over the diffuse sense of crisis and impasse that led in part to the undertaking of the present research. The very substantial advances on all fronts — economic, political, and cultural — that marked the three decades after 1936 fed a complacency about long-run national capacity among the leadership that was out of keeping with the urgency of social problems and the immediacy of new challenges. A principal aim of the Ahumada diagnosis was precisely to bring this situation compellingly before the national leadership in every sector. Ahumada's implicit thesis was not merely that it is possible to avoid past errors in facing historical transitions but, more importantly, that the chances for recovering from such errors does not extend indefinitely into the future.[55] In other words, for Venezuela — as

---

[54] Douglas Pike, *Viet Cong* (Cambridge, Mass.: The M.I.T. Press, 1966), p. 2.
[55] *SRSP*, pp. 3–23.

for other developing nations — the historical opportunities for strategic gains in the struggle to match the social capacity of advanced countries are not realistically to be regarded as inexhaustible.

Even taking into account the natural prejudice that inclines all of us to attribute overweening importance to the events that mark our own time, the importance for Venezuela of choices made over the next two decades seems indisputable from a historical perspective. The very fact that many of these choices have been consciously articulated, assigned approximate priorities, and that the basic instrumentalities for their achievement have been roughly mapped is suggestive of the qualitative change in national capacity at decision-making levels that this research seeks to describe, interpret, and further harness to useful purpose. This book is in effect an account of the formation, present composition, and changing qualities of Venezuela's first truly national elite. The long critical look backward taken in this chapter should not be allowed to overshadow the significance of major integrative processes in Venezuela nor should it lead to a casual dismissal of the nation's possible role in the larger scheme of Latin America's self-realization. Once before in a time of great trial and challenge, Venezuela contributed to a regional cause far in excess of what might have been expected in terms of its relative resources and sociopolitical experience.

The principal strands of elite change in the present century have been roughly outlined here and in the primary statement that defined the context for this research.[56] The particularities of Venezuelan development accentuated the natural tendencies toward differentiation and compartmentalization of elite formations in a society changing rapidly on many fronts. The consolidation of territorial control and the centralization of political power was the work of a single caudillo whose primary institutional legacy was the framework for a modern military establishment. This is perhaps the most stable, hermetic, and relatively autonomous power base for a contemporary subelite in Venezuela. The most diverse and permeable subelite, by contrast, is probably the political, wherein a wide range of ideological positions, personalist loyalties, organizational commitments, and international sympathies make themselves felt. However, the dominant tonality of politically induced change between 1930 and the early 1960's came from a moralizing, reformist, middle-class leadership, which over that period manifested an impressive tenacity of purpose and considerable organizational skill. With the support broadly

[56] Ibid.

of intellectuals and youth, and with a populist base in organized labor and rural areas, this leadership was able to construct a viable platform of political power that provided ostensible civilian dominance, an expansion of popular participation, and more effective political demands on the economic sector. The task of exacting terms of operation reasonably favorable to the nation from the foreign companies who developed the country's oil wealth consumed the energies of a generation of political leaders.[57] In the process the state became a major investor and an active redistributor of the national product. The enlarged economic role of the state and the entry into manufacturing and industry of local investors and entrepreneurs (often in combination with foreign capital but increasingly under terms set down as part of a global development strategy for the nation) brought new diversity and dynamism to the business class.

As this research was undertaken, Venezuela paradoxically gave every sign of being newly poised on the edge of disaster just as the conditions for major strides toward the solution of national problems were materializing at elite levels. A new kind of rapprochement, flowing in part from a generalized desire to avoid additional changes in government by force, was emerging among certain sectors of the political, economic, and military leadership. A broader acceptance of the need for the direct political expression of multiple sector interests through political parties and pressure groups and the abandonment by some leaders in both the economic and political spheres of the tendency to a unilateral working out of policy promised new bases for nonviolent reform. However, the efforts of the governing coalition to promote reforms through the negotiation and accommodation of interests brought with it a loss of revolutionary momentum and ideological appeal that made that coalition increasingly unstable and cut it off from the support of intellectuals, youth, and the nonunionized working mass in cities. These critics characterized governmental action as slow, piecemeal, and pusillanimous — as a surrender to powerful interests rather than a vigorous attack on social inequities. At the same time, those social sectors still committed to revitalizing old forms of political control remained determined to cut off the growing power of labor and middle-class groups and their parties and organizations. In this view, the scope and intent of ongoing reforms was menacingly revolutionary and socialist. Inevitably, Venezuela became an international test case for competing models of development. Venezuelan leaders themselves represent a

[57] The most detailed account of this struggle is still Rómulo Betancourt's *Venezuela, política y petróleo* (Mexico: Fondo de Cultura Económica, 1956).

wide range of ideological positions and international political commitments. At the same time there is an active interest and capacity to intervene on both the United States and Communist sides. The dilemma lay in the determination of the more extreme partisans on each flank to thwart any approach to solutions grounded in any version of the rival formula. These conditions imposed severe constraints on any genuine social experimentation in the rational search for ways to reconstitute the society on a more humane, autonomous, and productive plane.

Though the survival of a particular regime and of certain democratic forms was plainly at issue in Venezuela in 1963, this research was not intrinsically concerned with immediate outcomes of this nature but with the question of middle-run (fifteen to twenty years) elite capacity in relation to the external and internal constraints that have been described. Our effort will be successful to the extent that it is both imaginative and realistic in defining and assessing the variety and impact of such constraints. Much of what has been implied or surmised here concerning the quality and influence of past events can be substantiated only by a careful linking of biography to present actions and postures. That is the task of the next several chapters. At the same time these constraints clearly are not usefully to be seen as immutable conditions but as precisely the main objects of elite action and contention. From this point of view not individual actors, nor regimes, nor even relatively well-established political procedures can provide fixed reference points for any but the most trivial projective analysis. But that does not mean that we are totally at sea or cut off from any question or meaningful action that goes beyond predicting a limited range of outcomes on the supposition that all major conditions remain indefinitely the same.

In the broad context of this research, the analysis that follows asks simply, What can be said on the basis of intensive observation over a short period about the potential capacity of leadership to help bring about the new Venezuela prefigured in their statements to us and in key documents such as national plans? The historical challenge is given explicit form in these delineations of a Venezuela with a diversified and productive economy freed from overdependence on a single commodity and externally determined investment and production decisions, a Venezuela that can provide a useful and remunerative activity to all those who need or desire to work, a Venezuela in which disparities in earnings and consumption do not seal major blocs of the population into tight, alien compartments.[58] If the challenge continues to be posed and felt primarily in economic terms (and there is much evidence that this is the case at every social level), the instruments for the achievements of these goals clearly are perceived to be political. Part of the historical test of contemporary elites will lie in their responsiveness to new political possibilities — not to any "findings" this book may report but to the full research that lies behind it and the lines it points to for self-analysis, for communication, and for investing political action with a renewed sense of rationality and collective purpose. It is in this sense that the present research decidedly seeks a place not in time, nor within covers, but in life.

[58] Refer to Panel of Nine, Alliance for Progress, *Evaluation of the 1963–1966 National Plan of Venezuela* (report presented to the Venezuelan government by the Ad Hoc Committee), September 1963.

3 SOCIAL BACKGROUNDS, SPHERES OF ACTION, AND POWER STANDINGS

Historically, as has been suggested in the last chapter, one useful key to the changing social configuration of elitehood in Venezuela lies in the successive primacy of cacao, coffee, and hydrocarbons as economic mainstays.[1] Because each of these commodities connotes not only the national dominance of particular subsectors at various class levels but also the ascendance of specific regions, the list conveys a sense of the center-periphery tensions as well as the class conflicts that have been associated with major shifts in the economy. Every commodity can also lay claim to its own caudillos, each with his own coterie of the notable and notorious, and in this fashion has also enriched the record and the folklore of personalistic leadership.

But linking decisive transfers of power to critical economic turning points captures only a single form of periodicity in elite rotation or succession. Moreover, it focuses on relationships that help to order the broad sweep of events but sheds less light on the continuous process of renovation, recruitment, displacement, and ejection from elite status that marks a society with a turbulent past and a powerful commitment to change in the present. The intent here, however, is not to move directly to this "micro" level of elite movement but, in recognition of the multiple forces now impelling restratification and elite realignment, to probe more deeply into the social composition and experience of mobility characterizing present leadership. At this point the concern is not to individualize the variety of such experience but to uncover the class foundations of current elite formation and differentiation with a view to assessing

[1] An early version of this chapter was presented jointly with Philip Raup, Jr., to the 1967 meeting of the American Political Science Association. Mr. Raup's help in laying out the analysis and in performing the extensive data manipulations for this chapter, as well as the one that follows on elite careers, is gratefully acknowledged.

64

the relevance of class and mobility to the central hypotheses about elite structure and functioning that gave impulse to this research.

In this connection it is important to note that in almost all elite studies the main body of systematically worked data has been social background information of the kind to be treated here. The over-reliance on a single kind of information has made the results of elite research generally disappointing. The scrupulous analyst has ventured only with great caution beyond simple, descriptive statements; the more adventuresome often falls into drawing weakly supported inferences about the representativeness of elites, individual political behavior, policy preferences, power structures, and criteria for admission to elite status on the basis of sketchy and highly selective knowledge of individual attributes.[2] In the present case, independent information on policy priorities, values, behavior in power situations, and concrete group and clique structures exists and will be treated elsewhere. The facts of social background and present location discussed here are thus not approached as surrogates for other less accessible aspects of elite thought and action, and attention can turn exclusively on their inherent usefulness in terms of specific study objectives.

Concretely, one can begin to ask in what way this first body of data helps to confirm or qualify the ideas about the diffusion and compartmentalization of power and influence that were outlined in the Ahumada diagnosis.[3] At least four major issues concerning Venezuelan elites were raised in that diagnosis on which the information regarding social backgrounds has considerable bearing:

1. Elite recruitment to particular spheres — economic, political, cultural — was alleged to have become differentiated by class over the last few decades, with middle-class elements dominant in the political sphere

---

[2] Frederick W. Frey has written an excellent overview of the contributions and shortcomings of social background research. See "Social Background Research in the Study of Politics," mimeo (Massachusetts Institute of Technology, 1964). Dankwart A. Rustow's recent review article in *World Politics*, vol. 17, no. 4 ("The Study of Elite: Who's Who, When and How"), especially in Part 3 (pp. 697 ff.), critically examines several major "empirical" elite studies. An interesting effort to establish empirically the relative predictive power of social background attributes vis-à-vis opinions and attitudes is Lewis J. Edinger and Donald D. Searing's "The Comparative Study of Elite Socialization," *Comparative Political Studies*, vol. 1, no. 1 (January 1969). Mr. Searing has extended this comparative work to include data from certain samples in the set of surveys (CONVEN) that were carried out simultaneously with this research. See "Elite Socialization on Comparative Perspective," mimeo (University of North Carolina, March 1968).

[3] *SRSP*, Chapter 1, especially pp. 18 ff.

and in certain subsectors of cultural activity (especially education) while more traditionally favored elements remained dominant elsewhere.

2. The particularities of the class mix within each sphere were said to constitute an element in a compartmentalization of interests, values, and modes of political action that impeded coordinated elite action across spheres.

3. Within the functional compartments that have been noted, further fractioning, also related to class changes and differential mobility experiences, was cited as an obstacle to the effectiveness of leadership *within* spheres.

4. Another order of within-elite differentiation according to power scores was also posited. Though less clearly linked intuitively to class factors, this hypothesis attributed distinctive styles of evaluation to those at the very apex of power in each sphere as distinct from those near the top but just short of the very highest positions.

Indicators of Elitehood

Because the principal hypotheses rest on the supposition that the most critical dimensions of internal differentiation within the elite are power and functional specialization, a first task is to pin down and validate the bases on which these distinctions have been established among respondents. Power scores, a major criterion for the selection and ranking of respondents, are external to the main body of data, for the scores reflect the appraisals of outside judges concerning the relative capacity of individuals to contribute to the shaping of national policy.[4] In the majority of cases there was no question as to what a person's main sphere of action or functional specialization (economic, cultural, political) might be, and judges were not requested to make such a classification. The grouping by functional sphere shown here in almost every instance reflects the individual's principal salaried position at the time of the survey (with some exceptions, such as presidential candidates who were not professional politicians and individuals holding nonpaid offices in major organizations).

---

[4] *SRSP,* Introduction, pp. xiv–xviii. See also Chapter 1 in this volume. Although the power scores reflect the ratings of a panel of nine judges, inclusion in the first listing of 1,088 names submitted to this panel rested as much on the tenure of institutional positions and general visibility in policy decisions and other activities of national concern as on an individual's reputed influence. The approach taken to identifying Venezuelan men of power thus incorporated elements of the major conventional strategies for locating power wielders: reputation, decision participation, and the tenure of formal office.

The holding of multiple positions within a single sphere or across spheres and the combining of activity in paid as well as unpaid positions was, of course, commonplace. These issues are not by-passed in the analysis, but a primary step was to locate the main anchorage or institutional context of each respondent's action for this was believed to be a central axis of elite differentiation.

The first study evidence that the collection of people we set out to reach constituted a socially recognizable group came from the judges ranking themselves. The consistency of these ratings strongly implied that at least among this small number of knowledgeable individuals there was relative agreement as to who counted for how much in the higher circles of Venezuelan society. Wholly independent evidence that the group reached was not only socially recognizable as such but mutually self-aware came from an early examination of sociometric data. Among the 161 individuals in the final sampling who gave such information, the average respondent had at least heard of 88 percent of the other members of the set and about six in ten mutually claimed one another as friends or acquaintances. Within functional spheres such group recognizance was even higher, with better than nine in ten known to each other at least by name and better than seven in ten mutually acknowledging acquaintance or deeper friendship.[5] Even without any hard outside norm for assessment, it seemed reasonable to view these figures as reassurance that we were in fact dealing with a substantial part of a larger structure and that it would be possible to pursue meaningfully the kind of differentiated internal analysis necessary for our purposes. The fact that for the target group as a whole as well as for the group finally reached there was no relationship between main sphere of action and power scores further suggested that (1) we had obtained a reasonable sampling of the full range of power bearers within each sphere, and (2) power scores and sphere of action indeed constituted major independent dimensions on which to center analysis.[6]

The judges' power ratings and the early classification of respondents by spheres constituted in effect an effort to identify the population of relevant respondents and to order them along the two main dimensions of interest to the research *without* benefit of the extensive factual information about each individual that the study subsequently produced. From this perspective the extensive biographical or background data on respondents could

[5] *SRSP*, Chapter 9, pp. 225–237.
[6] The exact probability of association between power score and sphere as tested by chi square was 0.115 for the 276 persons in the target group and 0.389 for the 180 respondents discussed here.

be seen as no more than a device for objectifying and systematizing the information on which the surprisingly consistent, intuitive classifications of the judges had been based. Presumably such consistency was improbable unless the judges were attentive to roughly the same array of external signs of elite status and also were sensitive to the particularities of power base and style specific to each sphere of action. Confidence in the analytical usefulness of these classifications is bolstered by the few findings so far reported, but a more interesting line of inquiry is to see which of the many theoretically relevant indicators of elitehood that were investigated turns out to mesh most significantly with the summary judgments of the selection panel and the composite ratings of elite peers as expressed in the sociometric data.

At this stage the focus was on those attributes of power or influence that are most visible and presumably of common knowledge, especially among informed insiders, though for many of the more public figures, the circle of the knowledgeable with respect to some of these characteristics may be broad indeed. Among such external marks of elitehood are counted income, training, job experience, time in office or other positions of command, multiplicity of positions, ties to other elite individuals, contacts with other population groups, access to the public through mass media, and so on. In short, the aim in this first look at study data was to amplify and particularize the image of the elite in each sector before seeking to understand how elite status has been achieved or sustained.

Table 3.1 shows the relationship of twenty-two such variables to power scores and sphere of action. Only four reveal a strong association with *both* power ratings and sphere, three are linked to power but not sphere, eight to sphere alone, and seven manifest fairly weak ties to both field of action and power rankings.[7] The seven cases of relatively weak association are as interesting as those that help to further define configurations of intraelite differentiation. Among them are all the variables having to do with organizational participation — age at which high organizational office was first held (24), the variety of organizations in which the subject has been active for substantial periods in the past (23), and the number and variety of organizations in which office was held concurrently at the time

---

[7] As what constitutes a "strong" or "weak" relationship in these circumstances is partly a matter of taste and partly a matter of the intellectual or real world risks of placing confidence in or rejecting the significance of an observation, Table 3.1 shows all the calculated probabilities. The reader will readily identify the borderline variables whose placement on the table is arguable (for example, 15, 19, 21). The numbers in parentheses in the text identify variables in Table 3.1.

TABLE 3.1   *Indicators of Elitehood: Exact Probabilities of Association with Power Scores and Principal Sphere of Action*

Indicators Name	No.		1 Power	2 Sphere
CPICK	17	Number in group communicating with subject	1.000[a]	0.983
AGE	3	Age ++	0.992	0.951
BAGS	5	Multiple sources of income	0.959	0.999
MSIU	4	Frequency of contact with foreigners in Venezuela	0.952	0.961
ABROAD	15	Time spent abroad	0.937	0.732
LEGATE	16	Attendance at international conferences +−	0.951	0.764
FPICK	14	Number in group designating subject as friend	1.000	0.087
INCOME	6	Income	0.865	1.000
WHEEL	7	Number of group contacts	0.785	1.000
NOWYRS	8	Years in present position	0.811	1.000
CAPTAL	10	Years resident in Caracas −+	0.466	0.996
MAGRIT	12	Writes in magazines	0.361	0.996
NUSRIT	11	Writes in newspapers	0.093	0.993
FIELD	9	Field of specialization	0.672	0.980
HOPPER	13	Number of work spheres in which subject has been active	0.263	0.967
MATER	19	University attended	0.910	0.917
SCHOOL	18	Years of education − −	0.845	0.691
MEDIA	20	Mass media use	0.695	0.667
JEFES	21	Number of organizational offices held concurrently	0.323	0.916
TYRO	22	Number of work spheres in which subject is currently active	0.443	0.792
CREST	24	Age at which first held organizational office	0.668	0.646
JOINER	23	Number of organizational spheres in which subject has been active	0.610	0.766

[a] Values reported as 1.000 equal at least 0.99999. The probabilities indicate likelihood of association according to chi square tests. Power scores are mean ratings by judges and range from 2.4 to 4.0. The spheres are economic, political, and cultural including, respectively, businessmen; men in parties and government; and, in the more diverse cultural sector, educators, writers, and others in communications, a few churchmen, and heads of scientific or cultural organizations. Because almost all probabilities are derived from chi squares with the same degrees of freedom, these have been shown without troubling to calculate additional measures of strength of association.

of the study (21). Holding paid positions concurrently in more than one field (22) is also not specific to relative power standings or common to those with primary commitments at present to any particular field. Thus the multiple tenure of paid positions or offices in organizations is not a major mark of power standing within elite circles, irrespective of main field of action.

The generally negative results concerning organizational activity do not mean that these can be dismissed as a factor in high-level politics in Venezuela but rather that their role as a power base for individuals and as avenues to power for leaders is both complex and still taking shape.[8] Early experience in organizational office, as noted, does not in itself seem to count for a great deal. Participation in organizations over time (five years or more in at least two of the following: parties, chambers of commerce, professional colleges, social clubs, or international organizations) similarly does not help to predict power or sphere. Plainly some kinds of organization are focal for men in particular spheres (parties for politicians, chambers of commerce and social clubs for businessmen, professional colleges and international associations for cultural leaders); but on balance, neither past nor present activity in organizations seems helpful in making this first order of discrimination.

Less surprising, in a country with highly developed mass media and a generalized pattern of intensive media use extending well down in the social order, is to find that heavy and multiple use of mass media (20) is common to all subelite spheres and by no means distinctive of those with highest power rankings. Similarly, in a group in which more than seven in ten are university graduates, internal differentiation by years of schooling (18) and university attended (19) are tenuous, though of a higher order than those discussed so far. Though the statistical evidence on this score is by no means compelling, the circle of businessmen seems to have a somewhat higher concentration of men with university training in the United States as well as men with no university experience; those with postgraduate study or degrees seem to have gravitated to politics and government.

It is the latter kind of difference, however, that is most prominent in these results. A substantial number of the variables tested (12 out of 22, numbers 6 through 15 in Table 3.1) show a decided association with sphere of specialization, providing powerful confirmation at this first level

---

[8] Chapter 4 provides interesting detail on how organizational office figures in careers within the different sectors. Chapter 7 discusses the contemporary status of organizations by sphere.

of the main hypothesis attributing central importance to this factor as a source of problems for coordinated elite action. Business, political, and cultural leaders are markedly different on many critical and readily observable characteristics. Businessmen report the highest incomes (nearly nine in ten reported incomes above 100,000 Bs. in 1963 whereas the median for all others was about 76,000 Bs.). Businessmen have more sources of income than other leaders. In this respect the politicians, almost totally dependent on salaries, trail the cultural elite, which has somewhat more diverse although probably also less stable sources of income. The political sector has the most youthful leadership (median age 44); the economic and cultural group both approach 50 (median age 49). In line with these age differences but not entirely to be explained in these terms is the relative newness to present positions of power of the politicians, especially as compared with entrepreneurs. The proportion of men relatively new to Caracas, though small, is also heavily concentrated among politicians. Business leaders commonly have had long careers within a single sphere of activity; cultural leaders tend to have had substantial experience in diverse work spheres; politicians include the greatest proportion who have yet to complete ten years of work in any single field.[9] Those with training in technical fields, though not dominant in numbers among businessmen, are more visible there than among other groups.

The remaining variables that clearly set off elite spheres from one another have to do with communication patterns. Politicians and cultural leaders are roughly twice as likely to write for newspapers and magazines as are businessmen. Frequent contact with groups other than their own (union leaders, farm workers, the military) is more common among politicians than for others in this elite sampling. However, businessmen are more likely to claim being in touch with politicians than politicians seem inclined to acknowledge being in touch with businessmen.[10] This polarization of communications around politicians is further borne out by the sociometric data, which reveal politicians, as a group, to be the recipients of a greater number of communications from other elite individuals than

[9] This does not mean that political leadership is in the hands of immature individuals. The proportion of such "novices" among politicians is 28 percent, among businessmen 12 percent, and among cultural leaders 14 percent. The fact that groups seem to differ significantly with respect to a particular characteristic does not always mean that such differences point to dominant features of any group. It is not easy to keep all such details present in verbal presentations of complex quantitative results.

[10] This finding is based on responses to a survey question on group contacts and is distinct from analogous results derived from the sociometric data on communications between elite individuals in the sample.

the leadership of the cultural or economic sectors. It is only with respect to frequency of communication with foreigners in Venezuela that the business group outstrips politicians.[11]

So far only those variables that serve to establish differences among elite sectors have been described. Seven variables also discriminate among power levels as established by the judges' ratings. The fact that only four of these overlap with the twelve variables most clearly tied to sphere further supports the idea that we are dealing with separate although obviously interconnected constellations of elite characteristics. The analysis will return to this issue at a later point. At this stage it is important to get a first sense of the differences between these two sets of variables.

The most striking associations with power scores are in the sociometric data. The total number of those in the sample who at interview designated an individual as a friend or as a person with whom communication is maintained, is strongly correlated with the ratings made months earlier by the small panel of judges. Age is also related to power scores, though not linearly; the topmost rankings went to individuals between 43 and 50 rather than to the more youthful or elderly extremes of the distribution. Multiple sources of income also show a nonlinear relation to power scores; those with income from dividends and other property in addition to salary cluster at the top and at the bottom with respect to power status. Travel abroad, especially travel to international conferences, is a progressively distinctive mark of increasing status within the elite. By contrast, communication with foreigners at home is much more common at lower power status levels than at the top.

Obviously some form of interaction is indicated among power scores, spheres of action, and the four variables that are linked to both. Obviously as well, only a small fraction of the possible relationships among the twenty-four variables included in Table 3.1 has as yet been examined. But before attempting a more comprehensive treatment, it seems useful to summarize what has been gleaned from this first overview of a sizable

[11] In the more comprehensive samplings of the CONVEN survey conducted simultaneously with this elite research, the proportion of foreign-born among industrial executives was 60 percent. Forty-four percent of executives in commercial enterprises were foreign-born. These proportions are much lower for political groups (for example, high government officials = 10 percent, technicians in government = 9 percent, labor leaders = 1 percent). The only noneconomic group showing such a marked presence of foreign-born are parish priests (69 percent). None of the elite political figures and only one among the cultural leaders interviewed is foreign-born. Seven of the elite businessmen were born outside Venezuela, none in the United States. One of these was born abroad of Venezuelan parents.

array of indicators of elite standing regarding how power status and elite specialization take on social visibility in Venezuela.

1. In the large, the results to this point manifest a convincing coherence among the three major data sources treated: judges' ratings, the sociometric choices of elite peers, and the information given by subjects about themselves.

2. The multiple tenure of paid positions or the holding of multiple organizational offices seems to be of secondary importance as a base or instrument of elite action in Venezuela.

3. The most distinctive indicators of relative standing within the elite are the judgments of elite peers (especially the extent to which an individual polarizes communication claims from other influentials) and experience of or access to communications *abroad*. However, reported frequency of contact with foreigners *at home* is negatively linked to relative power status.

4. Differences by sphere of specialization generally bring into focus the distance between businessmen and politicians, with the cultural leadership by and large lying between these but closer to the men in politics or government with respect to the variables so far treated. Men in the sphere of politics are, as a group and in contrast with businessmen, more youthful, newer to power, more open to contacts with diverse groups within Venezuela (except foreigners), more focally the object of friendship and communication claims of other elite individuals, and have incomes both more modest and more limited with respect to source.

Systemic Qualities of Elitehood Indicators

Though some patterns among this first set of variables have been tentatively identified, so far we have sought only to establish whether the two variables at the center of the analysis (power scores and sphere of action) can be viewed as primary dimensions along which the remaining variables do take on some order. The possibilities of other forms of order is not to be discounted and is, moreover, implied in the results shown so far. As a glance at Table 3.1 will demonstrate, practically every variable listed there has been in theory associated with elitehood, high status, influence, or leadership in a positive sense. That is, even though some of them are merely nominal categories, it is the *presence* of these characterstics or their magnitude, where some ranking or scalar quality is present, that has been conceived in theory as marks of elite status. Some of the variables are posi-

tively linked to power standing. More show stronger links to sphere of
action than to power. A fair number show no determinate ties to these
organizing variables, and one or two show negative associations with the
power scores.

Of course, this merely opens the door, as was the intent of the research,
into the particularities of elitehood as it takes shape within specific arenas
of action and as it has been molded by the special conditions imposed by
Venezuela's past and current situation. Some insight into these may be
obtained from an examination of Table 3.2 and Figure 3.1, which attempt

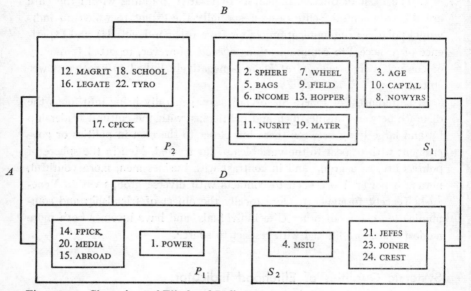

Figure 3.1   Clusterings of Elitehood Indicators

NOTE: Letters *A* through *D* indicate the links between clusters specified in the ordered
matrix in Table 3.2. *E* ($P_1 \leftrightarrow S_2$) is not shown because there are only two links; one
of these is negative MSIU $\leftrightarrow$ POWER) and the other is affected by a large no-informa-
tion (JEFES $\leftrightarrow$ MEDIA). There are no links between the P_2 and S_2 clusters (*F*).

to show the full set of 24 elitehood indicators as interconnected subsystems.
Table 3.2 identifies the main clusterings but is designed primarily to highlight the relationships that connect the main clusters. Figure 3.1 emphasizes the substantive composition of each subsystem and how it "decomposes" internally. The method used to identify the subsystems is an adaptation of HIDECS, a computer program for the hierarchical decomposition
of a set with an associated linear graph. The aim is by successive partition-

TABLE 3.2   *Ordered Matrix of Exact Probabilities of Association among Elitehood Indicators*

Indicators																							
No. Name	P_1			P_2					S_1											S_2			
14 FPICK																							
20 MEDIA	99																						
15 ABROAD	94	99																					
1 POWER	99	69	94																				
12 MAGRIT	*	*	—	*															89				
16 LEGATE	*	—	—	—	A														99	98			
18 SCHOOL	—	—	—	—															95	96			
22 TYRO	*	—	—	—															69	99			
17 CPICK	*	—	—	*					71										94				
11 NUSRIT	—	—	—	*	*	*	—	*	—	*									99				
19 MATER	*	*	—	*	*	—	—			*	99	92											
2 SPHERE	—	—	—	—	—	—	—	—		—	68	99	99										
5 BAGS	*	—	—	—	—	—	D	—	B	—	99	94	99	99									
6 INCOME	—	—	—	—	—	—	*	—	—	—	86	99	99	99	99								
7 WHEEL	—	—	—	—	—	—	*	*	—	—	99	98	96	99	97	93							
9 FIELD	*	—	—	*	—	—	*	*	*	—	80	97	97	96	97	99							
13 HOPPER	*	*	—	*	—	—	—	—	—	—	35	80	96	75	64	99	93						
3 AGE	—	—	—	—	—	—	—	—	—	—	38	99	95	91	83	99	99	94					
10 CAPTAL	—	—	—	—	—	—	—	—	—	—	83	94											
8 NOWYRS	—	—	—	*	—	—	—	—	—	—	78	95	99	85	98	85	99	91	95				
4 MSIU	—	—	—	—	—	—	—	—	—	*	—	*	*	*	*	*	*	*	*	*	94		
21 JEFES	—	*	—	*	*	*	F	—	E	—	—	—	C	—	—	—	—	—	—	—	81	99	
23 JOINER	*	—	—	—	—	*	—	—	—	—	—	*	—	*	*	*	—	*	*	—	80	99	99
24 CREST	14	20	15	1	12	16	18	22	17	11	19	2	5	6	7	9	13	3	10	8	4	21	23
																							97
																							23

Note: The asterisks indicate associations between clusters. Only probabilities larger than 0.95 have been marked. Table 3.1 gives the full specification of what each indicator represents.

75

ings to identify the subsets of variables that have the most correlations internally and the fewest across subsets.[12]

The partitioning displayed in the table and figure strongly supports the notion that the emphasis given to power and sphere is highly congruent with the "natural" or empirically established order of relations among these variables. Four major clusters emerge: two power clusters (P_1, P_2) of about equal size and two sphere clusters, one quite large (11 variables), the other with only four variables. The two power clusters consist almost entirely of facets of *communication* behavior or experiences: media use, extended travel abroad, writing in magazines, attendance at international conferences. The only two variables not directly of this nature (years of schooling and number of work spheres in which paid positions are held) are bound to the cluster P_2 by their strong association with communication variables — writing in magazines and participation in meetings outside the country. P_1 and P_2 are themselves strongly linked by a sociometric variable (the number of times an individual was claimed as a friend by elite peers) and by writing in magazines. The first of these is the dominant variable in the entire set ($P_1 + P_2$). In the final step of "decomposition," power score and another communication variable (the number of elite peers claiming to be in communication with a subject) emerge as relatively independent elements within the cluster.

The smaller of the "sphere" clusters, S_2, has no links at all to P_2. One of the connections to P_1, through the variable MSIU (contact with foreigners in Venezuela), is negative. It will be recalled that frequent communication with foreigners inside Venezuela was earlier noted as a negative associate of power scores. The other link to P_1, through JEFES (the number of different types of organizations in which office is held) to MEDIA (frequency of exposure in radio, television, newspapers, and magazines), is also negative in its implications, multiple office holding tending to go with moderate rather than intensive media exposure. As S_2 consists almost entirely of organizational participation variables, there is further confirmation here of the secondary place of this dimension in contemporary elite action in Venezuela.

The largest cluster, S_1, "decomposes" into three subclusters. The first of

---

[12] The partitioning was performed on a matrix of the exact probabilities of association between each of the twenty-four indicators of elitehood and every other as established by chi square. Refer to Christopher Alexander, *Notes on the Synthesis of Form.* The adaptation of the HIDECS program for the present analysis was made by Carlos Domingo, director of the Computation Center of the Central University of Venezuela, while at M.I.T. as a visiting scientist during 1967.

these seems to capture a time dimension that, as has been noted, distinguishes among action spheres — age, time in present position, years of residence in Caracas. A smaller cluster or dyad (NUSRIT and MATER) reminds us that few of those with university training abroad write in newspapers. It also underscores the point that in Venezuela to write in newspapers denotes only a field of activity whereas to write in magazines is a mark of power, MAGRIT being a central variable in the P_1 and P_2 clusters. The remaining subcluster highlights the distinctiveness of the several spheres in amount and sources of income, in field of training and diversity of occupations over the course of the working career, and in frequency of contact with diverse population groups in Venezuela other than foreigners.

A few of the variables that connect the power clusters with sphere (those links shown in boxes B and D in Figure 3.1) are of special interest. The three that seem to invite additional attention are age, university attended, and the variety of past work experience as manifested by the number of spheres in which a subject has worked at least ten years (HOPPER). There is a complex of age, experience, and training factors at work here which tie in with power and field of specialization in subtle ways. Almost the totality of subjects without university education are, not surprisingly, among men over fifty. Businessmen as a group are older than the leadership in other fields, but this sector also contains most of those with technical specialties. Leadership under 43 is all university trained, and those with graduate training and degrees are concentrated in the 43 to 50 age group. It is the latter group which was attributed most power by the panel of outside judges, though the friendship claims in the sociometric tests favor the older men. For this reason, the appearance is given that sociometric choices favor men without any university training at all as much as those who studied in the United States. On the other hand, those who studied at the Central University predominate among the "parochials" with little or no foreign travel. Because the study of technical specialties is pursued mostly abroad, another thread of complexity is introduced here. The weight of practically all of these factors on the diversity of fields a subject is likely to enter into during a working lifetime seems obvious and is indeed manifest in Table 3.2. It is through this experience variable (HOPPER) that the predominantly sphere-fixing age and training variables seem to get diffused to power related dimensions. Though elusive and perhaps impossible to capture in any single new index amenable to the kind of quantitative analysis being attempted here, one begins to scent at this point the intricacies of the clash of generations and cultures widely believed to be a major source of elite malfunction in Venezuela. This question will demand increasing attention as new types of data are woven into the analysis.

Class and Mobility

The relationship of class and mobility to power standing and functional specialization within the elite is obviously vital to an understanding of the prevailing structure of dominance or leadership in Venezuela as well as to an assessment of the potential for conflict stemming from this key source of social differentiation. The ambiguities and uncertainties in this respect are notable in Venezuela. This study began with a keen sense of the newness to power of many of the individuals to be studied and the organizations these men were simultaneously directing and building.[13] A short four years before this research a major political turnover had produced a complete renovation of incumbents at the upper levels of political action and multiplied the number of political parties, had shaken up and restructured the organizations of businessmen, especially in their dealings with government and parties, and had given impulse to fundamental changes in education and mass communications.

Nevertheless, a persistent sense that major structural changes had yet to come and that somehow, within the apparent flux of power, oligarchical elements continued to exercise subtle controls over public policy prevailed in much political debate and social analysis. The social imagery of this oligarchy was, however, quite complex. At one extreme stood simple affirmations that a tight clique of economically powerful families in combination with their military supporters and abetted by a pliant Church as well as by external economic powers was able not only to impose a veto on policies not to their liking but to manipulate those in public office almost at will. Others saw more complex adaptations and survivals of oligarchic forms within a system that had already undergone major transformation. The distinction had early been drawn between the social as against the cultural configuration of an oligarchy, so that even if it were apparent to some that the structural and organizational base for traditional oligarchical domination was absent, the existing power structure could still be seen as oligarchic in intent, style, and aspiration.[14] A rather long quote from a major political figure conveys the odd fashion in which this theme is simul-

---

[13] *SRSP*, Introduction, p. xiv.
[14] Refer to Chapter 2, pp. 50 ff.

taneously affirmed and rejected in contemporary appraisals by knowledge-able party leaders.

This is a strange country. This is a country in which oligarchic groups have never had influence as a deciding power. They have not had the influence to designate, to dispose; their influence has gone merely to moderate impulses. Oligarchic groups influenced Páez, who was a man born of the people, to impede his commanding a great process of transformation and total change. As regards Guzmán Blanco and Falcón, once the Federal Wars had broken out they acted as a brake, but not as a deciding force to raise [persons] to positions of command. Since that time in Venezuela . . . the oligarchic groups have not brought anyone [to power] because, moreover, power was transferred on the field of battle and the victor on the battlefield was always from the people [*pueblo*]. After 1858, the oligarchies in Venezuela were displaced from power . . . maintaining their capacity for influence through economic organization, the large landholders, the bankers, the capitalists, the importers who blocked the development of the country. But as a group in command at the top, no. . . . How did Castro reach power? Does Castro reach power in the hands of the oligarchy? No. . . . Later he defects and the oligarchies take refuge under his wing and begin to corrupt him. It is for this reason that General Gómez used to say that his comrade Castro was a good man, but that the Caracas oligarchies had corrupted him, and for that reason he was going to Maracay. What happened to General Gómez is that he became an oligarch and in his own turn created an oligarchy around himself, but it was not the old Caracas oligarchy.[15]

The data on class and mobility to be presented here cannot settle the multiple issues posed by these varied formulations, but they can serve at least to establish some senses in which the notion of oligarchy seems inapplicable in Venezuela today, leaving the way open to a clearer appraisal of how social power is in fact related to group and class interests.

One question that might be asked is whether those in the present elite are largely the offspring of traditional ruling sectors (large landowners and the military) now appearing in guises more suitable to the demands of the moment. Some support for such an interpretation seems to be given in Table 3.3. Nearly four in ten of the elite subjects do in fact have grandfathers who were landowners or military men, while another four in ten of the grandfathers were businessmen (largely in commerce). In the fathers' generation the proportion in the traditional sector diminishes substantially (to about one in four), although the business class approaches fifty percent. Among the present group of subjects the traditional sector is no longer visible. Of course, there are still military and landowning elites,

[15] Interview 062177, pp. 22, 23. These remarks summarize succinctly much of what is most relevant to the present analysis from Chapter 2.

TABLE 3.3   Intergenerational Differences in Main Occupational Sectors (Percentages)

		Subjects	
	Grandfathers	Fathers	First Job	Main Present Position
Agriculture and military	37	24	3	—
Business	42	47	31	29
Government and sciences	21	29	66	71

but the landowners no longer figure importantly at this level of power (if they ever did), and the military evaded our interviewers. However, the argument here is not primarily about changes in elite composition over recent generations but about the extent to which contemporary elites looking backward might have a basis for identifying with traditional ruling sectors.[16] These first data are inconclusive, indicating a substantial fluidity of intergenerational movement among occupational sectors, which may be interpreted as evidence of freedom of social movement across occupational boundaries but could merely manifest the adaptability of ruling groups to new circumstances.

TABLE 3.4   Intergenerational Differences in Occupational Status (Percentages)

			Subjects	
			First Job	Main Present Position
N =	Grandfathers (151)	Fathers (175)	(177)	(180)
High	17	22	28	100
Upper middle	33	41	59	—
Middle and low[a]	50	37	13	—

[a] Includes mostly white collar along with artisans, small shopkeepers, and a few skilled workers and small farmers.

Better evidence that the social reference points in the past for contemporary leaders are middle-class rather than oligarchic in any meaningful sense is shown in Table 3.4. The occupational status of the fathers and

[16] Because the parental generations shown here certainly cannot be taken as representative of elites in their time, the data are not a way of demonstrating structural change in Venezuela but only an aid in defining a generational space of social reference and awareness for these subjects.

grandfathers of present elites is by and large relatively modest. Lower- or working-class backgrounds are very infrequent among these subjects; a sizable majority come from middle- or upper-middle-class families and are status mobile vis-à-vis their fathers. It is interesting in this connection that mobility is characteristic of the present subjects but not of their fathers, seven in ten of whom are reported as holding the same or lower status positions than the grandfathers. Subjects are thus not only highly mobile as individuals but seem to represent the vanguard of a broad-gauged generational take-off in mobility. They have as a group outstripped their brothers in status gains, but the brothers on the average also show advances in status over the fathers.[17]

Although high mobility characterizes subjects in all elite spheres at present, a particular pattern of association between intergenerational mobility and present sphere of action is clear and consistent (Table 3.5). Those

TABLE 3.5 *Occupational Status Mobility: Exact Probabilities of Association with Power and Sphere*

	Power	*Sphere*
Occupational status of paternal grandfather	0.090	0.982
Occupational status of maternal grandfather	0.814	0.944
Occupational status of father	0.460	0.897
Respondent's status in first job	0.601	0.895
Index of intergenerational mobility[a]	0.468	0.998

[a] This index, one of several, groups subjects according to the number of the following characteristics: grandfather (paternal or maternal) with a high status occupation and father with high job status and/or high educational achievement.

now in politics show the most modest origins whereas the few with high status antecedents are concentrated among the top business leadership. No such pattern emerges with respect to power scores; the fact of status mobility does not imply advantage or disadvantage with respect to relative power standing within the elite once entry has been gained.

Yet another possibility may be explored in pursuit of the oligarchy thesis. It may be that these elite subjects are upwardly mobile middle-class individuals coopted through marriage into the inner circles of influence

[17] These gains are more marked in education than in job status. Of the subjects with brothers, half have brothers who on the average got more education than the father. Only a quarter have brothers who also on the average rose above the father occupationally. This implies substantial mobility at these middle-class levels but also means that elite individuals are tied by close kinship to men in modest situations.

and power. Little can be learned on this score from studying the women who share the family world of the respondents. Fewer than one in ten of the mothers of these men have more than primary school training. Sisters of respondents average slightly higher, the median lying in the incomplete secondary category. Only a handful of the mothers ever had any important occupational activity outside the home, and this remains true of the sisters of these men today. Fewer than one in ten of the wives have activities outside the home, and their median education also lies at the incomplete secondary level. Early marriage does not seem to explain the low education of these high status wives for the median age at marriage is in the early twenties.

Apart from an interesting first glimpse into the private lives of subjects, these facts suggest the marginal participation of women as individuals in their own right in the surge of middle-class mobility that their husbands symbolize. They also make clear that one must look to the *males* in the families of the wives for any inkling as to the significance for mobility of these marriages. On the whole these findings suggest that the elite figures under study have by and large married into families much like their own. Apart from the similarities in the women that have been noted, there is a high association between the occupational status of subjects' fathers and that of their wives' fathers. This is also true of the education of both sets of fathers. The education of the wives' brothers is on the average substantially below that of subjects, and relatively few of the brothers-in-law of the present elite are reported as holding high status jobs. Thus, both by origin and by marriage, elite subjects (except for a small group largely concentrated in the economic sector) are tied to a social world largely peopled by persons of modest, middle-class culture and accomplishments.[18]

Returning then to the fundamental questions posed in the opening paragraphs, some first answers can be given on the basis of the data on social backgrounds that have been presented.

1. The takeover of power by middle-class elements in Venezuela can be regarded on this evidence as complete within the cultural and political spheres and well under way within the business world. This process has taken place largely within the life-span of the subjects under study. Though

---

[18] Another question relevant to the oligarchy theme is whether present elites are passing on to their sons their own status gains. This seems to be the case. Practically all of the respondents' sons over eighteen have either completed university training or are in the university. These who are employed, especially economic sector sons, are in upper-middle or high status positions.

the matter cannot be discussed in detail here, it is important to keep in mind that this process did not involve the displacement of a well-structured aristocracy or oligarchy, but the overthrow of a system in which a favored subset of the groups now in power, organized loosely around a caudillo, managed the nation in their own interest.[19]

2. High mobility characterizes the top power wielders of all sectors, but it is the political sector that has been most clearly an avenue of ascent for men of modest origins and the economic sector that conserves visible traces of inherited power and status bridging several generations.

3. The marked presence of foreign-born individuals at all levels of economic activity in Venezuela is apparently only beginning to make itself felt in the ranks of the nation's top economic leadership. That is, outside the major international corporations, the foreign-born figure importantly at all levels of management but seem as yet to be excluded from the topmost circle of elitehood. Within the political and cultural sectors the penetration of first- and even second-generation immigrants is negligible.

4. Practically all factors of social background that differentiate elite sectors lend emphasis to the polarity between political and economic leaders.

5. Class and mobility, though related to main sphere of action, show no marked link to relative power standing. The power dimension, which, as has been shown, is most clearly tied to communication variables, may on this basis be viewed as probably more responsive to circumstantial factors of action *once within* the elite than to factors of social origin or the experience of social ascent.

6. Thus the data on social characteristics by themselves establish some probable grounds for intersector conflict within the elite but do not shed light on the bases of conflict between different power levels, which is also a central hypothesis of the research.

It should be clear at this point that the present discussion only opens the subject of how class and mobility are related to comparative power standing and specialization within the Venezuelan elite. Perhaps the most dramatic finding so far is the direct and intimate fashion in which the nation's top leadership is socially embedded in a primarily middle-class world of limited perspectives. What consequences this fact has for elite evaluations,

---

[19] Though no detailed data are available from the present research, the middle-class backgrounds of the principal elite sector that has been omitted — the military — and particularly of those officers who would have figured in the present sampling, are well established.

attitudes, and ideological orientation is the larger issue to which subsequent analysis will turn. Clearly, for example, the absence of sociological grounds for talking about an oligarchy in Venezuela does not foreclose the possible cultural survival of an oligarchic tradition in elite thought and action, however middle class the bearers of this tradition may appear.

4   PATHS TO ELITEHOOD

The foregoing analysis has provided a fairly detailed picture both of the power attributes of subjects in the positions in which the research found them and of the social contexts in which they began their ascent. However, it has yielded a much more sketchy image of respondents' trajectories on the way to positions of power. Some were seen to achieve high status at an earlier age than others, some had used periods of study and work abroad to advantage, some had moved about a great deal from one sphere of activity to another, all had gravitated to Caracas. For some the rise to eminence had been smooth, untroubled, and unfolded as a natural process clearly foreshadowed in early advantage. For others the way up had been marked with unpredictable swings of fortune, punctuated by violence, imprisonment, and exile.

The youngest among these men were in their middle to late thirties in 1963. The study thus covers careers that began at periods ranging over three decades — roughly from the mid-1920's to the period immediately after World War II. These subjects took up work and organizational roles in the period that spans the waning of the Gómez era and the imposition of a new dictatorship in 1948. The critical events of this period have been roughly outlined in Chapter 2 of this volume, accenting those aspects believed to be most relevant to an understanding of the emergence of the elite under study here and its role in those events.[1]

The study of careers is, of course, as old as biography. No particular difficulties would be presented if "career" were taken to mean no more than a description of a sequence of jobs or life situations for an individual.

[1] Chapter 1, *SRSP,* provides a more comprehensive, macroanalytical overview of events in this period. Early chapters in Volume 3 cover the same ground from the perspective of nonelite groups in the population.

But even the most primary or neutral of such descriptions tend to impute some characteristics to the individual involved, to groups with which he is identified, or to the society or subsector of the society in which such changes of position take place. Thus, as soon as a list of jobs is called "a career," a great many problems arise. Implicit in the idea of career is the notion of movement along a path, but this casually invoked metaphor introduces a great many ambiguities and demands for specification. What is the nature of the space traversed by such a path? What motivates people to move along it? Is such movement best envisaged as a calculated journey, as the conditioned running of a fixed maze, or as a random walk? Is the mobile individual a path *maker* or merely moving through a socially prestructured, life-shaping course?

Three basic types of information will be brought to bear on questions such as these. The first data source is the detailed occupational and organizational histories that have been treated summarily in Chapter 3. In addition to this simple job and organizational record, respondents were invited to discuss in considerably more detail the two or three job changes that they themselves believed to have been ultimately most decisive in shaping their careers. Part of that information has also been coded and will be examined in the aggregate for clues as to typical or distinctive career lines within elite subsectors.[2] Finally, these same accounts will be used to provide a more rounded, qualitative sense of the actual circumstances in which such critical shifts in activity occur and how they are experienced by those who live them.

Summary Career Characteristics

Some first clues to over-all career configurations came to the surface in Chapter 3, particularly in the cluster analysis that brought out the sub-

[2] In a study that accumulates such extensive and diverse data some choices are inevitably made about the treatment of parts of the information that are later regretted. Thus in the coding of job histories, details concerning intermediate jobs (positions between the first reported job and the main job at time of interview) were coded in aggregate. This means that the coding recorded how many such jobs there were, in what fields, in what kinds of positions within each field, and for what lengths of time in each field. This decision was made as an economy but also partly in recognition that at the time we had few good ideas about how to compare a career with ten changes as against one with three or four. By the time we began to get some hunches that seemed worth exploring, the cost of going back seemed prohibitive in view of the probably marginal gains in terms of the central interests of the research. Unfortunately, not having this detail also prevented a later matching of the complete job records with the more selective sequence of changes cited by the subjects as decisive in shaping their careers. The present chapter might have been materially enriched had that been possible.

groups of variables that tend to go with relative power as against those that signal main sphere of action (see Table 3.2 and Figure 3.1). Holding high positions in several organizations (JEFES) can be seen there to be closely tied to sphere and specifically to the economic sector. This particular cluster thus includes other characteristics that mark the business elite — high income, multiple sources of income, frequent contact with foreigners in Venezuela, and relatively low contact with nonbusiness groups within the country. In contrast to this, holding multiple *paid positions* in more than one sphere (TYRO) is more closely linked to power and communication variables — writing in magazines, travel to international conferences, and postgraduate study (again, usually abroad). This latter cluster of variables links into the political and cultural spheres rather than the economic.

However, the most obvious inference — that businessmen rise through and consolidate their prestige in organizations whereas the other two sectors rely more on occupational movement, advanced training, and communications — would be more accurate with respect to what happens once people are close to the top than with respect to how they got there. The fact is that businessmen achieve high status in their *work* sphere earlier than others and move into high positions in organizations only later. The reverse is true for politicians and men in the cultural sector.

Some of these relations, based on information on all jobs held, are shown in Table 4.1. Men in government and politics were younger than other elite individuals at the time of interview. But businessmen are in important managerial posts at an early age; half of the economic sector leaders interviewed were in such positions by the time they were thirty. Only about one in five cultural figures had achieved equivalent status by that time in their lives. As regards organizations, however, it takes businessmen nearly an additional ten years (around age 40) to get into command positions. When they do so, they seem to go into more numerous activities than other elite individuals.[3] Careers in the cultural sector, as they emerge here, take longer and involve greater movement from one sphere to another than do others.

Relationships to power scores of these same variables are more ambigu-

---

[3] It is probably somewhat misleading in this instance to speak of differences in reaching high positions in business firms as against business organizations as a time *lag*. The proliferation of business-sponsored organizations in Venezuela is recent and has been led by prestigious elder statesmen in combination with some energetic, younger men. Some of this qualitative detail is brought out later in this chapter. Refer also to Chapter 7 on organization.

ous and indirect (Table 4.2). The median age at interview of subjects with different power scores is about the same, but the age distribution within each power level is very different. Those with low power scores spread rather evenly over the full age range (from 34 to 80 years); the middle-level power group has a U-shaped age curve with young and older

TABLE 4.1   Summary Career Characteristics by Sphere

	Main Action Sphere		
N =	Economic (58)	Political (86)	Cultural (36)
Median age at interview	49	44	49
Median age at which high status position in present main field was achieved	29	33	33
Percentage achieving high status position in present main field before age 30[a]	50	35	19
Percentage with paid positions in two or more spheres	38	37	47
Percentage with five or more years experience in more than one sphere	24	27	42
Median age at which high organizational office was first achieved	39	37	40
Percentage holding high organizational office before age 40	53	62	44
Percentage holding three or more organizational offices	50	32	36
Percentage with five or more years activity in more than one type of organization	47	51	36

[a] Percentages in age groupings have been shown when some idea of the distribution is required to interpret the medians.

men predominating. The highest power group has as a dominant component men in their middle to late forties (43 to 50 years). Organizational experience and multiple tenure of office show moderate but not statistically impressive associations with power. Variety and movement in past and present paid positions, as already noted, is not a very good direct predictor of power scores but is tied in with numerous other experience and training variables that do link up with relative power standing.

Aggregating these many bits of information about the totality of positions held by elite subjects thus tells us primarily that there are some interesting differences in the paths traveled upward by businessmen as against

TABLE 4.2 Summary Career Characteristics by Power Score

		Power Scores	
N =	Low (45)	Median (67)	High (65)
Median age at interview[a]	47	46	47
Median age at which high status position in present main field was achieved	31	32	34
Percentage with paid positions in two or more spheres	42	34	43
Percentage with five or more years experience in more than one sphere	29	27	31
Median age at which high organizational office was first achieved	39	36	39
Percentage holding three or more organizational offices	31	39	43
Percentage with five or more years activity in more than one type of organization	36	46	54

[a] Refer to text for comments on age distribution within the three power levels.

those followed by the other two sectors. These differences have to do mostly with the timing and relative prominence in career configurations of jobs (paid positions) as against organizational office (in parties, chambers of commerce, professional colleges, unions). However, as we know that it is not useful to think of these "paths" as vectors through a well-defined space, very little more can be ventured by way of analytical inference from this first overview. Time and age here mean *change,* and often changes in opportunities and availabilities of work or organizational positions generated by these actors themselves. Elite individuals on the move do not merely have careers; they either make careers (that is, create firms, parties, offices) for themselves and others or simply ride the bandwagons of individuals with greater motive power. Group careers in this sense do not merely represent preferred options among available routes but a complex interplay of aspirations, capabilities, and contingencies. The following pages seek to push beyond the point at which most career analysis breaks off by introducing additional detail about sequences of jobs and offices and the circumstances surrounding such shifts.[4]

[4] There are only six items indexed to career in a recent bibliography covering books in print, other bibliographies, and 100 social science journals published in English (1945 to 1967). See Carl Beck and J. Thomas McKechnie, *Political Elites: A Selected Computerized Bibliography* (Cambridge, Mass.: The M.I.T. Press, 1968).

Important Job Shifts

Over a full lifetime of work or political struggle many job changes or ventures into organizational action occur that seem of trivial importance in determining final success. Nevertheless, as soon as one tries to think of jobs and job changes as *leading* somewhere, a sizable constellation of serviceable indicators of the relative significance of particular positions to the career comes to mind: the amount of time in the position, the stage in the career when the change takes place, whether the change involves entry into a new institutional sphere, the kinds of personal associations formed while in it, successes or setbacks, chances for the acquisition of new skills. All of these imply the enhancement in one way or another of personally controlled resources for self-advancement — skills, experience, motivation, material resources, influence.

No effort has been made in the present case to assess from this perspective each of the more than fifteen hundred jobs that figure in the complete work histories nor the similar number of organizational offices in the record of participation in such groups. Subjects were asked rather to indicate themselves the two or three among all the job changes reported that had been of particular significance in bringing them to the position occupied at the time of interview. Additional details were then obtained about the circumstances in which these changes occurred, factors weighing in the choice, experiences in the new position, and the gains or losses each represented in terms of career potential.

Of course, the criteria applied by subjects in designating changes in job or office as critical are varied, not always clear, and not necessarily more correct than those that might have been introduced by the analyst. Whereas the analyst is inclined to focus on resources and capabilities for forward movement, subjects see jobs or offices from many more perspectives and speak more as though they were concerned with opportunities to act or use skills than with advancing career goals. The idea of career itself is a hazy one in most such discussion except as it connotes diversely a diffuse socially esteemed achievement and an individually productive, ideologically correct, or a morally irreproachable public record. In a period of great flux, such as the decades under review here, the ground for a realistic evaluation of each opportunity as it arose in life even in terms of such vague canons are precarious indeed.[5]

---

[5] Changes other than those in job or office are, of course, relevant to careers as they are to the more general question of social mobility. Evidence concerning changes

Many obscure and subjective influences may thus reasonably be supposed to be at work in respondents' decisions to highlight some positions rather than others in recapitulating past activities. One very common feature in these accounts, nevertheless, was the tendency to attribute importance to job or office changes in mid- or late career and particularly to those involving changes of sphere. Among the 162 respondents who gave enough information about such decisive changes to warrant inclusion in this part of the analysis, a majority (52 percent) gave details about one or two such changes, about a third talked only about job changes within a single sphere, and a small minority (12 percent) reported three or more important changes of this kind. Interestingly, when *all* job changes are considered, the cultural sector emerges as the one with most diverse experience, though in this more selective account sphere is not related to the number of such changes. This further supports the impression that selective importance has been given in these accounts to changes that meant crossing over into a new institutional area.

Just as the earlier data seen in the aggregate suggested two main career lines — one for businessmen and the other more common to politicians and cultural leaders — so does this second data set point to dual, contrasting paths to the top.[6] One path emphasizes continuity in a single field, relatively long tenure of specific positions, and seems to lead to high income rather than to the higher power levels (Table 4.3). The second involves more variety, briefer tenure of positions, more purposeful movement from one position to another, greater vulnerability or sensitivity to political events, educational gains in mid-career, and leads more surely to high power standing than to high income. Though the relationship to main sphere is obscured by the selectivity factors in reporting that have been noted, these broad characterizations will be seen, on closer examination of the qualitative materials, to have added fresh facets to the basic picture building up here. That picture is one in which economic careers are

in education, residence, status gains through marriage, and so on, has been discussed in Chapter 3 and is presented here in an accessory way, but the emphasis has been consciously placed on tracing the more public trajectories of job and office. An incisive discussion of the need for more systematic treatment of the multiple facets of mobility patterns is Harold L. Wilensky's "Measures and Effects of Social Mobility," in Neil J. Smelser and S. M. Lipset, eds., *Social Structure and Mobility in Economic Development* (Chicago: Aldine, 1966).

[6] The tallies that support this section are based on some 500 job changes for 162 respondents. No extensive statistical testing has been done and none is shown in the single table included, though the analysis has been guided by results of an adaptation of Fisher's Exact Test incorporated in the M.I.T. ADMINS data-processing system. The commentary here is a summary of many such tallies.

*TABLE 4.3   Summary Characteristics of Important Job Changes
             by Frequency of Changes in Main Sphere of Activity*

		Changes in Sphere	
N =	*None* (58)	*One or Two* (84)	*Three or More* (20)
Percentage who have			
Power scores higher than 2.4	66	73	85
1963 income above 100,000 Bs.	48	42	30
More than five years in at least one of major jobs	43	38	30
Improved education between major job changes	28	30	50
Job changes related to political events	36	27	50
Mobilized personal influences to make job changes	65	75	80

increasingly set off from those in other sectors with respect to almost every dimension that has been explored.

Some additional clues to the play of elements in important career changes may be gleaned from looking at these alternately in the aggregate as above and seriatim (that is, first job, first important change, second important change, and so on). Economic leaders started their careers more often than others with fathers who were already achievers in their own sphere. Characteristically, little time was spent in the first position by men in any sector. But unlike businessmen politicians seem rarely to have held on to any job for as long as five years, whether early or late in the career. Gains in education between jobs usually occur early in the career and apparently slightly less often among businessmen. However, as will be seen, businessmen were generally substantially ahead of others in their schooling when they took their first jobs. Men in other sectors often began work just after and sometimes even before completing primary school. This helps explain the numerous short-term positions that mark the early occupational histories, especially of politicians.

Roughly four in ten of all job changes in all spheres are candidly reported to have involved some mustering of personal influences. It is in mid-career that the combination of a more prolonged job tenure and parallel gains in education seems to pay off most directly in the capacity to mobilize such personal networks. Though the proportion of changes in which politically related events or influence initiatives figure is fairly constant from early to late job shifts, the intensity of the impact on the career of such politically shaped circumstances and individual initiatives seems also to have been at its height in mid-career. It is in these latter moves as well that such resourcefulness also most clearly eventuates in solid status gains in job moves. Thus status gains are on the whole less marked in later jobs but are more clearly linked then to entry into new spheres, especially government, party, or cultural endeavors.

Finally there is some visible patterning in the movement among spheres of activity from one job to another. On each job change individuals moving out of politics go in roughly equal proportions to business or to cultural affairs (usually to university or media work). Businessmen leaving the field early in the game tend to move into the cultural sphere; later on they are more often drawn into government. Those who begin in the cultural sphere make early shifts primarily to politics and only in late changes do they begin to move into business as often as into governmental or party activity. It is as if constraints on certain kinds of cross-sector movement were only thrown off as individuals achieved a sufficiently secure anchorage in their own main sphere either to move about at will or to have freely transferable status resources.[7]

Business Trajectories

On the strength of the aggregate characteristics of jobs and job changes in the economic sphere an image of stability, smoothness, and security gradually takes form. It is careers in business, as has been seen, that bear visible traces of inherited status and advantage bridging generations. It is businessmen more often than others who begin employment with a palpably assured future. After relatively short and sometimes merely pro forma apprenticeships at the middle levels, these men are installed in positions of responsibility. As they mature, their positions multiply and they are increasingly drawn into the organizational politics of the business sphere, into the representation of business interests vis-à-vis government, into various forms of business statesmanship, and finally into government itself. Though some few still make the hard climb to business eminence

[7] It will be recalled that in *SRSP* the sociometric measures of cross-sector friendship and communication ties were all considerably higher between the political and cultural spheres than between the economic sphere and either of the former. See Tables 9.3 and 9.4, pp. 231 and 232.

largely on their own, the steady progression through a well-delineated path of advancement within the family firm, the business syndicate, or the large corporation is probably becoming more typical. This does not mean that business careers are uneventful or that individual capacities weigh little in career outcomes. However, in contrast to those who give most of their lives to politics or work in the cultural sphere, businessmen move in a world of considerable order, regularity, and steady satisfactions and tend to remain within it. Some of the contextual qualities of this privileged milieu can be conveyed by a brief overview of several careers in business.

The first subject, a young industrialist, comes from a family whose business activities in Venezuela date from the turn of the century. The wide-ranging financial interests of this group are managed by three generations of the family men and their associates. After schooling in a U.S. university, he entered the family business in the early 1940's. Ten years later, after enjoying some early successes, he was named vice president of one of the family firms. "At a given moment in those years my income was possibly the highest of any person in the region of my age, which was then 26." [8]

Over the years as the family industrial interests expanded and his own scope of activity broadened, he successively assumed duties on numerous boards of directors, was drawn into the intense political rivalries among business groups that are fought out in the Federation of Chambers of Commerce (Fedecamaras), and was delegated important representing functions for industrialists in a governmental body concerned with financial policy.[9] These activities finally brought him to a position outside the family network where at last he was able to savor a sense of independent achievement.

> This is a position that has filled me with satisfaction. I have been called by a very large economic group, a very important group, and I have found for the first time . . . that I am taken into account. Because, unfortunately, up till now I have worked in companies that I managed for relatives, many times because of one's youth one's opinion is not given consideration.[10]

---

[8] Interview 057167, p. 2.

[9] Refer to Chapter 7, pp. 76 ff., for some details concerning inner conflicts within the business community. Leadership functions within Fedecamaras have grown increasingly demanding: "One cannot be president of Fedecamaras and do business at the same time, because being president of Fedecamaras today is practically like being Minister of a private activity that demands a great effort to do it adequately." (Interview 057167, p. 27.)

[10] Interview 057167, p. 17.

The same kind of intergenerational conflict that is alleged to explain major schisms within political parties raises its head within family economic groups. Junior members complain both of being denied a voice in major decisions and being blamed for setbacks.

> I would call it [the problem of the family elders] an excess of personal pride and the opinion that they know everything, and the relatively narrow group within which they have their friendships, social and economic. In my opinion this did not give them the vision to adapt . . . to the growth of Venezuela.[11]

Despite such strictures and signs of restiveness among young, industrializing entrepreneurs, these family economic combines constitute a principal framework within which business leadership is formed and brought to maturity. Positions and opportunities are deployed, allocated, and met largely from within the circle of family and trusted associates.

Major corporations, especially the oil companies, constitute a second, even more controlled and apparently efficient, socializing milieu for the economic elite. Such companies have been recruiting carefully in the universities for several decades and, especially in the beginning, mainly from within the technical and scientific schools. A second business leader, today on the board of directors of a major oil company, began his career as a company geologist at about the same time that the man above took his place in a family enterprise. In this case older relatives and close family friends "interested" in his career were already well placed within the corporation as the young man took up his new duties. The ten years or so that the first man spent in apprenticeship (selling and submanagerial functions) the young geologist spent in tough exploration work and in oil camps. The decisive shift here (after eleven years in the company) is signaled by the transfer from technical to managerial functions:

> One morning in the most unexpected way the president of the company called me and told me that they had great interest in my accepting a position as assistant manager of a department that worked in a field totally unknown to me. Naturally I felt very honored but at the same time very fearful of getting into an entirely new field and in a management position, and I let my superiors know this with the greatest candor. They affirmed that they had no doubt that I would be able to further my career in this new activity, and, without giving it much thought, I answered that I accepted with delight.[12]

[11] Ibid., p. 42.
[12] Interview 323281, p. 8

Once onto the main line of ascent the subsequent rise and expansion in scope of action for this young executive was rapid and extensive. He carved out a distinctive set of functions for himself through specialization in the critically sensitive area of the industry's relations with government, with other oil companies, and within the national business establishment. In this way he moved quickly from a special assistantship at the highest level of management to the company's board of directors. Simultaneously his representative, organizational roles multiplied as did his opportunities to share in other business ventures and participate in the directorates of other enterprises. At this stage in the business career the service demands on business leaders ramify explosively, ranging over everything from housing to management training to the advancement of science to museum boards.

A particular mark of this special path to elitehood is the degree to which it is embedded in a formal apparatus of performance reviews, directed in-service training, evaluation, counseling, and studied rotation of functions. Moreover, the operations of this elaborate and inexorable machinery are justified in terms of an equally elaborated ideology in which individual aspirations and interests are fused with those of an abstracted "management" and an even more abstracted company "interest."

Those who have come up within the system defend it staunchly:

> All companies of our type are autocratic. Nevertheless, I have noted that in this organization, the individual who considers that he has been hurt by any measure has always had a chance to present his case. I am not going to say that generally or in most cases individual preferences win out, but in many cases the interest of the person is weighed against that of the company. If an individual does not want to accept a change or a position, I am sure that we have never forced him. . . . So that within all that autocracy or autocratic system individuality exists, the individual can speak, and there have been cases in which the individual has said: "I don't want to accept that. It is not in my interest." [13]

However, the roots of self-confidence are expected to rest on an implicit faith in one's self-worth as certified by the company's evaluation of the individual as a contributing factor within the larger scheme of the organization needs. Whatever technical and administrative provisions may be made to ensure the fairness and efficiency of this complex life-defining selection system, its smooth operation obviously hinges on high levels of acceptance and faith in the wisdom of the disposition being made of individual destinies.

[13] Interview 407305, p. 19.

If an individual has confidence in himself and trusts the company, if one is convinced that "I am valuable to the company, I contribute something to this," well, one is then already convinced that the company recognizes this. It may be that one is too much an organization man but one says "Well, they do it for my own good, for their own good.". . . Now if the individual for x reason does not have self-confidence . . . if he himself doubts whether he is valuable to the company, then it does rouse apprehension, it does cause an inner tremor. "Why can they be doing this? Surely they mean to . . . put something over on me [*echarme una vaina*]".[14]

The final product is a homogenized, all-purpose, international executive. The following comment is a description by a Venezuelan of a foreign-born executive filtered through this system. There is an unconscious self-depiction here. One may wonder whether this easy interidentification at the top among men of different nationalities is really explained by the advanced Venezuelanization of the outsiders or by common socialization in a broadly embracing corporate culture.

These are totally bilingual persons, completely adapted here, who have many years of service and many years of residence in the country. So that even though it might be said that this man is a foreigner and this other Venezuelan, he is a foreigner who knows how the Venezuelan thinks and how business is done here. He has the contacts with other firms in this field, with government. Thus, when you get to this level there is very little difference between one and the other.[15]

The self-made men in business are an earlier breed, more generally encountered among those who began their work lives in the middle or late 1920's. Small town and provincial beginnings are more common among them. They may have come up in tandem with successful brothers or other relatives but whatever family resources existed were in the process of accumulation during their rise. One such career begins with an apprenticeship as telegrapher in a small town. The father's intervention is critical despite the modesty of the position. The status implications of working for a foreign firm and the continuing relevance today of such considerations are candidly acknowledged.

My father had social contacts with them; . . . for that reason in a conversation with them he obtained that privilege. At that time it was considered a privilege for someone to get a job in the offices of [name of firm]. It was, for example, as if for someone who desires to learn office work and

---

[14] Ibid., p. 9.
[15] Interview 323281, p. 69.

gets a job in one of the oil companies, something that is synonymous with good organization, efficiency, it is one of those things that can prove a valuable experience.[16]

Two turning points give thrust to this career — the early discovery of a powerful talent for selling and, a few years later, a turning of that talent and drive to the promotion of national industry and the marketing of national products.

> I turned out to be a magnificent salesman because after that experience, all my life practically, I have been dedicated to selling something. Just as today I sell ideas for industrializing the country, at that time I sold . . . other articles. The times when I have made most money, let us say, most profit, have been those when I was selling. So that experience was very valuable to me . . . it helped me to discover my true vocation.[17]

The pioneering role in what they perceive as a more authentic industrialization of the country with effects reaching directly into life in the nation at all levels gives a missionary impulse and flavor to the efforts of these men that is absent among those who are younger and better connected internationally.

> To certain government figures [name of firm] seemed more like a subversive movement than an industrial enterprise because they talked about a series of new things that in the judgment of the governing group might even turn out to be revolutionary. All this business of incorporating the farmer into the national economy, of advancing and doubling the wages of persons in the haciendas, of buying and paying for crops in advance . . . all those measures were new and unusual and naturally revolutionary. They did not win us sympathy.[18]

Peaking in the career is here marked by the acquisition of full proprietorship in an industrial firm with collateral activities in investment financing and brokerage. As in other business careers, with eminence came public service demands both from within the business sector and from government. The aggressive economic nationalism of some of these home-grown capitalists, expressed in action both through government and private organizations, throws them occasionally into conflict with the younger group who think of themselves as more modern, sophisticated, and politically astute.[19] However, these internal differences are here less

[16] Interview 342237, p. 2.
[17] Ibid., pp. 3–4.
[18] Ibid., p. 14.
[19] Refer to Chapter 7, pp. 76 ff.

relevant than the over-all quality of regularity, smooth development, and strong convergence that characterize the march to elitehood in business.

Political Trajectories

It is this quality of order and continuity that most clearly sets off business careers from others and that most clearly symbolizes the detachment and distance from politics that businessmen have until very recently studiously cultivated as a public stance. Put most simply, businessmen have been committed to doing "business as usual" regardless of political events. Their most clearly articulated political aspiration and demand has been for "normalcy" — for the freedom of action and forms of protection that would shield them from the reverberations of political disturbances and conflicts. For the politician, by contrast, it has been precisely those breaks in "the usual" that are his main business, that shape and constitute his career. For this reason, political careers are the most public, the most deeply enmeshed in historical events, the most profoundly rooted in the mass experience of and involvement in the social change of the last few decades.

Because these lives are public property in a sense that goes beyond the mere fact of a very generalized and often intimate awareness of circumstantial details attending moments of personal crisis, it is a little more difficult to cite "typical" careers here without betraying the identity of persons who have spoken freely in confidence, even though hardly anything that is not in the public domain is likely to be mentioned.[20] Some liberties are therefore taken here in mixing up elements from similar careers and in keeping discussion in this section at a slightly more abstract level than in the immediately foregoing pages.

The political history of the past few decades in Venezuela is largely the history of the rise of a single party, Democratic Action (AD), and

[20] In citing interviews here and elsewhere no elaborate measures have been taken to mask identities, though we have been careful to eliminate all positively identifying detail. Individual subjects may occasionally feel they have been quoted or described in a way that betrays their identity. Knowledgeable persons may similarly be tempted to play a sort of detective game by collating scattered references to the same subject and seeking in this way to pin down individuals. Ideally, we believe, research such as this should be committed to full disclosure and bound to it by subjects rather than the reverse. However, we recognize that neither persons nor institutions are yet prepared to deal with open political communications of this kind in Venezuela or elsewhere. The option of embracing or rejecting the representations of individuals or organizations culled from study remains with our informants.

successive cleavages in its ranks. Aside from a small group who have held fast to early Marxist commitments and a Christian Democratic movement that emerged somewhat later, the political careers of all the men studied have been directly tied in one way or another with the fortunes of AD. Even groups such as the Communists and Christian Democrats who have been generally most resolute in opposition to AD and in maintaining a distinctive position of their own on national issues have either through tactical choice or by force of circumstance shared both moments of power and harsh persecution with AD. This process of intermittent coalition and political proliferation by inbreeding means that the lives, and particularly the early experiences in politics of men who today view each other across apparently unbridgeable ideological gulfs, have in the past been closely intermingled.[21]

The special mark of these political trajectories is their modest beginnings. Turning back the clock thirty-five or forty years and looking for the men at the top in Venezuelan politics today, one would find a scattering of adolescents in provincial cities, hard-pressed economically and working at modest if not menial jobs in efforts to help support themselves while continuing their schooling. The privileged exceptions have gravitated to political groupings other than AD or its main offshoots.

Among early occupations are apprenticeships in shoe-making, clerking in dry-goods shops, rent collecting, working as printers' devils, selling eyeglasses, and chauffering. But the classical path of beginning individual emancipation and ascent in Venezuela for this group has been teaching. Teaching careers in the Venezuela of the 1920's and 1930's began at an early age. The ink had hardly dried on a bright pupil's school certificate before he was back in the school teaching the course or grade he had just completed.

> Well, my interest in the profession was born after I was a teacher. In fact I became a teacher a little out of hunger. I had just finished my first year of secondary school (*bachillerato*) and was being supported by relatives; but as I was already nearly 18, I didn't want to continue being a burden to anyone.[22]

---

[21] Reference is made again to the several historical chapters in this series. Note especially Chapter 2 (pp. 58 ff) and also Chapter 7 (pp. 193 ff) in this volume. Accounts in English of the rise of AD include Robert J. Alexander, *The Venezuelan Democratic Revolution* (New Brunswick, N.J.: Rutgers University Press, 1964) and John D. Martz, *Acción Democratica* (Princeton, N.J.: Princeton University Press, 1966). Rómulo Betancourt's *Venezuela, política y petróleo,* cited earlier, remains the principal source narrative for these events.

[22] Interview 094184, Part A, p. 3.

On finishing primary school I needed some position, some work that would allow me to continue my secondary schooling. Then I was offered the second grade . . . and I began to work as a second grade teacher in the school where I had gone to primary school.[23]

Though these hardly sound like auspicious beginnings for careers in pedagogy, these early experiences were enlarged by teaching at higher levels and finally in the university. A diffuse mystique about the teaching function invests this aspect of the career, however marginal it may be in the over-all picture for a given case, with a particular value to the individual that is, no doubt, politically exploitable as well.

I have always been a teacher in all places, at all times; I have everywhere considered that the teaching profession is the one that entirely fulfills my basic vocation.[24]

In teaching I found myself. I found that it was a profession within which a personal ambition was realized . . . my goal of serving others, and I embraced the profession with great enthusiasm. Today I am absolutely convinced that my two main vocations are politics and teaching. I feel extraordinarily good when I have the opportunity of transmitting something I know to others.[25]

The process through which students, teachers, and workers came together in AD and other embryonic political forces of the time thus becomes clearer. A sizable number of individuals spent their teens and early twenties circulating from one group to another or were simultaneously active in more than one of these roles. For those who were to be professional party men two additional experiences are commonly shared at around this time that have important socializing implications. One of these is early participation in party life within the student context; the second is sharing in the distribution of offices and jobs that it was within the reach of the parties to use as rewards for their cadres.

I got that job by designation of the party to which I belonged . . . and which controlled the council. . . . As a consequence many party members were given administrative positions, preferably those who besides being well qualified for the positions had economic problems the party wanted to help them solve.[26]

Many such jobs as clerks, readers, and secretaries in various government offices were the means of subsistence for university students and a

[23] Interview 062177, Part A, p. 3. Only in the early 1940's did a primary school certificate become a requisite for teaching.

[24] Ibid., p. 6.

[25] Interview 094184, Part A, p. 3.

[26] Ibid., p. 7.

first foothold in and glimpse of government administration. Meanwhile within the student movement subjects were being schooled in the rudiments of party discipline and learning to savor the rewards and satisfactions of leadership.

> [I learned] in the first place to see things from the point of view of my party, which means to increase the political influence of my party among students in the mass at the national level. And from an exclusively student point of view, to keep student interest alive . . . in working in the ranks of an organization that apart from its interest in posing national political and social problems with a progressive, reformist perspective also frequently posed specifically student problems with the same forward-looking, leftist standards.[27]

A great watershed, though by no means an end to the uncertainties or dangers of political activity, is marked by the death of Gómez. This event is almost routinely taken as a landmark in recounting personal political histories.

> When Gómez died in 1935, I was working at my profession as a lawyer in contact with groups inimical to him. The death of Gómez caught me by surprise in [place] after I had been in [place] and [place] seeing other people who were enemies of Gómez in order to prepare ourselves for his inevitable death.[28]

But the long-awaited death of the tyrant brought only a brief pause in the drawn-out struggle that for a few had begun as early as 1914. The twenty-two years between 1936 and the overthrow of Pérez Jiménez in 1958 brought dramatic victories and occasional tastes of power for most of these men but also periods of imprisonment, exile, and economic hardship. A man could be a modest bookseller one day and Minister of Education the next, governor of an important state one year and bankrupt a few months later.

> When I took up the governorship . . . I did not have a cent in my pocket but I had no debts. I think I owed perhaps a month or six weeks for my lodgings. When I left the governorship I had a debt of nearly 20,000 Bs. even though the salary was more than satisfactory.[29]

Loyalties to comrades, desired objectives, and organization presumably provided the sense of continuity and consistency without which such an unpredictable and vulnerable pattern of life might have been intolerable

[27] Ibid., p. 18.
[28] Ibid., Part A, p. 15.
[29] Ibid., p. 21.

over such a long time span. The quotations that follow would have been more reassuring on this score had they not been spoken by men responsible for major schisms in their own organizations.

> In almost all these political activities . . . the positions reached are explained fundamentally by the fact of belonging to an organization. Plainly, one has to have some intrinsic merits . . . but it is definitely the organization that decides, determines, singles out, and designates the person to occupy a certain position. Naturally to obtain such a designation, to get oneself thought of as a person to be raised to such positions, it is necessary to have always carried on a great effort, realized great tasks, to have demonstrated capacity for struggle, a spirit of detachment, sacrifice, and loyalty to the organization. I hope you have understood exactly what I mean when I say that we cannot separate the strictly personal things from the political in referring to the achievement of certain positions.[30]
>
> The business of dissensions doesn't frighten us. We are not frightened by any of that. That may frighten another party that doesn't have our tradition of struggle. When I hear people remarking about two schisms in the party . . . for all I know this may be the nineteenth! And the party has emerged stronger from all of them.[31]

The balance between the will to serve a party selflessly and the gratifications of formal recognition is sometimes precarious. The remark that follows alludes to repeated nominations to the Senate and high party office:

> The party nominated me as a gesture of homage that I recognize is undeserved, naturally. Why should I say it's undeserved? It's not undeserved. Why shouldn't I deserve it since I have struggled hard?[32]

Obviously, the transition from accepting an office or other reward repeatedly from the party and coming to feel proprietary rights over such a post is not very difficult. In any case the professional party man is typically a permanent incumbent of party office who in time of opportunity or need is delegated to governmental or other party duty. Not a few such major figures would seem almost to have appropriated certain offices. Up till now, however, this in itself has not implied any greater stability or security in the career, but rather a more irrevocable linking of personal fortunes to those of the organization.

In this the party men differ substantially from party sympathizers who may have varying and quite deep involvement periodically in party life but who regard themselves as technicians or independents and are reluc-

[30] Ibid., pp. 17–18.
[31] Interview 062177, Part A, p. 52.
[32] Interview 308254, p. 135.

tant by temperament or principle to put themselves unconditionally at
the disposition of a party.

> As you can see, in [year] I detached myself from political activity. In fact
> that occasioned a small trauma. As a consequence of the struggle within
> [party] I lived continually protesting a series of issues and rebelling against
> discipline. The moment came when my situation became intolerable. I re-
> signed and asked to leave the party. Then they declared war on me.[33]

Such breaks thus involve risks and sometimes prolonged disconnection
from the main centers of political action.

> Well . . . I lived very modestly with the little I earned in my profession,
> especially in those first years getting through that period of being treated as
> a leper, and I made out.[34]

What sets these men off most clearly from the main core of party leadership may be their desire to work with governments (*"trabajar con el
gobierno"*) rather than to *be* the government.[35] In this sense they are
more dependent than any other elite subgroup on "the call" from above
with respect to opportunities. "I couldn't insinuate myself [as a candidate for a position]. I had to wait for them to call me." The careers of
these men can be synthesized as a sequence of such summons from above.[36]
On the border line between the political and cultural sectors are men
of strong ideological convictions (usually leftist) but little appetite for
party or government office who nevertheless remain for long years in
party ranks and are identified as leading party figures.

> I preferred not to accept any kind of public office and to retain my inde-
> pendence, the possibility of propagating my ideas in an independent way.[37]

For those in Marxist parties the sacrifice, at least as regards public
office over the last few decades, has not been great, for it has been only
in moments of crisis or national euphoria that they have won access to
government. Like the technicians, such political intellectuals are shielded
in some measure from political persecution and reprisals by their partial
detachment from the most sectarian elements in party ranks, but almost
all have nevertheless been subjected to exile, imprisonment, and periods
of clandestine existence.

[33] Interview 030087, Part A, p. 16.
[34] Ibid., p. 33.
[35] Ibid., p. 28.
[36] Ibid., p. 28. See also Chapter 7, footnote 14.
[37] Interview 014046, p. 67.

Somewhat better protected in this crossfire of party demands and outside hostility because of identification with party are union leaders, though because of the central importance to parties of labor support and the tandem development of parties and union, the careers of top labor leaders look much like those of party professionals. They too tend to have come up with their organizations and to have a quasi-proprietary hold on offices in party and union. Their power lies to a great extent in their personal following in labor ranks and their connections to party are similarly colored by personal loyalties.

> What attracts one is the attention of a leader, the quality of the leader that wins over masses. Well, I was an admirer of [name] and if [name] had gone into the Communist Party perhaps I would now be a Communist or if he were from [party] I would also be in that party . . . because it is only later that one begins to know party doctrine . . . philosophy, programs, objectives. But first one is drawn by a man, and it is this same attraction that a labor leader may also have. [Workers] join a union out of sympathy and fondness for a leader who listens to them, who calls them. . . .[38]

Because the union is both a critical element in party support and an outpost of party action, the union leader is also continually enmeshed in negotiation, accommodation, and maneuver not only with management and government but with other parties. It is within labor that efforts at interparty unity, formalistic sharing of power, and prorating of offices and other attributions have been developed to a fine art. The ideology of labor unity and the practical demands of collective bargaining and other forms of worker action constitute pressures both for interparty alliances and coalitions and for a certain dissociation from party on non-labor issues. The internationalization of labor organization has also fortified the extraparty bases of power available to labor leaders who have important party functions.[39]

Cultural Trajectories

The considerable differences between political and economic careers, as has been noted, reflect in part the determined effort by businessmen to insulate their activities from the shocks of the day-to-day political struggle. Though less shy of politics and much closer in social origins

---

[38] Interview 336287, Part A, p. 35.
[39] Refer to Chapter 7, pp. 228 ff. Further detail on differentiation of roles within spheres is given in Chapter 7. Discussion there emphasizes action in contemporary roles rather than modes of ascent.

and the concrete experiences of social ascent to political figures, those who have achieved eminence in the cultural sphere also seek detachment from the pressures toward certain kinds of sectarian identifications and loyalties. By and large all activity not directly centered on their own goals and values are felt as a distraction by men in this sphere. Thus despite the generalized stereotype of intense radicalism and political involvement of intellectuals as a class, cultural leaders enter into party activity as they do into business — half-heartedly, with uneasy reservations, and with one foot outside the door. This does not imply lack of commitment to political ideas or an unwillingness to rise to political responsibilities in crisis, but rather that partisan activity is accepted by these men as a perhaps necessary but nevertheless damaging interruption of their main work. Because all work outside the true vocation palls and may compromise the individual's talent or values of independence, jobs are taken carelessly or in consideration of factors having little to do with the positions themselves. If there is little fear of political ideas, there is great distrust and resistance to organization.[40] Yet the affinities to the political sphere are clear, and the careers of men in the two sectors intermingle and overlap. The career of the intellectual is a continuous flirtation with politics.

Like the subjects in politics, cutural leaders took employment early, often out of economic need, and well before their education was complete. First occupations are varied — but are more clearly linked in this case to early shows of talent or felt vocation. In the provincial towns where many of these men grew up, modest cultural achievement was a ready springboard to prominence even for the very young. The secondary school director who speaks in the following quotation was 22 at the time; the editor in chief was all of sixteen:

> Most of the professors in that school had been my secondary school teachers, who taught according to traditional methods. And I arrived to contribute something to a renovation along with three or four colleagues from the Pedagogico [normal school].[41]

> In my first job I was a proofreader; the following month I was both proofreader and first grade teacher in a night school for workers. A year later I dropped the proofreading and became editor in chief of a morning newspaper. . . .[42]

[40] More detail on these points is given in Chapter 7, pp. 207–221.
[41] Interview 043135, p. 6.
[42] Interview 111219, p. 4.

The point of convergence for all was Caracas and the university. It is of some importance in this connection that political events prolonged the presence within the university of the main protagonists of the 1928 political protests as well as young Marxist activists of a few years later, thus enlarging the effective span of this generation as a socializing agent and context for Caracas youth of the time.

> On the death of Gómez, all those students expelled in 1928 returned from abroad . . . and also those who had been expelled in 1931 on the discovery of the first student cell of the Communist Party. . . . So there came people who had interrupted their studies in 1931, people then in the university, and those of us coming from the lyces. There were great differences in age and in development [*formación*].[43]

Those who were later to find distinction in the cultural sphere entered eagerly into student activities but generally remained leaders of the second rank, engaged in propaganda or accessory cultural or educational efforts. Early ventures into this kind of activity — the publication of small literary magazines and the organization of cultural societies or informal literary circles — dated back for many to secondary school days and the provincial towns of early youth.

Various cultural subcareer types can be roughly identified. For those who take themselves most seriously as writers or artists the career is not so much a series of positions as a series of works or artistic products. It is these deeply self-involved men who show the greatest anxiety and remorse about the dissipation of energies represented by side ventures into politics or by the need to take jobs merely to survive economically. These tensions derive not merely from a preoccupation with economies of time but from fears of loss of perspective with respect to the more universal or intimately personal issues to which these men give a high priority.

> I reached the conclusion that Spanish American cultures did not exist. That we were passing from a primitive stage . . . to a state of civilization without passing through a cultural stage. We were acquiring the materials of civilization without having developed a culture organically. This led me to react against . . . mechanical civilization, . . . fundamentally against what, for example, the United States stands for, where material culture had reached a very high level. I believed that influence to be disastrous for America and that it warped our destiny. This led me also to approach the

[43] Ibid., p. 15.

people as possessors of a different measure of life. I recognized or thought that the man of the people, the Venezuelan campesino . . . the primitive man ruled by magic and ancestral beliefs and also by agrarian cycles, the march of the sun and the moon, . . . might rescue the notions of cultural truth for which I was fighting.[44]

There was a moment of hesitation in which I felt myself thoroughly penetrated by a certain existentialist philosophy with respect to the relativity of the human condition, with respect to the absolute need to be sincere with oneself, and not to occupy oneself with absolutely anything other than one's own self-realization.[45]

Others who have made careers in journalism and education are less troubled by commitments to such intellectualized and involuted quests for universal or private truths; still, they manifest a similar skittishness with respect to organizational involvements. The quotations that follow have special impact because they do not come from men who have been content to remain on the sidelines in times of political danger but who have in fact suffered prison, exile, economic hardship, and harsh public attack for standing firmly on their political principles.

At one time I believed that the writer should serve, should commit himself in a series of campaigns of a political kind, of a social kind. Today I do not believe this. I believe the function of the writer is fundamentally to write and that writing in itself serves a social function. I believe that is the fundamental . . . duty of the writer. . . . He should be alert formulating a critique of the human condition or trying to understand it and contributing in this way to developing man, man from within. That critique should be made freely and in that sense I favor an integral critique of our time . . . including within that critique capitalism and Marxism. . . .[46]

I believe I am more useful in the street where I am able to have the liberty to state criticisms and take part in a series of activities useful to the community that one cannot enter into when one has the ties and responsibilities of a position, because this creates confusion in which a man cannot give his views or point to errors because he is thought to have violated the trust placed in him.[47]

No, I never participated. In reality I have never entered a specific political group, political or party organizations. The only political organization which I joined was [name] while it was a civic group, but when it became a party, I got out.[48]

---

[44] Interview 112100, pp. 77, 78.
[45] Ibid., p. 79.
[46] Ibid., p. 80.
[47] Interview 111219, p. 35.
[48] Interview 015048, p. 26.

This apparent fear of compromising independence rises to a peak with respect to positions in business. The more secure and well paid a position, the more discomfort it evokes and the more it activates a nagging sense of complicity. This is compounded when the employer is one of the large corporations holding oil concessions:

> In the department of public relations I had a great many personal difficulties that never came to the surface, and that I have hardly ever spoken about. . . . I felt extremely bad. . . . In that department there were many foreign employees and Venezuelans with very little feeling for national problems, with stereotyped ideas about national problems, and with marginal opportunities to exert initiative.[49]

This visceral distress is not relieved by a willingness to look on the positive side of corporate intentions, nor by an appreciation of the favored situations of those within the corporate shelter or the considerable freedom of dissent insiders may be allowed.

> Positions in public relations are relatively comfortable; some people envy those who have them. . . . The philosophy of the department of public relations did not interest me because it was basically designed to highlight, seduce, and transform . . . Venezuelan public opinion, to make it favorable to [the company]. . . . The company believed that it was contributing to the social and cultural development of the country and my opinion was generally contrary. . . . [Things] were sometimes done in good faith by the company], but as I analyzed them I saw them differently in a way that produced friction. This friction never came out on a personal level. Life was not made uncomfortable for me. It was possible to dissent. . . . In fairness [the company] must be given credit for this; they practice up to a certain point a broad democracy within the company because internal criticisms are heard.[50]

In the end, perhaps the most galling ordeal of such experiences is to witness what one sees as corruption or mercenary behavior on the part of fellow nationals.

> I consider that some North Americans in management had a more patriotic perspective on problems, from my own standpoint, than the Venezuelans who were in those positions.[51]

Thus, although on the surface the careers of men in the cultural sphere

[49] Interview 043135, p. 18.
[50] Ibid., pp. 21, 22.
[51] Ibid., p. 23.

have many of the aggregate characteristics of some political careers —
modest beginnings, haphazard movement from one sphere to another,
repeated setbacks for political reasons, dependency on summons from
above — they are further troubled by a quest for ethical certainties and
an apprehension that the milieu itself cuts such men off from the realization of their full potential.[52] Economic insecurity and political disturbances not only sidetrack creative energies but actively subvert the canons
that should rule in cultural work and professional judgments.

> *El Nacional* in order to maintain its selective position has required from
> every party, from every group, . . . a columnist. They rotate these during
> the week so that only in exceptional cases would they reject the person a
> party designates as writer.[53]
>
> I have reached the conclusion that my successes as a writer are not attrib-
> utable to my work but to my personal and public conduct. That is, I have
> been read neither . . . when I was praised . . . nor . . . when repudiated.
> . . . Politics absolutely determines evaluations.[54]

Thus men of letters, educators, those in the mass media, and others
who are generally represented as the most honored elite within the Latin
American context seem in fact to have the most precarious and exposed
careers among the groups treated here. More than other men at the top
they have been often pressed into or have fallen heir to jobs that other
people rejected and they themselves claim they did not want. Though
they have made a fetish of independence, they perceive themselves often
as victims and dupes of the more powerful in other sectors. Whenever
unpleasant tasks are to be done that no politician will risk, the call goes
out for men of independent judgment and unassailable moral principle.
Whether the summons is answered or not, the anxious soul-searching continues.

> Now that I am in an important command position within the ministry, it
> has been my duty to combat and dismiss, to participate in or share respon-
> sibilities for sanctions imposed on many members of the *colegio* . . . per-
> sonal friends with whom I have close affective ties. . . .[55]

Some of the more ugly business of politics is delegated to the technician
and the politically independent intellectual, a function they earn precisely by placing themselves above politics.

[52] Refer to Chapter 7, pp. 207–221.
[53] Interview 111219, p. 13.
[54] Interview 112100, p. 96.
[55] Interview 043135, p. 35.

Careers and Social Structure

Elite career patterns have generally been studied to draw inferences about the individual characteristics of notables, about the nature of sub-groups most successful in competing for status positions, the institutional spheres in which such subgroups anchor and exercise power and influence, and macrofeatures of stratification and mobility.[56] In the present case it has been possible to treat careers in unusual detail, and there is less need to make inferential leaps from career configurations to other aspects of social structure. Direct links of this kind have been pointed out in earlier chapters, and many more will come to the surface in the chapters to follow. Still, without too much anticipating later findings and efforts at synthesis, a few remarks are apropos here about the broader significance of what has been brought out in these pages concerning careers.

In Chapter 1 these subjects were described as the vanguard of a movement of social ascent having both class and generational significance. Other study data on mobility patterns for a broad array of groups in the nation give further support to this idea, which at that point was based only on information with respect to the mobility of respondents' male siblings and in-laws. There are clear links or parallels between the mobility phenomena treated in the earlier chapter and elite "recruitment" as depicted here, though the latter term, despite its general use, is considerably more ambiguous. However, the comments that follow refer primarily to turnover in elite positions and only marginally to the general process of restratification in Venezuela that is treated at several points in these volumes.[57]

A first question that arises has to do with the historical specificity of the careers that have been described in this chapter. Though the potential for useful comparison is undercut by emphasizing the uniqueness of these experiences, it would be less than honest to sidestep the fact that these biographies strike one overwhelmingly as discontinuous with anterior patterns. One is thrown back to the original question of which metaphor

[56] Lester G. Seligman, in "Political Mobility and Economic Development" (Chapter 12 in Smelser and Lipset, eds., *Social Structure and Mobility*), catalogues a great many such hypothetical relations, primarily on the basis of African and Asian data, though the empirical support for many of his assertions is fragmentary and vague.

[57] Chapter 4 in Volume 3 explores the ramifications of broader changes on mobility and stratification patterns as they affect groups at many social levels. The most striking element in those results that does not figure within the elite is the great importance of immigration as a diversifying force within many middle and upper-middle status groups.

— the maze, the random walk, or the blazed trail — is most usefully to be invoked. Much elite theorizing seems to presume that offices or "functions" are constant and individuals with varying kinds of attachments to groups circulate among these positions. If the elite, like the present one, is alleged to have worked or witnessed some kind of revolution, the presumption is rather that a new group (modernizing or not) takes over, consolidates its situation, and proceeds to change all the offices and "functions." In the present case neither of these images is quite appropriate. The closer one gets to individual lives the more vivid the sensation that everything has been in motion at once, *especially at the higher status levels of the society.*[58]

Moreover, whenever a rapid ascent of middle-class groups is affirmed to have taken place, the immediate supposition is that a "traditional" oligarchy or a ruling class with aristocratic pretensions has been displaced. As the two previous chapters should have made clear, no such group or class has so far managed to consolidate its power in Venezuela and pass it on to a successor generation. The capture of power by the present middle-class incumbents of elite positions has given Venezuela its first ruling group since the time of independence that has some plausible claims to social distinction that are valid beyond its own borders and relevant to modern demands of national development. *Social advances over the last few decades have been concentrated at the top.* This may not speak well for the redistributive achievements of the alleged revolution under democracy, but it nevertheless brings out a transformation and potentially positive increase in the capabilities of those in leadership.

As regards the actual career configurations of present notables, at least two questions remain. The first is how different these may be from antecedent patterns of entry to elitehood. The second is to what extent they show signs of stability or institutionalization as regular conduits to higher position. A slightly different answer may provisionally be given for each sphere. Economic careers show the most convincing signs of falling increasingly into new and well-ordered paths. However, ascent in this sphere is still more selective and more concretely tied to initial connections within the business world than those in other institutional sectors. Nothing like this can be said with equal confidence for careers in party or government. The continued proliferation of parties and the disconnection between

---

[58] "That is, within each institutional locus be it cultural, political, or economic, the higher the status of a group, the higher the absolute vertical mobility experienced by that group." Volume 3, Chapter 4.

young people and the main body of elite political figures treated here implies that careers in this field will go on being made in the way they have been over the nearly four decades since 1930 — by the creation of new groups and defections from the established. It may be argued that this is a form of institutionalization. If so, it is an institutionalization that represents a frustration of the hopes and labors of a generation of leaders and that marks their rejection not only by today's youth but by substantial sectors formerly loyal to them.[59] The situation with respect to careers in the cultural sphere remains equally ambiguous. Despite the great expansion of education and growth of the university, the organizational underpinnings for careers in this sector remain feeble. There is little on which to fasten hopes for a change from the institutionalized improvisation and uncertainty dominant to this time.

[59] Such a judgment as concerns careers should not be taken to mean that no important forms of political institutionalization have taken place. This is a far more complex issue that may in fact be the root question of this entire research enterprise.

5   PRIVATE SENTIMENTS OF PUBLIC FIGURES

Thus far much time has been spent in describing the world into which Venezuelan leaders were born and how they have moved about in it on the way to elite positions. This research is a form of collective biography that looks primarily to common reference points in group experience, to the fact of having been somewhere or covered a similar trajectory, as a mode of identifying factors that may give a unique stamp and possible coherence to the attitudes and behavior of particular sub-sectors of the elite. However, this kind of social profile tells us much about the contexts of elite socialization, about the structure of stratification and the mechanisms of social ascent, and leaves almost everything about elite subjects themselves to be inferred or hopefully to be filled in from other sources. In practice, in most such research, similarities in social profile have been assumed to imply a unity of experience and response to events with little or no substantive verification.[1]

This chapter turns to the analysis of interview materials on childhood and family life, early religious and attitude training, and friendship. Regrettably this material is not complete for all respondents; these sections of the interviews were omitted for reasons of economy for about a third of the subjects. However, as will be seen, the material obtained is rich enough and sufficiently suggestive to reward attention.

The decision in the course of the research partially to sacrifice these materials rather than others, makes plain the lesser priority given in the study design to psychological or personality data as against other infor-

---

[1] Morris Janowitz in his review of the Hoover Institute Elite Studies, "The Systematic Analysis of Political Biography," *World Politics*, vol. 6, no. 3 (April 1954), explores some of the implications of this assumption. This question remains salient in Dankwart A. Rustow's 1966 review of more recent elite studies ("The Study of Elites").

mation which was counted on to reveal elite operations more clearly.[2] In fact, though this portion of the interviews was closely modeled on the qualitative work on authoritarianism by Adorno and others, the intent was never to try to use these materials as the basis for a treatment in depth of the psychology of subjects. The data were seen rather as a window into certain aspects of the private lives and more intimate sentiments and commitments of these individuals.[3] In other words, no elaborate framework of psychoanalytic theory was invoked, no assumption was made that touching on private or remote or heavily sentimentalized matters would automatically open up psychological depths, and no efforts were made to shock, seduce, or otherwise stir respondents to dredge up painful memories. The confidence built up over the course of the interviews nevertheless often invested this part of the conversations, which almost always came last, with a candor and directness that is refreshing and revealing.

Apart from whatever they may indicate about personality, these descriptions of early family life, religious experiences, and friendship have considerable interest from other perspectives. These are features of life around which essential differentiations of self-image cluster for Venezuelans as well as other Latin Americans. It is the richness of family life, the easy intimacy and lasting ties of friendship, the diffuse spirituality of a fundamentally religious culture that many in Latin America believe compensate for the gap between their collective achievements and those of the materialistic cultures to the north. Are these cherished and fre-

---

[2] This part of the interviews was covered with 124 of the 193 subjects reached. This subset is not a systematic sampling of the total target group for it is made up principally of individuals interviewed early in the field operation. It includes roughly half of those with power scores above 2.4 in each sphere and all of those with scores below 2.4. (Refer to footnote 4, Chapter 3, in this volume.) These materials were coded and processed in a more conventional fashion than other portions of the interview texts. The limited counts and cross-tallies that support this analysis were performed partly through standard IBM card sorting and partly on McBee cards.

[3] T. W. Adorno, Else Frenkel Brunswik, Daniel J. Levinson, R. Nevitt Sanford, *The Authoritarian Personality* (New York: Harper & Brothers, 1950), especially Part 2, "Personality as Revealed through Clinical Interviews." The present author used a similar approach in a 1957 study of Chilean student leaders. In that case the data on family, religion, and friendship were used to identify points of tension in private contexts and to support the hypothesis that student political activism of whatever ideological hue, in Chile at least, did not seem to represent a transfer to the political sphere of private pathologies. The student leaders by and large revealed quite balanced perspectives on family and religion but considerable anxiety and frustration with respect to friendships. See Frank Bonilla and Myron Glazer, *Student Politics in Chile* (New York: Basic Books, 1970).

quently invoked values given genuine substance in the lives of the nation's leaders? Does the attachment to such values displayed in talking about family and religion support the notion that the intrusion or inappropriate application of private standards to public affairs really may explain much institutional malfunctioning in Venezuela? Earlier chapters have also stressed differences in class origins and mobility, especially between the economic sector as against political and cultural leaders. In retrospect, does anything in the childhood of these men serve to augur their future prominence or the ways in which they would later move apart from one another?

Parents and Childhood

Two things stand out at once in a first examination of the composition of households in childhood as they emerge in these accounts. First of all, though grandparents and other relatives figure importantly as models and as important actors in some events, the typical household in which respondents grew up was not an extended family group but a nuclear unit of parents and children. The presence of other relatives in the home is rare, and allusions to supportive networks of kin, either with respect to practical problems or as a larger circle of conviviality and solidarity, are scattered and infrequent. The principal deviation from this modal pattern is the household in which the father is absent. About one in four of the political and cultural leaders and one in nine of the top businessmen report the absence in the home of the father.

It is in fact father-centered grievances that account for almost the totality of negative images and feelings concerning childhood in these accounts. The number of such allusions is imposing. Nearly half of the political, two in five among the cultural figures, and about one in three of the businessmen giving information were either orphaned at an early age or experienced some form of separation from the father which they felt as a deprivation and at times as a direct rejection. These include not only fathers who died young but also those who traveled, drank habitually, were deserters, took mistresses, or simply remained aloof and inaccessible. A few of the men were born out of wedlock and even when "recognized" and provided for by fathers, suffered the self-doubts and status ambiguities of their condition. No way of estimating the incidence of this kind of adversity in childhood for the population at large or for the social sectors these men represent is available to us, but these rough figures seem impressive nonetheless. An unapprised reader would be much more likely to associate comments such as those that follow with school dropouts, delinquents, or terrorists rather than with men of state or captains of industry.

I am going to relate an incident I recall with great pain. First, there is the fact that I never had toys, and then a time I went to a carousel and was not able to get in and I was never able to ride a pony. That is a thing that has never been wiped out and is a very painful memory. The only thing I recall with pleasure, a happy day, was the day of my first communion. Apart from that I had a hard childhood. My father abandoned us as infants. He did not meet his responsibilities, so I did not have happy moments in my childhood.[4]

When I was just about seven my father died and my mother had to abandon me and four brothers . . . and return to Venezuela to take care of my father's properties. At the same time the world economic crisis around the year '28 and '29 occurred and the uncle with whom we had been left . . . lost all his property.[5]

Well, it is somewhat difficult for me because, as I have said, my father died when I was sixteen. There were two periods of my life that can be . . . differentiated very violently. That period of childhood of plenty, of complete happiness . . . and immediately, almost cataclysmically, another of work, suffering, and problems. . . .[6]

My father thought like any peon and like any mountain farmer of the period. He looked to his sons as just work hands who should immediately begin to help solve his economic problems. . . . So I had no choice but to leave home so that I could separate myself, divorce myself from my home, and find my way on my own.[7]

My mother died when I was three. . . . He [the father] was a man of little culture or education and then left us pretty much on our own. For that reason we were educated in boarding schools. . . . He did not set up any kind of family organization to substitute for our mother. . . . When he had the opportunity, he sent us to school and stayed alone. . . . He was not oriented to the home; he lived with one woman and then another. He cared little about what happened and simply counted on those around him to take care of us. . . . My father never knew much about how I was doing in my studies.[8]

My father was a little indifferent in such matters [education]. . . . He had a mistress around somewhere . . . and two children somewhere else. He is a very roughcut individual. . . . Even though we had everything, he was a

[4] Interview 006002, p. 31.
[5] Interview 022065, Part B, p. 149.
[6] Interview 042134, pp. 155–156.
[7] Interview 043135, Part B, p. 124.
[8] Interview 327241, Part A, pp. 25–26.

man with whom we could not have the intimacy to present him with our
problems.[9]

My father was very violent, he didn't reason, very impulsive . . . and he
was not very proper in his outside life, as was the custom of the time. All
my uncles . . . had natural [illegitimate] children. It was said that one should
have as many women as one could support.[10]

When my father used to go to Europe, where we lived, he sometimes spent
half of the year there and half of the year here [in Venezuela]. He was
demanding with others and with himself . . . with great authority. . . .
There were moments when he did not want to accept something and he manifested this not vehemently but with violence.[11]

So many cases have been cited in order to convey the extraordinary
frankness of these statements, the range of situations they cover, and to
make plain that they occur even at the highest class levels. Loss of the
father, rejection by him, or failure by the father often imply economic
deprivation or setbacks, but mentions of poverty or material hardship
are considerably fewer than complaints about fathers. When the father
is present, moreover, the burden of responsibility for the family's poverty
is not imputed entirely to him. The same themes of absence and deprivation are transformed when there is some identification with the father's
difficulties.

From a very young age we began to suffer the persecutions to which my
father was subjected. And not only the affective blows but the economic.
My father never had any material fortune and we lived exclusively on his
earnings. Any time we were without my father, economic difficulties were felt
deeply at home. Aside from that my childhood was gay, peaceful as it was in
those days.[12]

No facile interpretation can be given regarding the significance of such
childhood conflict with fathers for later political behavior. However,
these depictions hardly square with conventional images of the traditional patriarch serenely in command of self and those around him.
Obviously there were some harsh components in traditional familiality
that reached into all class sectors. The powerful thrust of much of this
commentary and the relative ease with which it was elicited leave little
doubt that remote as these events may be, they retain a considerable
affective charge. On the whole such images of the father as distant, severe,
threatening, and rejecting coincide with the images of parents Adorno

[9] Interview 044138, pp. 164–165.
[10] Interview 054162, Part B, pp. 128–129.
[11] Interview 138163, pp. 88–89.
[12] Interview 113101, p. 113.

and others found among those high in authoritarianism. Others have seen radical party activity as a rebellion against such authoritarianism in fathers. Work on achievement motivation on the other hand suggests that the removal of authoritarian fathers from the home by wars, seafaring, travel, divorce, and so on may be a factor in promoting mobility and other forms of self-assertive striving. In general, however, efforts to connect childhood relations with parents to adult political behavior have demonstrated that a wide range of political outcomes is compatible with similar childhood experiences.[13] For the moment one may note that strong impulses flowing from this childhood source are at large in Venezuelan society and that they are apparently concentrated at the very top in the political and cultural realm.

The opposite face of this rebellious indictment of fathers and their substitutes, according to Adorno, is the conventional idealization and overestimation of the positive qualities and status of fathers.[14] It is this note of uncritical glorification that is dominant in practically all other comment of fathers, and particularly in the interviews with businessmen.

> My father is 76 today and he still maintains the activity and creative energy of a man of 20 or 30, and it is that quality of constant creative energy that has had a great influence on me. . . . Naturally, he has defects. Who does not? But all those defects are overshadowed by his trajectory, by his conduct, and by his positive influence over our development.[15]

> [What I most admired in my father] was his great responsibility to the family. In childhood I felt a different kind of admiration because it is different then, but I feel it now and always before this. . . . He always showed a great sense of responsibility toward the home and discipline in his work. He came up in the small town atmosphere of business and agriculture, of wholesome habits, of rising early, of discipline, always meeting one's obligations. . . . I don't believe [he had any defects]. All his life was one of work and to my knowledge he led a most regular life in the towns.[16]

[13] Some of this work is summarized in Bonilla and Glazer, *Student Politics in Chile*. In addition to Adorno et al., *Authoritarian Personality*, note the early efforts of the Institute for Social Research, Max Horkheimer, ed., *Studien ueber Autoritaet und Familie* (Paris: Librairie Felix Alcan, 1936). See also Gabriel Almond, *The Appeals of Communism* (Princeton, N.J.: Princeton University Press, 1954) and, of course, Harold Lasswell's groundbreaking *Psychopathology and Politics* (Chicago: University of Chicago Press, 1930). On the question of need achievement and the family dynamics that produce it, see David C. McClelland, *The Achieving Society* (New York: Van Nostrand, 1961), pp. 404–406.

[14] Adorno et al., *Authoritarian Personality*, pp. 339 ff. Among the surrogate father figures similarly portrayed as harshly intolerant and violent in these interviews are several priest-uncles who undertook to replace fathers who proved negligent or had passed away.

[15] Interview 340245, p. 121.

[16] Interview 330257, p. 94.

My, there are so many things I admire in my father. I have admired his capacity for work, his tremendous capacity for work. He is a man of astounding capacity for work. His clarity of mind, his sense of honesty, his sense of respect for others, including his respect for his children and all the problems his children have had in the normal course of life. We have had a large family. As you can understand there have been problems of every sort . . . and he has known how to manage and suggest things without ever intruding in anyone's life. And that is perhaps one of his strongest characteristics, a great independence and sense of responsibility and then a great civic responsibility. He has been a member of an infinite number of organizations.[17]

My father was always singled out as a man of great integrity, of a very serious character, very manly and at the same time kindly. . . . Despite my age at the time of his death . . . my respect for the memory of my father and my respect for my mother, who lives, lead me to take an ever more firm position in life before the moral and social problems of the nation.[18]

I remember his attitude of great lordliness and the letter which I still save indicates that he was a man of lofty spirit. That is what I most admired in him, and I saw that even in life . . . because he was a very neat man who always dressed in white, very careful of his person and in his manners at home, over which he maintained a careful watch. Then he taught me . . . sincerity and not to lie. For him that was the worst sin. Then there was his kindness. He was an extraordinarily kind person. At bottom he loved me more [than my brother].[19]

Rarely is any real balance or convincing insight interjected in these filial tributes, even when the interviewer insists on some attention to possible shortcomings, response is evasive or tends to lapse into condoning generalities.

. . . his will to face up to realities and make decisions in the light of them and see them carried out without fear of anything. To consider that every problem has a solution at its own plane, and that those that have no solution are merely those he has not faced. A great confidence in himself, a great character, a great ethical sense. By far what is called a man of many principles which are not only spoken but applied. [Interviewer: . . . any defects?] Well, perhaps that same confidence in oneself sometimes leads to excesses. At first when one is a child, one believes everything one is told as though it were the voice of the Bible. . . . Later, in the course of time, one discovers that there was a mistake here and a mistake there, because no one is infallible.[20]

This idealization is carried to even greater lengths with mothers, with respect to whom no real defect is acknowledged. The strongest reproaches

[17] Interview 304244, p. 45.
[18] Interview 014046, Part A, p. 5.
[19] Interview 060174, Part C, p. 337.
[20] Interview 004013, Part B, p. 216.

directed at mothers in all these statements are hesitant chidings for extremes of self-effacement or possible over-excesses of love, indulgence, possessiveness, or desire to shield children.

She was a very gentle woman and liked to give me and my brothers wholesome advice. But she never struck me. She lived serenely. . . . My mother had a unique spirit of tranquility and serenity. She was a great reader and at the same time a good housekeeper. She enjoyed having friends visit her with us. She was very beloved not only by all her relatives but by all those who knew her. . . . Frankly, I cannot recall any [weakness] in her.[21]

My mother is a person . . . I think that everyone speaks with great emotion about his mother . . . in our case my mother is a person known by all those who have dealt with her. . . . I have heard it said that she is the kindliest of persons, a woman who has never had a harsh word for anyone, who thinks evil of no one, who is most generous and careful never to trouble anyone, extremely Catholic, extremely responsible, watchful for persons who may be ill so she can go to their side to aid them . . . so that her principal characteristic has been her kindness.[22]

Well, my mother, granddaughter of [name], daughter of [name] and [name], led a life of great dedication to her home, but with the great merit that when my father died . . . she took charge of our education and not only as a mother but as adviser, inculcating in us the highest principles of morality and character, of resistance to all the eventualities of life.[23]

[I admire in my mother] her profound kindness, incapable of an egotistical sentiment, incapable of an unwholesome criticism of any kind, and a great resignation . . . in the face of the realities of life. . . . Her excess [was one] of weakness, an excess of kindness, if that can be called a defect.[24]

[I admire in my mother] her rectitude, her constancy, and a great sense of responsibility. . . . Perhaps my mother was too kind and tolerant with us and perhaps we were a little spoiled at first, not . . . too much. The truth is that we constituted a very united family group . . . each one tied to the destiny of the other . . . a small group, my mother, my brother, and I, and we have continued in this way. The truth is I find no major defects in her. . . . Perhaps because she indulged us so much, I lack a little aggressivity that I would say is always necessary.[25]

It was her abnegation with respect to us, and above all, that I never perceived in her . . . discriminations with respect to us, her children. She was very sacrificing because she was a woman who lived . . . permanently consecrated to the care of her home. My mother was not a woman who was

[21] Interview 072216, pp. 78–79.
[22] Interview 304244, p. 46.
[23] Interview 014046, Part A, p. 3. The allusions to well-known family names as a way of calling attention to lineage is another of the indicators of authoritarianism used in the Adorno studies.
[24] Interview 042134, p. 155.
[25] Interview 135105, p. 113.

excited by festivities, she was rather even aloof from social activities. She lived very much within her home, very dedicated to her family, her children and, of course, her husband, my father. . . . If I saw in her at any time what may be called a defect, it was her egoism with respect to her children. . . . She centered her attention and preferences in a marked way on us her children [as distinct from nieces and nephews].[26]

Mothers thus emerge as a body of sainted females, loving and self-sacrificing, symbolizing the security and warmth of the family circle, submissive but compensating with inner fortitude and decisive action, when necessary, lapses on the part of the husband. Nor, despite the allusions to nonpunishing mothers, does this one-sided exaltation of the female parent seem to result from differences in the disciplinary roles taken by mothers. Despite the reported irascibility of some fathers, the principal forms of punishment (and these seem to have been meted out only slightly more often by fathers than by mothers) were generally light physical disciplining, the denial of material things or privileges, and brief isolation. In retrospect, this punishment is by and large acknowledged to have been not excessive, and there are hardly any cited instances of defiance or rebellion in childhood. Neither the grievances against fathers nor the adulation of mothers seems to be importantly connected with the handling of offenses in childhood.

But the centering of affect on the mother as the domestic focus of nurturance in childhood does not produce a transfer of this central role to the wife-mother in the family of procreation. With very few exceptions (a handful in each sphere of activity) the principal satisfactions of present family life are counted in terms of relationships with children and with views of the home and family as a refuge from public life and a center of pleasurable group activities. The rewards of intimacy and companionship with the wife in an individualized way are infrequently mentioned. The same is true of the idea of the extended family as a solidary unit of social support or expansiveness. Allusions to the wife are few, vague, and couched in the same abstractly idealized language as the descriptions of mothers.

I believe that when a marriage is effectively fulfilled other relations lose importance. . . . They do not disappear but they take on a very relative meaning.[27]

The greatest satisfaction in family life is to live in complete spiritual understanding on both sides, to respect each other mutually and conceive life with

[26] Interview 002004, pp. 149–150.
[27] Interview 041131, p. 109.

the satisfactions that intimacy brings to small things and to more important things when they are accepted and respected.[28]

My wife, my sweet wife, whom I call the most noble and sweet of my mistresses, because I have had several, before her and with her, is a singular and extraordinarily beautiful case because of her conduct. She has domestic training . . . and she has admirable qualities. She is not a gossip, she is respectful with everyone, she is very discreet, very simple, she is satisfied with what comes, she accepts life, fulfills her duties as a mother . . . she is sweet, generous, good . . . she is not rebellious nor spoiled. . . . That is, I have full liberty for my development. I have no blocks or limitations with her.[29]

When pressed a few moments after this burst of sentiment to specify the greatest satisfaction in family life, the last respondent replied laconically, "Well, the children, that is obvious." And in fact, for the large majority of respondents, the ostensive focus of concern and satisfaction in present family life is the development and success of children and, more specifically, the consolidation of status gains by the new generation in education, jobs, and good marriages.

Up till now, one has had two kinds of family life, life with the paternal family and with one's own family. . . . In the paternal family one could see the effort parents made to educate one, so that one could be better than they were, for they had not had the luck to study. And in one's own life at present [it is a satisfaction] to see a family grow; one feels that one has made an effort on behalf of the nation by having a family with children that advance daily in knowledge, in their education.[30]

I believe that the greatest satisfaction of family life is to have a pleasant living space. . . . I don't mean merely one with certain material comforts, because there are many homes where there is much material comfort and the atmosphere is unbearable, but rather an atmosphere of mutual respect between the parents, between parents and children, of cordiality and esteem. I believe it is the most fundamental thing to make the home pleasant and to educate, in order that all can live agreeably and project themselves and develop well in every way, that there be a balanced base in the home . . . and marriage. The greatest satisfaction must be to see, as my father and mother have, all their sons who are professionals, who have married well, and have happy homes . . . to see the triumphs of the males in our professions and in our homes and to see also . . . the success of the husbands of my sisters and the home they all have.[31]

[28] Interview 118179, Part A, p. 62.
[29] Interview 322280, Part B, pp. 127–128.
[30] Interview 036120, p. 49.
[31] Interview 301234, p. 184.

. . . to orient one's children, to try to give society useful people: I believe that and I practice it.[32]

. . . to be able to give one's children the opportunity of an education and a sound training so that they may have the instruments to be useful in the future.[33]

. . . to see one's children grow not only physically but intellectually and also . . . morally. As they become men of substance, they bring new brilliance to their surnames and to their parents.[34]

One sees oneself sort of immortalized in them, as one's own experience can guide them and help them to improve. Then one sees oneself projected into the future. . . . I would have desired a male . . . the continuity of the family is attained better around the son.[35]

Several points of reference are available as approaches to an evaluation of these findings. One of these is the clinically derived configuration of attitudes toward childhood and parents of authoritarian or prejudiced personalities in the work of Adorno and others. There are striking elements of congruence between the group patterns observed in that research and those that emerge here. The fact that these are group *trends* and not fixed paths of individual development or attitude formation should be emphasized. Nonetheless, the alternative views of parents as distant, overbearing, and irascible or as extravagantly idealized and superlative models is common to both. So are the shallowness of affect and individuation with respect to wives, the conventionality of status goals for children, the preoccupation with conformity and consolidating social approval through the good behavior of all in the family.

The family and intrapersonal dynamics that support and that give a particular shape and political significance to such attitudes are obviously complex. In Adorno's work these patterns are associated with ambiguities of identity, manipulative attachments to persons, submissiveness or efforts to overcontrol others, surface conformity, and inner rebelliousness accompanied by flashes of violence. The poles of attraction and discharge for such feelings are authority figures and out-groups.[36] All of these tendencies are in accord with the psychological states that were intuitively associated with elite conflict in Venezuela in the opening diagnosis.

A second point of reference with respect to these group patterns is the case study of a Venezuelan revolutionary presented in the first volume of

[32] Interview 111219, p. 83.
[33] Interview 067202, Part B, p. 187.
[34] Interview 072216, p. 79.
[35] Interview 054162, Part B, p. 131.
[36] Adorno et al., *Authoritarian Personality,* pp. 384–389.

this series.[37] It should be noted here that in looking at these patterns by age group — comparing roughly three generations (those who came to public life in the late 1920's, in the early 1930's, and in the early 1940's) — no differences of any account emerged. That is, though one supposes that family patterns may be changing along with other social transformations, no strong evidence that this is the case is to be found in the childhood descriptions of leaders of varying ages. The clinical study of the young revolutionary, based on twenty to thirty hours of interviewing as against the four to eight hours of the conversations with elites, and who is at least a generation behind the youngest of elite respondents, also runs true to form. The mother emerges as a reasonable, loving person concerned with home and children, placating a father who is seen not as evil but as a distant figure with a propensity for violence, an unpredictable inclination to run out of control.

The repressed hostilities generated by the culturally imposed idealization of these relationships break out repeatedly in the fantasy materials collected in clinical tests with that subject. The analyst, Walter Slote, traces the ways in which these impulses find expression, fulfillment, and are newly reinforced or turned toward destructive directions within the realm of politics. There is some support here, then, for the idea that the pattern being explored is rather general and persistent in Venezuela, or at least that there may be within the society several pockets of such free-floating, politically charged motivation rooted in childhood or in current interpretations of childhood.[38]

A third point of reference is data from other parts of the study. Some very tentative evidence linking attitudes toward childhood with political behavior is shown in Table 5.1. That table anticipates materials to be treated extensively in Chapter 7, which covers the activity of respondents in their principal organizational roles. One of the key units of analysis in that treatment is a power interaction or PRAXIS. A PRAXIS here means a codable episode in which the respondent, usually as the agent for some

[37] *SRSP,* Chapter 10, especially pp. 254–269.
[38] Of three generations of student political leaders studied in Chile (Bonilla and Glazer, *Student Politics in Chile*), only ōne approximates these Venezuelan results. Though the number of cases is small, interviews with eight Chilean leaders of the famous "generation of 1920" tend to parallel the findings reported here with respect to childhood and parents. The 1920 generation in Chile was strongly influenced by (was responsive to) anarchist ideas. It is famous in Chile because it challenged all forms of organization and resolutely resisted entering directly into party life. Later student leader generations, which in the study were characterized as "party militants" and "student managers" as contrasted with the 1920 "agitators," show very different patterns in evaluation of parents and childhood experiences.

TABLE 5.1   Attitudes toward Childhood and Action in Power Roles

	Negative Views of Childhood	Mixed Views of Childhood	Positive Views of Childhood
Number of respondents	(25)	(23)	(73)
Number of PRAXES	(77)	(52)	(171)
Mean number of PRAXES	3.1	2.3	2.3
Percentage of power interactions in which			
Authoritative or coercive means are applied	55	33	29
Outcome of interaction is some form of social cleavage	33	17	16
Ideological or evil intent is attributed to opponents	28	25	24

NOTE: Five respondents do not figure in this tally.

organization, undertakes to perform some action involving an application of power, influence, or authority.[39] The table shows that respondents whose recollections of childhood are largely negative (it will be remembered that most childhood grievances are father-centered) gave accounts of more such episodes than others. Moreover, they are substantially more likely than others to have applied authoritative, command, or coercive means in seeking to gain their objectives. They are no more likely than others to attribute motives of evil intent, fear, or dogmatism to their opponents; nevertheless, the encounters reported by them clearly ended more often in some form of social rupture than in a cementing of social ties. Obviously in real life, individual dynamics of such processes are considerably more complex and varied in outcome. The question remains, as well, whether the social disruption produced was in some way positive for the system, destructive, or of trivial import. Still, these fragmentary findings fit in with the general syndrome prefigured in the work on authoritarianism and in the case study of the revolutionary. If these clues have any foundation, they imply that the family in Venezuela has been and continues to be an incubator of politically charged tensions at all class levels.[40]

[39] For additional details, see Chapter 7.

[40] Information on political ideas within the family is available for only about half the subjects, but the picture presented is very consistent and squares well with the rest of the data. Very few (about 12 percent) of the fathers are described as politically active, but even those who are said to have suffered because of opposition

Friendships

Both persons who claim to have no true friends and those who claim so many friends that their understanding of the concept comes into question are few among the responding group. In fact only two individuals declared that they had no friends at all. Few informants are willing to state exactly how many of their associations with others constitute genuine friendships; but a sizable majority make it understood that the number is small and that their concept of friendship is an exacting one. Two principal strands are intermingled in definitions of friendship: one criterion emphasizes easy and complete communication, understanding, and sharing of affect; a second, occasionally more pragmatically slanted demand, stresses unconditionality, a total and unquestioning availability in moments of need. Obviously, these are highly idealized standards that would seem almost impossible to meet. It is interesting in this connection that there are few explicit references to failures or deceptions. Most statements seem intended to let on that the high standards set for friendship are in fact realized.[41]

I am going to reply with a phrase from Cicero that I read as a boy. It said that friendship in life is like the sun. That is, one cannot live without it. I regard friendship as something fundamental that needs to be cultivated. A person without friends seems to me to be totally wretched.[42]

I have various intimate friends, people with whom I identify, let us say, on the most intense plane, on the spiritual plane; people with whom I have great affinity, people whom I trust. . . . I have a few intimate friends with whom I have lived such a long time. . . .[43]

. . . to find a person of exceptional qualities who will identify himself with our manner of being and our manner of living, with our qualities and with our virtues and defects . . . a person who understands one perfectly well and whom one can understand equally, who will even be capable of any

---

to Gómez are rarely described as democratically minded individuals. The most advanced views reported are a vague libertarianism tempered by a strong sense of hierarchy, a preoccupation with order, a desire for rectitude in government, and a fear of the chaos latent in the mass. Very few disagree with the political views of fathers, which are in fact generally recollected with some condescension. Mothers are a total blank politically. Though wives are credited with having political opinions much more often than the subjects' mothers, these views are almost unanimously affirmed to be mirror reflections of the husbands' thinking.

[41] In the Chilean student leader study that has been cited (Bonilla and Glazer, *Student Politics in Chile*), the same seemingly unattainable standards were articulated but evaluations as to their actual fulfillment were both objective and, on the whole, explicitly negative.

[42] Interview 006022, Part A, p. 37.

[43] Interview 135105, p. 118.

sacrifice in one's behalf just as one is capable of performing it for him, but above all who will make possible the establishment of that current of profound human understanding and sentiment. . . .[44]

The intense focus on intuitive intercommunication appears often in combination with or shades off into a preoccupation with forms of solidarity and support having more practical implications.

Relations are important first in an intellectual and spiritual sense because of the intellectual or spiritual exchange those relations may produce. Then they are important because we are all part of society and each relation that one has is, so to speak, an element in the construction of our lives. . . . One's relations can help in the attainment of an objective . . . or they may impede its realization. What one desires is to achieve one's goal, so one always tries to seek relations that will help one with that goal.[45]

I believe that the correct and exemplary life of the individual depends on the friends he chooses . . . on the opportune exchange of ideas and advice on both sides. . . . One often has friends whom one serves. At other times one demands to be served and is satisfied. I . . . have made a cult of friendship. In my view there is nothing better than a good friend.[46]

[Friendship] provides a number of emotional satisfactions with respect to the establishment of solidarity ties that are very valuable from the individual point of view in the satisfaction of certain spiritual needs. They are also valuable from a social point of view because they contribute to the ready solution of problems the individual faces. They bring about team action in certain circumstances, they create sentiments of cooperation. They even have an important influence on different aspects of professional life. Links are established which facilitate in many cases the achievement of tasks in which people have a common interest.[47]

[Friendship] is rewarded at the moment that one least anticipates. I believe in friendship, in faithful friends, and I regard that as one of the best investments a man can make. . . . Help in difficult moments — the opportunity that one has to come to their aid and support them in their times of difficulty — this provides great personal satisfaction. The opportunity to have someone to whom to confide intimate problems — these are wonderful things that friendship makes possible.[48]

Friendship in the first place offers companionship, solidarity. That is absolutely indispensable above all for persons like myself, who are interested in group efforts, whether political or social.[49]

Friends who will help one in any circumstances, that seems to me extremely useful and has great importance. . . . One doesn't always find people who

[44] Interview 308254, Part B, p. 198.
[45] Interview 339240, p. 31.
[46] Interview 009030, p. 57.
[47] Interview 015048, Part B, pp. 161–162.
[48] Interview 047145, pp. 55–56.
[49] Interview 007024, p. 68.

will help in any situation, who will look out for one and solve problems. That is very difficult.[50]

Friendship relations are likened to kinship ties, are regarded as in competition with them, or are foresworn as inferior to or threatening the more vital and reliable links of family. The politician who made the last statement quoted just above also remarked:

. . . I have friends, I have a great friend who is not a member of my party, who is anti [my party], but is a great personal friend, proven in circumstances that were extremely difficult for me and who, I can say, is practically a brother to me in everything, in social events, well, in everything.[51]

I respect loyalty in friendship. . . . That is, for me friendship is a new marriage that one performs with persons who are, well, external, just as one does with one's wife. . . . I am very true to my friends . . . think as they may. I respect them and help them. I have always been well received by my friends. . . . I also maintain my friendship steadfastly.[52]

[Friendship means] pleasant relationships that make for good times, a good meal together, an outing, and so on . . . but generally for many years I have asked no one's advice, I have not consulted any friend. I consult my wife, and I begin now to consult my children who have the same standards as I and accord with my opinions.[53]

Naturally, friends are indispensable, as long as they don't get mixed up with one's private life. I have many friends, men and women, but here in my home only those persons penetrate who have our confidence and share our intimacy. . . . I like to have friends and I have many . . . but I prefer not to bring into that intimacy persons who may disturb it for any reason. I consider harmony in the family of great importance. I believe this provides the basis for a psychological stability that is indispensable in the times we are living.[54]

There is thus at the same time a tendency to measure friendships by standards of intimacy both reserved to the family and often recognized as not attainable within it ("because it is also outside persons who are disinterested, who give one service as advisers, help, support, and orientation, without any self-interest"[55]). Thus the ready recourse to kinship-grounded metaphor in allusions to friendships both signals its importance and throws into question the degree to which the elevated canons for

[50] Interview 044138, Part B, p. 170.
[51] Ibid.
[52] Interview 118179, Part A, p. 63.
[53] Interview 072216, p. 80.
[54] Interview 007024, p. 67.
[55] Interview 024072, p. 41.

judging friendship ties are actually being met. The very strong emphasis
on loyalty and constancy as indispensable characteristics in friends further suggests considerable anxiety on this score.

> Well, sincerity is the most important thing for me, the friend who is truly
> sincere, the friend who joins me out of sympathy, without looking beyond
> that toward any other speculation. . . .[56]
> The most important thing in friendship . . . is loyalty in the most ample
> sense of the word. As long as there is not loyalty, generosity in friendship,
> the social relation cannot be sincere. . . . I find most offensive and dis-
> agreeable any insincerity, fictitious and accommodating positions, which are
> also a form of insincerity.[57]
> . . . loyalty to the friend. Being loyal does not mean thinking like the
> friend. . . . No, being loyal one has a friend, so that friend may provide
> one opportunely some advice, some help . . . save one from some mis-
> chance, give one moral support when needed.[58]

The guidelines from Adorno for evaluating the attitudes toward others
likely to characterize authoritarian types are not as transparently relevant here as they were with respect to childhood attitudes. Views of
friends among authoritarian, dogmatic, and prejudice-prone individuals
were found in that work to stress status acceptability, conventional moral
standards, elements of hero worship, attention to hierarchical relations,
exploitativeness, and distrust.[59] Because in the present accounts the
friends claimed never emerge as real people, we discover little about
their social attributes beyond the highly abstract ideals that have been
noted. We discover little about when in life most important friendships
were formed, the contexts and occasions in which friendships solidify,
or the relative duration of such ties. However, the almost strident insistence on sameness — *like* interests, *like* feelings, *like* life styles — implies
a very narrow social range in such relations. The parallel expectation and
demand for support, not only affective but for practical advice and backing in moments of crisis, equally implies a restricted range of persons
able to perform such a function for men at this level. Many of the
Adorno themes can thus very plausibly be seen as underlying the almost
ritualistic obeisance to the idea of friendship that have been cited. Such

[56] Interview 086084, p. 39.
[57] Interview 043135, Part B, p. 137.
[58] Interview 324282, p. 73.
[59] Adorno et al., *Authoritarian Personality*, pp. 405–406.

harsh definitions of "we-ness," for example, further suggest exclusivism and out-group rejection.[60]

Here again, group patterns seem to parallel in interesting ways the clinical study of the revolutionary.[61] In that case also the dubious metaphor of kinship-grounded intimacy was invoked as the model for relations with friends. Because, in fact, no true intimacy had been achieved within the family, both the persisting desire to find it elsewhere and the latent fear of a genuine exposure to intercommunication were exposed. On close examination, despite relatively effective, untrammeled, and cordial associations in work and organizational settings, the experiences of genuine intimacy with others turn out to have been fleeting and extremely rare. The very one-sidedness of these appraisals of friendship, despite the broad range of life experiences that lie behind them, lead one to sense the presence of an oppressive, culturally reinforced norm rather than multiple testimonials of individual fulfillment.

Religion

As noted in an earlier chapter, between independence and a very recent surge culminating in a new concordat between Rome and the Venezuelan government in 1964, the Church has had a generally passive and accessory role in the nation's politics. Though the conservative reaffirmation after independence early in the last century did not bring about a reimposition of Church power and privilege, the Church and, in particular, religious education have until recently continued to be identified with the diffuse traditionalism and political conservatism of landed wealth and the growing business class.[62] Religious education is in fact more common among business leaders and others, both for the total group of informants and among those who gave the more detailed information on which this chapter is based. For all the respondents the proportions having primary and secondary schooling in religiously operated institutions are for businessmen about four in ten, for cultural leaders about three in ten, and for politicians about one in four. These proportions are roughly parallel

---

[60] R. D. Laing comments on the interplay between family-based and external claims and opportunities for meaningful relations in *The Politics of Experience* (New York: Pantheon, 1967), especially Chapter 11.

[61] *SRSP*, pp. 273–275.

[62] Chapter 2, pp. 46 ff. For comment on contemporary links between business and Church, see Chapter 7, pp. 221 ff.

among the smaller group under discussion here, ranging in this case from about one half for the businessmen to one in five for the politicians.

Though this emerges as a fundamental differentiating life experience that compounds class differences between the economic and political leadership, attention to this factor alone would probably exaggerate the importance of religious differences in *childhood*. Because the religious atmosphere in the family at childhood is widely reported from all sectors to have been one of conventional orthodoxy and regular devotional observance, economic factors and simple accessibility (for example, the politicians have more provincial, rural, and small town beginnings) may account for much of the divergence in choice of school. By the same reasoning, of course, the fact of religious education possibly gains importance as an element explaining the persistence in later life of religiously grounded differences. But as regards the childhood context of religious feeling and practice within the family, the recollections of majorities from all sectors have much the same ring.

> [Religion] came to us by conviction because we saw that they were Catholic, that they always went to mass and took us. There were religious festivities and my parents would go and take us all though never by compulsion. Sometimes one as a child prefers to play rather than go to mass . . . "Go first to mass and then the rest," but we were never forced. We saw rather that it was a convenient thing because we saw them do it with such good will, with an enthusiasm that we found contagious.[63]
>
> My mother was very religious, that religiosity typical of the Venezuelan woman, but there was never any fanaticism in my home. Nor was there a [fundamentalist] atmosphere of prayer or religious healing.[64]
>
> To begin with I should indicate that all the members of my family . . . were baptized in the Catholic Church. As regards my religious training, I should say that given these circumstances I was also educated within a religious framework beginning with the religious instruction that is given in the home.[65]
>
> My religious education was entirely in the home. I never studied in any private school and therefore I was never in any religious school. But my father, my mother, and all my family have been eminently Catholic . . . and my religious education was always in the charge of my father and mother.[66]

The pattern far more commonly associated in popular thought with Venezuela and other titularly Catholic countries with Mediterranean

---

[63] Interview 086084, p. 27.
[64] Interview 337288, Part B, p. 144.
[65] Interview 002004, Part B, p. 128.
[66] Interview 024072, p. 32. Note the ready identification of private with religious schooling.

antecedents (the devout female and the skeptical or anticlerical male) crops up relatively infrequently in these biographies and is almost never reported to have been a source of conflict within the family.

My mother, naturally, was religious in the sense of complying with her religious obligations. In my home there was never any kind of fanaticism. My father was a man who never went to church. Nevertheless, he required us as children to go to church, to attend mass. My father always believed in God but he did not go around making a show of it. He respected God but did not practice the Catholic faith.[67]

[My religious education] was within the Venezuelan mainstream . . . of Christian doctrine and oriented by my mother who was a fervent believer. [The religious atmosphere in my home] was one of absolute freedom, of absolute respect. I am a little more like [my father] in my flexibility with respect to those beliefs.[68]

She [the mother] has her ideas and my father respects them, on the basis of the simple principle of respect, so there is no problem. Naturally, in my father's home no acts against religion were permitted in order to avoid problems in the family. . . . My mother is a special person. She prays every day and takes religion as an obligatory part of her life.[69]

My mother was a woman of profound religious sentiments, although far from being sanctimonious. She met her religious obligations in an absolutely normal way, without having, especially when I was a child, any kind of friendship with clergymen, with religious congregations. She belonged to none, but was nevertheless very religious. My father was what in that time was called a very anticlerical individual. He was not an atheist or a materialist. His education had been largely religious and some of that remained with him. My father was a Mason. At one time he was even excommunicated by the archbishop of Caracas.[70]

Even though explicit references to this kind of sex-linked cleavage in religious roles in the childhood family are infrequent, there are other signs that this second pattern may have been closer to the norm or at least that it constitutes a far more common alternative configuration than one would infer from such specific contrasting of parental religious attitudes: fathers are hardly ever mentioned as religious role models, though when they are their influence seems to have been lasting.

My father was a very religious man, and his example was very valuable to us in that sense. Naturally, my mother also was very devout. Moreover, our first teachers were also religious. . . . As in all Venezuelan families of

[67] Interview 033091, p. 99.
[68] Interview 042134, p. 157.
[69] Interview 036120, p. 42.
[70] Interview 034092, Part B, p. 137.

the time, I believe the father is the one who establishes the orientation of
the house and is the most vital example, especially for the male children, of
the conduct to be followed.[71]

Now my father is a man of great religious sentiment, and if I am going
to talk about my religious formation, I believe . . . the person who may
have most inspired me toward a certain religious pattern is my father. The
school may have been a complement because, naturally, I went to a school
run by priests . . . but I attribute more importance, insofar as my own
religious views are concerned, to the attitude maintained throughout his life
by my father.[72]

However, it is the female who dominates as the religious model, whereas
males entirely monopolize the field in representations of childhood exposure to areligious models. In addition, though few, those male figures who
are recalled as providing a first experience of counterreligious views are
without exception depicted as tolerant individuals, striving for some form
of rational accommodation of religious dissensus. This is far less true
of religious models, who particularly among informants now high in
politics, are portrayed as rigidly dogmatic bigots as often as they are
credited with an open, accepting view of religious diversity.

I belong to a very religious family. But in this regard my father was
always careful from the start to let each one follow his own inclinations. . . .
From childhood I felt a natural reaction against religious things. My father
never insisted that I follow any other path. He simply questioned me, observed me, and left me to myself. For my mother and my grandmother, my
disdain for religious things was an extremely discomfiting and disagreeable
thing.[73]

My mother is very Catholic, very dutiful with respect to her Christian
obligation. . . . We even abstained from meat at home on Saturdays in honor
of the Virgin, and all those things. My mother's religion is perhaps more
emotional. Mine is more reasoned.[74]

I think her defect [the mother] was a tendency to fanaticism in religion.
Perhaps that was a real defect.[75]

My religious education was guided by my mother who was a fervent
believer. . . . I am totally different from my mother with respect to that
almost dogmatic point of view of her faith.[76]

In short, once again, and from another perspective, we come upon a
representation of family life that radiates conventional orthodoxy, rou-

[71] Interview 309255, Part B, pp. 122, 130.
[72] Interview 004013, Part B, pp. 200–201.
[73] Interview 321278, pp. 91–92.
[74] Interview 006022, Part A, p. 28.
[75] Interview 036120, p. 48.
[76] Interview 042134, p. 157

tinized practice, and conformity. Only a handful of the informants report themselves as being seriously at odds with or deviating in principle from family religious views. There is practically no genuinely religious or moral content in any of the discussion that pretends to describe the thought and behavior of the most devout and exemplary religious role models. As deviants from the general disposition to affectless acquiescence, the informants encountered in childhood only a handful of free-thinking or indifferent males and a larger number of females whose mild religious excesses merely envelop them further in a faceless shroud of womanly virtues.

Current religious practices and orientations differ from those reported in childhood primarily in that they are more unequivocally weighted toward formal compliance, vagueness, and indifference (Table 5.2).

TABLE 5.2 *Contemporary Religiosity by Main Sphere of Action* (*Percentages*)

	Economic	Political	Cultural
N =	(39)	(53)	(23)
Individualized, principled, spiritually grounded religious commitment	13	—	22
Social commitment to the Church and to advancement of Church-defined interests and religious values	26	15	17
Formal compliance with religious obligations, conventional observances	41	26	—
Vague commitment to moral principles without formal compliance	10	29	22
Indifferent to religion	10	30	39

NOTE: Nine respondents could not be clearly classified for this tally.

Although not very much can be made of variations by sphere given the precariousness of these numbers, this table also shows a tendency to either strongly religious or outrightly indifferent views among cultural leaders. The politicians lean strongly toward the indifferent and vaguely principled end of the religious spectrum whereas businessmen cluster more substantially from a middle conforming position toward a more actively religious stance.

These markedly different patterns by sector may represent trends — that is, configurations that have been crystallizing over time — for the proportions of top leaders attending religious schools show a decline with age within the political and cultural spheres. The younger a politician or cultural leader within the present elite, the less likely is he to have had a religious education in childhood. This is not the case among business leaders, where even among those under forty-three a ratio of four to one is still evident in the number who have attended religious as against secular institutions in the primary and secondary grades. However, except for the single category of pro-Church activism, religious education does not prove to be a good predictor of religiosity in maturity (Table 5.3). In fact, among

TABLE 5.3   Contemporary Religiosity by Religious Education
(Percentages)

	N =	Some Religious Schooling, Primary or Secondary (58)	Never Attended a Religious School (55)
Individualized, principled, spiritually grounded religious commitment		5	13
Social commitment to the Church and to advancement of Church-defined interests and religious values		29	9
Formal compliance with religious obligations, conventional observances		18	26
Vague commitment to moral principles without formal compliance		15	24
Indifferent to religion		23	29

NOTE: Twelve respondents were not classifiable for this tally.

those who gave information, there are more presently showing principled religious commitment among those who never attended a religious school than among those educated within Church institutions.

As Table 5.3 also suggests, the paths to whatever present position is now taken with respect to religion have also been diverse. What is more impressive, however, is the uniformly shallow affect and conventionality of this religious biographical comment. By and large, whether or not the respondent presently conceives of himself as a religious person, remarks on the respondent's own religious experience convey no greater sense of involvement or insight than the descriptions of the religious life of parents or other figures taken as models. Claims to a reasoned secularism and an independently derived ethical position ring as hollowly as do the formalistic professions of faith.

I say that I am already a saint, therefore I don't need to practice [religion] any longer. . . . Well, that is because I have had for a long time a well-formed morality of my own which squares well with religious morality, religious formulas. I consider [religious] practice useful for many people . . . but if one is already responsible and has enough knowledge, . . . religion no longer has any function to perform. I demand more than religion. I make demands on myself and demands on others.[77]

Well, I am not religious, no . . . because I later became more independent in this respect. Naturally I didn't stop attributing [to religion] its due importance as a moral restraint, as a way of directing the spirit if it is well utilized just as any ideology might be. At least that is my view, that if the religious thing is used for good, it obtains in a way the same results that any faith might if put to the same purpose. . . . This matter does not bother me. I have a great respect for the religious ideas of others. Nor do I fight the Church. I am not a denouncer of priests.[78]

If you call religion the fact of going to mass, complying with formal ceremonies, I think my [religion] doesn't go very far. If you call religion an attitude toward life, toward the Divinity, toward the hereafter, toward conscience, then [my religion covers] a great deal. . . . I believe names are chosen conventionally. I find this second sense more serious than the first, but naturally names are chosen at the whim of the person who uses them.[79]

The affirmations of faith do not communicate any more convincing sense of depth of reflection or feeling with respect to religion.

The greatest beauty of the Christian religion is woman. It brought woman to the altar, it brought her to God, it raised her with the Virgin. That is the greatest thing that can be. I say to you that for me woman is the grandest thing that has existed on earth. . . . Every day before I come to the bank I go to mass . . . to greet the Virgin, to greet God, to greet Christ.[80]

What attracts me most about religion is precisely the philosophy, let us call it that, of Christ . . . which is a wholly human thing on the one hand, with a permanent spiritual loftiness that helps one, undoubtedly, to bear a series of adversities and problems with the very principles that define that religion.[81]

Later, after I left San Ignacio, I had something of a reaction. I tried to be a free thinker, though on a modest scale and mostly during the years I was in the university. Not because of outside influences, for I did not have any. I did not have conversations, I was not under group pressures, I simply considered that at that moment it was the best way for me to think. Later I returned to what I might call Catholic practice, and today I consider myself

[77] Interview 054162, Part B, p. 118.
[78] Interview 135105, pp. 115–116.
[79] Interview 095200, p. 63.
[80] Interview 049149, pp. 35–36.
[81] Interview 039127, p. 88.

a Catholic who meets his obligations, who is happy in his religion and feels at ease in it.[82]

Given the spectrum of positions taken with respect to religion, it is not surprising to find Church authority on issues such as divorce and birth control challenged on a broad front. Such challenges come about as readily from those with early schooling in religious institutions as from others. Moreover, they are stated not infrequently even among the most Church committed. Among those with more conventional attachments to Church who still comply externally with religious practices, a majority reject the Church's position on these issues so vital to the family (Table 5.4).

TABLE 5.4   Religiosity and Challenges to Church Authority (Percentages)

	Strong Religious Commitment	Conventional Religious Compliance	Noncompliance, Indifference
N =	(31)	(29)	(47)
Views on birth control and divorce			
Accepts Church position	68	31	2
Rejects Church position	32	69	98

NOTE: Eighteen respondents were unclassifiable for this tally.

The quotations that follow are not intended to convey the full range of opinions on divorce and birth control but rather to add yet another perspective on subjects' religious views and modes of adapting to religious proscriptions. The first citations are from conformists with strong Church ties.

I tell you this not as an opinion but as an experience. . . . Among the transcendental conversations that we had before marriage, the first was to accept all the children the Lord should send us. [Should divorce be allowed?] Certainly not. And never as the basis for a new marriage. They should not do it if they have children or if they have no children, because of a conception of life that transcends matrimony.[83]

I believe divorce is a social evil which today has been accepted and is dominant in many countries of the world. But between . . . two responsible persons it should not exist. It may be possible to accept separation for the Church permits it. . . . We always observed with absolute fidelity our Catholic duties in my home. We had eight children and we never thought of look-

[82] Interview 307253, p. 55.
[83] Interview 019058, pp. 71–72

ing for a way to control that except within the norms that the Holy Church itself accepts.[84]

Dissent on these issues from within the religious committed group stresses social responsibilities and duties, and the control of impulse even while calling for greater flexibility in Church doctrine. The latent fear and distrust of greater individual freedom sometimes breaks through and is made explicit as in the following quotations.

I believe it is necessary. . . . Today I think the Church and the State should permit birth control in families. . . . There are certain circumstances in which divorce should be permitted . . . but it would be bad to make divorce too easy because then there would be many people who would use divorce irresponsibly.[85]

With time it will be necessary to control birth rates everywhere. . . . The point is to have children who will later prove useful to society, who will not become a burden, and that the individual will be able to support. . . . A time will come when it will be necessary to establish the father's responsibility, to make it effective with respect to his children. . . . I believe that divorce is a just thing. Naturally, it should have its restraints . . . it should not be . . . like washing one's hands. It should establish responsibility with respect to the children of a marriage. . . . A man, if he does not divorce, continues doing as he pleases. There are male adulterers, but no one calls them adulterers.[86]

This moralistic tone is generally absent in the statements favoring birth control and divorce of the less religious, who tend to stress affirmations of individual rights and social realism in attacking such conditions on individual action.

I am in favor of birth control. I think a couple in particular circumstances has not only the right but the obligation to control birth. . . . My idea of the independence and freedom of the individual go so far that I believe simply that the independence or freedom of the individual in itself justifies his way of acting. I don't believe anyone has a right to interfere in such things . . . as long as the two people are in agreement.[87]

I believe a couple should have absolute freedom in all circumstances. Now, as in all forms of liberty, it should be a liberty based on knowledge and awareness of the implications of that liberty. . . . Divorce should be allowed, though avoiding it when possible. . . . I think divorce is a solution but like . . . amputating an arm or a leg.[88]

[84] Interview 310256, p. 57.
[85] Interview 330246, p. 30.
[86] Interview 065192, p. 70.
[87] Interview 128187, p. 41.
[88] Interview 321278, p. 93.

I believe . . . birth control has become a matter of social necessity in the world today. . . . One has to live realistically. I think religions cannot live on things that are not real. They should be directed toward man, toward the world, and not toward something that is outside him.[89]

If the challenge to Church authority and dogma on issues that bear so directly on private morals is widespread, the rejection of Church action in the political sphere is even more one-sided and absolute. Politicians particularly would deny any political role at all to the Church, and even Church partisans would claim for it only a detached, monitoring function over politics (Table 5.5).[90]

TABLE 5.5 *Political Role Appropriate for Church by Main Sphere of Action* (*Percentages*)

	Economic	Political	Cultural
N =	(39)	(46)	(22)
Church should function as a moral monitor, clarifying issues, guiding the people	56	26	46
Church should stay out of politics altogether	44	74	54

NOTE: Seventeen respondents were unclassifiable for this tally.

This is made even clearer in Table 5.6, which shows that even among those most committed to the Church nearly half urge that it remain entirely out of politics.

The political role envisioned for the Church by its partisans is primarily a defensive and educational one — defense against communism and other sources of anti-Church action, general orientation with respect to civic duties and political responsibilities. Partisan activity within the range of "legitimate" (that is, non-Marxist) political organizations is explicitly stamped as undesirable.

Naturally the Church should do everything possible to open the eyes of Catholics against this [communism], but with respect to other tendencies that are perfectly compatible with Christian and religious standards, and

[89] Interview 324282, p. 67.
[90] Table 5.5 shows the role informants feel the Church *should* have. There seems to be more uncertainty about the *actual* political role of the Church in Venezuela than active belief that it is intervening in a direct fashion. Even among politicians, who should be in a position to know and take a strong stand against such Church action, the number of direct accusations of interference is negligible.

TABLE 5.6 Political Role Appropriate for Church by Religiosity
(Percentages)

	Strong Religious Commitment (29)	Conventional Religious Compliance (28)	Noncompliance, Indifference (44)
N =			
Church should function as a moral monitor, clarifying issues, guiding the people	53	50	29
Church should stay out of politics altogether	47	50	71

NOTE: Twenty-four respondents were unclassifiable for this tally.

which are really a matter of personal taste . . . I think the Church should have no influence because religion is a much more permanent thing than all of that.[91]

In principle [the Church's responsibility in politics] is to be on the alert with respect to deceptive lures that might bring parishioners to become the gullible tools of ideas that go against the Church itself.[92]

These responsibilities have already been defined by the bishops themselves; they have just indicated them in a pastoral letter. The Church must be watchful that when parishioners vote in the election of any type of official they do so responsibly and conscientiously. . . . The Church should not, as it has not, espouse the cause of any party. But I do think it has the obligation to orient the laity as to the best way to vote and the selection of persons to be elected. The Church has an absolute right to ask parishioners not to vote for persons who in office will attack the very institution of the Church.[93]

The difference between such views and those that start out forthrightly proscribing the field of politics to the Church lie really only in shadings of emphasis. Though they start formally from a counterpremise, in the end these statements wind up dramatizing the existing consensus on this issue.

The Church should not try to influence in any way the political position of its members. . . . Thus when the Church tries to orient laymen in a political or partisan way, it is committing a fundamental error which sets up advantages that should not exist. For that reason I always recommend that the Church stay out of politics as such.[94]

I believe that the Church should remain withdrawn from all political involvement in a country. I think the two last papal encyclicals . . . are two

[91] Interview 323281, pp. 29–30.
[92] Interview 050150, Part B, p. 205.
[93] Interview 024072, p. 35.
[94] Interview 345261, Part A, pp. 52–53.

very modern documents. They have defined this matter in the following way: We Catholics have a duty to participate actively in the politics of our nations, but the Church's role is merely one of moral guidance and, of course, opposition to communism, which is very normal . . . for communism is atheistic.[95]

One of my great reservations with respect to the Church is the priest turned politician. We are a people that are profoundly Catholic but do not accept in any event . . . that the priest, the deacon, or the highest dignitary in the hierarchy should intrude into politics. This is a spontaneous matter that has been maintained until now. . . . We have the experience of Colombia in past decades. The clergy from the pulpit recommended voting for conservatives or for candidates they favored. We have not had those problems. Instead, we keep the Church exclusively away from the heat of political propaganda.[96]

We are, of course, not concerned here with Church action in politics as a public issue but rather with the quality and scope of religiously grounded loyalties and values.[97] On this evidence, one would judge these to be narrow and tenuous. For most subjects religion is not a politically motivating force. Apparently for most, it is not even very influential as a framework for defining moral stands on critical social issues. A small group that is strongly pro-Church as an institution is present, but these individuals are responding more to a social ideology or life view than to genuinely religious appeals. There are hardly any signs of reflective, individualized spiritual awareness in the abundant commentary on religion.

This absence of personally experienced belief accompanied by conventional orthodoxy in religious practice is also associated in Adorno's work with the authoritarian syndrome that he and his colleagues sought to pin down.[98] In an atmosphere that is religiously neutral or in which religion is not highly charged affectively or ideologically, he found both the strongly religious and the irreligious at the low or "democratic" end of his scale. It was the middle position, accepting authority or complying mechanically without accepting or seriously examining the claims to the truth of religious doctrine, that went with the constrained and constraining personality of the authoritarian. These relations are, however, tenuous and espe-

[95] Interview 007024, p. 63.
[96] Interview 318271, Part B, p. 130.
[97] For comment more relevant to the first point, refer to Chapter 7, especially pp. 220–221. In view of some of the political initiatives and efforts at social action being undertaken by businessmen in combination with clergy and religiously sponsored organizations, the general complacency of these assessments of the Church's political capacity and intent may not be entirely justified.
[98] Adorno, et al., *Authoritarian Personality*, pp. 727 ff.

cially likely to be affected by other variables when religion is not a salient commitment.

A tally such as that shown in Table 5.1, but ordered according to religiosity rather than feelings about childhood, showed no clear pattern of ties between present religious commitments and political style. In addition, we know almost nothing about why particular religious positions have been taken in maturity. Religious schooling, as has been seen, is by no means decisive in this respect, and the religious atmosphere in the *home* in childhood does not appear to have varied a great deal, whatever the class setting or locale. No clear moment of common religious crisis, such as adolescence, emerges in these recapitulations.[99] Yet there are important differences by main sphere of action in patterns of religiosity and response to religious issues. More detailed and carefully drawn religious biographies would be needed to get more precise notions of how religious feelings have been sustained, renewed, or effectively neutralized over the lives of these men: We know that a systematic campaign to revive religious commitments and directed especially at businessmen has been mounted in Venezuela. Religion is not now a major factor in politics but may yet become one.

The Ascendance of Middle-Class Values

The study data, as noted, are not used to make systematic efforts to connect specific childhood experiences to present political behavior among these subjects. But this chapter does provide a perspective on the private world into which elite Venezuelans were born and through which they have moved to prominence. In Chapter 3, that world was described as one peopled largely by those of modest, middle-class culture and accomplishments. That chapter also affirmed that persons from such backgrounds had completely taken over leadership in politics and cultural activity in Venezuela and that a similar process of penetration was under way in the economic sphere. These affirmations were made not only on the basis of an examination of the social backgrounds of respondents and their fathers but also on information about mothers, siblings, wives, and male in-laws of elite individuals.

The women, in particular, have considerably less education than the men in this circle. However, male kinsmen of elite respondents, whether

---

[99] In the Chilean research mentioned earlier, a falling away from religion in adolescence was repeatedly mentioned (Bonilla and Glazer, *Student Politics in Chile*).

direct or through marriage, are also generally more modest achievers in education and occupation. The human framework in which the kinds of relations that have been discussed in these pages take place is thus one of limited middle-class perspectives. Behind the thin overlay of technicism, sophistication, and intellectuality that marks the professional activity of these men, lies a world of private relations in which more simple formulas and modes of action dominate. It is worth remembering that this is the first generation of mostly university-trained elite incumbents Venezuela has had. These men are, by and large, the vanguard of a social group in ascent. Their private lives are still embedded in a class-marked milieu heavily pre-occupied with status, social propriety, and provincial canons of decorum. The conventionality, conformity, and relative shallowness of a great deal of this commentary — even when individuals are obviously straining to go beyond the commonplace in reporting and interpreting their lives — can be more readily understood with this social context in mind.

This middle class elsewhere has been called to task for investing the na-tion's politics with a great many negative features — an excessive frac-tioning of views and parties, reformism, individualism, sectarianism, and opportunism.[100] The survey covering numerous middle-class groups that is part of this study localizes a great amount of dissensus and conflict in Venezuela among these groups. If diversity and fragmentation are political characteristics of this class, the present chapter suggests considerable unity of experience and shared views with respect to vital life areas. Moreover, the findings do not, as in other sectors of the research, convey an impression of values, institutions, or behaviors in great flux. Nothing in what leaders tell us about the families they head suggests that these families are today very different contexts for socialization than the families into which these leaders were born. Little of what informants say about their religious views leads one to believe that, outside of a few who have opened them-selves to the stimulus of new currents in the Church, religious thought and practice have changed materially among men of this social level in the past few decades. The same may be said about the spheres of friend-ship. *In short, these have not been in the past nor do they seem to be becoming areas of life in which informed, principled, and emotionally ful-filling action patterns are taking root.* This substructure of culturally sup-ported and enforced overvaluation of unsatisfying relationships must cer-tainly constitute a heavy burden for individuals and is a submerged force

---

[100] Guillermo García Ponce, *Política y clase media* (Caracas: Editorial La Muralla, 1966).

at work within the society. Still, only a very intuitive feel about how some of these tensions are actually generated and work themselves out in the lives of individuals and elite subsectors can be elicited from these materials.

Again, some of the elements of the analysis of the case of the revolutionary seem apropos here.[101] Repressed hostility toward parents is apparent as well as the pressure to a shallow glorification of parent figures. Whether, as the psychological study in *SRSP* seeks to demonstrate, these early experiences motivate rebelliousness against authority figures, paranoid distrust, anticipations of malevolence in others, incapacity for sustained group action, and efforts to seek dominance through violence, the information available here cannot hope to prove. Negative memories of childhood do show some relation with political behavior that seem congruent with this view, as shown in Table 5.1. The socially mobile also seem to have more negative recollections of parents in childhood, though their political behavior does not seem to be any more "paranoid" or authoritarian, according to our crude indicators, than those of the status stable now in elite positions.

Revolutions alternately in expectations and more recently in "frustrations" have been seen as the driving force behind political demands in nations like Venezuela. These expectations and frustrations generally have been linked to appetites or aspirations for material improvement, though they are occasionally seen as having political and personality dimensions insofar as they manifest desires for autonomy and self-determination. But in general, the reference point or model on which such aspirations are presumed to be fixed lies in the developed nations. People are frustrated because they envy the material comforts and world power of more favored nations. The powerful outsider takes on the role and characteristics of the father in the fragments of life histories that have been reported here — remote, overbearing, exacting deference, demanding for himself a monopoly of impulse behavior.

Without challenging the importance of national development goals as a politically motivating force nor the tendency to impute individual characteristics to collectivities, an alternative view emerges in this material. Tensions here arise not from frustration over being unable to do what others do — creating and managing great industrial and war machines, juggling complex power systems at home and abroad — but rather from failing to meet one's own, culturally prized self-image. Many props to self-esteem can be assembled to meet charges of failure according to other

[101] Slote, *SRSP*, especially pp. 306 ff.

people's standards. Guilt and shame about the incapacity to give reality to one's own most cherished purposes, and in areas in which blame cannot be readily projected outside one's own circle, would seem to be far more corrosive individually and explosive politically. If family, friendship, and religion are in truth focal arenas of culturally valued fulfilment and achievement, then the need to study action in these frameworks at least as closely as economic and political behavior are now being observed is more than apparent.

A Note on the Interviews

Though some general comments on interviewing have been made in the opening chapter, the portion of these conversations dealing with the more private relationships treated in these pages merit a few additional remarks. Part of the reason for citing from the interviews so extensively has been to allow the material to speak for itself — to make plain that despite the many inhibitions, real and imaginary, that stand in the way of a free exchange between interviewer and respondents of such elevated status, something really happened in these encounters.

No one who sets out to obtain information on sensitive matters from persons whose privacy is normally guarded jealously fails to have second thoughts about how far one can go without becoming offensive or provoking the respondent to interpose an impenetrable defensive screen. All of us who are professional askers of questions spend almost as much time in anguished speculation about how to elicit certain forms of talk as in puzzling over its meaning once it has been produced. All of us have been schooled to watch for the many devices by which men shield themselves from self-knowledge and throw off unwanted probes into reserved areas. When the normal barriers to free expression in guided forms of introspection are compounded as in Venezuela by political and social tensions of great intensity, it is easy to make any research venture of this kind appear foolhardy and to instill great self-doubt in any investigator.

For all these reasons it seemed at the start somewhat presumptuous to pretend to penetrate significantly into the private lives and sentiments of subjects in this primitive way — with rather artless, direct questions; in only partially controlled settings; with interviewers who were gaining experience as they went along. No pretense is made here that this interviewing experience has been entirely successful, controlled, thoroughly sifted for useful insights, or properly evaluated. Our preoccupation lies precisely with such matters, for we have been unable to give a good answer to a question that has been asked of the research team many times: What made these important and busy men take the time to tell you so much about themselves? How were topics manifestly so remote from the main business of the study introduced into the interviews? How were subjects persuaded to put on tape so much information of a private and possibly damaging nature in a milieu so riddled with conflict and distrust?

Part of the answer we believe lies in the low-key, common-sense approach taken in this work. The assumption under which the study operated and which interviewers sought to communicate to subjects was that once the *bona fides* of the research and the interrogator were established, it was in the subject's best interest to get as much as possible into the record in precisely his own language. Once started, the interviewer worked gradually from the most simple forms of fact collection to increasingly individualized and subjective appraisals of life experiences. Questioning, though directed, was intended to be natural and sympathetic. Interviewers were free to express curiosity, compassion, skepticism.

However, a more important part of the answer to our unanswerable question probably lies in the material in this chapter, for it reveals a great hunger to talk, a great hunger for affect, a desire for self-knowledge that is not entirely masked by the awkwardness and inexpertness of some of these attempts at self-revelation. Many respondents readily volunteered that they had never had such an opportunity to think and speak about themselves at such length. At least a few had manifest difficulty disengaging from the interview.

Because these men are successful and intensely involved in the present, they rarely look back. The satisfactions of the present soften whatever rancors may survive from a past that tends to be idealized. For these and other reasons it is probably this chapter that will come most as a surprise to subjects who read this book. All of these men know the facts of social stratification and other inequities in Venezuela. They are keenly aware of political shortcomings. Most will admit that a working democracy remains a future goal that it may take the nation many detours to achieve. However, they will probably find it harder to believe that on their testimony as a group, the family in Venezuela is not the individual's securest refuge, that most friendships are barren, and religion an indifferently or mechanically honored institution.

Obviously this is a simplified and harsh summary of the complex picture of family, friendship, and religion that has been drawn in these pages.

Still it is important to note that most symptoms of bankruptcy in other institutions that may be uncovered elsewhere in this volume will be accepted with equanimity. But the implications of the present chapter strike directly at the heart of cherished symbols, fundamental loyalties, and areas of great emotional investment. Moreover they imply a need to look more closely within the self and among those most close to the self for the reassessment of intimate relationships that alone can answer the doubts and anxieties that we here give back to our subjects.

6   INTRAELITE LINKAGES

Much research on elites has floundered or at least opened itself to severe criticism by assuming that certain forms of social proximity or common experience mean in fact the existence of like interests, direct communication, and coordinated action among men in positions of power. In the absence of secure and comprehensive data on the actual existence and operation of such interconnections, quite different views of national and local power structures have been argued forcefully and at length, but with little active effect on the resolution of conflicting counterclaims.[1] Such constellations of intraelite linkages remain among the most inaccessible of social facts and the most difficult to assess once verified.

As has been reported in *SRSP*, 164 of the elite informants completed a sociometric questionnaire in which they indicated degree of friendship, frequency of communication, activities in common, and degree of kinship with each of the 276 individuals who constituted the original target group.[2] Though this body of data is probably unique for an operative elite, it obviously falls well short of an exhaustive mapping of intraelite ties. Nevertheless, it opens the way to an exploration of rarely treated approaches to obtaining partial views of structures known to be extremely complex and incompletely represented in the data available. Plainly the risks of study-

[1] A case in point is Talcott Parsons's review of *The Power Elite* by C. Wright Mills. See Parsons's *Structure and Process in Modern Societies* (Glencoe, Ill.: Free Press, 1960), pp. 199–225.

[2] Allan Kessler, who presented the first overview of these materials (*SRSP,* Chapter 9) also gave indispensable help in the preparation of data for this chapter. The present analysis rests importantly on conceptualization, measures, and computer routines devised by Mr. Kessler. His work in this area has been carried on in close collaboration with Professor Frederick W. Frey. Carlos Domingo, of the Computation Center of the Central University in Caracas, programmed the partitionings discussed later in the chapter.

ing political systems by this form of selective palpation are considerable. But again, the intent is to make as much as seems reasonable out of what information we have rather than merely to deplore its imperfections.

As the earlier report on these data specified, they were not collected with the idea of exposing the private network of relations lying behind the public façade of power nor of uncovering the secret machinators who really sit on top of the pecking order among notables.[3] The study's concerns lay rather in assessing capacity for collective action, in bringing into view the organization of organizations in Venezuela insofar as this might be represented in ties among a large number of the individuals in command positions in practically all sectors of organized activity. By themselves the sociometric data provide little ground on which to base judgments about the relative weight of office versus personalities in the establishment, maintenance, or operation of such social networks. These are analytic niceties not readily unraveled in natural situations. In the present case the analysis does in fact seek to uncover the bases of solidarity among elite subgroups, but the focus is on how ties develop among institutional spheres, organizations, social sectors, and particular roles rather than on the individualities moving in these circles. Such ties, of course, have implications not only as social bonds but as opportunities for issue confrontation and the necessary articulation of conflicts. A subsequent chapter on contexts of intra-elite interaction provides much of the qualitative detail that will be found missing here.

Kessler's early analysis provided first confirmation of various critical points in the research team's early speculations about elite structure. First, the respondents as a group could reasonably be regarded as a mutually self-aware aggregate — about nine in ten knew of one another at least by hearsay. Communication rates were much more modest — in only 8 percent of the possible links among these men was frequent communication reported. At least occasional contacts were registered for about three in ten of the possible interpersonal connections. In addition, as has been more fully verified in Chapter 3 of the present volume, sociometric characteristics (being a favored object of friendship and communication choices) were found to be positively associated with the power scores based on the ratings by judges collected months before the survey. This reinforced our interest in both the first reputational rankings and the composite scores based on the later, more comprehensive choices by peers.

[3] Chapter 9 deals with "invisible" elites — those not tapped directly in this research.

Outside the economic sphere kinship proved to be of negligible importance as a factor in intraelite ties, and even in the business world the matrix of kinship ties merely recorded the existence of family concentrations of economic power that minimally informed Venezuelans can readily name. Attention thus centered on friendship and communications and secondarily on activities in common. The first findings on sphere differences in density and concentration functions squared well with other results that were suggestive of the relative social distances separating men prominent in each sector.[4] Communication ties were most dense within the political sphere and least so within the cultural. The cultural sector appeared to be the least cohesive internally on all counts. Cross-sphere ties were strongest between the political and cultural sectors. In the economic sector, however, the number of friendship ties binding its members compensates for its isolation and the relative weakness of internal communication.

Concentration effects brought out further complexities. The internal disarray of the cultural sector was compounded or perhaps merely explained in part by the polarization of friendship ties on a few individuals. As regards communication, however, it was the economic sphere that stood out in concentration scores. In short, distinctive rates of mutual awareness and communication both within and across sphere boundaries readily came to the surface. Put most simply, the pattern was for the politicians, high communication but less friendship; for the businessmen, low communication and relatively high friendship; for the cultural group, weakness on both counts. Communication links, especially those between the specialized spheres of elite action, were being channeled through a relatively small number of individuals.[5]

The findings with respect to subsets based on power scores are also striking (Tables 6.1 through 6.4). Because the pattern is so consistent, it

[4] The principal sociometric measures used in the first analysis as well as in this chapter are density and distribution functions. "The density function is the ratio of the observed number of relations to the possible number that could occur among the elements or individuals. When every element is related to every other element, the density function has a value of one" (*SRSP*, p. 229). "When all the lines of a graph are concentrated on one point that relates to all other points and no other lines exist, the distribution function has a value of one, that is, all the relationships are concentrated on one point. When each point has the same number of lines from it, the lines are evenly distributed, and the distribution function has a value of zero" (Ibid., pp. 229–230).

[5] Refer to *SRSP*, Tables 9.3 to 9.6. All density ratios by sphere were larger than one, indicating that partitioning by main sphere of action did in fact locate subsets of more than average density of interaction.

*TABLE 6.1   Density Statistics for Inter- and Intraset
Friendship Contacts: Power Groups*

I. Mutual choice of "friend"

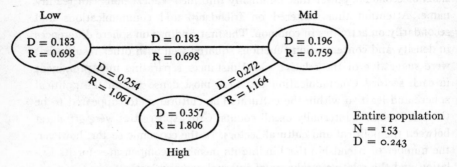

Entire population
N = 153
D = 0.243

II. Mutual choice of "friend" or "acquaintance" or combination of either

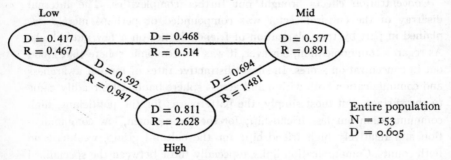

Entire population
N = 153
D = 0.605

III. Mutual choice of "friend" or "acquaintance" or "heard of him" or any
combination

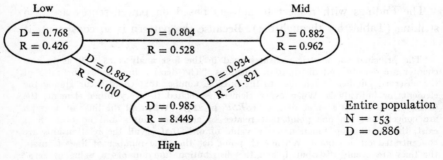

Entire population
N = 153
D = 0.886

D = Density function, R = Density ratio
Set size: High power score = 52
              Mid-power score = 62
              Low power score = 39

TABLE 6.2   Density Statistics for Inter- and Intraset
            Communication Contacts: Power Groups

I. Mutual choice of "often"

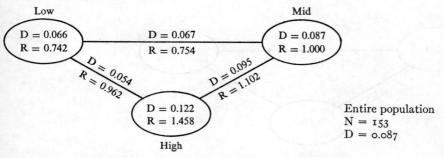

Entire population
N = 153
D = 0.087

II. Mutual choice of "often" or "occasionally" or combination of either

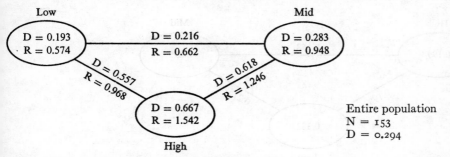

Entire population
N = 153
D = 0.294

III. Mutual choice of "often," "occasionally," or combination, or one-sided choice
     of "never" and other side "often" or "occasionally"

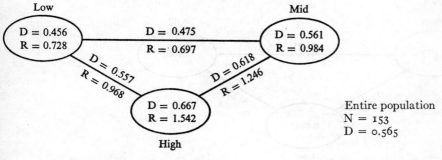

Entire population
N = 153
D = 0.565

D = Density function, R = Density ratio
Set size: High power score = 52
          Mid-power score = 62
          Low power score = 39

TABLE 6.3   *Distribution Statistics for Inter- and Intraset Friendship Contacts: Power Groups*

I. Mutual choice of "friend"

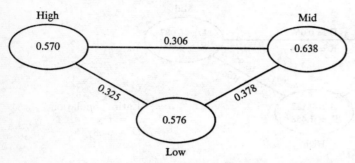

II. Mutual choice of "friend" or "acquaintance" or combination of either

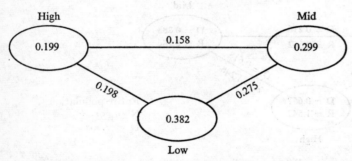

III. Mutual choice of "friend" or "acquaintance" or "heard of him" or any combination

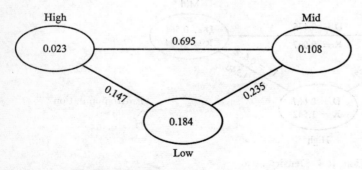

Set size: High power score = 52
          Mid-power score = 62
          Low power score = 39

TABLE 6.4   Distribution Statistics for Inter- and Intraset
Communication Contacts: Power Groups

I. Mutual choice of "often"

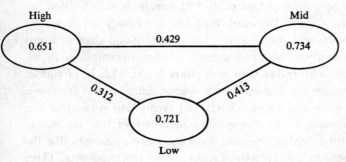

II. Mutual choice of "often" or "occasionally" or combination of either

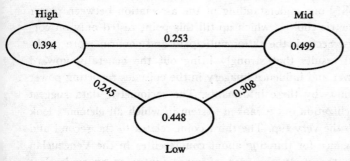

III. Mutual choice of "often," "occasionally," or combination, or one-sided choice of "never" and other side "often" or "occasionally"

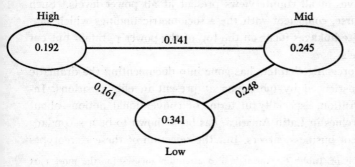

Set size: High power score = 52
          Mid-power score = 62
          Low power score = 39

can be stated quite succinctly. Only men in the very highest power level manifest above average densities of relationships. For both friendship and communication these densities are roughly twice as high among those at the very top as among those closer to the lower periphery of the power spectrum brought into view in this study.[6] Moreover, communication between power levels is oriented upward. Both low and middle power scorers have more friendships and contacts with the highest group than with one another. The distribution functions suggest greater concentration in sociometric choices at mid- rather than high power levels. This is, of course, congruent with the density findings, which suggest diffusion and dispersion of choices at low levels and a more closely and evenly knit network at the highest level. The analysis, of course, must move deeper into the nature of internal structures within the elite to trace more systematically the genuine implications of this pattern of links among power subsets. Three observations seem worth making at this point. First, these density ratios confirm and amplify our understanding of the association between power scores and sociometric choices, which up till this point rested only on correlational findings. Second, the ratios anticipate and confirm more qualitatively grounded results that strongly bring out the generally upward orientation of power and influence imagery in the episodes reporting power or influence attempts by these informants. The sociometric data suggest not only a hierarchization but a ranked system in which all elements look for direct links to the very top. The third point relates to the second and pinpoints its relevance for thinking about counterelites in the Venezuelan context. Early in the study the idea of counterelites as an underclass sharply stratified by power had been questioned in favor of a notion that saw representatives of all counterviews present at all power levels.[7] Such a view is, of course, congruent with these sociometric findings which suggest that intraelite linkages focus on the top of the power pyramid but cut across power levels.

Much in the foregoing chapters has gone into documenting the dramatic social ascent experienced by most men at present in elite positions. Inherited social position, especially in terms of conventional notions about traditional oligarchies in Latin America, has been shown to be a secondary factor in all except business careers. But the rejection of these stereotypes

[6] In the discussion of Tables 6.1 through 6.10 attention focuses for the most part on results at levels I and II which include for friendship, at least mutually acknowledged acquaintanceship; for communication, at least occasional mutually acknowledged contacts.

[7] Refer, for example, to "Venezuelan Men of Power: A Study Plan" (CENDES, July 1963), mimeo prepared by the present writer and Julio Cotler.

about social structures merely opens new questions about how in fact social relations among the powerful are colored by status antecedents. As
Table 6.5 indicates, friendships and acquaintances show above average
densities within subsets based on the number of high status antecedents
an individual possesses. They are stronger as well between the most
favored subset and the one having at least one mark of high status origins
than between the former and the largest group of respondents, who have
no links to high status groups in earlier generations. These differences are
roughly paralleled in communications but not as clearly or consistently
(Table 6.6). The distribution statistics here fail to bring out any additional facets of such ties and have not been shown. But in this case, sociometric findings direct attention back to a variable that in terms of previous
analysis might have been put to one side.

In these data, age emerges as a distinctive factor both in friendship and
in communication bonds (Table 6.7 and 6.8). In general the density of
friendship ties is greatest among the older age groups and feeblest among
the younger men among power wielders. Ties between the older men and
the most youthful within elite circles are also less numerous than between
the top and middle subgroups. Though the differences in question are not
entirely consistent nor very large (see also Tables 6.9 and 6.10), they suggest greater capacity in friendship nets for the oldest men (over 50) and in
communication nets for the middle-aged (43–50)— the group that also has
the largest proportion of high power scores.[8]

In addition to the major dimensions of intraelite differentiation that
have been reviewed (sphere, relative power standing, class of origin, and
generation), density calculations were performed for two other variables
— university attended and party affiliation. Nothing remotely as elaborate
as the U.S. preparatory school, Ivy League complex or the British public
school has been operative in Venezuela as a socializing context for elitehood during the lifetime of these respondents.[9] There are, nevertheless,
some notable secondary schools in the country with a reputation for producing men of prominence. In fact, about one in three of the respondents
attended one of five such schools.[10] However, not much can be said on the
basis of our data about the contemporary significance of this experience,
though the matter merits more attention than it has been given in this

---

[8] Chapter 3.

[9] C. Wright Mills in *The Power Elite* (New York: Oxford University Press, 1956)
seeks to document at some length the particularities of the education of the very rich
in the United States. See pp. 63 ff.

[10] San Ignacio de Loyola, La Salle, Andrés Bello, Caracas, and Fermín Toro. All
these schools are in the capital city.

TABLE 6.5   *Density Statistics for Inter- and Intraset*
             Friendship Contacts: High Status Origins

I. Mutual choice of "friend"

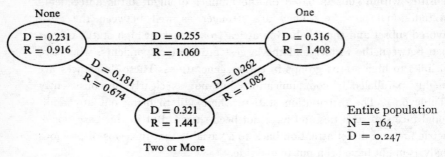

Entire population
N = 164
D = 0.247

II. Mutual choice of "friend" or "acquaintance" or combination of either

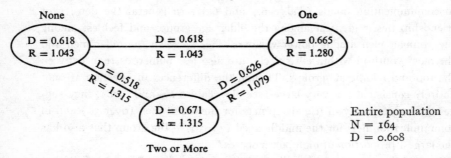

Entire population
N = 164
D = 0.608

III. Mutual choice of "friend" or "acquaintance" or "heard of him" or any
     combination

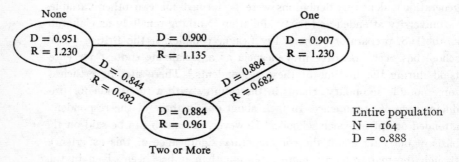

Entire population
N = 164
D = 0.888

D = Density function, R = Density ratio
Set size: Number of high status antecedents[a]
          None = 74
          One = 55
          Two or more = 35

[a] The high status antecedents counted include father's occupation, father's schooling,
and the occupations of both grandfathers.

TABLE 6.6 *Density Statistics for Inter- and Intraset Communication Contacts: High Status Origins*

I. Mutual choice of "often"

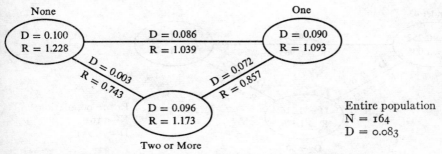

Entire population
N = 164
D = 0.083

II. Mutual choice of "often" or "occasionally" or combination of either

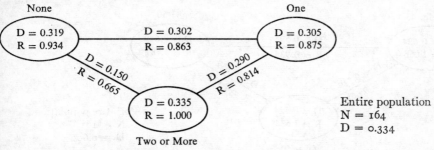

Entire population
N = 164
D = 0.334

III. Mutual choice of "often," "occasionally," or combination, or one-sided choice of "never" and other side "often" or "occasionally"

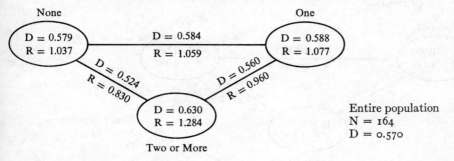

Entire population
N = 164
D = 0.570

D = Density function, R = Density ratio
Set size: Number of high status antecedents[a]
    None = 74
    One = 55
    Two or more = 35

[a] The high status antecedents counted include father's occupation, father's schooling, and the occupations of both grandfathers.

TABLE 6.7   *Density Statistics for Inter- and Intraset*
             Friendship Contacts: Age Groups

I. Mutual choice of "friend"

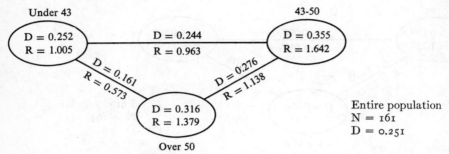

II. Mutual choice of "friend" or "acquaintance" or combination of either

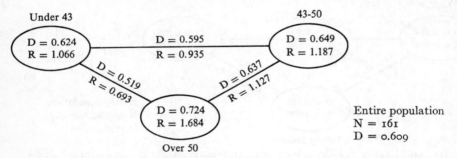

III. Mutual choice of "friend" or "acquaintance" or "heard of him" or any
     combination

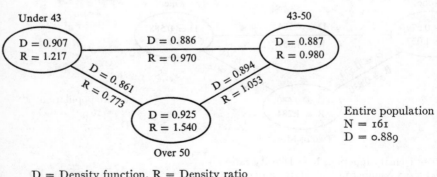

D = Density function, R = Density ratio
Set size: Under 43 = 55
          43–50 = 49
          Over 50 = 57

TABLE 6.8   Density Statistics for Inter- and Intraset
Communication Contacts: Age Groups

I. Mutual choice of "often"

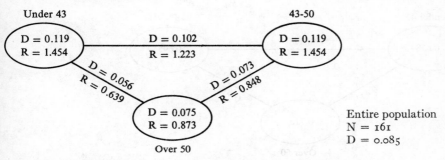

Entire population
N = 161
D = 0.085

II. Mutual choice of "often" or "occasionally" or combination of either

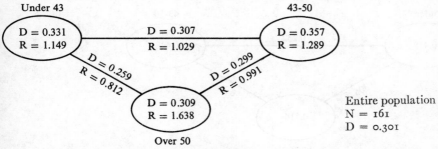

Entire population
N = 161
D = 0.301

III. Mutual choice of "often," "occasionally," or combination, or one-sided choice
of "never" and other side "often" or "occasionally"

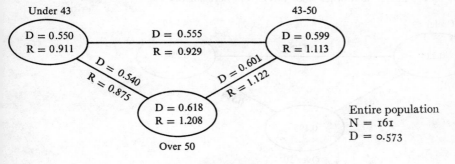

Entire population
N = 161
D = 0.573

D = Density function, R = Density ratio
Set size: Under 43 = 55
         43–50 = 49
         Over 50 = 57

TABLE 6.9   Distribution Statistics for Inter- and Intraset
Communication Contacts: Age Groups

I. Mutual choice of "often"

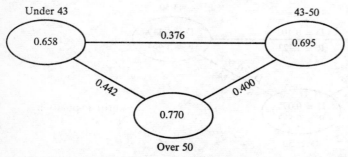

II. Mutual choice of "often" or "occasionally" or combination of either

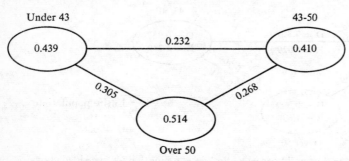

III. Mutual choice of "often," "occasionally," or combination, or one-sided choice
of "never" and other side "often" or "occasionally"

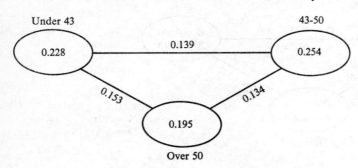

Set size: Under 43 = 55
43–50 = 49
Over 50 = 57

TABLE 6.10   Distribution Statistics for Inter- and Intraset Friendship Contacts: Age Groups

I. Mutual choice of "friend"

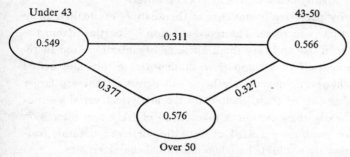

II. Mutual choice of "friend" or "acquaintance" or combination of either

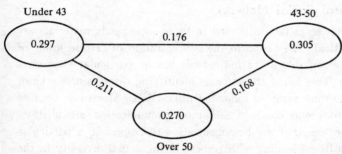

III. Mutual choice of "friend" or "acquaintance" or "heard of him" or any combination

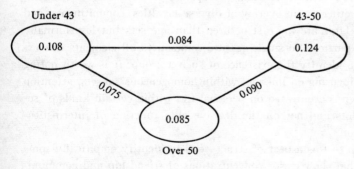

Set size: Under 43 = 55
        43–50 = 49
        Over 50 = 57

research. As regards the university, the sociometric data at this level indicate above average within-group densities for friendships among those who studied at the Central University (UCV), in the United States, and elsewhere abroad. Links between UCV alumni and those who studied in the United States are slightly below other cross-set densities.

The partition by party really anticipates the analysis of smaller, more compact groups that is to come. The representation by parties within the sample is irregular in size and very small for some organizations and therefore does not lend itself to a comparison of densities within and across parties. It does, however, immediately bring out densities that are larger than all but one or two of those elicited by the analytical variables considered so far. Clearly these networks take on an entirely new dimension when we consider genuine organized collectivities or more natural, real-life groupings rather than subsets based on individual characteristics.

Locating Natural Social Networks

The kinds of order so far uncovered in these sociometric materials are principally analytical. They confirm the concentration of certain kinds of social linkages among subsets of individuals having particular characteristics in common. This is not the same as identifying discrete networks or cliques within the total array of indicated interactions. Moreover, because these measures of group cohesion and intercommunication are abstractions about aggregates that are homogeneous with respect to a particular quality, they can be misleading with respect to the actual diversity in the composition of the "real" groups or networks of associated individuals operating at elite levels. These "real" groups are complex entities — small, diffuse, held together by an overlay of diverse loyalties, commitments, and identifications. They are more structured than age sets but less formally organized than parties. No single feature common to all elements can explain or serve to identify the existence of such a group. It is worth noting finally that by focusing on linkages within homogeneous subsets, attention thus far has been concentrated on personal ties within certain kinds of social compartments and not on the decisive elite function of interinstitutional articulation.

One approach to this aspect of structure is to identify empirically some of the subsets that show major concentrations of friendship and communication ties and then examine closely the composition of some of these subgroups. Two such partitionings, one for the friendship or mutual awareness matrix and the other for communications, are given in Tables 6.11 and

TABLE 6.11 HIDECS Partition of Friendship Sociomatrix

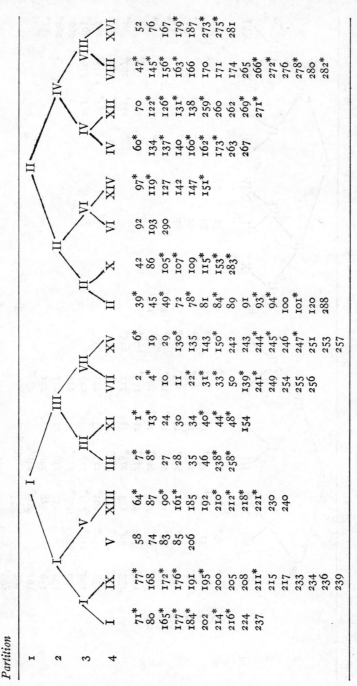

NOTE: The asterisks indicate an additional, fifth-level partition. At each stage in the partitioning a measure of redundancy is brought to a minimum (that is, the subset is divided at each partition into groups that maximize internal interconnections and minimize cross-group links).

TABLE 6.12 HIDECS Partition of Communication Sociomatrix

Partition

1															

Partition 2: I, II — Partition 3: I, III, II, IV — Partition 4 (leaf groups):

IX	I	V	XIII	III	XI	VII	XV	II	X	VI	XIV	IV	XII	VIII	XVI
7	2*	8*	10	85	86	1*	29	72		31	27	44	47	34	35
101	4	11	22*	161*	176*	50*	33*	83		39	28	153*	163*	48*	42
107	6*	13	119	185	184	91*	64*	84		40	30	160*	167*	49*	45*
109	105	19*	120*	200*	192	93*	90*	89		87	187	170*	177*	58	52
115	127	24*	122	205	202*	100*	92*	142				171	179	70*	60*
139	130*	46*	126	208*	206*	191	94	147				173*	271*	76	71*
	134*	74	131	212*	210	195*	97*	193				174	272	78*	77
	135	80*	143	215*	214	211	245*					288*	273*	267*	81*
	137*	151*	145*	216*	230	221	249					290	278*	269	262
	138	172*	165*	217	233*	241*	253						282*	275*	263
	140*	238*	255*	218	234*	243							283	276	265*
	150	259	256*	224*	237	244*									266
	154		257	236	239*	247									280*
	156*		258	240	242*	251									281*
	162		260*	246*		254*									
	166														
	168*														

NOTE: The asterisks indicate an additional, fifth-level partition. At each stage in the partitioning a measure of redundancy is brought to a minimum (that is, the subset is divided at each partition into groups that maximize internal interconnections and minimize cross-group links).

6.12.[11] By examining the nature of the relationships among individuals in some of these partitions as well as the aggregate characteristics of partitions at different levels, we get further insight into the structure of intraelite interconnections, and especially the current modalities of bridging institutional spheres. The principal point in displaying the actual partitions is to convey a clear idea of what this process involves and to bring out the very substantial differences in the results of partitioning on the basis of friendship as against communications choices.[12]

All of the cautions noted earlier concerning the interpretation of sociometric measures are equally pertinent here. We are working with only part of the full structure of interconnections among elite individuals; we surely are missing some of the polarizing figures who contribute importantly to giving a well-defined shape to this structure. Some individuals who are isolates, near isolates, or who are merely "leaderless" because the study failed to reach their subset stars, are floating around in the matrix with no apparent social anchorage. For this and other reasons peculiar to the technique used, many slightly different partitions can be produced from the same data. It is important to keep in mind that the analysis is not much concerned with the precise locations of individuals but rather with determining what may reasonably be inferred from the partial views of the structure represented in these data.

Looking first at the partitioning into four subsets as established at the second level (this can be seen in the heading for Table 6.10), a first sense can be obtained of how existing friendship and communication clusters within the elite may be differentiated. Tables 6.13 and 6.14 show information on eight variables for the quadripartite division of both the friendship and communication matrices. A great many other variables have been tested in this connection, but it is chiefly those proved to operate as strong discriminators in other contexts that here also produce results of interest.

The most striking feature of these nets, both for friendship and communications, is that in every case they straddle in about the same proportions the three main spheres of activity. They are all interinstitutional networks in this sense, though they need to be examined more closely to get

---

[11] The same technique used in Chapter 3 for the cluster analysis of social background variables has been applied in this partitioning. Refer to footnote 12, Chapter 3.

[12] More detail on these differences will be reported as the analysis unfolds. Note, however, the substantial overlap in some of the partitions, for example, partitions 1 and 3 (at level 3) in the friendship and communication matrices respectively and also both partitions 7 (also at level 3). In the friendship partitions a full range of values (0–4) weigh in the calculation of linkages. With regard to communication, only reciprocally acknowledged links were taken into account.

TABLE 6.13   Characteristics of Friendship Nets: Level 2 Partition

	F. Net 1 (42)	F. Net 3 (46)	F. Net 2 (31)	F. Net 4 (34)
Sphere	Mixed	Mixed	Mixed	Mixed
Power score concentration	Mid	Low	High	—
Mean age	48	49	49	50
Party affiliation[a]	Left	COPEI	Independents	AD-Right
Percentage holding multiple organization offices	38	52	58	26
Percentage with high status origins	26	22	32	9
Concentration of friendship choices on net members	Mid	Low	High	—
University attended	UCV	—	—	—

NOTE: The numbering of the nets matches that in Tables 6.11 and 6.12, which follow the successive branchings of the partition process.
[a] Left here includes Unión Republicana Demócrata (URD), Democratic Action Opposition (AD-OP), Leftist Revolutionary Movement (MIR), the Communist Party of Venezuela (PCV), and supporters of Admiral Wolfgang Larrazabal. The right includes supporters of Arturo Uslar Pietri, the Venezuelan Association of Independents (AVI), and other independents.

a more meaningful grasp of what this may imply. Men in politics are numerically dominant in all the subsets, so that differences show primarily in the relative weight of cultural versus economic figures. Specialization within sector begins to take on some importance at this level. In general, it seems to be political or power related dimensions that most clearly set apart the several friendship and communication nets. Political affiliation, relative power standing, the number of organizations in which high office is held, the frequency with which individual subset members are chosen as friends — all of these lend distinctiveness to each network of association or communication. One net (friendship net 2) has a concentration of members with high status origins; both nets 4 have a disproportionate representation of individuals with modest beginnings.

At this level of abstraction the profiles of the equivalently numbered nets in terms of the variables treated here are fairly similar despite substantial differences in the specific elements that populate them. The principal variations between friendship and communication nets also lie in the relative saliency of power scores and particular political groups. This underscores again the primacy of communication and sociometric variables as factors in relative power standing and the far greater significance of other variables related to social location and experience of change as associates

TABLE 6.14 Characteristics of Communication Nets: Level 2 Partition

	C. Net 1	C. Net 3	C. Net 2	C. Net 4
N =	(50)	(53)	(14)	(44)
Sphere	Mixed	Mixed	Mixed	Mixed
Power score concentration	Mid	—	—	Low
Mean age	49	48	50	49
Party affiliation[a]	AD	COPEI-Left	—	—
Percentage holding multiple organization offices	42	42	57	39
Percentage with high status origins	20	36	14	9
Concentration of friendship choices on net members	—	—	—	Low
University attended	—	—	None	—

NOTE: The numbering of the nets matches that in Tables 6.11 and 6.12, which follow the successive branching of the partition process.
[a] Left and right are defined as on Table 6.13.

of main sphere of action as well as normative orientation and evaluation.[13]

These second-level partitions still represent sizable aggregates that (with the exception perhaps of communication net 2, with fourteen members) are not likely to operate as functional action groups.[14] One may ask whether coming down an additional step to an eighth subset, third-level partition brings into view groups that are more homogeneous or well defined. Some such phenomenon would have to be present to support any general proposition about compartmentalization within the elite, at least insofar as such compartmentalization is presumed to rest on or produce actual barriers to contacts among individuals. As regards the friendship or mutual awareness nets, the distinctions that can be made at level 3 in terms of the variables that have been discussed so far are few and scattered. Communication nets show considerably more consistency or differentiation, again primarily in terms of power, party affiliation, the range of friendships, and status origins, and secondarily in terms of age (Table 6.15). At this point the repeatedly advanced hypothesis about sectorial compart-

[13] Refer to Chapter 3, pp. 72 ff., where these differences are first noted.
[14] The magnitudes of density functions for level 2 partitions are approximately those shown for the analytical variables earlier in this chapter. As will be seen in the more detailed analysis, as one moves into smaller partitions with much higher density functions, the groups tend to greater heterogeneity with respect to most of the analytical variables that have been explored. Table 6.16 shows some density ratios for a level 3 partition.

TABLE 6.15 *Characteristics of Communication Nets: Level 3 Partition*

	C. Net 1 (23)	C. Net 5 (27)	C. Net 3 (28)	C. Net 7 (25)	C. Net 2 (7)	C. Net 6 (7)	C. Net 4 (19)	C. Net 8 (25)
1. Sphere	−	−	+	−	−	−	−	−
2. Power	+	−	−	−	+	+	+	+
3. Mean age	+	+	−	−	−	−	−	+
4. Party affiliation	+	+	+	−	−	−	+	−
5. Percentage holding multiple organization offices	−	−	−		−	−	−	−
6. Percentage with high status origins	−	+	+	+	−	−	−	−
7. Concentration of friendship choices on net members	+	−	−	−	+	+	+	+
8. University attended	−	−	−	−	−	−	−	−

NOTE: A plus sign in the table indicates that the net in question shows some distinctive features with respect to the row variable.

mentalization within the elite becomes less tenable or requires a radical reformulation. The image evoked by these elite clusterings is not that of a society with three or four functionally specialized and relatively isolated power pyramids but rather one of a considerably more complexly articulated superstructure. This superstructure would appear to the eye much more like the skyline of a city of skyscrapers, where each point reaching up represents not a single institutional sphere but a diverse aggregation most clearly defined by its political components.

A closer look at a few such networks will convey some of their essential features, the variety in their composition, and a much more realistic sense of the quality of subgroupings within the elite than can be captured by density statistics. Network II (level 3, Table 6.12) has seven members — three businessmen, two politicians, a labor leader, and a clergyman. The density function for the subset, taking into account only reciprocal ties of frequent or occasional communication, is 43 percent. This is about the maximum density level reached for at least occasional communications in the partitions by power score and by sphere. Density scores for mutually acknowledged acquaintance or friendship also match the highest reached for analytical variables, which lie around 70 percent. The businessmen form a solid subclique within the network and are linked to the political subclique (a senator, deputy, and labor leader) through ties to the two legislators (Figure 6.1). The prelate has a marginal position within the net, figuring only on the basis of alleged communication to him by the politicians. The labor leader also figures here only as part of the political subclique and has no direct ties to the bankers and industrialists. The banker and the senator who dominate the two subcliques have the highest power scores and the highest number of reciprocated friendship and communication ties. The union leader's friendship claims were not acknowledged in three out of five relationships. Within this net of older, very well established figures, there are no mutually acknowledged claims of shared political activity even between politicians. Two thirds of the relationships are defined as exclusively business based. In the remainder, one party claims that a political dimension is present in the connection which is denied or not registered by the second party.

Communication net IV (level 3, Table 6.12), which is larger and has additional internal partitions, may be used to illustrate the way subnets are meshed (Figure 6.2). The net has twenty members representing every sector of activity, and within the four subpartitions suggested by the HIDECS decomposition all three sectors are presented except in the core clique,

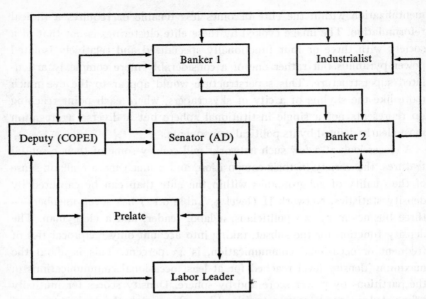

Figure 6.1   Links among Elements in Communication Network II

NOTE: Refer to Table 6.12, level 3. Arrows indicate the direction of communication claims.

which is exclusively governmental and economic. This core clique appears to represent a major component of the nation's economic planning and coordination apparat. The dominant figure in the core clique (net IVA in Tables 6.16 and 6.17) has reciprocal friendship relations with every one of the other nineteen individuals in the net. The dominance of the core clique is such that the density functions between it and the partitioned subnets are somewhat larger than the densities within the subnet.[15]

Several points of contrast exist between this net and the first one displayed, which seems a more typical combination of political and economic elements with fringe participants from the cultural sector. In the present case the political element is dominant and the economic participants do not constitute an independent subclique but articulate directly through

[15] This, of course, brings out a difficulty with respect to the partitions. The allocation of some elements to one or another subnet is quite arbitrary, for every element has to go somewhere and marginal individuals are not accumulated or filtered out as isolates. This means, of course, paying more attention to core cliques and their members but it is also important that certain kinds of people (for example, cultural leaders and low power scorers) tend to be found on the fringes of cliques or in cliques that are attached to core groups of larger nets.

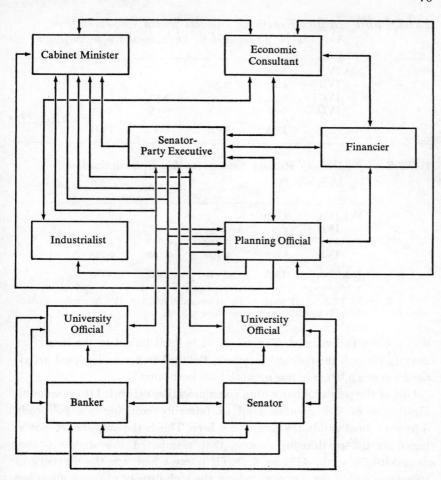

Figure 6.2 Links within and across Two Subnets in Communication Network IV

NOTE: Refer to Table 6.8, level 3, for communication net IV.

the core political figure. However, the dominance of the political figures may be more apparent than real. The economic members receive practically all the unreciprocated claims (eight out of ten). The banker in the subclique, especially, is held within the net almost exclusively by unreciprocated claims made on him both from within the subclique in which he lies and from the core group of government officials. The planning official by contrast makes the largest number of outwardly directed claims

TABLE 6.16 *Density Functions: Subnets within Communication*
             Network IV (Frequent or Occasional Communication)

Net IVA	0.67			
IVB	0.47	0.30		
IVC	0.37	0.40	0.30	
IVD	0.57	0.25	0.25	0.33
Net	IVA	IVB	IVC	IVD

TABLE 6.17 *Density Ratios: Subnets within Communication*
             Network IV

Net IVA	2.983			
IVB	1.303	0.630		
IVC	0.863	0.979	0.630	
IVD	1.947	0.490	0.490	0.733
Net	IVA	IVB	IVC	IVD

NOTE: Refer to Table 6.12, level 3, for communication net IV. A similar pattern exists for friendship links within and across these subnets.

that are not reciprocated. The subclique is itself linked to the larger net directly through the political members. Political and organizational activities loom much larger in this network than in the first.

One of the subpartitions within communication network III provides an illustration of still another kind of intraelite grouping — a politically oriented subnet within the economic sphere. This is the only subnet emerging from the partitioning process that manifested this degree of homogeneity by sector (Figure 6.3). Of interest here are the diversity of subsectors within the economic sphere, the high density of communications claimed (57 percent), and the linkages to another subclique within the net composed of major oil executives. A political and organizational dimension is claimed to exist in these relationships by at least one of the parties in about half the cases. Most of the members of the net are relatively young and have low- or middle-range power scores.

The same is true of the political-cultural subnet shown in Figure 6.4. This subnet has various interesting features. The first of these is the role of the journalist as key figure in the core subnet and as link between the two subnets. The strong connections of the journalists to both AD and COPEI subcliques and the general diversity of political and cultural elements present in the net bear remarking, as does the concentration of ties

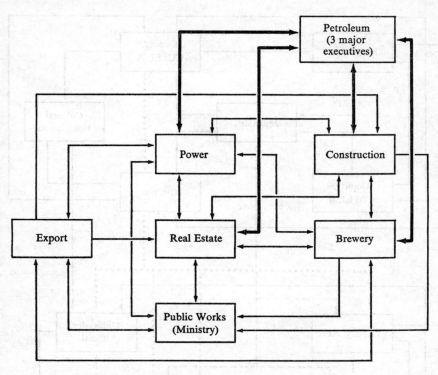

Figure 6.3 Sectors Represented in a Political Subnet within the Economic Sphere

NOTE: The subnet is one of the level-five partitions within net III, level 3, Table 6.8.

on two individuals ([Deputy, COPEI, A] and the journalist). The businessman operating a cultural foundation appears in a secondary, fairly isolated position in this context. The presence of the highest university officials within this subnet of relatively young and generally dissident politicians marks that institution's estrangement from the very top circles of power.

Numerous additional examples could be shown and further interpretations wrung from these illustrations, particularly by introducing more information about the individuals in each subnet. However, the shortcomings of the data and the crudeness of these methods do not really justify pushing much beyond the kinds of inference about structure that have been ventured so far. Many fundamental problems of interpretation (for example, what do friendship and communication really mean in this con-

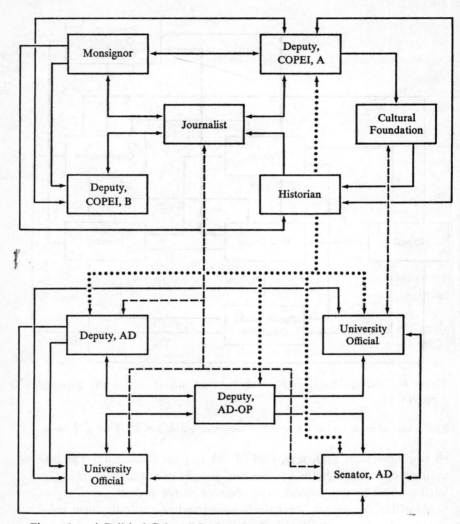

Figure 6.4   A Political-Cultural Communication Subnet

NOTE: The two subnets shown lie within net VIII, level 4, Table 6.8. Only the key interconnections between the subnets have been shown (dotted and dashed lines).

text?) have been glossed over in this discussion because we have been more concerned with the facts of connectivity than with the content or quality of communications. In this sense the present chapter provides a good transition from the previous materials on elite backgrounds and careers to the qualitative treatment of intraelite interactions that follows immediately.

The importance of the present materials is that they have permitted a reasonable if not fully conclusive test of the basic hypotheses concerning communication among institutional sectors and across power levels in a way not ordinarily possible in elite research. The early pages of this chapter and the work reported in the earlier volume substantiate the distinctiveness of communication patterns within and across such subsets. But we have sought to avoid assuming, on the basis of such aggregate statistics, that social reality conforms in a simple way to such primary notions of compartmentalization. Without challenging the basic facts of greater affinity or distance between groups as reflected in density statistics, an effort has been made to demonstrate that "natural" groupings maintain such interlockings but nevertheless permit considerable intermingling of diverse elements. The illustrations have been intended both to bring out the existence of specialized networks and to convey the root features of heterogeneity and the dominance of political factors (the relative power of members and political affiliation or, perhaps, ideology) in defining the distinctiveness of particular networks.

No hard and fast reference points are available for judging whether the interaction rates observed here are sizable or modest, compatible with efficient coordination across spheres and power levels or a serious block to the rational identification and implementation of desirable policies. Overall communication levels seem modest indeed — just under one in ten of the communication links possible among informants is mutually stated to be frequently active. However, looking more deeply into functional subgroups hardly leaves the observer with the feeling that this is an elite crippled by lack of access to one another. A better sense of the implications of the observed interaction rates and the selectivity factors operating may be obtained from an examination of what elite individuals say actually occurs in their encounters with each other.

7   ACTION IN POWER ROLES: CONTEXTS OF INTRAELITE RELATIONS

The foregoing chapters have, each in its way, sought to place the set of Venezuelan notables we have been studying within some meaningful social space. We have looked at the group successively from various perspectives: (1) in a historical context, (2) in terms of changing relationships to a complex stratification system, (3) in terms of the particular qualities of the individual experience of movement through the world of occupations and organizations on the way to elite positions, (4) within the framework of early family life and other childhood experiences, and finally (5) in terms of location within the network of associations and contacts that knit together individuals who have penetrated the circle of elitehood. The following pages draw principally on the material in the interviews dealing with activities in positions of power. Substantively, these discussions yield in varying detail and richness,

a. Descriptions of how power wielders view and carry out their command roles in organizations.

b. Descriptions of organizational action, structures, and relations with other authoritative and power-generating individuals and social aggregates.

It is important to distinguish the present analysis from the discussion in a more generalized form of role performance and organizational functioning as contemporary *issues*.[1] The aim in the section of the interviews to be treated here was to tap respondents' perceptions, attitudes, and broader values concerning action in authoritative and power relationships. The focus here is on action and appraisal of performance in contexts in which

[1] See especially the analysis of role performance as a public issue given in Gabriela Bronfenmajer, "Elite Evaluations of Role Performance," Chapter 8 in *SRSP*.

respondents are intimately involved rather than on evaluation of how the behavior of individuals and organizations, in many cases at a considerable social distance from respondents, was seen to affect broadly gauged collective interests. In the main, respondents are providing here information about their own action in primary roles and in the lives of organizations they themselves head. The interactions recorded are principally those in which the respondent as an individual or as prime agent for an organization was the initiating power actor, and secondarily those in which respondents felt themselves to be the objects of power attempts by others.

The code categories and analysis, as will be seen, gloss over most of the circumstantial detail concerning personalities and substantive events in the power confrontations and in the somewhat more formalistic and abstracted depictions of roles and organizational structures. In part this is necessary to protect the anonymity of respondents and confidences made in the course of the interviews. Fundamentally, however, the decision to pitch the discussion at a rather high level of abstraction reflects the basic position taken in this research that our critical perspective, particularly in these general analyses, should be structural rather than topical. This does not imply self-imposed censorship nor a disposition, out of fear or complicity, to protect men in power. In fact, very little of a private nature that is not known or that cannot be surmised from other sources is present in our data.[2] Our belief is simply that insofar as such material comes to the surface in an inquiry such as this, it can be put to use more constructively in other contexts that are within the reach of institutions like CENDES.

So far much has been said about factors that might incline these men to behave in certain ways. A substantial array of predisposing social models from the past, career experiences, putative interests, and loyalties has been mapped. However, except for the information in the sociometric chapter dealing with frequency of contact and the nature of activities in common, almost nothing has been said about what elite individuals *do*. The total weight of the evidence from each perspective has been to further solidify and elaborate the specifics of the starting hypothesis concerning intraelite

[2] Awareness of this fact among respondents probably contributed to the generally free climate of exchange and information giving that characterized the interviews. "Fortunately in this country people talk a great deal," remarked one respondent (Interview 029086, p. 80). Another noted, "Venezuela is not yet a country where things happen and one does not know who does them. Things here can still be identified and we can know their source" (Interview 007024, p. 78).

differentiation and its consequences. But we have been in effect amassing evidence the plausible causes exist for a phenomenon that remains unsubstantiated or at least very incompletely and intuitively portrayed.

This curious inversion of logic has not been especially troublesome because the problem does seem on the surface self-evident or open to intuitive appraisal. A few readers will recall that Ahumada's 1962 diagnosis opens with the simple affirmation that "no research is required to support the conclusion that something is wrong with Venezuelan society." [3] In the years between, none of the symptoms of political malaise to which he pointed — sporadic terrorism, the collapse of coalitions, schismatic movements within parties, recurrent threats of coups by the military — has been more than briefly absent. Plainly we are dealing with a heterogeneous elite, some parts of which are given to a murderous and self-defeating competition. Yet in other settings and according to much contemporary democratic theory, it is precisely the permeability, diversity, and energetic action at the top, which in part are manifested in these ways, that are presumed to guarantee the survival of civility.[4] How do such forces actually make themselves felt in political action at the upper reaches of Venezuelan society?

Our information on terrorists and military conspirators is fragmentary and indirect. However, we have already rejected on other grounds the idea that it is useful to think of the sector of the elite within our reach as a sensate nucleus hemmed in by extremists of the right and left while facing strong demands from a recalcitrant and unproductive mass. As the materials on national perspectives show, respondents themselves take a more complex view of their own situation, the sources of demands on them, and the factors behind the recurrent recourse to violence.[5] Most do not see themselves as living in a political world apart but consciously recognize that they are enmeshed in a total system that generates, lends meaning to, and rewards impulses that weaken the capacity for collective action at many levels.

This chapter approaches this range of problems by examining closely a large number of interactions among powerful men and major organizations. The objective is to achieve some qualitative sense of the differences between encounters of this kind that seem to have positive consequences

---

[3] *SRSP,* p. 3.
[4] Peter Bachrach, *The Theory of Democratic Elitism* (Boston: Little, Brown, 1967) discusses the motif of elite pluralism or contention in current theorizing about developmental democratic systems.
[5] See especially the discussion of terrorism in Chapter 7, *SRSP.*

for the society as against those that are disruptive. Part of the difficulty, of course, is to decide when consensual or conflictful actions can reasonably be evaluated as socially productive or disruptive. But the first task is to get some kind of representation of the main lines of everyday elite action that goes beyond the headlined bombings, suppressions of coups, detentions and exiles, suicides and schisms.

Elite and community power studies have ordinarily turned to the examination of decision-making or issue-oriented activity by leaders in order to get at the distinctive modalities of elite action and to obtain a sense of the differences in scope, motivation, opportunities for intervention, and effectiveness of individuals and subgroups within the elite.[6] This path was not entirely closed to us though it was not a methodically pursued aim in the interviewing. Much information on leaders' issue orientation was obtained but these data do not add up to careful case studies of how specific issues have been resolved at high levels. Numerous critical decisions of national import or of vital concern to major organizations are discussed in the interviews in considerable detail and from numerous, contrasting vantage points. These materials have in fact been used extensively in the preparation of background studies of parties and pressure groups. However, the choice here has been to take as the basic unit of analysis not an issue or a decision but what we have called a *power interaction*. Information about present positions (ROLES) and the organizations in which they are lodged (BODIES) has been independently coded and will be presented as a mode of entry into the larger topic of action in power roles (PRAXIS).[7] But it is the last of these that is the major focus of concern.

Each PRAXIS constitutes a codable episode or incident described by the respondent in which, as the incumbent of a power role, he figures centrally as the object of action or as key actor in an interaction involving power. The word "episode" is used here to make plain that we are not trying to

---

[6] Nelson Polsby presents a well-argued defense of this "pluralistic" approach to power structures in *Community Power and Political Theory* (New Haven, Conn.: Yale University Press, 1963). We also have a root concern with heterogeneity but we are preoccupied as well with not losing sight of the over-all structural coherence or articulation of elite action.

[7] The words in capitals within parentheses are the code words that lead off each of the corresponding coding sequences or "trees." The basic mechanics and principles of the coding scheme applied to the textual material from the tape-recorded sections of the interviews have been described in detail in Chapters 6 and 7 of *SRSP*. The system basically reduces interview text into lists of linked symbols or code words that are computer manipulable. There are one thousand such words in the glossary for power roles and organizational structures.

represent interactive processes in detail. Each "episode" may be made up of many interactions that are only partially reported in the interviews and may represent an as yet incomplete or unresolved chain of exchanges.

The fact that we are concerned in the coding with standards and styles and not with quanta of power allows us to sidestep at least some of the difficult issues regarding the definition and measurement of power. We thus are not concerned with the minute scrutiny of outcomes in efforts to gauge the extent of change effected by particular actors nor with how much power anyone has or expends in a given power attempt. Independent procedures have identified these respondents as relevant power wielders and have served to order them according to power scores. Some differences in outcome related to power levels do appear in the present data, but the codes here do not seek to discriminate the exercise of power from the generation or discovery of power. In our view, outside of extreme situations infrequently present in these data (for example, the application of overbearing force, or unconditional submissiveness) every interaction sequence in which power figures is a test. This should be the case particularly in situations of weak institutionalization as well as high turnover and inexperience in leadership.

Although power as a central concept or unit of analysis does not figure directly in these codes, the code categories without exception relate in some fashion to the social uses of power. Underlying all codes is the notion of sets of behaviors, attitudes, interactions, and outcomes linked to power acts, positions, or roles with collective import. These are actions, or ideas about actions, in which one actor, as agent for a social unit of some kind, seeks to work some transformation in his social milieu through influencing others. In simplest terms we are talking about how social units through their leadership seek to structure their world.

In view of the heavy emphasis given throughout the full body of this research to cultural variability and changes in political values and evaluations, we understandably tend to think of many such power attempts as efforts to restructure symbolic relationships, that is, to change the *images* of the world and existing relations rather than the world itself. This is part of what Talcott Parsons describes as transforming what is available into what is needed or what others have seen as transforming the inevitable into socially desired goals.[8] In any real life process this involves, of course,

---

[8] This point is also related to the observation in D. Goldrich, R. E. Agger, and B. E. Swanson, *The Ruler and the Ruled* (New York: John Wiley, 1964), that the significance of non-decision-making politics has come to be underestimated, as well as to Karl Deutsch's plea that the prevalence of game and war models of politics not be allowed to

changes in leaders' self-images and many other adjustments that cannot be understood as mere manipulations of thought or feeling.

Concretely, the interviews ranged broadly over many aspects of organizational life, inviting free descriptions of aims, structures, and operations and dwelt deliberately on events (setbacks, achievements, internal factionalism, alliances and confrontations with external groups) calculated to elicit accounts of interactions couched in power terms. In this way it is possible to take as evidence a much broader range of power related commentary and not just responses to inquiries self-consciously placing the individual in a "decision-making" posture.

By being able to code many such diverse incidents within a common framework of power related variables, a sizable "stock" or sampling of them could be built up, thus expanding the opportunities of numerical manipulation and of checking for the consistency of patterned actions or responses for individuals or groups. As Table 7.1 shows, although we have

TABLE 7.1 *Number of Codable References to* ROLES, BODIES, *and* PRAXES

		Elite Sector				
		Political		Cultural		Economic	
N =	*High* (64)	*Low* (18)	*High* (25)	*Low* (12)	*High* (38)	*Low* (19)
PRAXES	144	70	42	47	88	29
Mean	2.2	4.4	1.7	3.9	2.3	1.5
BODIES	80	23	33	18	52	26
ROLES	80	24	30	17	64	27

more than one codable role or organizational description for only a few respondents, the number of multiple PRAXIS accounts is generally considerably higher, especially for the respondents within each sector who are low in power scores.[9] The single reversal of this tendency (among

over-shadow the concept of politics as *debate*. See Deutsch, "Recent Trends in Research Methods in Political Science," in James C. Charlesworth, ed., *A Design for Political Scope, Objectives, and Methods* (Philadelphia: American Academy of Political Science, 1966). Peter Bachrach and Morten S. Benaty, "Two Faces of Power," *American Political Science Review*, vol. 56, no. 4 (December, 1962), emphasize non-decision-making politics in still another sense (the mobilization of bias or power in order to close out options or prevent issues from crystallizing).

[9] Each sphere is here divided into those above and below power scores of 2.4. The scores range from 2.0 to 4.0. The small variations in number of cases between these

second-ranking economic leaders) is not unexpected in view of the very different conditions of ascent in that sphere. On the basis of the earlier findings with respect to mobility (Chapter 3), for example, one would be tempted to guess that ascent via the economic route being more controlled and more selective, those in positions short of the top in business might be less involved in an aggressive scramble to stand out or be more inhibited from taking bold initiatives than those on the way up in other sectors.

But before plunging into the substance of the exposition, there are still a few preliminaries to be cleared away. It is useful to have as a starting reference a global sense of the kinds of roles and organizations respondents occupy and command and have described for us (Table 7.2). This over-

TABLE 7.2 Number of ROLES *Descriptions by Sphere*

	Elite Sector					
	Political		Cultural		Economic	
N =	High (64)	Low (18)	High (25)	Low (12)	High (38)	Low (19)
Total ROLES mentioned	80	24	30	17	64	27
Sphere:						
Economic	3	—	3	1	51	15
Government	36	10	3	1	2	2
Parties	37	10	—	2	1	1
Cultural	1	1	17	10	1	3
Associational	3	3	7	3	9	6

view establishes roughly the approximate scope of the material available and makes plain the modest leverage the analysis can derive on the basis of numbers alone. Here the quality of observations must count for much more than their number. Coverage of the highest positions in business, government, and parties is good; for cultural and associational leaders resources are more spare. Some basis for contrasting high and low power wielders is present in each sphere. There is less chance for systematically contrasting the self-views of men with positions in a single sphere with those of their colleagues whose main power anchorage lies outside that sphere (for example, do politicians who are also in business view themselves differently as businessmen than do those men who have only business

---

groupings and those shown in the chapters on national perspectives reflect the fact that small numbers of respondents completed one part of the interviews and not the other. Refer to Chapter 4, pp. 93 ff., for a discussion of business career paths.

roles?). The associational roles described in each sphere tend, of course, to be extensions of the sphere itself — the associations mentioned by politicians are labor unions, those by businessmen are trade associations or chambers of commerce, those by the cultural leaders are the colleges of professionals. Business roles cover primarily top managerial executives and secondarily board members and proprietors, with a strong representation of the financial field and industry and lesser numbers of men in construction, the oil industry, and commercial agriculture. The bloc of government roles includes roughly equal numbers of cabinet ministers, senators, members of the Supreme Electoral Council, deputies in the legislature, and other high officials. The party roles described are all positions at the national level, chiefly party executives and national committee members, mostly AD but also COPEI and a few URD with a scattering of figures from other splinter groups. The cultural roles divide roughly evenly between mass media executives or professionals and academics but include two churchmen as well. Because, as should be emphasized again, these are role descriptions by incumbents, this rough account of the various corners of the elite world into which our respondents will guide us can also stand as a more detailed description of our sample than we have had until now and as a listing of the kinds of organizations that will be simultaneously exposed partially to our view. In other words, if Table 7.2 had been drawn up on the basis of descriptions of organizations (BODIES), the numbers would be just about the same. As the accounts of roles and organizations are intermeshed in the text, they will also be treated in tandem here.

The fact that this research was carried out a few years after a major political turnover that had repercussions on power constellations in every department of national life sensitized the planning group to the factor of newness in the leadership — newness in the men in office, in the organizations they manned, and in the canons for leadership by which they were guided.[10] These rather simple propositions bear some reconsideration on the basis of the data on roles and organization.[11] These men are indeed

---

[10] Refer to *SRSP*, p. xiv.

[11] Each chapter in this volume presents rather different problems with respect to the balance between quantitative and qualitative elements in the analysis. This has to do (1) with the levels of aggregation set in code categories and the extent to which detail is pursued beyond those categories, as well as (2) with how often counts or tallies are performed or shared with readers. The general technique of moving from global COUNTS to sets of words (LINKS) associated with a given analytical unit (a role, an organization, an issue) and finally to STRINGS (an interesting combination or patterns of symbols) has been exemplified in Chapter 6, *SRSP*. As a rule, the numbers dwindle and claims of representativeness or modality in response are more tentative or are explicitly discounted as more detail is given. *Who* speaks and

new to power, especially the politicians (Table 7.3). Very few of the political leaders have been in their present positions as long as five years, and roughly half among those with high power scores have had even briefer tenures. However, taken as a group and especially as concerns

TABLE 7.3   Newness in Roles (Percentages)

	Elite Sector					
	Political		Cultural		Economic	
	High	Low	High	Low	High	Low
$N^a =$	(64)	(18)	(25)	(12)	(38)	(19)
Role institutionalization						
Old role, old organization	76	76	74	86	88	78
Old role, new organization	20	19	22	6	6	23
Time in role						
Less than five years	84	90	67	46	33	55
Less than three years	48	68	41	33	23	27
Time in organization						
More than five years	50	72	45	80	75	46
More than ten years	39	62	34	67	60	41

ᵃ All figures in the table are percentages based on the total roles for which the pertinent information was given. The bases from right to left are 72, 21, 27, 15, 48, and 22. See footnote 12 for an explanation of the institutionalization code.

party office, they occupy positions in organizations or agencies that pre-date by a considerable period the 1959 power shift and that have a fairly well-defined institutional character.[12] Several currents stand out in connection with this interplay of role and organizational and institutional elements. It is the top business leaders who have the smallest proportion of men new to their present positions, and only in the business sector

what is said become increasingly important. We have tried to balance the desire to expose clearly the mode of work against the danger of producing only tedium or exaggerating the extent to which such work processes are in fact precisely reproducible from one analyst to another.

[12] Needless to say, the degree to which any role or organization is "institutionalized" in this sense is an empirical question that is most difficult to establish. The reference here is simply to a code category in which a distinction was drawn between "new" and "old" (pre-1958) roles and organizations in order to estimate degree of institutionalization. The supposition is, for example, that the head of a planning agency lacked both established local role models and an organizational context (this turned out to be a rare NEWNEW situation) whereas a bank president (unless in a specifically innovative venture) was in the majority situation of an established role in an established type of organization (OLDOLD).

are men new to office more frequently found among *low* than high power scorers. The figures on time in the organizations in which present positions are held amplify this image of *newness at the very top* in the political and cultural as against the economic sector. Approximately two in three of the low-scoring political and cultural leaders have more than ten years in their present organizations as against one in three of those in the very highest positions. These figures are just about reversed for the business sector. Newness to office thus does not appear to be a major factor in the world of business and even in the political and cultural sectors seems to be compensated by a reasonable continuity of organizational involvement. Interestingly, though, the evidence here points to considerable permeability at the top in government, parties, and the cultural sphere but considerably less in business firms.

Government Leaders

Looking closely at the materials on ROLES and BODIES in order to get a more differentiated perspective on the self-images of each sector, it becomes apparent that newness to office is most relevant for those in government.[13] Only a handful of these men have been with their current agencies or in their present office for more than five years, and there are no differences here between those rating high and low in power scores. This, of course, does not mean that they are innocent of political experience or are working in an institutional void. These men are new to office but seasoned in political struggle. Many see themselves as a triumphant, reformist vanguard bringing the hope of honest and efficient government to the country for the first time. By and large, they emphasize technical capabilities in describing both strengths and weaknesses of the agencies they command. Their sense of mission and self-conviction is perhaps best reflected in the fact that level of motivation and moral qualities figure prominently in references to points of strength and much more rarely in connection with felt deficiencies. Many show an awareness of being central actors at a very special historical moment, one that is perceived both as a unique opportunity and as a time of great difficulty and danger. The

---

[13] The brief commentaries on each elite sector that follow are based on summary listings of LINKS — that is, of all the code words or concepts that were explicitly associated in responses with the respective set of roles. The tables on pp. 183, 186, and 188 of *SRSP* are examples of such listings. These remarks are a way of introducing each group. Many of the observations will be amplified and specified in the quotations that follow and in the later analysis of interactions.

opportunities are associated with a particular constellation of support elements rarely brought together in Venezuela before this time — possibilities of coordinated action within government and paragovernmental agencies, diffuse public support, assistance from international organizations and foreign governments, backing from the military. None of these sources of support, however, is entirely assured. The threat, of course, is linked primarily to the political and armed action of the MIR and PCV, though more subtle pressure and resistance from the business sector are also reported.

A few differences in function and perceptions between high and low power scorers in this sector are hinted at in these data. Low scorers are concentrated in the economic ministries and autonomous institutes and, quite plausibly, seem to have heavy administrative implementing functions in contrast to high scorers, who spend more time in fixing policy objectives and coordinating activities with groups other than their own. The organizations of high scorers, as the main activities just noted would imply, have broader publics and are more concerned with the mapping of policy and operational procedures. Low scorers feel disadvantaged by government duty in terms of excessive demands on their time and economic loss whereas high scorers more often show preoccupation about interruptions to their professional activities. But in discussing their own roles and satisfaction in them, moral and affective qualities again come to the fore both for high and low scorers. In short, it is the sense of being engaged in a trying and complex task of technical and moral rehabilitation in government while under determined siege and with only grudging and unpredictable support from within and outside its own sector that most clearly marks this group.

Newness to office, as noted, does not mean newness to politics or government. Most of these men have been close to party life and in and out of government at various levels for more than two decades.[14] What it does mean is being in the forefront of government at a moment when major innovations are being undertaken on every side. The scope of these deliberate efforts to restructure the governmental apparatus and the

---

[14] Chapter 4 traces in detail the principal career lines for each elite sector. The pattern of repeated, rather unexpected "calls" (*llamadas*) to office noted there extends to positions at this level. Appointments come upon the individual ". . . just like a person who walks down the street and is struck on the head by a falling flowerpot" (Interview 050154, p. 183). At this level, however, the call comes much more frequently from the very summit (the President of the Republic) and is much more difficult to resist.

extent to which responsibility in this connection has been entrusted to men of a technical rather than purely political mentality needs to be understood to grasp the complexity of forces at play.

Some allowance must be made in reading the quotations that follow for the natural inclination to magniloquence of high officials describing their pet projects. Throughout this period, the government was under sharp attack for being overcautious, pusillanimous, and accommodating entrenched interests in the carrying out of promised reforms. But it is important to have a sense of the range and magnitude of changes being pursued simultaneously from within government. None of the numerous projects described or alluded to in the excerpts that follow has been fully implemented. They convey, nevertheless, a sense of the prevailing mood in this sector and the kinds of tasks it had set for itself — in short, its own definition of the grounds on which it justified its own action. The speakers are generally the individuals with the top responsibility, officially, for the activity described.

> I consider the [agency] a dynamic center for national development that will come with increasing intensity to complement the action of the oil industry. . . . I always have the hope that our industry may have resources or means of expansion that are unknown or as yet uncontrolled and that will be discovered in future years.[15]

> In the immediate future the Congress has several goals to attain: first to maintain and expand its autonomy; second, to become an organ of legislative work . . . ; then to exercise political control, not irascibly but in a more constructive manner, to control the administration also in a stricter and less polemical way and also, as regards the Congress's role, to move toward a modification of the way national bodies are managed, including the Congress itself.[16]

> It was decided to study down to the last detail the entire administrative apparatus of government, not only national but also the state and municipal government, with which we collaborated. Under my direction all the projects for the legal revisions necessary to achieve administrative reforms were elaborated. . . .[17]

> Here we finance the building of factories or equipment for a factory but the preparation of a project is not financed via the state credit system. If we want to promote the creation of a new entrepreneurial class, of young entrepreneurs rising from the ranks of middle-class professionals, we need

[15] Interview 334258, Part B, p. 1.
[16] Interview 011033, p. 12.
[17] Interview 113101, p. 22. At the time of the interview all these projects for new legislation were being held for presentation to the Congress at a more propitious moment.

to promote a program of financing for industrial investment *projects*. I believe that is the best way to fight for the democratization of industrial property.[18]

A nucleus of men in the Supreme Electoral Council gave themselves wholly to the labor of bringing about the elections over and above any other consideration and closing their eyes to any circumstance that might intervene.[19]

[Our greatest success has been] the reform and the organization of the police and all the auxiliary services, the coordination with other bodies, and above all the new conception of the policeman, who is an armed agent of the citizen who acts with great energy when necessary but who normally should be a guide, friend, and protector of the citizen.[20]

The idea of universal coverage is a fundamental principle in this. Once this problem is resolved, social security will be one of the largest and most important organisms in the country, above all as a political instrument, because it will have effects on the lowest strata in the country and those most distant from the centers of population and civilization.[21]

Standing starkly out of context and read seriatim as they appear here, some of these comments, as has been noted, sound ingenuous or like more of the conventional, artless put-on that frequently marks the discourse of official spokesmen. However, most of the statements are in fact linked to reasonably realistic accounts of measures, actions, achievements, and setbacks. They are informed as well with a sense of urgency and mission that has a dual source — on the one hand, a feeling that the present provides a historical opportunity that must be grasped *now* and, on the other, a perception of the dangers, collective and individual, that surround the politician.

I consider myself fortunate to belong to a generation and to live in a country and a world where the resources exist to accelerate social progress in a way that few communities in the world have within their means to achieve.[22]

This project is one that would sweep aside any opposition, on the supposition that any might exist, because it is within the natural order of the growth and development of Venezuela. [The project] is necessary because oil has its limits, and as its power to propel the economy diminishes, it will became almost impotent for further development. It is the same as with our children. We carry them, throw them in the air, toss them about up to a certain moment. Then we can't move them. We need a crane. Then they

[18] Interview 030087, p. 69.
[19] Interview 052154, p. 184.
[20] Interview 091143, p. 35.
[21] Interview 315265, p. 57.
[22] Interview 091143, p. 31.

lift us. Then we have to hitch another factor, another horse to pull the load.[23]

I would say that our greatest success has been to survive. This is an organism that was fiercely attacked in its first years; to have survived that struggle . . . and to have won a little, I would say the respect of public opinion, including that of major agencies and the government itself.[24]

[We are walking] a path to be traversed with a dagger between the teeth, and that is our situation not merely with respect to extremists of the factions that have dedicated themselves to violence and arson but of all parties. The violence is extraordinary, in the relations of party to party, in all fields . . . it is almost a war without quarter. All that is missing is the knives carried in the teeth.[25]

The particular array of pressures, resistances, and sources of support from within government itself as well as from outside that is experienced depends, naturally, on the specific front of innovation an individual commands. Confidence and motivation are sustained by the strong presidential backing given certain major efforts and by diverse signs of diffuse public responsiveness. Obviously as well, the threat posed by armed action against the government has crystallized a countercoalition of forces, domestic and international. That coalition is precarious, at cross-purposes internally, and is maintained at a certain sacrifice not easily reckoned in the scope and pace of reform. The outlines of this system of forces as perceived from the government sector can be seen in the following comments.

In those circumstances [clashes within the government], we have had to appeal to the maximum authority, the President of the Republic, and present him the problem and he tells us that we should not embark on this or that [project] because it is going to tie up such a volume of resources that the development plan will be distorted.[26]

The [agency] has been free of political influences and interventions of this kind, we must confess, because of the protection it has always had from the President of the Republic. . . . They are aware of what this means and have been genuinely responsible, we must confess. I report this as a simple fact and mean to praise no one.[27]

[23] Interview 334258, Part B, p. 15.

[24] Interview 030187, p. 60.

[25] Interview 052154, Part A, p. 22. The dangers described are not hypothetical. In early 1967, one of the respondents, Julio Irribarren Borges, president of the Social Security Administration was "executed" by the FALN in retribution for the alleged assassination by police of FALN leaders. Irribarren was also accused of defrauding workers and acting as an informer to the political police. Of course, the dangers faced by those who have chosen the path of insurrection are no less real.

[26] Interview 030087, pp. 48–49.

[27] Interview 334252, Part B, p. 6.

There was very effective collaboration [in the 1963 election] from all official organisms, the whole official apparatus, beginning with the government through the Minister of the Interior, all other agencies, the armed forces, and finally the decision of the people who wished to vote as was demonstrated by the turnout. . . . The Aero Club cooperated during voter registrations distributing leaflets from airplanes manned by private pilots, and on election day they left a squadron at the disposition of the council for whatever might be necessary. It was not used. . . . All the private firms in the country with their own radio networks also put these at the disposition of the council and these were ready in case there should be any break in the official communications system.[28]

Naturally in these reforms there is strong resistance from people, and in a country like ours, with certain cultural lags, people don't understand well nor value greatly a general reform in administration. Many ministers feel it is to their advantage to retain their small clientele of bureaucratic employees faithful personally to them or the party.[29]

[Factors favoring police reform are] the present circumstances of anxiety and danger (which meant that the role of the police had to be taken seriously) and the good fortune to have had good collaborators, competent men, and generous assistance from democratic countries, technical missions from Chile, the United States, England, France, Mexico . . . strong backing from the government and especially the president and his ministers, and the prior state of backwardness that allowed us to make a clean sweep.[30]

There [the oil industry] nothing can be done. There, let us confess, there is no planning. There is the planning of the oil companies themselves which we do not know because they never inform us. With respect to petroleum we limit ourselves to fixing growth rates that we consider probable within the world market, the evolution of the world oil market and the play of interests that influences the diversification of sources of supply in the global strategy that oil companies employ to gain adantage on one side or the other.[31]

Here in Venezuela . . . because our professional class is young we do not have as in other countries these great droves of professionals, these untouchable vestals. One can say rather that the mass of professionals is young. I believe this group is disposed to give its best to collaborate in an effort of importance and benefit to the nation.[32]

The ones I count on most are workers, the unions. They have best understood and know best what they want and the goals they pursue even though they don't have the culture of other groups.[33]

[28] Interview 052154, Part B, pp. 184, 189.
[29] Interview 113101, p. 23.
[30] Interview 091143, p. 36.
[31] Interview 030087, p. 101.
[32] Ibid., p. 93.
[33] Interview 315265, pp. 50, 52.

Party Leaders

Thus, large ambitions coupled with a sober awareness of the tentativeness of achievement to date as well as the precariousness of support and the implacability of opposition from certain quarters serve to define the arena of struggle for those who have accepted leading roles in government. Politicians with primary responsibilities to *party* and the management of party organizations are, of course, equally embedded in this conflictful framework of idealized objectives, perceived perils, and opportunities. But the concrete problems they face and the kinds of power confrontations in which they figure differ substantially from those of men in government who almost always claim and at times pointedly exercise a certain independence from party discipline. These men in government tend to represent themselves as technicians in sympathy with a party's program or policies or bound by friendship to major party figures. Even when they occupy party posts, they are likely to describe these as *pro forma* actions intended to publicly certify their association with a party rather than as essential services to the organization. Generally, this association, albeit episodic or marginal, is of fairly long standing. Nevertheless, whatever the uses of independence may be in this connection, at the time of the survey the primary, visible anchorage of power in government remained in the parties.

In contrast then to the men in government, the party leaders interviewed are almost all founding members of the political groups they lead. Thus, although here again the median time in present office is about three years, a sizable majority (heavily weighted, as is to be expected, with AD leaders) have been in their present political organizations for more than fifteen years. Characteristically, except for those party figures representing groups (especially businessmen) whose emergence into politics is itself recent, these men have been continuously absorbed in party activity throughout adulthood and often from early youth. The friendships and rivalries among them, whether within or across party lines, are colored by forty years of struggle and contention, shared persecutions, betrayals, achievements, and setbacks. Even the more youthful are drawn at times vicariously but often in very direct ways into conflicts and antagonisms that predate their entry into politics. Some sense of the quality of that experience has been given in the chapter on career patterns. *Issue*-oriented as against *organization*-focused conflict is treated in the chapter on national perspectives. Of more central concern in the present chapter are some of the conditions that govern action within and among political organizations.

The success of the parties in resisting military regimes, universalizing the vote, institutionalizing regular electoral procedures, and imposing civilian-based party-regulated governments stands at the heart of this set of problems. The two pertinent processes that have accompanied these successes are on the one hand a variety of experiences of concerted action through coalition and on the other a steady fragmentation of political forces both through schismatic movements and the entry of new, specialized interests into the political arena.[34] The various forms of action in coalition, arrayed roughly in order of their efficaciousness, might be stated as follows:

1. Coalitions to resist or oppose illegal governments.

2. Coalitions intended to strengthen the stability or range of actions open to elected governments.

3. Coalitions of minority forces in order to contest elections or form opposition blocs within the government.

By early 1964 the process of fragmentation and differentiation of political forces had advanced to the point at which it had become clear that, short of a major reconcentration of power via a coup of some kind, *government by coalition* had to become a central feature of the political system for an indefinite time. This meant that the history of factionalism and aborted alliances was beginning to take on critical significance. In fact these two themes dominated the discussions by party leaders of the inner workings of their own organizations and relations with other parties. The following remark might be more heartening if it had not been made by a man who was about to abandon his party with the full expectation that it would collapse on his withdrawal.

[34] Manuel Vicente Magallanes, *Partidos políticos venezolanos* (Caracas: Tipografía Vargas, 1959), provides a chronology of the efforts to found parties in Venezuela up to the formal appearance of AD in September of 1941. COPEI and URD followed in 1946. The Communist Party (PCV) dates from 1937, though proto-party efforts go back to the 1920's. Two fractionings of AD, the first in 1960 and the second in late 1961, produced the MIR and AD-Opposition groups respectively. Loose alliances of variously designated forces supported Arturo Uslar Pietri and Wolfgang Larrazabal in the 1963 presidential election. The full lineup of candidates, parties, and voting coalitions in that election are compactly presented in *Venezuela Election Factbook* (*Elections: December 1963*) (Washington, D.C.: Institute for the Comparative Study of Political Systems, 1963). Yet another major division within AD occurred in late 1967 apropos of the designation of candidates for the 1968 presidential election.

I believe that in Venezuela — not to state the ideal, which is three — at the very most *four* political parties could be organized. More than that is a kind of carnival. We have to stop thinking that each Venezuelan is a political party in himself and put to one side our pride and flawless ideas and recognize that if one wants to work in politics one can find a place within the policy framework of some party.[35]

The older parties, especially AD and URD, were feeling deeply the divisive effects not alone of personalism of the kind alluded to but more importantly of generational and ideological factors.

They want the Youth Vanguard of URD to be independent of the party, with an autonomous constitution, to be like a little party outside the party. These are the pretensions of youth, of a group, not of youth but of a group in URD. We cannot consent to this. . . .[36]

The top leaders of the party . . . some in exile, others in prison, some killed in clandestine activity, could not have permanent contact with our youth. The latter, in the daily clandestine struggle, were in permanent association with Communist leaders. Subsequently, there was confusion . . . difficulty among them in assessing reality correctly in the light of the dialectical method of analysis. They gravitated toward the orthodox strategy of the Communist Party rather than the strategy and tactics of AD as a result of this Marxist indoctrination, which is not beyond the margin of AD principles for the organization gives its militants ample freedom ideologically.[37]

To be sincere, we have noticed a small group, very small, of certain young men who disagree with these formulations . . . and who today have one foot outside the party and a few have already left. This is no more than a small group; it doesn't even amount to twenty.[38]

For some party leaders, within and outside the government, the preoccupation over the decision of large numbers of their youth to follow the MIR and PCV into insurrection has more to do with the consequences of this choice for party life and constitutionality than with the fear of terrorism itself.

The fact that in a democratic regime the state and a democratic party such as AD . . . , that had no interest in ideological discriminations, has been obliged to take coercive measures against a party . . . is in itself negative. The fact that as a consequence a party progressive in doctrine such as the Communist Party should have disappeared . . . is also negative, because it has left without expression . . . a dense sector that by conviction had its hopes and confidence in those doctrines. At present that sector finds itself

[35] Interview 087094, Part B, p. 2.
[36] Interview 088102, p. 73.
[37] Interview 108070, p. 108.
[38] Interview 324232, p. 93.

blocked from expressing its opinions as a consequence of what I and my party [AD] regard as a tactical error of the Communist Party, to have taken to insurrection, which has also diminished its chances of penetration with the masses.[39]

The same right that the president has to complete his period in March of 1964 is also ours [the legislature]. Because there is here a distortion or disfigurement because of presidentialism and our tradition of strong executive leadership, government and state are identified with the executive power and within that with the President of the Republic. Constitutionality is identified with the period of tenure of the president, but constitutionality is not only the president's period in office but respect for the constitution and the established juridical order.[40]

It would be useless also to try to explain whose was the first violence. We believe that if the legality of these two parties had been guaranteed, which is now very difficult because things have reached an irreversible extreme . . . , this would have forced the Communist Party and MIR to agree not to have recourse to violent methods. There would be a good base for understanding, not between the extreme left opposition and the government but with respect to the conditions of political struggle, and the government would have been in a better position with respect to the Communist Party.[41]

As noted in the chapter on careers, for AD leaders the experience of 1948 remains extremely vivid and has colored their approach to government and coalition in this second ascent to power. Especially after the modest plurality achieved in the December 1963 vote (31 percent), AD actively sought to pull together a broad-based combination of parties to lend solidarity and drive to the Leoni presidency.

It seems to me that we were too romantic [in 1945–1948]. We were not sufficiently skilled or astute to avoid, by following a more flexible political line, raising as many enemies against ourselves as we did. . . . We perhaps romantically committed the error of being very little permeable to other sectors.[42]

Given the coalition of forces produced by the recent elections, it is indispensable to have other forces join in to give the actions of the state consistency and projection. Thus the party [AD] is disposed as before . . . to sacrifice what one might call the orthodox, pragmatic line in government and to make concessions, concessions naturally of a tactical kind to other sectors . . . parties or important economic and social sectors.[43]

Our objective [in proposing coalition] is not that AD be helped but rather that Venezuela be helped to reach basic goals. In this case the merits are

[39] Interview 108070, p. 116.
[40] Interview 316267, Part A, p. 58.
[41] Ibid., p. 70.
[42] Interview 124142, Part B, p. 10.
[43] Interview 108070, p. 117.

shared, the failures are shared, and the errors are shared. Naturally, for people from outside the party and from other political organizations to collaborate they have to be brought into the government and this might be considered a retribution — ministries, presidencies of autonomous institutes, state governorships.[44]

Ironically, it was just at this moment of maximum receptivity in AD that its most stable coalition partner, COPEI, decided to go it alone.

The party has been very careful to be consistent politically and ideologically in the years that it formed part of the governing coalition, from 1959 to 1964. It gave a demonstration of absolute loyalty not only to the country but to the allied party and to President Betancourt, under whose government this test of democratic coexistence and understanding was carried out. . . . In the course of the present year, we have ratified fully that despite the break in our alliance with Democratic Action, we continue to accept publicly the responsibility that we acquired through our collaboration in the previous five years of government.[45]

The fundamental reason [for the break in the AD-COPEI coalition] was that we were denied the right to participate, to influence the basic decisions and orientations of the present government. It was not a bureaucratic difference, because we were offered very much more than can have been offered to any other group with expectations of joining the government. But we regarded it as fundamental, in order to enter a new coalition, to make a type of governing alliance in which we would participate in those decisions.[46]

The difficulties of achieving a coalition to govern are compounded in the efforts to structure an effective combination to act in opposition to the government. Here, where the effects of fragmentation are perhaps even more palpable, the same incapacity seems to be present no matter what the contingency.

We understand as a unity candidate a candidate for a united *opposition*. That candidate was not viable because the other opposition parties, and basically URD, did not accept that coalition. Outwardly yes, but they insisted that their candidate had to be Jóvito. Now, we could not . . . oblige our people to vote for the leader of another party because that is very dangerous in a political organization.[47]

Every one of them [opposition parties] has its own program, its own strategy, and its own tactics to reach government or influence it. At this specific moment, for example, there is no possibility of combination or alliance with any other political force.[48]

[44] Interview 068205, p. 68.
[45] Interview 029086, pp. 65–66.
[46] Ibid., p. 69.
[47] Interview 316267, Part A, p. 61.
[48] Interview 094184, Part A, p. 94.

The incestuous character of the process of party proliferation and the apparent belief within each faction that it bears the most authentic expression of an original truth rather than newly discovered alternatives seems to inspire both nostalgia for an earlier unity and a determined intransigence. The remarks that follow were made by men who had publicly broken with the AD party.

> Our program has its fundamental roots in many of the old principles of Democratic Action, that is, the principles gathered in what has been the program, the fundamental ideological instrument of the party conceived at its beginning.[49]
>
> I say this was a problem of strategy and tactics [the AD-ARS schism] because deep in our hearts we cannot say that the Old Guard are traitors or bandits. I believe that is an incorrect position. . . . They can make mistakes as human beings err. History will judge their position, not we. It may be that we are the mistaken ones . . . but I do believe that the economic policy and other government activities were not correctly run and that led me to stay with the fraction that I believed truly represented the doctrine and ideals of AD. . . . I was born *adeco*. I am not sectarian as it is bandied about that *adecos* are. But I will die *adeco*. I cannot die any other way, whether or not I am a militant of the party.[50]

Given the clear awareness of the party's waning forces as a lone actor and the apparently insurmountable barriers to acceptable coalition, some AD leaders reverted to a dogged and somewhat baffled reaffirmation of the correctness and root strength of their position. The obviously shallow foundations of improvised electoral counterforces help to sustain the faith that in the long run the party's intimate connections with the whole process of the nation's political development will once again find mass vindication.

> What explains the survival of a party? A party cannot be improvised. That is why they are mistaken who think that with money, with little bells, and with much propaganda a party can be made. That is not the case. A party is a social phenomenon that responds to very clear sociological processes. This business of running into the street shouting that one is forming a party, come this way — that just doesn't work. Everything has its reasons for being, its historical moment. AD corresponds to a historical moment in this country. Then it made a very clear and objective programmatic formulation that cut deeply into the popular mentality. Because if we had not penetrated into the spirit of the people, we would not have survived.[51]

---

[49] Ibid., p. 89.
[50] Interview 302236, Part B, pp. 122–123.
[51] Interview 313262, pp. 30–31.

If the people [*pueblo*] in a majority had not been in agreement with the democratic regime, they would not have turned out for elections. The fact that a majority came out to vote proves that they prefer the regime of alternation in office that has been put in their hands. Then the party [AD] acted correctly in defending the regime it had promoted and which the people had ratified in each election.[52]

[The] group of workers in the party is the spinal column of AD, around which cluster the professional sectors, the student sectors, the intellectual sectors, who do not properly have a class consciousness. The workers and rural groups, yes, and in any case they constitute the revolutionary foundation of the party.[53]

However hollow such reaffirmations of revolutionary intent by AD leadership may have sounded to the party's youthful opposition, there is no question that the political parties as a bloc continue to view as their primary enemy and danger not one another but the possibility of reaction from the economic sector.

The extreme sectors of Venezuelan society will continue to oppose not only the electoral victory of the party but also its remaining in power. The Communists each day more desperately try to bring about the destruction of Democratic Action as government and party, and the most reactionary sectors of our economy, those we designate as the oligarchy, are also I believe ready not only to oppose us as they are doing now, pouring torrents of money into the candidacy of Arturo Uslar Pietri, but are ready for any adventure, any adventure that eliminates the danger to them of Democratic Action's remaining in power.[54]

There is also economic fear among the most representative capitalist groups, because they have the clear conviction that when we speak of a service economy, or an economy at the service of man, we do not make such pronouncements demagogically or to please but in all sincerity. Therefore, many of them fear a triumph of COPEI more than any other victory because they know that COPEI, without being possibly accused of Marxism or communism, which are the epithets that some reactionaries employ against social progress, COPEI could perfectly well achieve some basic structural change in the country.[55]

Unfortunately, the press, radio, and television in our country are in the hands of the interests against which we are struggling. They represent, if not entirely, in many cases partially, powerful economic interests that they believe would be affected if we could influence national policy either by occupying the government integrally or influencing a governing team. Our nationalist, revolutionary, anti-oligarchical position frightens them and naturally they exert

[52] Interview 108070, p. 115.
[53] Interview 068205, p. 59.
[54] Interview 113101, p. 67.
[55] Interview 029086, p. 74.

the influence they possess over these organs . . . to impede or limit news
. . . of our activities.[56]

If the historical necessities of the country require a collaboration . . . between oligarchic sectors and democratic sectors, if this is desirable and bene-
ficial to the nation, we are ready in any case to reach specific agreements that
do not compromise our principles or harm popular interests. But this . . .
would have to be transitory, in the very short run, and at one moment or
another the clash between these contradictory forces will have to occur.[57]

Business Leaders

Though by no means complacent about the main thrust of political
intent as crystallized in such party statements, business leaders cultivate
a detached equanimity vis-à-vis what they perceive as the errors and
excesses of political intrusion into the business sphere. In contrast to the
sense of struggle, risk, strong commitment, and precarious attainment
that permeates the remarks of politicians, businessmen — albeit somewhat defensively — radiate solidity, continuity, self-assurance, and success.
The men in this group are bankers, industrialists, and major importers.
A majority have been in their present position for more than five years,
and for the high scorers this is true of about four in five. Though the
number who do so is small, this is the only group that mentions long-
term planning as an important part of their activities. They enjoy their
work and its rewards — money, prestige, conviviality, and a sense of
service. Though the present situation is by no means regarded as unprob-
lematical, few allusions are made to pressures. Many more mentions are
made of allies and sources of support than of opposition or hostility.
The latter, appropriately enough, are generally seen as coming from government or the parties. Businessmen themselves do not fail to make a
connection between the stability, regularity, and assured satisfactions of
their own milieu and the differences in their own approach to public
issues as against those of politicians.

> If one analyzes coldly why a person reacts in a certain way at a given
> moment and why I react differently . . . one puts oneself in the position of
> saying that if I had been in the shoes of one of these leaders of today and in-
> stead of going peacefully to the university as I did, instead of finding a peac-
> ful job, marrying and having my children and a home and an organized life
> . . . , if I put myself in his situation, and at the age of fifteen he was put
> in jail, in irons, and exiled and he suffered hunger and then returned, didn't

[56] Interview 094184, pp. 83, 84.
[57] Interview 068205, p. 65.

know how to do anything, lacked connections, and so entered politics and again landed in jail and was again exiled — that is an individual who logically, no matter how cool or objective he may be, has to have something against the society that denied him what it gave to others.[58]

The lives of businessmen have in fact been generally unmarred by this kind of setback or frustration. The lone sour note in the bullish climate of industrial expansion is sounded by men in those few firms or product lines that are finding themselves displaced or by-passed as the economy is restructured.

I am pretty much in favor of the industrial development of Venezuela. It is the only way to make jobs. But you have to take into account that we [importers] are the victims of that development. Until recently we have been able to get enough profits to maintain the organization, but I doubt very much that we shall be able to keep our nearly 400 employees in the future.[59]

Well, the principal difficulty with competition is that the market is saturated, which means that the industry's capacity [textiles] is greater than consumption and always creates difficulties for these firms cannot operate at full capacity, which increases their costs beyond the level of possible profit. . . . There are some small firms that when they cannot sell at normal price liquidate their inventories at prices that undermine the price structure of the entire market.[60]

Far more characteristic is a sense of optimism and preparation for an open and guaranteed future. Technical innovation, extensive training at all levels, and a concern with the improvement of management and the Venezuelanization of technical and managerial staffs are the keynotes in this buoyant, expansionist mood.

We have given special attention to manpower and we have today 80 to 100 students, 20 to 25 are in universities. . . . Those employees work five hours daily and study the remaining time, and when examinations come they get a month and a half for review and examinations. . . . We have carried on a management course for seven months, with the collaboration of the Central University, that was attended by 28 executives from our banks.[61]

We have a school at our own plant with regular classes for our personnel. We teach electricians, mechanics, machinists, press operators and all the specialists that we need for our field. . . . We also have courses for supervisors, from foreman on up, in order to teach our personnel how to better manage workers . . . using the most advanced leadership methods. Our higher man-

[58] Interview 323281, Part B, p. 59.
[59] Interview 305247, p. 14.
[60] Interview 330246, pp. 16, 17.
[61] Interview 013045, pp. 2–3.

agement people get every opportunity to attend seminars, management courses, and training by correspondence.[62]

Today it is not possible to improvise a bank employee. One must undergo a very rigorous period of training over a period of years and a series of positions in order to come out with executives of quality. Above all, technical capacity. Then high morality. Staff are chosen on the basis of their private conduct, the success of their homes, the equilibrium of their family, the correctness of their behavior.[63]

I am studying now . . . a computer experiment using one of the IBM electronic brains at the Ministry of Mines. What we are doing may turn out to be something useful not only for this industry but for many others of this type that have plants located in various parts of the country but sell throughout the nation. They should study the optimum production levels for each plant and, according to transport costs, how far the [product] of one plant should be taken.[64]

In the last eight years technology in Venezuelan industry has improved much more than in the previous twenty-five or thirty years as a fruit of the necessity, of the pressure to survive. Agricultural techniques, in our own case [sugar], have improved substantially and this is being used to advantage by others and in manufacturing. . . . I am not making a patriotic speech. Industry has lived through five or six years of very tight margins and that put management under tension by need.[65]

I personally contracted those technicians in Germany in 1949. I was criticized. The majority are now naturalized Venezuelans with Venezuelan children. . . . With them we trained and improved workers in the plant and improved the knowledge and capacity of supervisors to the point that we have in a plant . . . that has close to 350 persons, a Venezuelan . . . who is considered one of the finest technicians . . . in Venezuela and who was trained 100 percent in the firm. In the same way in all the other departments we have been training Venezuelan personnel under excellent technical conditions.[66]

The programmatic views of businessmen with respect to government's role in the economy have been treated at some length elsewhere.[67] In the context of discussions of day-to-day business operations comment on this score is somewhat more tempered, though still plainly a matter that generates visceral discomfort. Within this somewhat more realistic and circumscribed framework, the progressive encroachments of government seem more readily accepted as inevitable. Though with obvious distaste and occasional flashes of anger, the tendency here is toward a cautious

---

[62] Interview 307253, pp. 81–82.
[63] Interview 340245, p. 89.
[64] Interview 035107, p. 13.
[65] Interview 067202, Part B, p. 124.
[66] Interview 005019, p. 78.
[67] *SRSP*, especially pp. 191–196.

and calculating adaptation to a presumably irreversible process rather than to ideologically grounded and elaborated attacks as was the case in more broadly gauged discussions of the Venezuelan economy of the future.

I believed at one time that through pressures in the Federation of Chambers of Commerce, conversations with ministers, politicians, articles in the press, this could be modified. Unfortunately, in the last two or three years I have seen that this is a process we have been unable to arrest and I rather think it will increase. I believe unfortunately that this is a factor of modern life. I believe the private sector will have to adapt to ever-increasing intervention of government.[68]

The state should create loans that make the economy function rather than loans that become a straitjacket to the economy. Here it always happens in that way. The legislators have already failed in business, otherwise they would not be in government positions. They try to think of something to make others fail as well.[69]

When in a banking system a superintendent of banks tells you "the volume of credits should be reduced because I think there is going to be inflation," I, who am the banker and who am feeling the needs, the pulse of the nation, in my hands as different petitions cross my desk, I find that an outsider is giving me an order of that kind — everything of the banker and man in me rebels because he is at his bureaucratic desk and I am in contact with the people who are trying to develop the nation. But unfortunately that is our institution today. State interventionism makes itself more apparent each day.[70]

I personally believe that Venezuela is in an enviable position because industry here, private industry in the first instance, has demonstrated a certain degree of maturity in confronting this kind of problem intelligently and not in an emotional but in a patient and calculating way. At the same time the size of private industry here is of such a magnitude . . . and the internal market is so small that to think that Venezuela could in a short term or even in the long run totally substitute the present form of oil exploitation in a radical way such as nationalization is such a utopian idea that it cannot be accommodated in any thoughtful human mind.[71]

Whether or not the relentlessly extended imposition of fresh controls and regulations will eventuate in some form of state socialism, one of the main counterpoises to pressure on this front has been a growing affirmation of collective concerns and social commitments by businessmen. Although this new ideology and the actions to which it gives impulse find primary expression in business organizations rather than through individual firms (these organizations will be discussed in later pages),

[68] Interview 057167, p. 29.
[69] Interview 305247, p. 28.
[70] Interview 340245, p. 83.
[71] Interview 323281, Part B, pp. 33–34.

business leaders go out of their way to emphasize the social contributions
that are side products of the activity of their companies.

We try to influence the stock market to strengthen the exchange institutionally, to strengthen the capital market, to strengthen stock values in benefit of
the national economy. . . . We have taken part in exchange operations, we
have operated with the Central Bank and the Ministry of Fiance (*Hacienda*)
at times of emergency in order to prevent panics and stabilize the stock
market. . . . This effort has been publicly acknowledged by the Exchange.[72]

We try to cooperate in every way possible in the industrialization drive of
the present government of Venezuela in a way that pleases us, by not requesting loans from the government so that the funds may be used for other industries.[73]

[Our greatest achievement has been] the consolidation of national savings.
None of the commercial banking institutions in Venezuela had ever undertaken
to develop the disposition to save among Venezuelans. . . . In tropical countries, where nature is so generous, the inclination to save is very limited and
in Venezuela specifically with very rare exceptions has anyone troubled to
promote national savings. This persistent and continuous campaign . . . stimulating savings — via the press, radio, and television — [combined with] a
housing program in which with a very small deposit the bank grants credit
for home construction . . . has been the most positive labor of our board
of directors.[74]

Our satisfaction is that we are going to leave a good number of well-trained
men in this country because there is no reason to wait for the government to
do everything or have the inclination [to act]. We have created a love for
that [secondary and university training] in the bank.[75]

One of the basic aims of every firm in the world is to make money, because if it doesn't make money it has no justification within our capitalist life.
Now, we believe — from a spiritual point of view — using the financial means
available to us, that we can help Venezuela grow industrially and in that way
offer more welfare and more job capacity in the nation.[76]

Businessmen's sense that they are playing a positive social role is
considerably shored up by the unusual cordiality that has marked labor
relations during the last few years. Despite the close links to party
of almost all union chiefs, business leaders exempt them from the distrust
and deprecation with which they approach politicians. No social group
is more highly praised by businessmen for their sense of responsibility and
reasonableness than are the heads of unions.

[72] Interview 301234, p. 148.
[73] Interview 010031, p. 21.
[74] Interview 340245, p. 68.
[75] Interview 013045, p. 13.
[76] Interview 057167, p. 19.

In the oil industry I believe that industrial peace is based on the good worker-management relations that exist rather than on the political factor of [labor] leaders who want to maintain industrial peace to please the government.[77]

I am convinced, for example, that groups like CTV, that within CTV, there are sincere groups of good will who prefer a thousand times that their workers be employed in private industry than become a little like parasites on the government. As regards our own employees, you can be sure that we can count on them with our eyes shut.[78]

Banks in general operate under particular or group collective contracts but relations are perfectly harmonious. On the contrary we have had an immense collaboration in all these crises . . . the collaboration of our employees has been extraordinary. We have nothing but words of praise for them.[79]

Considerably more controversial for businessmen than the fact that they should be sensitive to and publicize the social contributions of private capitalistic effort, is the idea of more direct and active involvement in social and political action. Some of the ways in which this issue is being fought out within their own interest organizations will be seen in the section on voluntary associations. For the moment it is enough to note that the range of opinion in this connection among business leaders runs from absolute rejection to enthusiastic involvement.

I have entered increasingly into social action functions. . . . I think all the changes the country has experienced since the twenty-third of January [the fall of Pérez Jiménez] have brought into the open problems that we had tried to hide before. There has been an awakening of conscience in the nation that has affected all of us in one way or another. . . . Apart from the fundamental change I mentioned, brought about by the *cursillo de cristiandad,* I have been influenced undoubtedly by the favorable climate, because there has been a change of attitude in business, in government, among the clergy, among technicians in all respects. When one sees the possibilities and the resources that exist, one is encouraged to get into more and more new things of this type.[80]

I believe the position of many professional and business leaders was wrong in taking the stand that political affairs should be decided by others who were the professional politicians. There is a group of people who, though they are

[77] Interview 033091, p. 22.
[78] Interview 089109, Part C, p. 106. The CTV is the Workers Confederation of Venezuela, affiliated with the AFL-CIO's regional confederation ORIT.
[79] Interview 340245, p. 74.
[80] Interview 301234, Part B, p. 154. The *cursillo de cristiandad* is a program of brief (usually weekend), carefully structured, spiritual retreats designed to revitalize the faith of Catholics and stimulate them to join in Church-related social action programs. They appear to have been of considerable importance in bringing numerous key business figures into this kind of activity.

not lined up with any party, represent a way of thinking and acting in Venezuela that should be heard in politics either through the parties or directly as a way of trying to influence certain ideas in the parties. [The idea] was not to limit these representations to the personal opinion of one or two persons, but rather to offer a path or vehicle for the expression [of this voice] in an organized way before the parties and the government.[81]

The other day I was offered a position as delegate to the last convention of AVI for the Federal District. At first I accepted with pleasure because I was interested and it seemed to me very necessary to go because there was an internal conflict to resolve. But later I began to think about my commercial position . . . about my family's businesses, and also about my position in the bank and that these stood in the way of accepting. My grandfather had the idea that one should be disconnected totally from politics if one was a merchant. I think, unfortunately, that this was a good idea in another age, but today politics intrudes on one and one has to begin to intrude in politics. But I think one has to be careful . . . not to assume too outstanding a role.[82]

Don't talk to me about that because that is politics. I am not a politician. I don't know anything about politics.[83]

A final, somewhat unrelated point can close this quick review of some of the critical parameters of the situation of businessmen and their perspectives on action. All comments from businessmen regarding direct associations with foreign investors, sources of capital, equipment, or technical support are uniformly favorable. This point has some importance for it suggests that there is little ground in the direct experience of businessmen to expect them to formulate or to respond to nationalistic appeals in defining economic issues. Such appeals are in fact generally absent in these interviews except in the scattered allusions to the training of Venezuelan technicians and managers.

An economic study was made, the amount of money required was determined, and I went to the United States and presented the proposal to the company, which offered and in effect took 40 percent of the stock, and I placed the other 60 percent here in Venezuela.[84]

I believe that the fact that we are able to make products of that quality . . . , the fact that we have been able to train Venezuelans in this art, all that is the result of technical assistance that is foreign for it is unobtainable here. . . . The principal advantages are that we are obtaining an experience, a

[81] Interview 067202, Part B, p. 151.
[82] Interview 057167, pp. 33–34. The Venezuelan Association of Independents (AVI) was an effort to organize business interests in order to influence the selection of candidates and elect some "independent" business representatives to the congress in the 1963 election.
[83] Interview 049149, p. 16.
[84] Interview 307253, p. 74

laboratory capacity, a technical capacity that we here in Venezuela could not obtain because of its high cost and our lack of personnel and because at the same time it would be senseless to spend forty years trying to discover methods already developed by other persons. . . . There are problems of adaptation to Venezuela of much of the knowledge, methods, and systems that have been developed abroad. Those are the disadvantages, I believe, for us.[85]

They maintain their original interest in the bank and they provide, above all, technical assistance. Because it is an institution with more than 100 years of life, you can imagine that they have banking experience and they transmit that experience to us. They provide us help through qualified staff people sent to Venezuela to work at certain levels. Moreover, when we sometimes ask for help on a special problem, they are always ready to collaborate with us.[86]

Cultural Leaders

The propensity to self-criticism within the cultural sector noted in the preliminary discussion of issues comes dramatically into focus when attention is turned on day-to-day activities. As university officials are the most numerous single group among the cultural leaders reached, it is the problems of the university that come to the fore here. Nevertheless similar themes are echoed by men in the mass media and in nonuniversity cultural institutions (foundations, museums). Many of these men in fact move in and out of the university or maintain continuous ties to it. The two churchmen interviewed, though they may be substantively at odds with others in this sector with respect to concrete approaches to the work of cultural renovation, are nevertheless prey to the same preoccupations and structural constraints that impinge on educators and communicators as well as on creative individuals detached from organizations. For these men, though certainly in varying degrees for each subgroup, the world in which they move is hostile, refractory, unpredictable, and capricious in its rewards. In this they are more akin to politicians than to businessmen. But for the cultural leaders it is also a world of *dependency,* in which action is circumscribed by and subject to the dispensations of those who command resources. Much of the time of men in this sector is in fact spent on the soliciting of such resources rather than on properly intellectual activities. Perhaps in part because of this combination of acute self-awareness and the need to continually justify themselves to prospective patrons, the search for *relevance* (capacity to contribute to genuine national needs) and for *authenticity* (to accomplish this in ways that

[85] Ibid., pp. 97, 99.
[86] Interview 018052, p. 13.

elicit and preserve distinctively Venezuelan values and modalities) is also centered in this sector. It may be no more than the twin desires for relevance and authenticity that explain the disposition, palpably present in this sector, to accept and patiently work against problems not of their own making and which other sectors aspire mainly to proscribe or excise.

The multiple problems of the university are incisively catalogued by its own members in ways that are more revealing than the bitter denunciations of outside critics.

The university, as we should acknowledge, does not answer to everything we would like to be . . . not because of faults attributable to the university itself, but rather as a consequence of a general growth crisis in the country that reveals itself most visibly and sometimes most explosively in the university. I believe that problem, like all the nation's problems, can't be solved by any single measure but with time, study, seriousness, peace, coexistence, all those things that sound hollow but are the basis of life and progress in a nation.[87]

In Venezuela there is only a limited number of good professors and even fewer researchers. For this reason we have had to turn in great part to foreign personnel from other countries and continents. . . . The lack of personnel is a result of the meager scientific development of our universities and the absence of truly professional teaching bodies. The majority of our university professors are professionals who give themselves partially to education. . . . With respect to professors there is a difficulty that is not only internal but national. Young professionals don't have much desire to dedicate themselves to university teaching because it is less attractive and less well paid than professional activity in most fields.[88]

Then there is the anguishing problem which is an immorality . . . [that] of the repeaters. Because you can understand that it is not just that a student who comes to the university, to whom the university or the state gives free training . . . it may be all right for him to repeat one year but after that there is no reason for the state to continue paying an individual who has not responded. . . . And what is even more serious, he is denying a place to other students who we know are better. This is immoral from every point of view. It is one of the most anti-university and antipedagogical things.[89]

I believe this is a more democratic way of seeing the university, because I don't think the weight and high cost of the university, its maintenance, should be borne by the people in behalf of persons who have no interest in collaborating or showing the responsibility that a student should have. It would be preferable to invest those funds in cleaning up national problems, in building housing for workers. There is a misapprehension in the fact of seeking to have the largest number of students possible, even if they don't study

[87] Interview 095200, p. 59.
[88] Interview 055165, pp. 38–39.
[89] Interview 117224, p. 93.

and are there as though they were in a permanent club spending most of their time only on politics. It would be much more democratic to have the university operate at maximum efficiency with as much responsibility as possible from students, that needy students be helped and that the funds being wasted by this excess of irresponsible students be put to other uses.[90]

The university has grown so steadily and it was designed for 6,000 students and 500 professors . . . and it has encountered difficult problems of plant or enlarging budgets to absorb more students. . . . One of the proposals is for quotas established by law . . . simply limiting the number to the capacity of a faculty or school. . . . I have been substantially against the quotas, not so much the quotas but the number to go in the quota. I believe the country needs a marked increase in education and that the university cannot begin limiting itself on the grounds that this implies lowering educational standards. We have money and the present capacity to absorb the largest number possible, and we should turn Venezuela's national wealth to advantage to give a socialized culture in the most general terms.[91]

Student representatives systematically blocked all measures to eliminate repeaters. . . . In this there is a badly conceived solidarity among students. . . . Students need also to engage in some self-criticism here and understand that the repeater is a drag on the university's progress and consecrates the tremendous injustice of denying places to other young people . . . who may be poor but more productive.[92]

This was not the moment to seek a solution such as this [enforcing university regulations against repeaters], a moment when the university is struggling against such powerful enemies, against enemies against whom we cannot even speak because we lack the means. Then instead of presenting a united front, we present two antagonistic fronts, because today when the professor feels endangered he must be against the students and the student body feels itself menaced by the faculty. Then a lamentable spectacle of disunity and antagonism is presented.[93]

One is always struggling in the university . . . not against politics, but against the form that politics takes in the university from the practical point of view. I do believe that politics should be discussed, ideas exchanged but from a university point of view . . . not in the terms of the street politician nor that of political proselytism.[94]

Unfortunately, the university today is made up of a series of small universities within the university, if it can be called that. There is no concept of the universal in the proper sense of the word but rather small isolated groups that don't maintain genuine relations with each other.[95]

There are schools where they [the professors] of the first and second con-

[90] Interview 311259, Part B, p. 54.
[91] Interview 118179, Part A, pp. 31–32.
[92] Interview 117224, pp. 102, 103.
[93] Interview 128187, p. 11.
[94] Interview 311259, Part B, p. 65.
[95] Ibid., p. 56.

secutive classes were absent. The youngsters leave at the third hour . . . not the youngsters, the students, because many of them are adults. . . . Naturally those students left at the end of the second hour feeling sure that the professors of the third hour would also be absent. So they missed the third and fourth hours. This has to come to an end.[96]

This sense of confusion and inadequacy, of urgent problems running out of control or beyond present capacity to manage in ways that are not self-destructive, extends to areas of cultural effort outside the university.

The internal element that causes the greatest sense of malaise [within the Ministry of Education] is the existence of our anachronistic administrative machinery in relation to the development of education. No relation is present between the administrative instrumentality and the ample expansion in the development of education.[97]

In our country where there are no publishing houses, where that filter does not exist, anyone who goes to a printer and pays from his pocket . . . feels himself a writer and this establishes that here any person can do that. . . . Everyone is a writer, everyone is mixed together, the good and the mediocre. There are no incentives for the good and on the contrary great advantages for the bad. . . . Because there is no discrimination in the absence of the filtering action of the editorial house, a chain of literary patronage is stimulated, all standards for ranking break down, literature falls into the hands of small sects . . . public opinion finds itself absolutely without bases of judgment . . . criticism does not function because it lacks appropriate materials to which it can address itself . . . and finally literary creation is debased and finds the level of the poorest product.[98]

[The Association of Writers] has a fairly passive attitude at bottom. We cannot say that it is a dynamizing or dynamic organism of Venezuelan intellectual life . . . nor is it a professional group. . . . It is not seeing to it that writers earn more, that bad writers don't publish. . . . Sincerely it is a pretty anodyne entity. I prefer to say no more.[99]

Particularly among those responsible for the university, the sense of urgency and frustration is magnified because these men perceive themselves to be under enormous pressures. Although the reality of these pressures is in no way to be minimized, their effect is no doubt heightened by the intensely developed, critical self-consciousness of the sector's leadership and by diffuse feelings of helplessness to penetrate the felt

[96] Interview 325235, p. 96.
[97] Interview 043135, p. 165.
[98] Interview 112100, Part A, pp. 82, 83.
[99] Ibid., p. 95.

intolerance and shortsightedness of opposition from the government and economic sectors as well as from some students.

The fall of the dictatorship brought a moment of great violence in the university, especially on the part of students. There were strong pressures to expel all the professors who had occupied important positions during the dictatorship. The University Commission then expelled all those persons who had been ministers, and I don't remember exactly but I think it also included all those who had been deputies and senators. . . . But students took advantage of that moment to pressure for the expulsion of professors who were regarded as incompetent and also . . . some who were disliked or were very severe in their demands on students. . . . Given the violence of these demands there were difficult moments, but we were able to overcome these by talking to students, convincing them that this was not the way to get what they wanted, that the way was to present formal charges and prove them.[100]

The fundamental thing has been this campaign to discredit [the university], which is a relative matter because I do not believe it is really an offense or a discredit to the university to say some professors are Communist; that is normal. In the University of London there are Marxist professors and in U.S. universities there are Marxists. During the decade of the most ferocious McCarthyism they were almost all expelled from American universities. . . . This kind of John Birch Society in Venezuela, constituted of adventurers of many nationalities, especially exiled Cubans, . . . some of them directed by U.S. businessmen and by employees of the U.S. embassy, with the stimulus and tacit approval of the Betancourt government . . . [created] a wave of McCarthyism in this country unmatched in its history. Apparently, this line is being rectified, among other things because it is a policy that has failed. McCarthyism did not take root.[101]

The antagonism that we have seen in the university was on the one hand between the students, a majority of whom are leftist with a leaning toward certain lines of action, along with the political parties who tried to use that student mass in behalf of certain points of view, and on the other hand the groups of professors, among whom the conservative sector is dominant, who tried to apply certain measures, in part responding to academic considerations and in part moved fundamentally by hostility toward a student mass that did not meet with their aspirations. Those are the two important elements of pressure at work in the university.[102]

For us [the university] . . . all channels of information are closed. We send out a press release and most newspapers do not publish it. We cannot buy a television program from the commercial stations. We cannot appear on the National Television. We carry on important work and it is not reported in the press. The books published by our press and the publications of the

[100] Interview 311259, Part B, p. 46.
[101] Interview 045139, p. 97.
[102] Interview 015048, Part A, p. 52.

various dependencies of the university are quite good; we have made substantial progress on this front, in most cases are not even commented on by the various organs of public information. . . . That campaign against the university . . . was active for three years. . . . Then began the other phase of the campaign, which we are still living, which is the stage of silencing the university, that is, pretending the university does not exist.[103]

What we did was to begin organizing some visits for representative persons from different sectors so they could observe the work of the university, its successes, the development of research, educational plans. . . . A few persons came, but in many cases there were persons who refused or simply didn't come. . . . The opposition congressmen all came but only a few from Democratic Action came from the governing coalition. Some didn't complete their visits. They realized that at the end of their visit they might be asked, "What did you see in the university?" "Are things going well at the university?" "Has there been progress or not?" [104]

Similar pressures are experienced by government officials responsible for secondary and primary education, though for them decisive and even drastic actions (for example, mass dismissals of politically suspect teachers, suspensions of student government) are available outlets even though these are seen realistically as only short-run measures with decidedly negative side effects.

Our greatest success during my time here . . . is to have normalized classroom activity last year after the death of a teacher in a school insofar as the general opinion among all sectors in the country was that classes should be suspended for a prudent period while the tide of exaggerated reactions subsided. Contrary to that opinion, the Ministry group . . . opened classes and we concluded the year without incident. . . . Last year was the only year within the present constitutional period that developed normally.[105]

It was possible to make much progress in the program to depoliticize the classroom through two approaches: the first was persuasion, to try to convince diverse sectors of the harm, of the negative aspect, of using the children as political instruments. . . . The more drastic method . . . was the dismissal of a large group of teachers who had active political participation in the classroom and in the community. The presence of these teachers, the activity they promoted, and their preaching in the classroom was a source of continuous agitation. So with their extinction, their dismissal from the classroom, political activity diminished and this served as an example to the professors remaining in the classrooms and they took a different position.[106]

The elimination of the student centers [in high schools], which was a temporary measure, contributed momentarily to calming the student situation.

[103] Ibid., pp. 56, 57
[104] Ibid., p. 60.
[105] Interview 043135, pp. 158, 159.
[106] Ibid., p. 160.

Neither I nor the Ministry consider this *the* formula for a solution, but for the moment it did calm passions especially in those schools where the functions of the student centers had been completely disfigured. . . . To prolong that situation could bring evils, so the solution does not lie in eliminating the student centers. . . . For that reason in the present school year the centers are authorized to function. . . . The idea is to regulate the functioning of the student centers, to put them in operation as extracurricular activities under the supervision of teachers and with very precise rights for students without limiting their initiatives. . . . We believe a teacher has more command over students, and that they can contribute more to the solution of problems in the schools than outside forces. In other words, when repressive forces alien to student activity [were present], activities generally became more confused and took a direction that was not desirable from our point of view.[107]

The general climate of insecurity and intransigence permeating the working milieu of educators as evinced in these comments is, if anything, even more pronounced in the remarks of journalists. Professional newsmen, some of whose careers reach back to the time of Gómez, have long experience with the many varieties of the more subtle as well as brutally coercive means of keeping the press in line that have been practiced in Venezuela. Although major dailys, according to these accounts, are not subjected to any systematic censorship by government, the range of pressures acting on the media seems not to have diminished greatly and the menace of regression to more primitive forms of control is ever present, at least in the minds of the likely victims.

At bottom the fact that the government and all the political parties complain that the paper does not give them enough importance or feature them adequately is proof that we have not surrendered to anyone. . . . From a political point of view certainly each group tries to influence the paper in its favor. This is logical, some groups more than others, but all seek to influence the paper. I do not consider this immoral but rather a normal process. *Cada quien arrima la brasa a su sardina.*[108]

I believe the newspaper has enough freedom. There are some limitations in that freedom that are not imposed officially or by any group but rather by a sense of the common interest. . . . As, for example, the tremendously alarming items that were circulated abroad with respect to the dangers that surrounded our electoral process. . . . No one came to say to me "Don't publish that," for my own sense of the common interest told me that they shouldn't be published. In the same way, a piece of news that I may consider to come from a reliable source, if it is inconvenient for the collectivity, is a matter of personal conscience not to publish it.[109]

[107] Ibid., pp. 160–161.
[108] Interview 140215, pp. 25, 29.
[109] Ibid., p. 40.

There was a small problem with Betancourt, who threatened to expel the owners from the country . . . because of editorials, one by me. We criticized the fiscal policy of the government but in an elevated and truthful fashion. But that produced displeasure in the government; it provoked disturbances. . . . We cannot publish, unless they are articles that come from abroad, anything concerning national defense . . . but apart from that there is no censorship. . . . We were asked once as a favor not to publish news of the [terrorist] bombings, but as the *Daily Journal* published the news we decided to do the same . . . and nothing happened.[110]

We are going to analyze freedom of expression not only in the light of how it is affected by executive or official action but also by business enterprise and other pressure groups. I am not in agreement, for example, with the fact that *El Nacional* was brought almost to bankruptcy by a pressure group that sought to destroy it. Similarly, newspaper chains take a particular line and eliminate a certain political segment. . . . They put one on a black list and one can't be touched even if one discovered the cell that produces cancer. . . . At this moment we are living an incredible situation . . . with pressure groups that are much more nefarious than decrees of the Ministry of the Interior sending twenty newsmen to prison.[111]

There ensued a strong McCarthyist movement. . . . We were subjected to a powerful campaign, canceling advertising and forcing the owners, or at least the principal stockholder, to cede his stock to his brother and an economic group around him. . . . The most serious thing was that *El Nacional* . . . had to surrender before this pressure. We could not get out of the crisis. . . . The truth is that with that serious experience, with the pressure of advertisers, the liberty of the press in Venezuela was truly affected. This is a most serious experience that can extend to radio and television and not just the press. I want to inform you that this same McCarthyist pressure was applied on a more modest scale to a radio station, to the point where several leftist newscasters were ousted. But the radio stations responded more readily to the requirements of the advertiser. . . . They did not find themselves involved as in the case of *El Nacional* in a prolonged campaign.[112]

I am not in accord with the idea that a press organ . . . sustained by business, by people who believe in the democratic system, neither socialist nor totalitarian, should serve as a mouthpiece for those who seek to destroy the system. I agree that extremists, Communists, should have their own press. I agree that they should be allowed their press. But that they should have the advantage of using the press maintained by interests diametrically opposed to their own does not seem to me just but rather foolish.[113]

A banker will allow me to cover the story of a bank robbery, but that night he calls the advertising agency that handles his account, he calls the publisher

[110] Interview 141222, p. 76.
[111] Interview 317269, p. 51.
[112] Interview 022065, Part A, pp. 37–38.
[113] Interview 140215, p. 33.

of the newspaper, and blocks the publication of my story. This is very common in Venezuela. In Venezuela we have two serious problems: there is much mystification about the sources of news and not only with economic, scientific, or publicity types. Also with the political — here the politicians work with incredible mystery. Everything is mysterious.[114]

It is hardly a surprise to find such pressures and risks equally present in more literary endeavors, but the intrusion of politics into intellectual and aesthetic life sometimes takes bizarre forms. The museum director, who in the following quotation describes an unexpected crisis in the process of opening an exhibition, was shortly after to see the most valuable pieces in a show of paintings on loan from abroad removed at gunpoint from his galleries by terrorists. The paintings were subsequently recovered undamaged.

> One of the publications . . . was a famous book that had as a consequence the disappearance of the author, that is, his disappearance from Venezuela . . . , the exile of the author, and the imprisonment of the person who wrote the prologue . . . who was, by the way, an excellent writer. . . . He was imprisoned for a while. It was a kind of punishment, one of those things the present government likes to call "learning experiences." . . . The author . . . has not entered Venezuela again, or if he has, it has been clandestinely. In any case he can have no public activity.[115]
>
> The truth is that political and social life in Venezuela asphyxiates the possibilities of internal growth through which a writer becomes great and finds himself. This is a negative country in that respect, a country focused on the struggle for power. The Venezuelan, in general, is sensitive to power . . . and power is obtained through politics or through business. The great majority of Venezuelans have as an ideal the achievement of power via politics . . . or via money. This is a country where the values of the marketplace and political struggle predominate over the values of the spirit and beauty, or at least the values of self-realization through creation.[116]
>
> At the last minute there was a sort of ultimatum from a pretty large group of painters, who said they would withdraw their works if the hunger strike [by university students protesting limits on registrations] didn't end. . . . That was a problem that we discussed a great deal — first with the board to see what position would be taken and then with the participants. A solution was found. We asked for an extension. . . . I had the exhibit almost mounted and it was to be inaugurated the following Sunday. . . . I asked the painters to leave their works, that I could not open the show that Sunday, and that if by the following Sunday the problem had been solved, there would be no

[114] Interview 022065, Part B, p. 56.
[115] Interview 041131, p. 70.
[116] Interview 112100, p. 91.

reason not to open the salon. That same Saturday . . . the problem was solved and we worked all night and opened on Sunday as had been announced.[117]

The significance of these multiple pressures and the conflicting interests and value standards that converge on and are played out within the cultural arena is, of course, compounded by the fact that these pressures stem largely from the principal "patrons" of such activity, those who hold the purse strings of government and the possessors of independent means, whose support is indispensable in giving reality to any new initiative. The state of economic dependency of these men and the institutions they manage combined with their vulnerability as individuals to economic setbacks seriously compromises their capability to function in any genuine sense as an autonomous elite sector.[118]

> What I have tried to achieve unsuccessfully is a form of insurance for journalists, a system whereby newspapermen, as we are generally improvident, with little sense of the future — almost always when a newspaperman dies we have to get together and bury him, taxing ourselves five or ten bolívares. At times really tragic situations arise, men who die leaving a widow and nine children. . . . My great ideal is to create a system of aid . . . so that when a newspaperman dies his family is not without help . . . , that if he is unemployed he is also not forced into transactions that compromise his dignity.[119]
>
> The other objective is to form a college of newspapermen, to free our profession from invaders. Because due to the same conditions . . . journalism is a profession without protection; anyone who fails in any other field thinks it is very easy to be a journalist, and the companies encourage this.[120]
>
> Finally we wrote a prospectus which [the donor] found interesting to back financially, and he is backing this project. If it were not for his support, the magazine would not exist, above all because it is so hard to get advertising for a magazine of this kind [a literary review].[121]
>
> Shell [the oil company] very generously bought this press . . . and gave it to us. Creole itself, for example, for certain publications, Creole as well as Shell . . . helps us on occasion with certain editions.[122]
>
> The Association of Venezuelan Writers has no official subsidy but is maintained on the basis of members' dues, which are not very high. They used to be five bolívares; they are ten today, but the number of dues-paying

[117] Interview 303239, Part A, p. 38.
[118] The problem of the dependency of the cultural elite in the broader Latin American context is discussed at some length in Frank Bonilla, "Cultural Elites," in S. M. Lipset, ed., *Elites in Latin America* (New York: Oxford University Press, 1967).
[119] Interview 317269, p. 47.
[120] Ibid., p. 49.
[121] Interview 041131, p. 63.
[122] Interview 046140, p. 51.

members is no more than 200. Well, with an income of this kind it is impossible to face up to maintaining an institution.[123]

Well, the condition of the writer in Venezuela is lamentable. . . . There are a number of negative aspects in our country from the point of view of the creative work of the writer. In the first place this is an inattentive milieu, very little attention is given to reading. Therefore there is no market for books, there are no publishing houses. An editorial house to a certain point helps the writer to act as a writer. Here there are no publishers.[124]

The Venezuelan Church is a poor church; and there are dioceses of profound poverty, that are barely able to subsist in some cases in situations almost of misery. . . . Some eastern [dioceses] have small subsidies, but the situation is very difficult in some dioceses, very precarious. . . . It depends on who is governor; there is nothing fixed or obligatory. It depends on the good will of the governor who may grant it but the next one can withdraw it.[125]

A third factor [in the university's success] has been the support of the state through the Ministry of Education . . . even though from an economic standpoint it has not been possible to obtain all the support necessary. . . . [Reasons for] economic difficulties have to be sought in the fact that we came to life just at the time of an economic recession that came after the dictatorship with the subsequent need on the part of the government to make important readjustments in outlays even for initiatives that it supported.[126]

As regards the university particularly, the question of financing has critical ramifications and is linked to a long-standing hemisphere-wide struggle for university autonomy which has never even approached a viable solution to the building of an independent financial base or endowment for universities. In the 1959 reorganization of the Central University, the principle of autonomy was reaffirmed and preliminary steps were taken to ensure the institution some independent income. These have never been fully implemented, and, as the remarks following manifest, the principle of autonomy itself is newly at issue, with quite sophisticated arguments put forward in behalf of new limitations on the university's independence.

Autonomy is a concept that arose fifty years ago in Latin American universities as a response to the aggressive and domineering attitude of dictatorial governments. In democratic regimes and even in advanced systems such as the socialist regimes, autonomy tends to diminish and to disappear because it is believed that the university should form an integral part of the educational system. In that sense we do not believe that the university should have

[123] Intervew 332275, Part B, p. 124.
[124] Interview 112100, p. 81.
[125] Interview 132076, p. 78.
[126] Interview 055165, pp. 37, 39.

absolute autonomy to govern itself and plan for itself independently of the rest of the educational system. . . . On the other hand, I consider that the university should have relative autonomy in the sense that once the general lines of coordination with the state have been established, the university should be free to organize its curriculum, name professors, minor authorities, and so on.[127]

I believe that one of the most important things is the reaffirmation of university autonomy . . . and I consider this of great value not only for the university and its consolidation but also for the life of the university. The possibilities that autonomy opens up for the progress of the university are very substantial because, in addition to the fact that political influences tend to a more adequate equilibrium and that academic standards are expressed more freely, there also exists the possibility of using the best talents in the nation regardless of their political or ideological position and this is an influence toward the maintenance of a more liberal climate within the institution. At the same time I think it is valuable in a milieu such as ours where authoritarian ideas predominate in many of the social expressions that take root. I believe the impact of the autonomous university on the collectivity is going to be a very positive factor in the improvement of democracy here in the nation.[128]

The awareness that the institution's claim on the society and on the youth it serves must be validated in meaningful action is very present in the thinking of university authorities. This search for relevance directs priorities toward the identification of national and individual needs and ways to meet them.

Our primary aim . . . is to apply new systems of work to the university in accordance with national needs, as objectives derived from these. I might note some of these: first, to achieve a good selection of students with rational limits according to the facilities of each school; then the organization of a school giving preprofessional basic courses, the creation of a predominantly technological school in line with regional and national needs, and the attainment of a full-time teaching staff and an entirely full-time student body as well.[129]

I don't even want to touch on the problem of the market for sociologists and anthropologists, from the point of view of work and from the point of view of the utility as a means of subsisting to an individual of bearing the title of sociologist or anthropologist. . . . I would just like to raise the fact of the degree to which an individual studying a field does so with the con-

---

[127] Ibid., p. 44. The issue is a complex one that can be noted here only as one more dimension in the general precariousness of the intellectual's situation and that of his major institutional haven. Refer also to *SRSP,* pp. 215–224.

[128] Interview 015048, pp. 66–67.

[129] Interview 055165, p. 40.

viction that it is what he wants, that it is what is good for him, and that it will make him a socially useful individual.[130]

I believe that we could carry out these projects and offer them to the state as proof that Venezuelan specialists are genuinely able to carry out certain kinds of work for which as you well know foreigners are imported for various reasons, among them the allegation that Venezuelan professionals have not begun to work as teams on projects that demonstrate their capacity for that kind of work. . . . I believe the university is obligated to demonstrate that *its own* people can be trained in this fashion.[131]

The quest for a mission genuinely responsive to present necessities is firmly coupled to a call for realism, tolerance, and a critical sense of proportion with respect to national pretensions in the cultural realm. Authenticity is sought here through harsh self-judgment, the resolute pursuit of locally relevant values, and a refusal to sidestep unpleasant issues.

Because our universities are democratic, we cannot hope to have them function as might private universities, where only people from a single sector able to pay are in attendance. Here we have people of all social classes; consequently it is logical that there be people of all ideologies and, in effect, we have people of all political ideologies. . . . Now I say, we are professors in universities in which students are political. Our problem is that as professors we are obligated to teach students who are political, even though they are political and *because* they are political. We are obliged to teach them. This then presents different stumbling blocks than a milieu in which students are not political. . . . I say that as professors we are obligated to try to overcome these obstacles and try to understand this reality so that within that reality our teaching can be fully efficacious.[132]

We cannot deceive ourselves. Venezuela signifies absolutely nothing in the development of contemporary thought, art, or letters. That is, Venezuela constitutes nothing. . . . Our literature fails because of its localism or provincialism or because of flashes of pretention. If in one case one sins through provincialism, in the other one sins through inorganicity, plagiarism, mimicry, because in reality forms cannot be copies. Thus our arts suffer in principle two main dangers: being behind with respect to more advanced contemporary currents or copying, feigning, simulating, in order not to lag behind. Between those two dangers are found the truly creative possibilities that have produced writers of stature in Venezuela.[133]

This is exactly one of the things that possibly sets off today's youth. In other times young people would have been satisfied merely to express a political attitude . . . that is, that their work have what used to be called a message; today they demand that the literary form be of genuine quality,

[130] Interview 128187, Part B, p. 9.
[131] Interview 325235, Part A, p. 86.
[132] Ibid., Part B, p. 110.
[133] Interview 112100, p. 86.

even though there are all these expressions that older people regard as obscene or vulgar and that young people like, not out of a mania for filth, but as a direct expression or apprehension of life.[134]

As an independent, I can demonstrate to anyone that I contribute with all the honesty of a Venezuelan to maintaining the principle that we must respect the ideas of others, to build our culture, to evolve, and help our people to evolve. I don't believe this is an unimportant labor or struggle; it is not directly political, but it is an effective struggle in favor of the culture of the people.[135]

Within the more inclusive effort of secularly based cultural construction and renewal, the Church too affirms its desire to enter more adventurously and imaginatively into contemporary social problems. For this task, as clerical spokesmen acknowledge and manifest in their self-appraisals, the Church is unevenly prepared. Perhaps more assured than other purveyors of ideas as to its capacity to influence high policy, the Church and its hierarchy in Venezuela remain locked in struggle symbolically with contrary ideologies and subject in much the same way as others in the cultural sphere to a play of individualities in which the decisive power lies with others.

Our immediate objective [the Church's] is our own internal renovation toward a more efficacious adaptation to the modern world. That has to be our immediate objective . . . the base of everything and for that reason we are awaiting directives from the [Vatican] Council to begin on a more concrete program . . . because we see that it is necessary to make our action on a social plane more effective.[136]

The opinion of the Church is transcendental in diverse fields, not in all. For example, in politics very little, because luckily the Church in Venezuela is not political. It pays attention to politics and participates in seeking to orient policy at high levels. . . . Of course, you can be absolutely assured; it is a certified and consummated fact that the opinion of the Church carries weight.[137]

Democratic Action was in power and it attacked private education and, as the largest percentage of private education in Venezuela is in the hands of the Church, all the troubles took shape. But at least we escaped the danger. . . . We escaped the danger with the fall of those people, you see, but we fell into another problem which was the dictatorship. But at least the educational problem was solved at that time.[138]

The number one enemy among all those is communism, but the Church is

---

[134] Interview 041131, pp. 65, 66.
[135] Interview 306249, Part A, p. 28.
[136] Interview 132076, p. 72.
[137] Interview 085083, p. 46.
[138] Ibid., p. 48.

also the number one enemy of communism. So they are antagonistic forces that will struggle permanently as long as the world lasts . . . because they are based on contradictory principles. Communism rests on historical materialism and the Church on historical spiritualism . . . , the Church defends the integrity of life whereas communism denies it. . . . Here no reaching out of hands can avail, nor silk gloves. The day communism adapts to the Church, communism ceases being communism, and the day the Church adapts to communism, it will cease to be the Catholic Church.[139]

In Venezuela matters between Church and State are resolved almost from one person to another. For this reason we representatives of the Church must be very attentive to see who is who. When we know that a person is anti-Catholic or anticlerical we avoid confrontations, clashes. We want to avoid frictions for the good of all. . . . We are still in a very individualistic phase . . . in which one has to pay much attention to persons to get along well.[140]

Voluntary Association Leaders

The extensive quotations presented thus far have been used to evoke a sense of the differences in mood, felt capacity, and substantive preoccupations of top men in government, parties, business firms, and the world of ideas, primarily educators and communicators, in the intimate context of action in their primary power roles. The men who guide and stand behind the organizations to be briefly surveyed here do not constitute an additional, discrete subsector within the national elite. They represent, rather, a small number within each of the spheres already covered who enter into a particular kind of activity related to the advancement or defense of the interests of a given sector or into efforts to mobilize sector capabilities in behalf of specific causes, national or other, that may be only tangentially linked to sector interests. Such organizational participation and leadership, as noted in earlier chapters, does not as yet have any clear relation to power standing within the elite. Though a few such leaders hold paid positions in these organizations, few of the professional staffs of such bodies figure within the elite. The principal impulses and the philosophy guiding these efforts come from the elite individuals who put their money and influence behind these organizations rather than from the men who run their day-to-day affairs. In this sense, each of the spheres we have been systematically analyzing — the economic, cultural, and political — can be seen as having its unique extensions into the world of voluntary associations. Though material is lacking for any-

---

[139] Ibid., pp. 72, 73.
[140] Interview 132076, p. 87.

thing like a full discussion of the important problems such a statement opens up, even a brief look at such associations helps to bring out essential and as yet unmentioned features of both intra- and intersector conflict and cooperation.

The most important single development in this connection is without doubt the gradual entry during the early 1960's of business groups into more direct and public forms of political and social action. This movement produced not only numerous new business entities with professionalizing, political, and community service objectives but vitalized and transformed the internal functioning of traditional business representation groups.[141] It is in this context that the inner tensions within the business community come to the surface in their most frank expression. The strains between the few nationalists and the large majority who are highly receptive to foreign participation in the economy, the resistance to involvement of those who would like to keep business as removed from politics as possible as against those calling for more direct action, the clashes between industrializers as against importers — all come into plain view here. Some plausible explanations for the absence or relatively muted quality of nationalist affirmations among this top business group are given here.

In theory and according to the statutes of the Federation, what it does is defend the interests of its associates. . . . It is evident that the Federation of Chambers is an almost unique case in the world, in which interests that are generally in opposition, especially in developing countries, sit around the same table. . . . The problem of the man in trade is generally opposed to that of the industrialist because the first prefers to continue to import and represent a foreign manufacturer whereas the industrialist wishes to produce locally. . . . Modern agriculture generally is an activity dedicated to the production of raw materials for industry, and naturally the cultivator is interested in the highest price for his raw material whereas the industrialist wants to pay the smallest price possible. . . . The banker is the enemy of all . . . and the man in transport is not seen in a friendly light by the industrialist. . . . So it is very interesting that Fedecamaras has survived and not only survived but become stronger over the years and that even though in an incipient form a consciousness has been created among businessmen . . . there are some higher level problems that are genuinely shared.[142]

[141] An idea of the scope of these programs and the degree to which religious and entrepreneurial ideologies and motivations were intermingled in them, particularly in social action initiatives, can be obtained from a review of the documents of the International Executives Seminar on the theme, "Business Responsibility in the Social Progress of Venezuela," held at the Macuto Sheraton Hotel on October 4–5, 1963.

[142] Interview 323281, pp. 23, 24.

There are two groups. There is the group which believes . . . that businessmen should solve their own problems and precisely on the basis of our own competence and at the same time demonstrate to government that we represent a certain force, that we act according to certain principles. And there is the other group which wants to take the easiest path and says let's ask for protection, let's ask for subsidies, let's ask for privileges, and let the government be the one to grant them because we deserve them.[143]

Generally, the most nationalistic groups are the medium and small entrepreneurs; the big businessmen . . . who for understandable reasons have to enter into contact with big bankers . . . naturally tend to moderate their nationalism and subordinate it always to their own convenience in manipulating credits. . . . The nationalist, who may not always have commercial relations on a large scale, cannot express a strong nationalism because that affects his interest by alienating men in commerce. . . .[144]

[People] saw there [Pro-Venezuela] the creation of an institution to defend industrial as against popular interests. The industrialists want protection in order to profit — that was the theme which was taken up by intellectuals, newsmen, and which was backed and promulgated by the sectors hurt by nationalism, for example, by importers and chambers of commerce. . . . The import sector [attacks Pro-Ven] via campaigns . . . preaching the disadvantages of industrialization, emphasizing . . . that industrialization increases the cost of living, that industrialization goes against consumers . . . and by hiring intellectuals to defend a kind of liberalism that is anachronistic but suits them perfectly because it preaches free enterprise, according to which the country should have no tariff barriers and everything should be determined by comparative costs. . . . Foreign capital uses other instruments . . . of subtle pressure . . . stimulating these campaigns among importers, behind the scenes with government officials, and pressuring powerful members of the institution [Pro-Ven] to undermine their help to the organization.[145]

As regards Pro-Venezuela, unfortunately, . . . there have been other kinds of frictions between the two business organisms, frictions that above all have first and last names [i.e., involve individuals].[146]

The central importance that is given to the Federation of Chambers of Commerce (Fedecamaras) is reflected in the heat and combativeness that accompany elections to its directorate. These contests are colored not only by the factors dividing businessmen themselves but also by the intrusion of external political interests and ambitions.

One of our greatest successes has been to achieve and salvage . . . unity in Fedecamaras . . . . I was referring specifically to unity this year because the problem that arose in the board of directors before elections was fairly

---

[143] Ibid., p. 26.
[144] Interview 003006, p. 94.
[145] Ibid., pp. 90, 96.
[146] Interview 323281, p. 49.

serious and I think if the situation during that period hadn't been managed with considerable tact Fedecamaras could have disappeared.[147]

On repeated occasions one witnessed the persistence of the government in trying to capture the Federation and have it as one more organism within the political complex. On one occasion . . . it was only by a single vote that a certain slate won against another with a manifestly official brand. Naturally . . . this only brought unnecessary frictions and cooling of relations.[148]

I think every banker has means of exerting pressures on other groups . . . because we all know that the majority of executives have bank accounts or their firms owe money to banks. I think, unfortunately, that this year very powerful pressures were brought to bear through the banks to bring [to office in Fedecamaras] a large group of persons who do not represent their sectors. Today, of the individuals who were there, one said, "I need to be a director of Fedecamaras to round out my curriculum vitae. I know that those directors who are bankers have not worked and won't work because Fedecamaras is not a Monday board meeting. Fedecamaras is with the Confederation of Workers from two in the morning if there are serious political problems, it is going to the interior, going to Miraflores [Presidential palace] every time there is a problem of public order. There are all kinds of problems, and one has to work.[149]

Apart from the nationalist-tinged thesis of industrialization advanced by Pro-Venezuela, the guiding orientations of the move by business into community action are an amalgam of recent Catholic social thought and free enterprise liberalism. The substance of these ideas will be discussed in the pages on elite reviews of the mass. Here we need merely to note the main impulses behind this very substantial, elaborately conceived, and potentially highly influential effort at organization. As they emerge in conversation with the principal promoters, these aims are the forging of a more sophisticated and ideologically efficacious anticommunism, the inculcation of a new political and social sensibility among businessmen, stemming the steady march toward nationalization of the economy and the threatened exclusion or imposition of further limits on foreign investment. The principal instruments are to be education and religious renewal or reengagement.

In addition to this [publication of an economics journal], we have held seminars and countless lectures among groups in Venezuela and abroad, among students, workers, labor unions, professionals, sometimes on television. We publish articles in newspapers and in general we carry on a daily struggle to

[147] Interview 082042, pp. 9, 10.
[148] Interview 323281, p. 38.
[149] Interview 057167, p. 53.

disseminate these ideas . . . to demonstrate to the world that thought has advanced since Marx. . . . In Venezuela we have been very successful. We have also had the cooperation . . . of similar institutes in Latin America and throughout the world. At present there are similar institutes in Argentina, Brazil, Colombia, Panama, . . . Costa Rica, Mexico, and one is being created in the Dominican Republic. There are two similar institutes in the United States and several in Europe.[150]

Then a group of persons (and here is the origin of my participation in AVI) made an agreement, at first naturally a very small group, and began to analyze the situation. Well, gentlemen, what are we doing in this country? For better or worse we constitute a group, some more, others less, of the men who produce in this country, who have commercial, industrial, or professional activity and have always been deaf to politics. Venezuela is living a difficult political moment. Every day enemies of the basic structures of the country arise. Why should we continue to be indifferent?[151]

The only way to strike back was in a positive way. It was not simply to declare, "I am anti-Communist," but to present a positive thesis which we know we had not put into action. . . . Something that to my mind has been the seedbed of much of this has been the movement of *cursillos de cristiandad*. This really shakes up a person, makes him aware that he cannot continue to live in a comfortable, selfish position, but that there is a duty toward others that is the Christian foundation of charity.[152]

We cannot deny that the tendency in Latin America and in other countries is to want to nationalize foreign capital, which to me is a complete and total imbecility. . . . Now that tendency can be reversed through education and the formation of man, bringing him to understand that from a socioeconomic point of view it is much more interesting for the country to have some gentlemen who take all the risks and give us most of the profits than to have us Venezuelans take all the risks and probably through poor management have lesser gains.[153]

The natural leaders . . . in all localities, and especially in the small towns of the interior, should be the business people who for reasons A or B have had some success in life and it is for some reason that they have been successful. And normally in the Venezuelan case it is not because they have had

[150] Interview 410316, pp. 66, 67. Norman A. Bailey, "Organization and Operation of Neoliberalism in Latin America," in *Latin America: Politics, Economics, and Hemisphere Security* (New York: Frederick A. Praeger, 1965), pp. 193–238, associates several of the groups in Venezuela to a continent-wide network of business-financed and -coordinated organizations engaged in political and social action programs that range from armed "white guards" and the blacklisting of political undesirables through many forms of propaganda and education designed to ensure the long-term survival of free enterprise in Latin America. On page 236 Bailey lists among the Venezuelan groups Acción Venezolana Independiente, Instituto Venezolano de Acción Comunitaria, and Asociación Civil Dividendo para la Comunidad.

[151] Interview 420308, p. 27.
[152] Interview 031089, Part C, p. 206.
[153] Interview 339240, pp. 107–108.

more education than others . . . but generally because they are competent persons — a competence they have developed in their own business. . . . If the businessman is content to make his modest profit, pay his taxes, travel and have a nice home, we are not achieving what a businessman should be. That consciousness is what I believe Fedecamaras needs most to stimulate.[154]

I think . . . we should have a continuous program because it seems to me that helping certain cultural groups in the country contributes to the creation of a peaceful atmosphere by deflecting the attention of many people from politics to much more beautiful things.[155]

Along with the course in sociology . . . they [students in community action program] are also given catechism. For example, they are taught Christian doctrine and the doctrine of the Church. . . . No one is forced to attend the religious practices the course includes. The course, as a Christian institute, has as one of the course facilities a chapel, and attendance at chapel is maintained. There is mass every day. There is no obligation or anything like that in a disciplinary way . . . nor is lack of attendance at mass reason for expulsion for anyone.[156]

A basic tenet of all such efforts in education and community organization is that they be nonpartisan or "apolitical" in the sense of not having ties to any of the existing parties or perennial candidates to high office. However, it does not foreclose, as noted in the earlier remarks regarding AVI, the pressing of business "independents" as candidates in the regular parties. Still, the more overtly political a line of action, the less likely it is to be readily approved by business leaders at this level.[157]

To maintain IVAC in contact with campesinos while a vigorous political campaign was under way, as elections were approaching, would have been to expose IVAC to some suspicion. We suspended our outside work. . . . We maintain IVAC completely detached from politics. This doesn't mean that among our collaborators there may not be persons who belong to parties . . . but IVAC is definitely not connected with any political force. . . . We have many people from a great diversity of parties. Well, the only thing we don't have, naturally, are characters from the Communist Party . . . because there you have a total philosophical contradiction with us.[158]

The strategy of an organization of this type is, I believe, and above all in our countries, basically tied to apoliticism because our politics are politics with so many ups and downs and the entrepreneurial function should not be subject to ups and downs but should have a maximum stability. Whoever ties himself to a political wagon . . . some day will be down and the busi-

[154] Interview 323281, p. 43.
[155] Interview 339240, p. 99.
[156] Interview 031089, Part B, p. 193.
[157] Refer to footnote 82.
[158] Interview 031089, Part B, pp. 197, 198.

nessman should never be down and not even up but simply in his position as businessman.[159]

One reason, perhaps, for the studied apoliticism of much of this kind of action is its obvious inspiration in the social service and community-oriented corporate ideologies of U.S. business philanthropy and public relations. In these new endeavors the Venezuelan entrepreneur has had as mentor and model the top executive talent of the major oil companies, numbers of them Venezuelan. They could hardly wish for a more experienced or sophisticated source of guidance in these new ventures. A small number of local business-sponsored foundations are already operating very much in the image of their U.S. counterparts.

> The Foundation is deeply engaged in a series of studies. . . . The Foundation staff and myself in particular are in a number of groups of men who are working actively on this aspect of the resolution of social problems . . . the philosophy of the resolution of these social aspects. For example, all this movement in private enterprise, of the responsibility let us say of private enterprise in the solution of these problems, is a movement that was born mostly through discussions in which the Creole Foundation participated. The seminar, for example, that was organized in February in Maracay, called "The Responsibility of the Entrepreneur in the Social Development of the Nation," is a program entirely promoted by us and in which we subsequently became associated . . . with the Association of Executives and the Mendoza Foundation. The principal success of the Foundation has been by its influence, by its pressure . . . in conversations, conferences, in committees . . . so that private enterprise in Venezuela participates much more actively in the solution of the socioeducational problem of the nation.[160]

Whereas the business sector or groups within it have begun to experiment with a wide variety of approaches to action on the political and cultural fronts, the cultural leadership is turned inward in a generally defensive stance, intensely preoccupied with the disarray within its own ranks and the precarious situation of its institutions and the persons who man them. No autonomous initiatives with the kind of drive or potential behind them implied in the thrust by business into the field of action appear in these data. The few efforts in this direction reported from within the cultural sector constitute little more than transient cliques or coteries with limited objectives and scant projection. The only major organizations outside the framework of government and the parties, aside from those sponsored by businessmen, are the professional associations

---

[159] Interview 323281, p. 40.
[160] Interview 339240, pp. 90, 91.

(*colegios*) and the labor unions. The *colegios,* though penetrated by the parties and sensitive to political issues, or perhaps for that reason, rarely bring collective pressures to bear on more than narrow questions. Except in moments of crisis, when political forces are pressed to muster the maximum support available to them, such groups rarely enter into political calculations at all save with respect to problems directly touching on professional or class interests. Thus, the only other major organization type that requires some comment, however summary, is labor.

The labor movement tends to be seen as an extension or appendage of the parties, and this view is by no means inappropriate insofar as it suggests an intimate interpenetration or symbiosis in which dominance relations are by no means clear or stable and the alternation of identities (political and syndical), especially in the leadership, is managed effortlessly and with stunning rapidity in the many settings in which the contemporary labor leader finds himself acting. The labor movement experienced and in part propelled the surge of unity felt by the political parties at the fall of Pérez Jiménez in 1958. The collapse and progressive fragmentation of that momentary coalition inevitably have been reproduced step by step in labor circles, but labor nevertheless felt itself in 1963 at a high point in its power in Venezuela.[161]

> All sectors try to influence an organism that has such an extraordinarily potent force as the CTV. Whoever does not, commits a grave error. So there are external forces that try to influence the minds of CTV directors . . . political parties, employers, the state, religious forces . . . all those sectors always try to exert influence. But our policy has been to maintain our organization in a position of independence. We do not accept impositions by parties or other forces external to the labor movement. Our policy is a working-class policy . . . it has as a foundation the struggle for the constant improvement of the standard of living of laborers and farm workers. . . . We support the government in matters of principle, in the defense of the constitutional system, in all those things that contribute to maintaining the realization of the program the government offered.
>
> Outside the CTV there are organisms that see [us] with great sympathy, especially the democratic political parties. . . . Independent personalities, managerial groups, groups of executives, even the Federation of Chambers has publicly recognized that the CTV has played not an important but a decisive role in the destiny of the nation and in guaranteeing labor peace, which by itself constitutes most of the public peace.

[161] A 1964 U.S. Army handbook describes the Venezuelan labor movement as "the most effective in Latin America." See *U.S. Army Area Handbook for Venezuela* (Washington, D.C.: Special Operations Research Office, American University, 1964). A compact summary of the situation of the labor movement is given from pp. 411–430.

We also have some members with positions in the government. For example, there is a representative of the Confederation in the social security agency, in the petrochemical plant . . . . We are trying to have one in the Telephone Company of Venezuela, in the National Development Corporation. In the National Agrarian Institute there are two representatives, and we are urgently requesting the same in all agencies that orient the economic and social life of the country.[162]

Despite such optimistic statements regarding autonomy, political factors patently continue to figure centrally in labor affairs, and remarks such as the preceding ones are seen even by those who most favor such a role for labor as exhortatory rather than as fact.

We ought to be a . . . true organization, with more power of decision and autonomy. However, because the labor movement is so politicized, ordinarily, in my view, the decisions of labor groups . . . are basically a result of agreements formed previously by workers but from a determinate political position. . . . This is not always the case. There are problems that arise at the moment that a meeting is under way and among all those present a plan of action or position is formulated. But for the more important matters it is customary to have consultation at the party level. . . . In other matters there is more independence. . . . I don't even want to say more independence because this process is not in my judgment a loss of independence. . . . Neither the union nor the higher level labor organizations is a simple bargaining agent. . . . In addition to obtaining some improvement or other for workers, they necessarily must have a revolutionary stance. One is in disagreement with a situation . . . this one has to be supplanted by a new order. . . . It is necessary to create new structures. These structures cannot be conceived from a strictly technical base, with a benefit-bargaining attitude, but rather in keeping with canons of ideology and doctrine, and this basically has to be discussed with one's comrades who vibrate on the same wavelength, the comrades who share the same ideology.[163]

The moment of unity after 1959 was short-lived even though events in other countries (Chile and Bolivia) fed the hope that a multinational move toward unification from the grass roots would force the labor internationals to seek a new entente.

In the unity meeting that we held at the end of 1959 . . . , which saw the birth of the single confederation, there were present delegates from CIOSL (Confederación Internacional de Sindicatos Libres), ORIT, FTM (Federación de Trabajadores Mundiales), CTAL (Confederación de Trabajadores de America Latina), and the Social Christian unions. They all came as our guests and they were informed at this congress that we would have friendly

[162] Interview 025074, pp. 70, 71, 78, 79.
[163] Interview 023071, Part A, pp. 30, 31, 32. The word "comrade" (*compañero*) is the general term for fellow members in labor, student, and political organizations of all ideological shades in Venezuela.

relations with them all but that the new national confederation [Central] would not affiliate with any of the labor internationals. So that we were able to bring together . . . all those people who on a world scale are like oil and vinegar. . . . This is what, on the international plane, made it possible . . . for AD supporters, COPEI backers, and Communists, and so on, to be together. . . . The resolution made at that congress was not to affiliate with any international and to work for the unity of the world labor movement. That is, we didn't just say [to the several internationals] that we were not with them but that they should unite and that they were going to have problems because if what was happening in Venezuela occurred in all countries, what would become of them? . . . Today the CTV is affiliated with ORIT . . . where it was before and the CUTV (Central Unica de Trabajadores de Venezuela) is again affiliated with the FTM. . . . Today we find ourselves, as far as international relations are concerned, just where we were ten years ago.[164]

The mechanical quality of the integration achieved is manifest in the allocation of slots in the executive committee by party and the subsequent jockeying for either dominance or, at a minimum, a neutralizing coalition. Still, it is not to be overlooked that much complex business of interest to workers is carried on with dispatch beneath this overlay of political stalemate.

It is logical that the structure of the executive committee [of the CTV] had to respond to that composition, that balance of forces. Thus in a committee of fourteen, seven were AD . . . three for the Communists . . . two for URD and two for COPEI. . . . Later things became more complex . . . two of the AD members went to MIR, thus AD was reduced to five. The Communist Party, URD, and the two from MIR began to make common cause. For many things, especially on positions of a political nature, they were converted into seven. Now as the fundamental issue was the acceptance or not of the democratic system, there were concrete proposals that democracy was no longer any good, that violent change was necessary, that the President of the Republic should resign. Then the five from AD and the two from COPEI also added to seven who said that this could not be done. There were interminable meetings . . . with each side trying to impose its views on this mattter, and no agreement was reached because we were seven against seven. Naturally we would be deep in this wrangle and suddenly another problem would arise, such and such workers have this or that problem . . . then there was rapid agreement among us.[165]

Much the same pattern of formally allocated voting power at the top, relatively easy collaboration on genuine labor issues, and a tendency to

---

[164] Interview 425328, pp. 7, 8. A brief history of international labor organization in Latin America is given in Robert J. Alexander's "Labor and Inter-American Relations," *Annals of the American Academy of Political and Social Science*, vol. 334 (March 1961), pp. 41–53.
[165] Interview 023071, pp. 37, 38, 40.

stand-off solutions or postponements of showdowns with respect to fundamentally political questions continued to characterize relations within
the CTV after the break within the movement in December 1961 that
was the prelude to the formal appearance of a rival confederation (CUTV)
in the spring of 1963.

> The composition is seven from AD, that is to say, they retain their initial
> number, and four from COPEI. We have doubled our earlier figure. Before
> there were fourteen members, now there are eleven.[166]

> Many propositions that we present unexpectedly, and I say unexpectedly
> not to imply a maneuver or tactical ability but rather because these are
> things that arise at the moment a problem is being discussed, we state and
> they accept, and at the same time they may propose something and we accept
> it. Almost always when one of the participants makes insistent objections, a
> decision is postponed.[167]

The problem for labor, then, was how to move from a position of
considerable strength to one of greater autonomy, a question of how to
approach unity in view of the political pull internally of parties and
externally of the labor internationals, and finally of how to recapture the
militancy and mass appeal that had been consciously sacrificed in deference to party concerns or through fear of plunging the country further
into crisis.

> For them [Marxists] it is unity at all costs; for us [COPEI labor leaders]
> it is liberty at all costs. Now we strive within that freedom to have workers
> understand the need for unity and that rather than set up a new organization
> when a union is no good they should strengthen their own position within
> the organization and make weigh their own points of view . . . but if we
> are unsuccessful and do not convince them, they have a perfect right to do it
> [set up a new organization].[168]

> As affiliates [of CIOSL] we can present any problem that arises and obtain
> support. The labor school that operates in the Confederation, in which we
> are training nearly sixty-five labor leaders every six months, gets economic
> aid from this organization and from ORIT [Organización Regional Inter-
> americana de Trabajadores].[169]

> Now the working class has to take a more revolutionary posture than be-
> fore. Previously we gave first importance to the maintenance of formal
> democracy over a series of workers' aspirations. We have braked . . . workers
> themselves have spontaneously braked a series of aspirations in view of the
> circumstances lived by the country. Because these difficulties are now over-

---

[166] Ibid., p. 45.
[167] Ibid., pp. 38, 39.
[168] Ibid., p. 36.
[169] Interview 025074, p. 79.

come, not entirely, it is not that there is no longer any danger, but because
the danger has been minimized, it is necessary to popularize democracy. . . .
The CTV, as the most representative labor organization, has to become the
engine of a genuine campaign of achievements in the new government. . . .
It is now necessary to have integral agrarian reform, struggle against unemployment, perhaps even reform in the tax structure.[170]

Such then are the specific pressures acting on each organizational sector
and its leadership. Though all the organizations are embedded within a
larger political context that is manifestly conflictful, each confronts a
quite different array of internal tensions and is moved to action by very
different impulses. The large ambitions of men in government are sobered
by their awareness of the precariousness of their support, the implacability of part of their opposition, and the fear of regressive reactions from
the military and the economic sector. The same climate of struggle, risk,
commitment, and fear that past achievements may only too easily be
reversed prevails in the party sector. Cultural leaders are more oppressed
by feelings of dependency, doubts about the relevance and authenticity
of their product and organizations, feelings that problems in their field
are fast moving beyond their control. Businessmen, though looking to the
future with buoyant optimism about economic expansion, are considerably
more perplexed and unsure of themselves with respect to the political
and social role of the business community in the new Venezuela they see
emerging before their eyes. This is the concrete reality that lies beneath
the surface eruptions of violence, repression, resistance, and rebelliousness that punctuate public life. However, the over-all articulation or
structural coherence of these disparate lines of elite action seem to be
dictated much more by self-imposed limitations and fears of overstepping
bounds than by any conscious accord bridging elite sectors and setting
well-defined limits on the nature and pace of change.

PRAXIS

Turning from these efforts to visualize the specialized contexts of day-to-
day elite action in power roles to a more quantitative appraisal of some
characteristics of elite behavior in such roles, one is struck at once with
the marginal relevance of many conventional ideas about power to an
understanding of elite operations at this level. As has been noted, almost
all the accounts of power or influence attempts (PRAXIS) in the interviews

[170] Interview 023071, pp. 55–56.

portray incidents in which the respondent figures as protagonist, almost always while in the main position occupied at the time of interview. Except for a handful of politicians no one other than the respondent is individualized in the descriptions of these encounters, either as main actor or as the object of action. On the whole, rather, these episodes have to do with the efforts of individuals, generally as agents for organizations, to work some change in their own organizations or in other organized entities — parties, government bureaus, business firms, or universities.

The fact that respondents almost universally chose to structure these accounts in this way means that the rhetoric of power and command figures hardly at all in these materials. When men of power and authority are asked to describe their major successes and setbacks they do not talk about the exercise of power or authority — that is, about obtaining or forcing compliance with authoritative decisions or commands — but rather about *the generation of support or acquiescence from other power wielders*. In practically all such incidents the principal alter is a peer or superior in the same or in another organization (Table 7.4). The only

TABLE 7.4 *Hierarchical Relation of Goal-Seeking Actors to Alters (Percentages)*

	Elite Sector					
	Political		Cultural		Economic	
	High	Low	High	Low	High	Low
Respondents	(64)	(18)	(25)	(12)	(38)	(19)
No. of PRAXES	(144)	(70)	(42)	(47)	(88)	(29)
Alter is a superior[a]	17	7	24	21	21	21
Alter is a peer in own organization	29	41	20	28	10	17
Alter is a peer in another organization	48	59	51	40	54	62
Alter is of lower status	3	4	12	19	2	—

NOTE: Coded only when relationship was clear and occasionally for more than one "alter."

[a] These divide for every group almost half and half between superiors within and outside the respondent's own organization.

exception is among the cultural leadership and reflects primarily efforts by professors at negotiation with students. Here, of course, though formally it seems appropriate to view students as subordinate to teachers,

political realities tend to put such confrontations on a plane of considerable equality. Such relations, indeed, have for all concerned much more
the quality of intraelite conflicts or accommodations. In fact, when student
demands begin to be depicted as acts of insubordination, this is usually
a signal that communications have broken down.

The matter of who is a peer or a superior of men of this stature has
been determined in this instance more crudely than was the case when
treating the relative rankings of men within the elite sampling. Peer in
the present case means simply a person of a comparable position in the
same or a parallel organization not formally subject to the respondent's
authority.

The overwhelming reliance on persuasion rather than other means — on
efforts to change the perceptions of alter's goals or values — serves to
fill out this image of the primacy of conciliatory, information-giving, and
esteem-disapproval manipulating activity among men at or near the top.
The explicit threat of authoritative compulsion figures almost not at all
in these interactions. The relatively high incidence within the cultural
sphere (about 12 percent) of threats of violence without institutional
sanction reflects the climate of insecurity and unpredictable threat that
colors life in the university and intellectual work generally (Table 7.5).

Elite goal seeking, then, as revealed in these interactions, is primarily
persuasive in approach and oriented upward toward superiors or toward
peers. Peers here obviously cannot mean persons of identical elite ranking but refer rather to the class of individuals who surround and work
closely with persons of recognized elite status, who occupy similar positions, and who enter into relations with them on a basis of rough equality.
For example, only some senators figure within our elite group. Presumably there are differences in the way highly prestigious senators deal with
one another and the way they might deal with relative newcomers to
senatorial ranks. Nevertheless, for a broad range of actions such junior
individuals and even employees of the legislature without senatorial rank
are not likely to be treated as mere subordinates by senior or more influential men.[171] Such interactions are likely to be even more hazy or
vague with respect to the relative status of actors when they cross organizational or institutional lines, that is, when a senator approaches the

[171] In this respect it is important not to confuse research operations with social realities. The fact that we have given a large number of men "power scores" and then arbi-
trarily designated those above a certain minimum as elite does not mean that we
should necessarily expect to find sharp differentiations in the way men above and
below such an arbitrary line deal with each other.

TABLE 7.5 *Means Applied by Goal-Seeking Actors (Percentages)*

	Elite Sector					
	Political		Cultural		Economic	
Respondents	High (64)	Low (18)	High (25)	Low (12)	High (38)	Low (19)
No. of PRAXES	(144)	(70)	(42)	(47)	(88)	(29)
Money or material inducements	2	1	7	6	19	3
Authoritative command or instruction	17	11	26	6	11	21
Persuasion: efforts to change perceptions, goals, values	62	82	79	89	57	76
Activation of commitments[a]	8	—	2	—	8	—
Use of violence without institutional sanction	8	6	12	13	2	—
Passivity: let time run its course	3	3	—	4	4	3

NOTE: Percentages add to more than one hundred because several means were applied in some instances.
[a] These are primarily commitments to organizations (party, firm) with a few appeals to national loyalties. Loyalties to family, friends, or local community are very rarely mentioned as factors in persuasive efforts.

head of an autonomous government agency or the publisher of a newspaper.

Such reaching across institutional lines is in fact given a very secondary place in these accounts. The nature of interinstitutional power cliques emerging from the sociometric data, as distinct from verbal depictions of past efforts to act politically, has been discussed in the previous chapter. Cliques of this kind exist. But here we find little foundation for viewing this kind of major cross-institutional coordination as a central ongoing function of such cliques.[172] The most common object or referent of reported power attempts here is the organization of the elite protagonist himself (Table 7.6). Approximately one in four such episodes portrays actions intended to produce changes in organizations in an insti-

[172] Arthur J. Vidich and Joseph Bensman, "Power Cliques in Bureaucratic Society," *Social Research*, vol. 29, no. 4 (1962), have elaborated in the greatest detail the operation of such personal networks linking diverse organizations as a common feature of social structure. Anthony Leeds has collected some empirical evidence for the Brazilian case, "Brazilian Careers and Social Structure: A Case History and Model" in Dwight B. Heath and Richard N. Adams, eds., *Contemporary Cultures and Societies of Latin America* (New York: Random House, 1965).

TABLE 7.6   Social Unit which Is Referent of Goal-Seeking Action
            (Percentages)

	Elite Sector					
	Political		Cultural		Economic	
	High	*Low*	*High*	*Low*	*High*	*Low*
Respondents	(64)	(18)	(25)	(12)	(38)	(19)
No. of PRAXES	(144)	(70)	(42)	(47)	(88)	(29)
Organization of actor	47	41	59	64	48	52
Another organization in same sphere as actor	16	20	7	4	12	10
Organization in another sphere	19	23	24	19	23	28
Social unit cutting across organizations[a]	24	20	19	21	18	10

[a] These units are specific population sectors (women, youth voters, the well-educated, and so on) or the general public.

tutional sphere other than that of the respondent. More will be said later about this class of PRAXES. For the moment, the point to note is that most reported actions are directed inward to the main actor's own organization or to other organizations within his institutional sphere.

As transactions fitting mainly within the normal, ongoing operations among top officials of organizations, relevant communications tend to be direct — mostly transmitted through formal institutional channels or on a person-to-person basis (Table 7.7). When indirect pressures are mounted, which happens in about a third of the incidents in the case of political and cultural leaders and somewhat less often among businessmen, efforts are as likely to go toward mobilizing the influence of other individuals or organizations as toward more general appeals to public opinion.

Both the numbers and the extended comments reflect a tendency to search for a resolution of conflicts at the top without engaging larger groups. Even among political leaders only about one in ten power initiatives include references to mobilization of support from broad publics and these allude primarily to elections or general uprisings rather than to support for particular political decisions or policies.

The fact that the referents of most of the actions we are discussing here are specific organizations should not obscure their political or public relevance. This may seem obviously the case with respect to actions

TABLE 7.7 *Channel of Communication Used by Goal-Seeking Actor* (*Percentages*)

	Elite Sector					
	Political		Cultural		Economic	
	High	Low	High	Low	High	Low
Respondents	(64)	(18)	(25)	(12)	(38)	(19)
No. of PRAXES	(144)	(70)	(42)	(47)	(88)	(29)
Direct, personal communication	24	23	19	17	22	14
Personal intermediary	3	3	2	2	8	—
Formal, institutional channel	33	40	45	41	35	48
Mobilizing pressure of organized groups or selected influentials	14	17	17	17	6	10
Agitation, efforts to mobilize mass public opinion	10	11	19	15	3	7

NOTE: Percentages add to less than one hundred because the main channels of communication were not explicitly stated for all PRAXES.

taken within government and the parties but is also true of a great many such actions within the cultural and business sphere, as has been made apparent in earlier portions of this chapter. Classifying the goals of such actions presents many more difficulties than coding any of the other aspects of these confrontations. Given the fact that goal seeking is often singled out as a distinctive human characteristic, the poverty and imprecision of the verbal and analytical tools available for describing or analytically distinguishing among goals is staggering.[173] No very clear pattern emerges with respect to goals in terms of the classification finally adopted (Table 7.8). Percentage distributions vary somewhat from sector to sector and by power level but in general goals range over the full array of categories. These run the gamut from over-all definition of goals (given relative emphasis in the political sphere) through questions of allocation of resources (more salient for business leaders) or to matters of policy implementation, management of personnel, sustaining motivation and commitment, and coordination with outside groups.

[173] In the present case our primary aim was to strike a level of abstraction that could encompass a broad range of organizations and yet represent something more concrete than hypothetical system functions or requisites. This is one of the areas in which we feel our efforts have proved least satisfactory. The deficiency of organization theory in this respect is, of course, notorious.

TABLE 7.8   Goals of Power or Influence Attempts (Percentages)

	Elite Sector					
	Political		Cultural		Economic	
	High	Low	High	Low	High	Low
Respondents	(64)	(18)	(25)	(12)	(38)	(19)
No. of PRAXES	(144)	(70)	(42)	(47)	(88)	(29)
Definition of objectives, programs	25	34	29	17	16	35
Obtaining, generating, allocating resources	15	14	7	26	39	35
Implementation of policies or goals	17	3	10	15	14	3
Management of personnel (training, placement, coordination)	10	11	24	13	23	3
Maintaining motivation	17	16	19	17	19	28
Coordination, alliances with other social units	10	19	5	11	13	3

NOTE: Percentages do not add to one hundred: in most cases several goals were indicated, in a few, objectives were not stated and could not be safely inferred.

However else tensions and animosities may work themselves out in this group, they do not tend to do so in all-out attacks on opponents. Of course, the sampling dwindles as one approaches the extremes of right and left where such inclinations are presumed to be most intense. Still we know from the abundant quotations already reviewed that the group we have reached is deeply implicated in the nation's problems, committed and partisan. It is interesting thus to find here again considerable detachment and discrimination in discussing the motivation of oppositions (Table 7.9). Because this was the case generally even when discussing the impulses behind terrorist activity, it is less surprising here.[174] In any case, whatever other shortcomings the Venezuelan elite may manifest or whatever blocks may exist to more effective, coordinated action among them, paranoid distrust of opponents seems to be a minor impediment to more rational accommodation except possibly in the very top cultural group and perhaps among second-rank politicians.

The most decisive way in which the free-flowing recapitulations of elite .action depart from most conceptualizations of the behavior of the power-

[174] Refer to *SRSP*, Chapter 7.

TABLE 7.9 Attribution of Motives to Alters (Percentages)

	Elite Sector					
	Political		Cultural		Economic	
	High	Low	High	Low	High	Low
Respondents	(64)	(18)	(25)	(12)	(38)	(19)
No. of PRAXES	(144)	(70)	(42)	(47)	(88)	(29)
Principled, legitimate differences of opinion	26	23	5	30	15	14
Individual or group material interest	8	10	12	9	21	17
Individual or group power or prestige interests	25	20	17	17	3	17
Ideological convictions	9	17	17	4	1	3
Evil intent, bad faith, destructiveness	12	27	22	9	11	10
Other motives	9	9	12	8	9	21

NOTE: Percentages do not add to one hundred because information regarding alter's motives was not given for every PRAXIS.

ful and prestigeful is in the relatively low index of successes they report (Table 7.10). Most models of power and influence focus on imbalances in the capacity to affect outcomes and tend to define power in terms of probable control over intended effects. In the incidents covered in these materials political leaders were able to achieve complete or partial suc-

TABLE 7.10 Outcome of PRAXIS from Perspective of Goal-Seeking Actor (Percentages)

	Elite Sector					
	Political		Cultural		Economic	
	High	Low	High	Low	High	Low
Respondents	(64)	(18)	(25)	(12)	(38)	(19)
No. of PRAXES	(144)	(70)	(42)	(47)	(88)	(29)
Complete or partial success	55	46	68	62	64	70
Stalemate	12	17	7	15	16	14
Setback or defeat	29	33	24	24	11	14

NOTE: Percentages fall short of one hundred because the outcomes of a few interactions were not clear.

cess in only about half of their efforts. Cultural and business leaders fared slightly better but only moderately above the chance or fifty-fifty level struck by politicians. When businessmen fail to achieve their goals, outcomes seem to divide fairly evenly between deadlock or stalemate and genuine defeat or setback, that is, cases in which the protagonist not only falls short of this mark but suffers some reversal as a consequence of his venture. The cost of misadventures is higher for politicians and cultural leaders. For them, unsuccessful sallies into the world of action terminate more often in defeat than in impasse.

There is, of course, no outside norm by which such relative "success" rates can be judged for individuals or bodies of elites. However, differences by sphere and power score in this connection are minor and congruent with the differences in decision climate or context in each sphere as they emerge in the extended comments cited earlier in this chapter. Taken together these materials elicit a picture of an elite whose initiatives, whether intended to produce change in their own or in other organizations, are to a substantial degree tentative, circumscribed, and unpredictable in outcome. This may be a more common feature of elite action than one would suppose from examining most formal models or conventional ideas about the behavior of power elites, but we have no basis on which to decide whether the Venezuelan case is atypical or close to others in this regard.

Apart from what they may suggest about the mood, efficaciousness, or levels of confidence among leaders, it is tempting to think of these rates as indicative in some sense of system states. Though guidelines for this kind of assessment are also largely unavailable, it is obvious that from this perspective it is not so much success *rates* but rather the *nature* of successes as against failures that is decisive. Judging the significance of particular successes or failures for specific organizations and even more for a whole political system is plainly a complex matter that can be approached here only in a most tentative way. But if one accepts the notion that a major function of an efficacious elite, especially one oriented toward reformist change, is to generate and maintain linkages among organizations and institutions in order to enhance the system's capacity to manage and absorb desired changes, then it is reasonable to focus in such judgments on the consequences of successes or failures for the maintenance of such social connections. All such linkages in a society like Venezuela are, of course, by no means supportive of social change. Desired changes in many cases require a break in some existing institutional combinations or a forestallment in establishing certain new ones. It is nevertheless and considerable interest to look at the interactions we have been analyzing in terms of their outcome as regards the formation of new bonds among organizations or the production of new cleavages. Tables 7.11, 7.12, and 7.13 summarize respectively the characteristics of PRAXES that end in deadlock, defeat, and success from the point of view of the initiator or main actor.[175] Each of these outcomes seems to have quite different and not altogether foreseeable consequences on interorganizational connections.

To be noted first is that many of these power interactions have no visible consequences of import for the kind of social connections being explored here. In roughly half the cases, and this was true for all sectors, no change in the nature of interpersonal or interorganizational links was noted by the narrators in the accounts of their efforts to act in behalf of or on their own organizations. Nothing can be said with much assurance with respect to how often these omissions are merely cases of incomplete information having been given or reflect a true absence of impact on social bonds. The materials are by no means exhaustive in this regard and the coding is not very refined. Still, it seems both plausible and worth remarking that only *some* of the actions of elite individuals, whether successes or failures, have these kinds of consequences.

The second point of note is that success, failure, or stalemate each has a different probability of leading to a strengthening or a rupture of social ties. It is *deadlocks* or stalemates (Table 7.11) that lead most consistently to outcomes whose implications for social cohesion are difficult to judge (being most often vaguely reported and inconclusive in nature) or that point most clearly to cleavages in old relationships or to the emergence of fresh barriers to concerted action. Repeated or prolonged impasse seems more destructive of social unity than clear-cut failure. In addition, such deadlocks occur more often in the case of politicians and cultural leaders with respect to actions taken within their own organizations whereas businessmen meet with this kind of impasse mainly when they venture out of their own field, generally in approaches to government agencies. In contrast to the typically well-balanced and confident tone that characterizes businessmen's accounts of their dealings among themselves, their descriptions of unresolved conflicts with government bristle

---

[175] These tables summarize listings of concepts or code categories linked to particular outcomes. Similar tables in *SRSP* (for example, p. 183) show the lists of actual linked code words with their frequencies. A simplified, verbal presentation has been preferred here as the mechanics have already been explained and exemplified elsewhere.

TABLE 7.11   *Characteristics of Power Interactions Ending in Deadlock*

	Main Sphere of Protagonist		
	Political 29/214[a]	*Cultural 10/59*[a]	*Economic 10/117*[a]
1. Social unit which was the main referent of action	Action typically aimed at protagonist's own organization. In about one in three cases action was directed externally.	Pattern identical with that noted for political sphere.	Externally directed actions predominate. Pattern exact reversal of that formed in other spheres.
2. Means applied in power attempts	Persuasive argument the principal modality with some manipulation of information and display of disapproval.	Equal mention of persuasion, rebuke, and authoritative instruction as means of obtaining compliance.	Persuasion and economic incentives are the principal means used. The patient waiting out of opposition is also mentioned here.
3. Mode of communication	Direct personal approach mentioned as often as formal channels. Secondary use of other influentials.	Very like political with somewhat stronger dependence on formal channels.	Very heavy reliance on formal channels. Direct approaches and recourse to alternate influentials infrequently mentioned.
4. Motives attributed to alters	Opponents are most often viewed as acting from reasoned preferences and secondarily out of regard for power or ideology.	Desire for power, plausible principles, and evil intent figure equally in estimates of alter's motives.	Bad faith and irrational fears are attributed to alters as often as reasoned rejection.
5. Outcomes in terms of effects on social linkages	Consequences for social ties of deadlocks were codable for about 1/5 of cases. All cases coded indicate new cleavage or rupture of former ties.	Same as for political.	Same as for political.

[a] Proportions indicate the number out of the total PRAXES in each sphere ending in deadlock.

TABLE 7.12 Characteristics of Power Interactions Ending in Setbacks or Defeat

	Main Sphere of Protagonist		
	Political 64/214[a]	Cultural 21/89[a]	Economic 14/117[a]
1. Social unit which was the main referent of action	In a majority of cases the main actor's own organization. Secondarily and in about equal proportions: other organizations of the same type, organizations in other spheres (here mainly government and broad population sectors).	Same as for political. Other spheres in this case refers mainly to government and political parties.	Same as for political. Other spheres here means primarily government.
2. Means applied in power attempts	In about half the cases persuasive actions dominate. In the remainder authoritative command and disapproval or exposure of guilt figure about equally.	Similar to political in priority on persuasion but more emphasis on exposure, disapproval, or ostracism of alter.	Same emphasis on persuasion; information giving preferred over the withholding of esteem or disapproval as secondary persuasive means.
3. Mode of communication	Institutional channels dominant; personal approaches and mobilization of other influentials principal accessory modes.	Agitation and generalized appeals to mass opinion indicated as often as more formal communications. Some efforts to mobilize influential groups and individuals.	Formal channels in almost all cases with some direct, personal contacts.
4. Motives attributed to alters	Power motives most often cited with evil intent and principled positions competing closely for second place.	Evil intent and ideological conviction prominent with rational or principled motives a close third.	Economic motives or legitimate principles highlighted with secondary emphasis on desire for prestige or power.
5. Outcome in terms of effects on social linkages	Codable outcomes (a little better than half the cases) are all cleavage or indicate a failure to establish any new links.	Similar to political with an even greater propensity to further cleavage.	Here alone defeats eventuate in new links almost as often as in further social rupture.

[a] Proportions indicate the number of the total PRAXES in each sphere ending in defeat or setback.

TABLE 7.13 Characteristics of Power Interactions Ending in Success

	Main Sphere of Protagonist		
	Political 111/214[a]	*Cultural 59/89*[a]	*Economic 76/117*[a]
1. Social unit which was the main referent of action	About 2/3 of these actions are directed externally, dividing about equally among similar organizations (parties and government agencies), organizations in other spheres, and broad sectors of the public.	Actions divide about equally between self- and externally directed, and external focus is on diffuse population sectors and noncultural organizations.	Internal/external break as for cultural group but external actions are aimed at other organizations (mainly government and other business firms).
2. Means applied in power attempts	Persuasive efforts first, with the passing on of instructions second and manifestations of disapproval third.	Persuasive efforts first, with information giving, passing on of instructions, and disapproval vying closely for a second place well below that.	Persuasion: information giving, economic inducements, and authoritative instruction all mentioned with equal frequency.
3. Mode of communication	Institutional channels prime mode, backed by personal contact. Pressures from other influentials and mass opinion make up about 1/3 of the channels mentioned.	Modes approximately as described for the political sector.	Formal channels and direct contacts dominant. Infrequent recourse to indirect pressures.
4. Motives attributed to alters	Reasoned position and good intentions perceived in most cases. Desire for power and material gains main other motives.	Principled preferences, material interests, and ideological conviction cited in close order as chief motivation of opponents.	Desire for profit or other economic gain seen as dominant; other reasoned objectives and desire for power cited respectively in 1/3 and 1/4 of the cases.
5. Outcomes in terms of effects on social linkages	About 2/3 of the episodes produce new interorganizational ties or reinforce old ones. In the remaining cases success is won at the cost of new cleavages.	Results approximately as described for the political sector.	Results approximately as described for political sector.

[a] Proportions indicate the number out of the total PRAXES in each sphere that ended in complete or partial success.

with imputations of bad faith and irrationality. They also suggest a heavy reliance or dependence by businessmen on formal channels in approaches to government. It is principally in this connection, and almost exclusively by businessmen, that mention is made of waiting out the enemy as a tactic in handling opposition.[176]

Initiatives that fail similarly lead more often than not to various forms of rupture in social relationships (Table 7.12). However, and particularly in the case of businessmen, reversals are sometimes fruitful in that they lay the ground for later, more rewarding opportunities. The emphasis by businessmen on acceptable economic interests or legitimate principles as factors motivating opponents in this subset of PRAXES helps explain why they are often able to salvage something from such momentary setbacks. This is far less the case with the instances of failure recounted by cultural and political leaders. Themes of conspiracy and betrayal, ambition for power, and ideological rigidity dominate in these episodes. Most of the breaks alluded to by political leaders and within the cultural sphere are tied up in one way or another with the successive schismatic movements and chronic factionalism in parties. These already have been described in some detail in this chapter. It is hard to tell whether the attributions of evil intent that crop up so frequently here are after the fact forms of self-justification or are themselves elements in the chain of reaction leading to failure and rupture. What seems clear is that once motives are questioned and, more importantly, once recourse is had to open manifestations or manipulations of disapproval or to the exposure of error or bad motives in oppositions, the chances of reconstituting connections are practically nil.

Individual and organizational success too has its price in terms of social disruption. One useful outcome of looking at power interactions as treated here is that awareness of this basic fact of social life is heightened. In about a third of the success stories in leadership, an immediate consequence and one not ordinarily foreseen or desired, was some form of social cleavage or disconnection (Table 7.13). Success antagonizes, success alerts other actors to the growing capacity of a political rival, success is sometimes achieved in ways that expose basic weaknesses and vulnerabilities, success stimulates groups once amenable to coalition to try to operate independently. All of these consequences of success can be observed at work in every sphere of elite action in Venezuela but especially in the political.

[176] The encounters in question are primarily between oil company executives and government officials.

Some interesting facets of the nature of success as against failure come to view in this analysis — for example, that politicians fail more often when dealing with their own groups whereas businessmen face setbacks mostly when they venture into other fields, that in describing successes leaders attribute varied but always legitimate motives to oppositions. However, the question of what the success or failure of individual leaders or organizations means for a whole political system is seen to be extremely complex and has been approached only tentatively here.[177]

Nevertheless this long chapter provides both a graphic and differentiated image of the real life context in which Venezuelan leaders must operate and a quantitative appraisal of certain features of their experience as political actors. In these pages the attention of elite informants has been turned inward. These are accounts of *intraelite* relations — of movement within that small world of the mutually aware and prestigious and the sizable circle of people around them who because of their proximity to the powerful are accorded similar forms of deference and consideration. Within this narrow compass, in which powerful individuals turn their efforts on superiors or on others they must treat as peers, a politics of persuasion, compromise, accommodation, and perhaps even excessive caution seems to prevail despite the surface climate of conflict, intensity, and willful or impulsive action. Intuitively one scents the play of unarticulated restrictions on political action at this level, restrictions that are perhaps only vaguely perceived or acknowledged by the actors themselves. The chapter that follows, which turns to elite perspectives on social reform, amplifies the scope of political relationships brought into view. The focus on reform issues brings into the open some of the constraints that seem to be silently at work here. Do the rhetoric and modalities of power change when elite-mass or simply elite-nonelite interactions are at center stage?

---

[177] In the VENUTOPIA numerical experiments (*SRSP*, Chapter 12), a more direct approach to this problem is made by basing measures of over-all states of the system (for example, levels of antagonism, polarization potential) on particular configurations of evaluations by the groups sampled in the survey. A similar procedure could be followed by representing elite individuals as actors in such numerical experiments or simulations.

8   ELITE VIEWS OF THE MASS

An earlier chapter on national perspectives stressed the duality of this research's interest in elite evaluations of the state of the society.[1] Because these are the views of highly placed men, they take on weight substantively in the play of forces that must be considered in calculating the prospects of any development policy. Thus efforts to weigh elite capacity hinge only partially on information about the range of communications and opportunities for confrontation or coordination open to diversely situated influentials or the quality of interactions among such men. These matters have been surveyed in the immediately preceding chapters. At issue as well are equally complex questions concerning the role of knowledge and self-consciousness as modes of self- and collective liberation. The desire to exercise purpose and foresight innovatively stumbles here against the awareness of the social determinateness of such cognitions. The wide-ranging search over the biographies and present context of action of these informants has sought to pin down some such determinants or sources of order in elite appraisals of the world and modalities of dealing with it. Material or class interests, common experiences of change, normative predispositions, interpersonal linkages, and ideological commitments all have been mapped against the main grid of institutional specialization and found to pattern in distinctive ways for men in each sphere of action. But the notion of order is ambiguous here for it must encompass both indispensable simplifications of reality and normative or ideological integrations of standards of judgment as well as rigidities and constraints that make for the persistence and proliferation of irrationalities in collective decisions. How can a people arrive at a sense of the true constraints — objective and

[1] Chapter 7, *SRSP*. The essential points covered there and relevant to the present discussion are summarized in these first pages.

subjective — that need to be accepted in order to maximize certain forms of collective self-realization? Do the world views of Venezuelan leaders support the hope that rational and humane considerations will inform the options formulated for the nation at large? On what grounds is the social scientist to affirm that one or another world view or ideology falls within or outside the range of viable or rational constructions? [2]

In the first overview of these data only the top power group was examined and only differences by sphere were explored. The questions raised had almost entirely to do with what could be gleaned about intraelite relations from the way men in each sector analyzed national problems. Do men in each sector tend to locate major problems outside their own main area of responsibility? Do men in each sphere rank internal problems differently than do outsiders looking in? Is there a particular elite sector with a special propensity to a negative view of the society?

The cultural sector was found to be the only one that stressed problems within its own sphere more than did elite individuals whose main responsibility lay elsewhere. The cultural sector also had a slight edge over politicians who in turn exceeded businessmen in the number of social malfunctions they identified with only very moderate prompting. The relative ranking of issues within institutional spheres, however, proved to be surprisingly uniform irrespective of the informant's main institutional locus.

Substantively, the national problems reviewed in *SRSP* were also all malfunctions located within the middle or upper class, within the most developed sectors of the society. That is, they were issues of elite contention that had to do with the performance, motivation, interests, and values of the social groups most proximate to elite informants. These issues — the basic structure of the economy, the existence of terrorist activity, and the persistence of traditional and humanistic rather than technical orientations in secondary schooling — were not remote abstractions but urgent matters of everyday business for many of the men being questioned. Similarly, the chapter on role evaluations — covering businessmen, university students, and government officials — had reference to evaluations of position in which all informants could see themselves implicated in fairly direct ways.[3]

[2] William E. Connolly, *Political Science and Ideology* (New York: Atherton, 1967), reviews some of these long-standing issues from a timely perspective. In a more psychological vein, Harold Walsby, *The Domain of Ideologies* (Glasgow: William Maclellan, 1947) asks simply: Why do people have so many different ideas on so many things?

[3] *SRSP*, Chapter 8.

That selection of themes, as was made clear, allowed an exploration of hypotheses central to the research but did not reflect the relative weight or priorities of issue concerns among informants. In particular it glossed over the high frequency of mentions of problems seen as rooted in conditions among the mass of Venezuelans — poverty, unemployment, illiteracy, family disorganization, the lack of adequate socialization for modern work or political life. In citing these symptoms elite informants generally made it plain that these were problems at a certain social remove — of concern to informants as responsible leaders, as conscientious citizens preoccupied with national growth and integration, as moral and humane individuals sensitive to the sufferings of the less privileged. Of course, the personal histories of informants had not been untouched by the direct experience of such social mishaps. Nevertheless, the essential point is that in the interview context they were discussing *other people's* problems and that those others were an abstract, disassociated mass observed from a distance. This means, fortunately, that without violence to the data, the discussion of issue perspectives in this chapter can emphasize elite-mass relations just as the immediately preceding chapter on power roles turned out to throw light primarily on intraelite interactions.

Even though the earlier analyses did not bring out details of elite views on mass problems, they provided a preliminary sense of contrasting viewpoints on this score within the elite. Political and cultural leaders, it was said, approached such issues from the stance of individuals actively engaged in deliberately opening up the nation to expanding forms of mass sharing and participation in national life. Economic leaders, though pointing to similar needs in the nation and beginning to embark on a variety of social action programs, spoke much more like persons hedging against being overrun by uncontrolled demands. It was in this political-institutional area, in the task of defining roles in the desired future society for the state and the mass of Venezuelans, that ideological tensions were sensed to be most pointed. Technical solutions, political accommodations, and even more difficult adjustments of values seemed to be within the range of potential consensus on many concrete issues (for example, with respect to the ordering of functions for the university). Hard-core resistance to such adaptations to technically supported information, the realities of political capacities and alignments, or diversity in values (such resistances being tentatively identified as ideological in nature) came to the fore with respect to the basic institutional arrangements that have been mentioned, particularly as regards the scope of state action in the economy. It will be

the task of this chapter to bring out in clearer detail the interplay of views
of present reality, preferences as to future states, and favored options concerning means and main actors as these relate specifically to elite and mass.

Reform Priorities

In the folk wisdom of polling, a variety of theories are regularly invoked
to guide probes into the relative importance of priorities of people's interests or preferences. The most candid, most salient, or the most genuine
response is alternatively affirmed to be the first one given, the one elicited
most spontaneously, the one occurring most frequently, the one elaborated
in most individualized detail, or the one expressed in most affectively
charged language. In an open and prolonged exchange covering issues, however, several of the items mentioned may meet any or several of such
criteria in contradictory ways. In the end, the informant himself may insist
that an issue, belatedly introduced in what could well be taken for an
afterthought, is in fact the one that really occupies first place in his own
thinking. Therefore, no single stratagem for ranking issues is appealed to
in this analysis, though a variety of such indicators of the relative salience
of issues will be treated. As elsewhere, we have selected the approach that
seems to provide as open a context as possible for information giving and
for sifting through all the data obtained in as much detail as is manageable
and useful.

On two counts elite perspectives can be directly compared with those of
the samples taken in the polls run concurrently with this study.[4]
Like all other Venezuelans, elite informants are overwhelmingly optimistic about the future of the nation and the prospects for their children.
Just over half also expect their personal situation to improve. Given the
privileged status of those speaking, there is little reason to interpret much
gloom or pessimism in the responses of the remainder, most of whom expect no change in their personal fortunes, with a few unsure of doing better
in the near future than they are at present. Such lingering uncertainties
about what is to come are not concentrated at any particular power level
or in any action sphere.

This generalized buoyancy of mood cannot be explained by a lack of
awareness of the dimensions of national problems. There is also rough

---

[4] See Volume 3, especially Chapters 6 and 7. The latter treats the question of reform
priorities. No group in the surveys registered under 70 percent optimistic about the
future of the nation or that of their children, or about improvements in their own
situation.

agreement at all social levels on priorities within a tough agenda of reform policies.[5] Among elite groups, as among all those in the CONVEN sample, the creation of new industries and improvements in the quality of education vie for first place. The consolidation of democratic practices through the stabilization of elections uniformly ranked last for every group sampled. Elites, particularly within the economic sector (like business groups sampled in the larger survey) give somewhat greater importance to the effective protection of citizens against violence than do practically all other social sectors, who rank this objective just above last place.

TABLE 8.1 *Reform Priorities by Main Sphere (Percentages)*

	Economic (58)	Political (86)	Cultural (36)
	N =		
Improve the quality of education	64	42	58
Create new industries	55	55	50
Accelerate agrarian reform	41	47	47
Eliminate unemployment	34	28	28
Protect citizens against violence	41	21	19
Construct more housing for the poor	29	15	10
Stabilize the electoral system	17	13	11

NOTE: The table shows the percentage placing each reform in first, second, or third place.

Looking at reform priorities by elite spheres (Table 8.1) provides a first impression of an arresting phenomenon — an apparent concentration on mass or popular needs among the business leadership. Economic leaders endorse improvements in education over the creation of new industries and indicate substantial support for priority efforts toward agrarian reform, the elimination of unemployment, and the construction of more housing for the poor. Only the link between these goals and the accent on protection against violence signals a pattern that is different in ideological tonality from the not dissimilar priority ratings of other sectors. A first appraisal of the ideological substructure underlying this priority set can be obtained from viewing Table 8.2. Though two parties are identified in the table, the intent here is principally to demonstrate patterning of priorities

[5] The question asked of elite informants was, "Here is a list of things that many people believe Venezuela needs urgently. Would you please tell me which you consider to be the most important, which follows that in importance, and so on for each successively until you have ranked all these measures?" The list of policy alternatives is shown in Table 8.1. A slightly modified wording was used in the larger survey.

TABLE 8.2   Reform Priorities by Party (Percentages)

	Left (21)	AD-Gov (31)	COPEI (15)	Independents (84)	Right (29)
N =					
Create new industries	71	65	33	50	59
Improve the quality of education	48	29	40	60	66
Accelerate agrarian reform	81	52	7	45	31
Eliminate unemployment	24	26	53	33	17
Protect citizens against violence	14	13	33	31	38
Construct more housing for the poor	—	13	53	23	10
Stabilize the electoral system	5	19	—	14	21

NOTE: The table shows the percentage placing each reform in first, second, or third place.

on an ideological, left-right dimension and, most importantly, to establish the conservative and rightist connotations of the emphasis on popular, and especially educational, reforms evidenced in the business elite responses.[6] The further to the left one goes the greater the emphasis on the structural changes presumably implicit in agrarian reform and industrialization. At the other end of the spectrum hope is rooted in changing and controlling people. The extraordinary bulge in COPEI ratings for housing can be said to reflect commitment to an electoral strategy rather than a basic ideological orientation. These are obviously the crudest of simplifications, justified only because they introduce rather than summarize an effort to differentiate elite views of a mass population to which, short of a political cataclysm, they are irrevocably bound.

Outside the framework of a forced choice among fixed policy alternatives, a somewhat different but not inconsistent pattern emerges.[7] First tallies of the global characteristics of responses make patent the weight of preoccupation with the condition and capabilities of the mass of the population but do not immediately invite analytical probes in the direction suggested

[6] The same marked emphasis on education and the control of violence is encountered in the responses of elite informants who say their first loyalty is to the family as against those who say they have a primary commitment to the nation.

[7] The long section of the interviews dealing with perspectives on national problems opened with the question, "Would you tell me what you regard as the three or four most important problems the nation faces today?"

by the ranking of policy alternatives already described. The free-ranging identification of problems tells us something different about the particularities of sector views than does the direct plunge into establishing priorities for solutions. In general, "mass" problems are mentioned about twice as often as symptoms of malfunction that point to intraelite tensions or deficiencies. This ratio, contrary to the earlier finding, is slightly lower for businessmen than for other informants. Mass problems, as shown in Table 8.3, have been broken down into human and environmental difficulties.

TABLE 8.3 National Problems: Mass versus Intraelite Referents by Main Sphere of Action

	N =	Economic (57)		Political (84)		Cultural (38)	
Mass Problems			2.64		3.15		3.50
Human		129		226		123	
Environmental		21		38		9	
Intraelite Problems		103	1.82	113	1.34	52	1.37

NOTE: Within the table the actual number of mentions is given to the left. To the right is the average number of mentions per respondent.

The environmental problems cover references to substandard housing and services (power, water, sewerage) as they affect primarily the urban poor. Human problems refer to such things as the instability of marriages, the irresponsibility or incapacity of parents, poverty, illiteracy, unemployment, delinquency, and so on.

The problems tagged here as intraelite issues refer primarily to institutional and organizational deficiencies. They have been so designated on the ground that the allusion is ordinarily to areas of malfunction that are the direct responsibility of elite individuals or persons operating under their guidance. Economic and political breakdowns or insufficiencies are generally described in terms of incapacities or irregularities in the behavior of middle- and upper-echelon individuals (for example, venality, inefficiency, personalism among politicians) or as the result of irreconcilable conflict or misunderstanding among such persons. By contrast, references to human problems in the mass of the population generally point to social conditions and characteristics that incapacitate individuals for productive work or supportive action as citizens at a very primary level. These distinctions are not always clear cut even analytically and have been per-

formed mechanically by computer count in the present case.[8] The objective
has been to make it possible to round out the extensive materials on intraelite relations with data on policy orientation toward problems of leadership and elite appraisal of the quality of the human resources present in the
nation.

TABLE 8.4 *Summary Tally: Mass Problems by Main Sphere
of Action (Percentages)*

	Economic	Political	Cultural
N =	(57)	(84)	(38)
Family disorganization	30	38	71
Substandard living conditions	25	39	16
Illiteracy, poor education	52	65	72
Rural backwardness	21	52	48
Poverty and unemployment	62	110	87
Excessive population growth and migration to cities	27	23	18
Social disorganization, delinquency	25	27	45

NOTE: Percentages are those who mention a given problem as among the three or four
most important confronting the nation.

Looking at Table 8.4 would not set off immediately the kinds of speculation about latent ideological effects inspired by Table 8.1. Businessmen
here, it could be surmised, essentially focus on job factors — wage scales,
unemployment, and education for work. These identical concerns might
be said to dominate even more markedly the thinking of politicians, who,

[8] There is inevitably a certain arbitrariness about the manner in which tallies based
on qualitative findings are performed. When a coding scheme with several nested levels
such as the one applied here has been used, decisions have to be made which in conventional survey analysis are obscured or already fixed in the questionnaire design.
The counts in Table 8.3 are based on the number of times a particular institutional
area was mentioned as problematical rather than on the next lower level of abstraction,
which recorded the exact symptoms of social malfunction cited by the respondent. A
problem arises because there were, for example, only six coded symptoms of family
malfunction but thirty-five for political breakdowns and twenty-seven for signs of
economic malaise. Counting on one level as against another substantially affects the
"results" obtained. In the present case the reported ratio of mass to intraelite references
would be just about reversed if the tally shown in Table 8.3 were performed at the
symptom level. The tally displayed has been given preference partly on the basis of
its congruence with other findings and partly on the basis of other characteristics in
the data dealing with issues. Some of these will come out in the course of the analysis.
The facts noted do not mean that the answer is simply to peel away misleading over-
lays of abstraction until the core of truth in the data is exposed. There is some truth
but also trivia and false leads at every level. Table 8.4, giving more detail on "human"
problems, is pitched at the more concrete symptom level.

however, more frequently indicate preoccupation with rural and housing problems (key areas of commitment for two of the major parties). The cultural sphere might be again revealing, as in the earlier analysis of perspectives, its very generalized concern with the situation of the mass, its readiness to open up problems within its own domain (especially education), and the inclination to highlight moral issues (the decline of the family and other symptoms of social breakdown).

Such institutionally anchored dispositions are probably in fact operative. However, it is of even greater interest that despite the surface differences with the earlier data on preferred priorities for major reforms, much the same configuration of ideologically grounded options and emphases appears here when party alignments are introduced (Table 8.5). Once again it is

TABLE 8.5 *Summary Tally: Mass Problems by Party (Percentages)*

	Left (19)	AD (30)	COPEI (14)	Independents (80)	Right (25)
Family disorganization	21	53	71	45	60
Substandard living conditions	16	43	71	19	32
Illiteracy, poor education	42	50	86	62	92
Rural backwardness	100	83	—	29	36
Poverty and unemployment	120	126	113	78	68
Excessive population growth and migration to cities	10	33	14	21	24
Social disorganization and delinquency	42	23	28	29	28

NOTE: Percentages are of those who mention a given problem as among the three or four most important confronting the nation.

the left end of the party spectrum that most insistently highlights structural factors of unemployment, maldistribution of income, and anachronistic rural institutions, whereas on the right both problems and solutions tend to rest relatively more on the regenerative powers of education and the strengthening of the family. Once again, the duality between changing the system and improving the people comes to the surface.

So far we have only reaffirmed with different data the crude generalization with which the main body of this analysis opened. Within the widely diffused concern with the condition of the mass of the population present in all elite sectors, two major, though by no means discrete, orientations seem to be present. One of these stresses the victimization of the mass by rigidities of the existent framework of social organization. The second dwells on characteristics of this population that imply incapacities in the mass and burdens on the developed sector of the nation. Both sphere and party or ideological factors seem to weigh in inclining individuals to one or another of these major orientations toward the mass. Clearly, in stating priority problems, informants were only opening their arguments, though they may have been providing some clues as to what was to come. The remainder of this chapter will pursue in some detail differences by sphere, by party, and by power level in approaches to both kinds of formulations of the elite-mass problem.

None of the foregoing should be taken to imply that individuals, by and large, focus on either VICTIM or BURDEN problems exclusively. But as the following tally by party demonstrates (Table 8.6), there is a definite tend-

TABLE 8.6   Summary Tally: BURDEN *or* VICTIM *Mentions by Party*
           (*Percentages*)

	Left (21)	AD (31)	COPEI (15)	Independents (84)	Right (29)
N =					
VICTIM mentions only	37	12	27	12	3
BURDEN mentions only	—	—	—	12	21
Mention both	29	45	40	24	34
Mention neither	34	42	33	52	42

NOTE: Refer to Table 8.9 for a list of parties included under the left and right designations.

ency for exclusive mentions of one or another set of problems to cluster at the extremes of the ideological spectrum. This suggests that even when both types are mentioned there is likely to be a dominant tonality to the comment.

At issue here, of course, is a fundamental feature of self-image among elites and a keystone of any ideology or theory of political development. As a result of the consolidation of elite power in countries where democracy has survived longest, such groups have come to be widely regarded as the most genuinely dynamic and innovative force and as the guarantors of continuity in national systems. In this view, the vital functions of the gifted, the expert, and the entrepreneurially able require that they be shielded from mass pressures. This means most concretely that the mass must not be available for casual mobilization by interlopers or dissidents.[9]

Such elitist ideas have been absorbed readily into theories of development in which a variety of elite types figure as hero whereas the mass appears as a dead weight or as a permanent, explosive menace. Even within the Marxist stream, where the place of the proletarian as protagonist of national liberation might be taken to be most secure, the penetration of elitist ideas has not been absent. In Venezuela, the preoccupation with the psychology of the mass and the alleged primitiveness of its political responses antedates contemporary disputes about development strategies.[10] In 1963 it seemed that every possible hypothesis about capacity and potential responsiveness in the mass was being entertained and acted on by some elite sector. Political parties, labor organizations, national and internationally based community development experts, terrorists, military action teams, the Church — all were actively engaged in diverse efforts to capture mass support for various forms of activity alleged to be of first importance for the nation and for the mass itself. What ideas supported such disparate approaches to the same group of human beings?

The section of the interviews on national perspectives was specifically intended to bring out the quality and substance of elite orientation toward such problems. Although the interview guide for this section did not presume or rigidly impose a fixed order on discussion, very specific landmarks were established for interviewers in guiding exchanges. These landmarks or checklists constitute a rough definition of the essential components of an ideology or world view. The degree to which elite thought would in fact manifest such coherence and structure was, of course, an open question. Whether or not the structures revealed would coincide with generally familiar and formally elaborated ideological constructions was a second open question. In any case, the interview opened with an invitation to list serious symptoms of malfunction in the society (that is, a statement of belief about the state of the system with an implicit indication of preferred future states). It went on to probe ideas concerning the causes of the presence and the persistence of symptoms (theories of how the system works) and the nature of actions to be taken, including details about the principal agents of such actions, the resources required, time spans involved, and the consequences of such initiatives (rationales and strategies

[9] A compact and wide-ranging overview of these problems is given in Peter Bachrach, *The Theory of Democratic Elitism* (Boston: Little, Brown, 1967). The ideas about elite-mass access are from William Kornhauser, *The Politics of Mass Society* (Glencoe, Ill.: The Free Press, 1959), who is cited at length by Bachrach, pp. 42 ff.

[10] Refer to Chapter 2, pp. 55–58.

of action). A final portion of the conversations, often inconclusive, pressed for a sense of personal involvement in actions intended to eradicate malfunctions or bring about desired future states. This final component of commitment is most elusive, and it probably most clearly separates those diagnoses that may be appropriately taken as ideological statements from others of more questionable or indirect political weight.

Mass as VICTIM Problems

The few tables shown so far in this chapter have presented only counts of the incidence of certain symbols or codes denoting mass problems. The relevant parts of the interviews have been reduced to lists of such words or symbols in a manner that retains some of the logical relationships among such concepts as they occurred in the interviews.[11] Among other things, this technique permits a very rapid listing of all the concepts or symbols associated with any single code word by any particular group. Tables 8.7 to 8.9 show such summary tabulations of all coded ideas linked to the set of problems we have been calling "mass as VICTIM" symptoms. Such a tally provides a good first sense of the over-all configuration of response in a group's total commentary on a given theme. It also provides clues to patterned internal divisions of opinion within groups as well as from one group to another. Comprehensive listings of associated words such as these can be produced in a matter of seconds in response to a simple command from a computer console.

A glance at the figures in the left-hand margins (stubs) of Tables 8.7 to 8.9, where the ratio of respondents to VICTIM mentions is given for each analytical group, conveys clearly the relative emphasis such problems receive from one interview subset to another. This ratio is two to one for political figures and about one to one for businessmen, with the cultural group falling just about dead center between them. A similar range is present in the array of responses from left to right as based on party alignments, with the groups from center to left giving twice as much attention proportionally to symptoms that point to the damage being done to individuals by social conditions as do those on the right.

However, what the tallies of linked words dramatize most is the remarkable symmetry of views among those from all spheres who agree that VICTIM problems merit the highest priority. There are hardly any differences observable, for example, between economic and political leaders

[11] Details are given in *SRSP*, Chapter 6.

TABLE 8.7 *Linked Associates of Mass as* VICTIM *Problems* (*Elite Spheres of Action*)

Elite Group	Nature of Action		Agent of Action		Consequences for System		Time Span		Resource Availability		Resource Type		Causes	
Economic 57/61	PRIZE	21	STATE	61	REFORM	93	UNDER 5	17	ENOUGH	24	ECOMAT	51	MARX	24
	STUDY OR CHART	15	BUSINESS	18	CHANGE	8	5-20 YRS	44	AVAIL	39	DRIVES	25	STYCOS	19
	BEGET	13	PEOPLE	5			OVER 20 YRS	39	NUEVOS	31	TECNIC	13	WARREN	19
	CUEIN	12	ELITE	4					ABSENT	6			PARSON	17
	RULES	11											SCHUMP	11
	ROUSE OR ENROL	11												
Political 84/176	PRIZE	23	STATE	60	REFORM	94	UNDER 5	28	ENOUGH	15	ECOMAT	47	MARX	30
	STUDY OR CHART	14	BUSINESS	16	CHANGE	6	5-20 YRS	34	AVAIL	70	DRIVES	16	WARREN	23
	CUEIN	13	ELITE	9			OVER 20 YRS	38	NUEVOS	11	TECNIC	26	STYCOS	21
	RULES	13	PEOPLE	5					ABSENT	4			PARSON	16
	BEGET	13											SCHUMP	7
	ORGAN OR TWINE	9												
Cultural 38/57	CUEIN	18	STATE	84	REFORM	85	UNDER 5	16	ENOUGH	50	ECOMAT	20	PARSON	33
	STUDY OR CHART	18	BUSINESS	11	CHANGE	15	5-20 YRS	8	AVAIL	7	DRIVES	32	MARX	25
	PRIZE	15	ELITE	4			OVER 20 YRS	76	NUEVOS	39	MEDIA	22	WARREN	25
	BEGET	14							ABSENT	4	ORGANS	17	STYCOS	6
	RULES	11									TECNIC	7	SCHUMP	5
	ORGAN OR TWINE	11												

NOTE: Mass as VICTIM problems include poverty, unemployment, maldistribution of income, scarcity and substandard quality of housing, lack of public services in urban slums, and backwardness of rural institutions. In the figures below the group headings, the number before the solidus indicates the number of respondents in the group; the number after the solidus indicates the total mentions of VICTIM problems by that group. Numbers in the table indicate the occurrence of each symbol in association with VICTIM problems as a percentage of the total mentions of each subset of symbols as associates of these problems. This in effect takes as the unit of comparison within the table everything each group said about VICTIM problems, adjusting in this way for the differences in the volume of interview output on this subject from group to group.

TABLE 8.8 Linked Associates of Mass as VICTIM Problems (High and Low Power Scorers)

Elite Group	Nature of Action		Agent of Action		Consequences for System		Time Span		Resource Availability		Resource Type		Causes	
High power scorers 131/224	PRIZE	18	STATE	58	REFORM	94	UNDER 5	15	ENOUGH	33	ECOMAT	38	MARX	29
	BEGET	15	BUSINESS	18	CHANGE	6	5–20 YRS	33	AVAIL	41	DRIVES	23	WARREN	23
	STUDY or CHART	14	ELITE	9			OVER 20 YRS	52	NUEVOS	22	TECNIC	17	PARSON	20
	CUEIN	13	PEOPLE	5					ABSENT	3	MEDIA	11	STYCOS	15
	RULES	12									ORGANS	9	SCHUMP	7
	ORGAN or TWINE	9												
Low power scorers 48/74	PRIZE	28	STATE	84	REFORM	86	UNDER 5	38	ENOUGH	8	ECOMAT	43	MARX	27
	STUDY or CHART	17	BUSINESS	8	CHANGE	14	5–20 YRS	19	AVAIL	49	DRIVES	27	WARREN	23
	CUEIN	15	PEOPLE	3			OVER 20 YRS	43	NUEVOS	36	TECNIC	14	STYCOS	20
	NORMS	11							ABSENT	8	ORGANS	13	PARSON	17
	RULES	9											SCHUMP	10
	ORGAN or TWINE	8												

NOTE: Refer to note on Table 8.7.

TABLE 8.9 Linked Associates of Mass as VICTIM Problems (Political Groups)

Elite Group	Nature of Action	Agent of Action	Consequences for System	Time Span	Resource Availability	Resource Type	Causes
Left 19/45	PRIZE 16 CUEIN 16 RULES 15 BEGET 13 ORGAN or TWINE 12 STUDY or CHART 13	STATE 81 ELITE 8 PARTY 6 PEOPLE 4	REFORM 87 CHANGE 13	UNDER 5 44 5-20 YRS 44 OVER 20 YRS 11	ENOUGH 19 AVAIL 38 NUEVOS 29 ABSENT 14	ECOMAT 35 DRIVES 31 LEGAL 19 MEDIA 11	WARREN 33 MARX 28 STYCOS 7 PARSON 7
AD-Gov 30/77	PRIZE 25 STUDY or CHART 13 CUEIN 13 RULES 13 BEGET 13 ORGAN or TWINE 12	STATE 48 ELITE 23 BUSINESS 16 PARTY 5 PEOPLE 4	REFORM 98 CHANGE 2	UNDER 5 31 5-20 YRS 18 OVER 20 YRS 51	ENOUGH 17 AVAIL 73 NUEVOS 6	ECOMAT 49 TECNIC 38 DRIVES 9	MARX 28 STYCOS 28 WARREN 17 PARSON 15
COPEI 14/26	PRIZE 33 STUDY or CHART 22 RULES 12 CUEIN 8 ORGAN or TWINE 8 NORMS 6	STATE 53 BUSINESS 19 PEOPLE 8 CHURCH 7 PARTY 5	REFORM 100	UNDER 5 7 5-20 YRS 29 OVER 20 YRS 64	ENOUGH 8 AVAIL 75 NUEVOS 8 ABSENT 8	ECOMAT 45 DRIVES 36 TECNIC 9 ORGANS 9	MARX 30 PARSON 23 STYCOS 19 WARREN 17
Independents 80/99	PRIZE 20 STUDY or CHART 15 RULES 14 CUEIN 13 ORGAN or TWINE 13 BEGET 12	STATE 73 BUSINESS 10 PARTY 10 PEOPLE 6	REFORM 73 CHANGE 26	UNDER 5 10 5-20 YRS 37	ENOUGH 56 AVAIL 36 ABSENT 8	ECOMAT 57 DRIVES 35 TECNIC 8	WARREN 30 MARX 30 PARSON 25 STYCOS 7
Right 25/34	PRIZE 18 ROUSE or ENROL 17 BEGET 15 STUDY or CHART 15 CUEIN 14 RULES 5	STATE 64 BUSINESS 20 ELITE 6 PEOPLE 3	REFORM 90 CHANGE 8	UNDER 5 10 5-20 YRS 15 OVER 20 YRS 75	ENOUGH 35 AVAIL 13 NUEVOS 50 ABSENT 2	DRIVES 27 MEDIA 25 ORGANS 22 ECOMAT 17	WARREN 24 PARSON 23 MARX 22 STYCOS 14

NOTE: Refer to note on Table 8.7. Left here includes Unión Republica Demócrata (URD), Left-ist Revolutionary Movement (MIR), the Communist Party of Venezuela (PCV), and supporters of Admiral Wolfgang Larrazabal. The right includes supporters of Arturo Uslar Pietri, the Venezuelan Association of Independents (AVI), and other independents.

with respect to the kinds of actions required, who the main agent of such actions should be, the relative time span within which recommended actions are likely to produce results, and even with respect to the major causes behind existing inequality of material advantages. The principal differences between the two sectors evidenced at this level have to do with the availability and nature of the resources required to do the job. The cultural sector, by contrast, takes a more distinctive stand, stressing more than others the role of the state, the importance of research and planning, and the central place of education as elements in breaking existing molds of institutionalized poverty. They are less sanguine than men in other spheres about the time it will take to effect meaningful change, much more concerned with factors of motivation, communication, and organization as basic resources in an efficacious attack on inequalities of income, opportunities for work, and living conditions generally. Their view of causes gives weight to social over political and economic factors as elements in maintaining the present situation.

Later pages will bring out the substance and quality of these differences in the words of the informants themselves. Obviously, many shadings of perspective are present both in response patterns that strike one here as quite similar and in those that at first view signal the presence of disaccord. Still, on the basis of these global tallies of links, it seems reasonable to infer tentatively that VICTIM problems are salient for substantial numbers in each sphere, and that this shared concern is supported by broad consensus with respect to major aspects of strategies for solutions. Focal points of tension with respect to policy are more visible in power level and party patterns of discourse on VICTIM issues.

Differences by power level convey a sense of urgency and a pressure for a mobilization of resources among low scorers that is absent at the very top. There is, however, no particular tendency among those lesser in rank to accent VICTIM problems more than do those above them in the power hierarchy. Nor do they stress any special order of causes or courses of action, except to insist more often on the quick provision of material assistance and incentives in the solution of the problems of the poor. The primacy of the state's responsibility is almost undisputed among these second-level leaders. Their time schedule for the achievement of reform (under five years for nearly four in ten low-scoring informants) is consistent with their call for a large-scale mustering of new resources. Interestingly, whenever a group has a high percentage affirming that the resources to tackle a problem are already available (ENOUGH), they are also likely to think a solution will take considerably longer than do groups that are counting on the allocation or generation of new resources.

But the most suggestive differences, because they bring out the sharpest cleavage of opinion, come to the fore in the tallies by party. The most crucial divergences lie in the time estimates for reform action to achieve effects. Twenty years or more is the modal expectation among all but the leftists. Wide differences are also registered in the proportion who would give groups other than the state prime roles in bringing about changes. Those with centrist orientation prescribe greater diversity in such agents whereas the two ideological extremes assign the responsibility for action almost entirely to the state. From no political perspective do more than a few respondents call for the poor themselves to take a role in working out their own future. Calls for basic changes as against extensive reform are few and come from both the far left and right. However, on the left they are coupled with demands for massive investment and quick results whereas on the right the claim is that change can be achieved with present resources albeit over a substantially longer time.

Mass as BURDEN Problems

In shifting to a review of code symbols present in the discussion of BURDEN problems, it is worth reverting to Table 8.6 to obtain a clear sense of what this represents in terms of the corpus or subset of informants whose ideas are under examination. The third row of that table (56 respondents mentioning both VICTIM and BURDEN symptoms) figure in both the tallies in Tables 8.7 to 8.9 and in those to which we now turn (Tables 8.10 to 8.12). Individuals in the top row (VICTIM mentions only) drop out here and the second row is picked up (BURDEN mentions only). However, for all those included in the present tabulations, the data under consideration are fresh in the sense that we are not building on general responses to policy issues but exclusively on the symbols or concepts directly associated with BURDEN symptoms by the respondent in the course of his conversation. It should be clear that there is overlap of people but not of the textual material under analysis except insofar as the respondent may himself have chosen to generalize.

The ratios in the stubs reflect this shift of persons and topics. The cultural sphere comes into its own here with nearly twice as many references to BURDEN problems per respondent as other spheres. As with the earlier tables for links, there are no differences by power level in these mention

TABLE 8.10   Linked Associates of Mass as BURDEN Problems (Elite Spheres of Action)

Elite Group	Nature of Action	Agent of Action	Consequences for System	Time Span	Resource Availability	Resource Type	Causes
Economic 57/75	CUEIN 26	STATE 43	REFORM 95	5–20 YRS 24	ENOUGH 50	ECOMAT 35	PARSON 29
	PRIZE 19	BUSINESS 13	CHANGE 4	OVER 20 YRS 76	AVAIL 25	DRIVES 35	MARX 24
	RULES 16	PEOPLE 9			NUEVOS 25	TECNIC 30	WARREN 15
	NORMS 16	EDUCATORS 8			ABSENT 5		DURKH 7
	STUDY or CHART 11	FAMILY 7					
	ORGAN or TWINE 10						
Political 84/138	CUEIN 19	STATE 47	REFORM 100	UNDER 5 6	ENOUGH 9	ECOMAT 43	PARSON 32
	PRIZE 16	FAMILY 10		5–20 YRS 65	AVAIL 61	TECNIC 37	MARX 27
	STUDY or CHART 15	BUSINESS 9		OVER 20 YRS 29	NUEVOS 30	DRIVES 16	WARREN 20
	NORMS 14	PEOPLE 7				ORGANS 4	DURKH 6
	ORIGIN or TWINE 14	CHURCH 7					
	RULES 13	EDUCATORS 6					
Cultural 38/98	CUEIN 30	STATE 53	REFORM 97	UNDER 5 8	ENOUGH 35	ECOMAT 24	PARSON 33
	NORMS 17	BUSINESS 11	REMAKE 3	5–20 YRS 25	AVAIL 12	TECNIC 13	MARX 25
	PRIZE 14	PEOPLE 8		OVER 20 YRS 67	NUEVOS 53	DRIVES 45	WARREN 17
	ORGAN or TWINE 13	ELITE 7				ORGANS 5	STYCOS 10
	RULES 10	EDUCATORS 6					
	STUDY or CHART 10	CHURCH 5					

NOTE: Mass as BURDEN problems include instability of marital unions, incapacity of parents to raise families properly, illiteracy and low education, delinquency, uncontrolled population growth, mass migrations into the cities, and other problems of social disorganization. In the figures below the group heading, the number before the solidus indicates the number of respondents in the group; the number after the solidus indicates the total mentions of BURDEN problems by that group. Numbers in the table indicate the occurrence of each symbol in association with BURDEN problems as a percentage of the total mentions of each subset of symbols as associates of these problems. This in effect takes as the unit of comparison within the table everything each group said about VICTIM problems, adjusting in this way for the differences in the volume of interview output on this subject from group to group.

TABLE 8.11 Linked Associates of Mass as BURDEN Problems (High and Low Power Scorers)

Elite Group	Nature of Action		Agent of Action		Consequences for System		Time Span		Resource Availability		Resource Type		Causes	
High power scorers 131/213	CUEIN	23	STATE	42	REFORM	97	UNDER 5	5	ENOUGH	21	ECOMAT	37	PARSON	33
	PRIZE	15	BUSINESS	13	CHANGE	3	5–20 YRS	49	AVAIL	54	TECNIC	32	MARX	26
	NORMS	14	PEOPLE	9			OVER 20 YRS	46	NUEVOS	25	DRIVES	22	WARREN	16
	ORGAN or TWINE	14	EDUCATION	7									STYCOS	5
	STUDY or CHART	11	FAMILY	7										
	RULES	11	CHURCH	7										
Low power scorers 48/78	CUEIN	24	STATE	66	REFORM	97	UNDER 5	8	ENOUGH	17	ECOMAT	32	PARSON	30
	NORMS	18	EDUCATION	6	RETURN	3	5–20 YRS	40	AVAIL	22	DRIVES	45	MARX	24
	PRIZE	15	PEOPLE	5			OVER 20 YRS	52	NUEVOS	57	TECNIC	19	WARREN	24
	RULES	14	FAMILY	5					ABSENT	4	IDEOL	3	STYCOS	7
	STUDY or CHART	14	CHURCH	4										
	ORGAN or TWINE	9												

NOTE: Refer to note on Table 8.10.

TABLE 8.12 Linked Associates of Mass as BURDEN Problems (Political Groups)

Elite Group	Nature of Action	Agent of Action	Consequences for System	Time Span	Resource Availability	Resource Type	Causes
Left 19/20	CUEIN 18 NORMS 18 STUDY or CHART 15 RULES 13 PRIZE 13 ORGAN or TWINE 13	STATE 80 FAMILY 12 EDUCATORS 4	REFORM 100	UNDER 5 3 5-20 YRS 2 OVER 20 YRS 2	ENOUGH 1 AVAIL 1	ECOMAT 1 DRIVE 1	MARX 37 WARREN 37 LENIN 10 PARSON 16
AD-Gov 30/48	CUEIN 23 PRIZE 18 STUDY or CHART 16 NORMS 12 RULES 12 ORGAN or TWINE 10	STATE 73 BUSINESS 12 LABOR 9 EDUCATORS 3 FAMILY 3	REFORM 100	UNDER 5 9 5-20 YRS 55 OVER 20 YRS 35	ENOUGH 1	ECOMAT 1	MARX 33 PARSON 24 WARREN 18 LENIN 6
COPEI 14/28	CUEIN 18 RULES 18 PRIZE 18 NORMS 14 ORGAN or TWINE 11 STUDY or CHART 9	STATE 42 CHURCH 17 PEOPLE 8 FAMILY 7 ELITE 5	REFORM 100	5-20 YRS 100	AVAIL 69 NUEVOS 31	ECOMAT 41 TECNIC 43 DRIVES 16	PARSON 30 MARX 28 WARREN 18 DURKH 13
Independents 80/117	CUEIN 25 NORMS 18 PRIZE 15 RULES 12 STUDY or CHART 12 ORGAN or TWINE 9	STATE 39 BUSINESS 13 EDUCATORS 10 PEOPLE 8 FAMILY 8 CHURCH 5	REFORM 98 CHANGE 2	UNDER 5 2 5-20 YRS 21 OVER 20 YRS 77	ENOUGH 32 AVAIL 27 NUEVOS 37 ABSENT 3	ECOMAT 31 TECNIC 20 DRIVES 38	PARSON 34 MARX 23 WARREN 17 DURKH 6
Right 25/51	CUEIN 27 ORGAN or TWINE 19 PRIZE 16 NORMS 12 STUDY or CHART 11 RULES 8	BUSINESS 42 PEOPLE 17 EDUCATORS 11 ELITE 8 STATE 8 LABOR 5 CHURCH 5	REFORM 89 CHANGE 11	UNDER 5 3 5-20 YRS 72 OVER 20 YRS 25	ENOUGH 54 AVAIL 18 NUEVOS 28	ECOMAT 3 TECNIC 3 ORGANS 3 DRIVES 1	PARSON 41 MARX 23 WARREN 16 SCHUMP 5

NOTE: Refer to notes on Tables 8.9 and 8.10. The italicized numbers are raw frequencies which are given when there are too few cases to warrant percentaging.

ratios. However, the relation of mentions to ideological lineup is reversed.
Informants on the right are twice as likely as those on the left to dwell at
length on these instances of human failure in the mass. As will be recalled,
an exactly contrary tendency was observed with respect to mentions of
structural rigidities making for inequality.

A similar broad consensus on prescribed actions is present here from one
action sphere to another, though emphasis on all fronts shifts to educational efforts, with the provision of material means or incentives taking a
second place. Though the state still tends to overshadow all other recommended agents, there is a consistently broader assigning of roles to diverse
groups with respect to this family of problems. Sociological and economic
interpretations prevail in all spheres with political causes being cited in
fairly close third place. Again one can observe the peculiar relation in
which the affirmation that necessary means are at hand is coupled with
the anticipation that solutions will be a long time in coming, whereas the
more remote the means the greater the optimism about a timely success.

As regards power levels, no differences of any account are to be observed
in these tallies except a greater insistence on state action and an apparent
reluctance to concede much of a role to business in the job of cultural and
moral regeneration that is mapped out by those in lower echelons. Ideological differences on these moral and cultural issues are also more diffuse
and complex, hinging most decisively on disagreements about the principal agents rather than on ideas about correct actions. Economic causes
are highlighted on the left whereas social factors lend anchorage to rightist
rationales of the dynamics underlying breakdown in the institutions of
socialization.

Ideas as Clues to Actions

The impression conveyed by the summary tallies — that policy dissensus
among groups with widely divergent views does not particularly center on
prescriptions for action — is not found to be misleading when the rather
abstract code for types of action is put aside and the textual replies themselves are considered. In various ways informants themselves recognize
this. The more self-conscious among them, aware that they are hardly
breaking new ground in action recommendations, find ways to acknowledge
this and to insinuate or affirm other bases of uniqueness or distinctiveness
in their position or that of the group for whom they are presumed to speak.

I think this type of solution is in the minds of people of different parties.
I don't believe we have a monopoly over it. The difference lies in the presen-

tation of problems and, of course, in the presentation of solutions. . . . The timidity [in other groups], not to judge them harshly, was due to the fact that they thought this might bring them into a face-to-face political show-down. . . . Those opposed are the ones our people call the "it can't be done" family — all those who said it could not be done because of the money . . . because it was a demagogic promise; in short, all those who had a defeatist attitude before the magnitude of the solution.[12]

People say, "No, that cannot be done. That is done badly." And when they get into power they do it exactly the same. A corn muffin [*arepa*] is made in only one way and whoever tells you that he is going to do it another way is no more than a demagogue. When he has to make *arepas*, he becomes convinced that there is one formula and not two.[13]

Speaking honestly, many of the solutions of [party] are not exclusively its own heritage. Our party does not have a monopoly over them. They belong to other organizations as well. What I am sure about, and I am stubborn in upholding, is that I do not believe other groups . . . put the same sincerity or wholesome objectives into the application of these ideas.[14]

Thus one may learn more about the policy implications of the views of men of power from the language in which they diagnose a problem than from the specific kinds of action for which they call. The VICTIM-BURDEN duality in looking at the mass turns out indeed to be more than a mere arti-fact of the coding or a feature of aggregate units that proves elusive when individual cases are sought in order to provide examples. Each view comes through in succinct statements devoid of ambiguity as well as in more com-plex combinations in which a substantial part of the total argument must be reviewed in order to get a clear sense of where the balance lies. How-ever great the overlap in action suggestions may be — particularly in the many cases where both VICTIM and BURDEN symptoms are discussed in the same interview — the way the balance inclines will be shown to have a very distinct relation to perhaps even more critical dimensions of policy such as resource allocation and the timing and intensity of action. The gulf that separates these two appraisals of the situation of the oppressed majorities in the country by men at the top is rarely made as clear as in the contrast between the quotations that follow. It is of some importance to keep in mind that even when the lines are less dramatically drawn the apparent impact on policy orientation is equally great.

But there is another kind of violence, which is the violence generated by

[12] Interview 011033, pp. 83, 84.

[13] Interview 062177, Part B, p. 129. Though this statement seems the most dogmatic of the three cited, it is close to the empirical facts. Despite the general agreement as to necessary action, criticisms of previous policy focus almost entirely on the allegation that wrong actions were taken in the past.

[14] Interview 102195, p. 28.

social injustice, by the problem of underdevelopment, by the poorly developed economic structure, and these are permanent problems. The fact that there exist here more or less two and a half million rural families that receive no attention from the state, the fact that there exists a high unemployment rate, the fact that there is great misery and hunger is not the immediate problem of violence . . . but is a structural problem. This one really requires an immediate solution.[15]

Well, the campesino is the victim. No responsibilities can be demanded of the campesino because the country has done very little for him. The campesino is cannon fodder for recruitment, the provider of servants to good families, provider of raw material for the amorous debuts of young dandies in the cities, victim of the landowner. The campesino is the most exploited group, the most tightly corralled, the one that has suffered most the heartlessness of men and nature. They cultivate the little they can, what they know. They do what they can.[16]

Our campesino is a *conuquero,* an individual who has no idea what agriculture is. Nor is he an individual who loves nature. He is an individual who was born in the country, who plants corn in the primitive way, but when he plants corn he doesn't know why or how it's done in one way rather than another . . . he is a completely primitive raw material. It's for that reason that I fear so much the plans for agrarian reform, if we are going to carry it out on the base of our present campesino. I believe the present generation of our campesinos is a lost generation and that all the government's efforts toward a true and effective agrarian reform should be carried out thinking about the children of campesinos, that is, in educating them. . . . To attempt to educate a present campesino to convert him into a farmer is a labor that would cost too much money without any true benefit.[17]

The assertion that a whole generation of rural Venezuelans — amounting to a substantial proportion of the national population — be put aside as unsalvageable is rarely stated as baldly as in the interview just cited. But the blanket indictments of the society made by the other two informants are also rare. Quoting at considerably greater length from an interview with a legislator from one of the parties in the "democratic" (nonviolent) opposition will convey more realistically how both BURDEN and VICTIM themes are interwoven in more thoughtful diagnoses. It is important as well to note how in this mingling of concerns one set of images (in this case the VICTIM theme) remains dominant.

Any observer can see that the population of Venezuela is a young one and that any national policy . . . cannot ignore this fact. I am dubious about the

---

[15] Interview 064186, p. 49.
[16] Interview 110191, p. 35.
[17] Interview 033091, p. 86. The *conuquero* is a seminomadic squatter who practices subsistence farming.

attention it has been possible to give this problem, though I recognize that there have been both legislative and executive measures such as the law defining as a crime the neglect of a child's nutrition and the law for the protection of the family, both intended to meet these problems. In Venezuela there is a very high birth rate . . . every year more than 300,000 children are born, and, according to data for the last few years, more than 150,000 of those children have unknown fathers. This phenomenon of illegitimate birth occurs primarily among the population strata who are most defenseless economically, in the population sectors with the least general culture, where the integral and coordinated action of public power has not made itself felt. This problem is very serious not only because these children who are among the poorest class begin to grow with notable deficiencies of diet, but also because the need among mothers to work in order to survive . . . makes them separate themselves from children at an early age, without providing the necessary training and affection that the child should have. How often do we read in the press about tragedies produced by the imprudence of children in situations in which the mother, in order to earn something, must leave the children at home, often putting infants in the care of four-, five-, or seven-year-olds. Then there is the cultural problem, even though in Venezuela after the decree of June 27, 1870, primary schooling is free and obligatory and this government in the five years between '59 and '64 has preoccupied itself very much with the extension of education. Still, the percentage not in school . . . because of economic reasons is still very high. Children who cannot buy books, decent clothes, sandals (*alpargatas*), or shoes. . . .

For this reason we have thought a form of beginning to develop a policy for the protection of children could be through a family subsidy . . . even if it were not national to begin with but could grow progressively, selecting first the most impoverished areas. . . .

The juridical provisions tending to protect children must be completed and at the same time the official bodies dealing with children who grow up with such antisocial tendencies should be improved and modernized. They should receive a much larger part of the budget than, for example, the Consejo Venezolano del Niño gets today. . . .

This problem of children who grow up abandoned comes to light in many of them in antisocial expressions. . . . They are children who have received no moral training, and their very poverty . . . and the environment in which they grow pushes them progressively toward delinquency. Most of these are juvenile delinquents . . . because they have not had the opportunity to be useful. . . . Many of those who are adolescents or young men in 1963 did not as children have a school within reach . . . and also they get nothing out of going to school to acquire theoretical knowledge if they cannot get a useful job. In this sense the multiplication of schools of arts and crafts, technical-industrial schools . . . could be a great contribution to finding a path for these youngsters, the majority of whom possess a great natural intelligence and, of course, a great precociousness. . . .

We have to face the necessity of regularizing consensual unions in Venezuela. It is necessary to distinguish here between out of wedlock children
(*hijos naturales*), who are the fruit of occasional or very transitory unions,
and those who are born to more or less permanent consensual unions (*uniones
concubinarias*). Here, unfortunately, even though since the discussion of the
Civil Code of 1916 there has been insistence on the need to regularize consensual unions . . . , of course with state control and satisfying certain obligations with the public registers through the action of priests . . . , it has
not been possible in the small towns and in the rural areas to do anything
really positive nor has a publicity campaign been carried out to persuade
people of the need to move from concubinage to marriage. There are unquestionably bad social effects, above all in these sectors of low culture. People
have a . . . union which lacks only the formalities to be a marriage, who
have the sense of monogamy, the sense of fidelity, of fathers who meet their
obligations to their children, but who think they shouldn't marry. This is
fundamentally a male prejudice because they feel the woman will be spoiled
by marriage. The woman acquires certain rights, because the situation of
concubinage is always provisional. Thus it seems to them that on getting
rights through marriage, something that had been functioning more or less
regularly and peacefully might go wrong.[18]

Characteristically, and even though this informant was deeply involved
in an unsuccessful legislative fight to establish income subsidies for poor
families, respondents find it difficult to explain what array of political
forces stands on each side of these issues. No clear opposition is identified,
but the focal point of controversy is said to lie in the clash between those
who want to mount a massive, centralized attack on these problems and
others who, as this legislator puts it, "are still thinking in terms of canasta
teas." As has already been seen in Chapter 7, private sector efforts have
in fact gone well beyond the level of charitable teas and are supported by
a well-elaborated ideology with international ramifications. More will be
said on this presently. For the moment the point to be noted is that the
root source of dissensus is quite consistently felt to have to do with resources, and that opposition, or at least a diffuse resistance, is perceived
as coming from the business sector by almost all propounders of the
VICTIM thesis.

I don't believe there are groups in opposition with respect to this problem.
The difference lies in that some want this centralized in the state and others,
although accepting national planning, want private individuals as well as the
state to contribute to the solution.
If by sacrifice [in order to mount a massive push on housing and employ-
ment] you mean the need to invest, which I do not believe to be the case,

without doubt it is the most powerful economic sectors that would have to make sacrifices, particularly those economic sectors who are too much influenced by the profit economy and at the same time have very conservative, almost avaricious ideas about money.[19]

The unfailing optimism about the future registered by Venezuelans of all conditions is hard to square with the expectations of disaster that all associate with inaction or insufficient action in this sphere, especially because few seem really to believe that action on the necessary scale will be taken.

> Inattention to these problems will produce . . . disastrous consequences for the country . . . , all of which follow from the lack of a correct availability of material means for large sectors of the population . . . because these masses who are today impoverished, who are underconsumers, who are unemployed, have been very patient until now. But we have no guarantee that they will be able to continue bearing with such calm and so much patience a burden that is so heavy.[20]

Part of the answer to this seeming dissonance lies in the fact that among VICTIM theorists, apocalyptic anticipations are accompanied by an overwhelming faith in the powers of social transformation. If the basic conditions of a man's life are changed, he will be "resurrected." As man is inherently worthy and whole, his prime needs are for self-awareness and audacity.

> The Venezuelan population grows at a faster pace than do industry and commerce and all sources of employment . . . and because economic development is carried out in a more technical way than the cultural development of the general population . . . a large part of the population presenting itself for work does not have sufficient training.
>
> When political democracy gives man freedom and with freedom the awareness to each citizen of his own problems, this means that every unemployed person can reason on the basis of his hunger and his need. When the mind reasons for a stomach that is in misery, the result is explosive.
>
> The campesino is both the object and subject of the problem. They are the fundamental object because the campesinos are men who are richest in the miseries of the nation, but they are also subject because to the degree that the campesino is incorporated into the active citizenry, is incorporated as an element of economic value, and is incorporated as a political power, in that same degree he will contribute more to his own benefit and that of the country.[21]

[19] Ibid., pp. 5, 26.
[20] Ibid., p. 16.
[21] Interview 011033, pp. 77, 78, 100.

The scale and intensity of action have more than a technical relation to the magnitude of the problem being attacked. In themselves they express and generate a state of mind.

> Above all it is necessary to give each defeated man the sensation of resurrection. It is a matter of style that has a strong influence on these matters, so that the solution in time depends on the courage, the style, and the audacity of those who govern.[22]

When a VICTIM theorist focuses on BURDEN problems, there is a reverse adjustment or accommodation of time perspectives. That is, the expectation of quick success by decisive action on a grand scale toward major structural changes goes with a great tolerance and patience for momentary setbacks or slow gains with respect to the stubborn process of re-educating the victims of neglect and deforming social experiences.

> Unemployment is a serious problem that stems basically from the economic structure of the country and has an impact on the life of the entire nation. Our unemployment is not like that of developed countries . . . but results from the incapacity of a people to intervene in the process of change of the nation. We have not had schools, we had very high illiteracy, there was no technical education in the schools. . . . It is commonplace that when we ask a Venezuelan what he knows how to do, he replies, "Anything." That is because the person who knows how to do anything is the person who knows how to do nothing.
>
> The agrarian reform is also a reform of man to teach him to live, to teach him to use his capacity to advantage, to put him in conditions proper to a human being so that he can learn the forms of hygiene that will help him to avoid illness, so that he can learn the forms of social sharing that will help him to work with others. This is something our people do not know.
>
> We have a tenth of the technicians we need. Therefore, it's not a matter of having a technician there but rather of a permanent insistence, a permanent education that slowly changes people. If you put a technican at all times behind each campesino, a moment will come when he will unlearn rather than learn as a result of this pressure. That is, the pressure produces a negative attitude toward the technician. He [the campesino] has to be convinced slowly, he has to be changed through the normal influences of friends, work-mates, of the person who directs groups, the leaders. For this reason I have given very great importance to the formation of leaders in rural areas and in the cities and have insisted that the teacher must have a function in the community he serves.
>
> The campesino . . . has lived long years without schools, without sanitation, without human attention, very close to the animals. It is only a short time back that campesinos began to receive attention. . . . Thus the

___
[22] Ibid., p. 80.

campesino changes as a function of the help he is given. Their manner of cultivating the land was the only one they knew; they could do nothing more
because they knew nothing more. No one had taught them anything else.[23]

A number of recurrent themes of the contrary BURDEN thesis are exemplified in the first string of comments by a leading business statesman. To
be noticed is the general sense of satisfaction with the pace of present efforts to produce change, the great caution about risking strains on the
economy by excessive demands on capital resources and the wealthy, a
harking back to an alleged historical heritage of social virtues centered in
the family, and in describing the better qualities of the mass the stress on
their patience, stamina, and great capacity to endure hardship cheerfully.

> I believe that the intellectual improvement of our people is achieved by
> what we are trying to do, that each year there be more children enrolled in
> primary schools, in secondary schools, to make education accessible to the
> largest number of persons. Now within that one also has to see what kind
> of education [is given]. We gain nothing by the mass production of *doctores*
> . . . that is, lawyers, engineers, and physicians who have been the traditional
> *doctores* in our country. I think we need to . . . train specialized draftsmen
> for our industrial development. We gain nothing by importing a boy from
> a farm village unless he is a tremendously intelligent lad who manages on
> his own initiative to reach the university. Normally we should provide him
> an education useful in the setting in which he is going to develop.
>
> You know that income taxes have increased considerably over the last
> three years. I believe that in these things it is necessary to wait a bit to see
> what happens in actual practice. That is, if we see that the rate of growth
> of the gross national product and industrial and economic activities of the
> nation continue to progress, then there is no doubt that the income tax is
> not ruining them. But I think naturally that a certain trial period is necessary.
> I don't think a country can, let us say, change income tax rates every other
> year because then people don't know what to count on.
>
> Now, I want to be very clear about something. I believe the government
> has the obligation to see that all Venezuelan children receive [an education]
> and the obligation to provide the means for that education to reach those
> children. But I am a great believer that the parent is in the last instance
> the person who chooses the way of educating his children. And in that I am
> very categorical because I believe it is a fundamental principle in the unity
> of the family, and it is on the unity of the family that all that social develop-
> ment will rest, because if the country loses those foundations it will move
> slowly toward the bestialization of its citizens.
>
> We are obliged to direct our education toward guarding our traditions, our
> historical heritage. . . . I don't believe we can suddenly renounce all that
> and permit the imaginations of our youth to be captured completely by

[23] Interview 062177, pp. 109, 112, 113, 115, 183.

unorthodox ideas. I believe we have the duty to demonstrate to our youth that we are not children of the cave . . . that we have a heritage of nobility and dignity that has characterized us throughout our republican era and that we simply have to take pride in that, and no person is going to come suddenly and try to infiltrate our youth with strange ideas that in no way defend the interests of youth or the nation in which they live.

I believe that the rural Venezuelan really is a good man, *par excellence.* The Venezuelan campesinado [who] makes up almost half of our population is an individual who should get the most attention. We have to see with how little that individual has lived. One has to see that this man has been content with no more than is indispensable to his subsistence and despite that he continues to be charitable, he is still friendly. . . . Many countries would like to have a rural class like ours, and it is for that reason that we always seek to improve their conditions.[24]

Such idealization of the mass, which depict it as docile and undemanding in its natural state, are coupled to another theme that is insinuated in this first citation by the allusion to the subversion of youth by unorthodox ideas. This is the theme of the susceptibility of the mass to demagogic appeals. In the quotation that follows, the comment on the political gullibility of the mass is taken as a springboard to a more current image in which demographic growth is visualized as a cancerous proliferation of the basest elements in the society.

The tendency to stay in power or to win power is to offer things free. You win the vote of the majority telling them that you are going to give everyone a family income subsidy, that everyone will get a house.

The population of the plains [*llanera*] . . . is the population with most defects in Venezuela, because it is a population that inherited and suffered malaria and hunger for very many years. By reason of the elimination of malaria it is this population that is growing most rapidly today. The populations . . . in which family structure is more important, in which there is more tradition, such as the people of the Andes, for example, have a much lower growth rate. . . . There [in the *llanos*] there aren't even families. There are women who have children and do not know exactly whose they are.

That population that has the most defective family structure and who physically is most defective is growing faster than the other Venezuela . . . , the population of people of the lowest quality is growing fastest.

There is no doubt that illiteracy is very widespread. On the farm [*hato*] it is not possible to give instructions to anyone . . . ; they don't even know numbers and it is a tremendous handicap. You can't even leave a written instruction there. . . . Those people from the *llanos* can do hardly anything with their hands. They can barely ride or rope a steer . . . because they are not even the good horsemen that history has told us about. They are mediocre

[24] Interview 335283, pp. 21, 22 (Part A) ; pp. 3, 15–18, 24 (Part B).

and extremely careless. I think one of the great problems of Venezuela is the great indolence. Where it comes from, I don't know. Perhaps it's a result of bad nutrition.[25]

BURDEN problems here are not so much explored and delimited as a way of estimating the magnitude of resources required but rather depicted as simply beyond the reach of any array of resources reasonably to be imagined. Setbacks tend to be read less as signs of mistaken approaches and more as certification that no solutions are really available.

I believe that an agrarian reform with the granting of lands and eventually a little credit does not solve the problem because of the same educational defects. Even the functioning of the civic mechanisms within a democratic system require an educational level more adequate than we have.

Growing unemployment and abundant unemployment have historically been the source . . . of totalitarian type regimes, and I believe Venezuela would not be an exception to that. A sizable mass, impoverished, concentrated in the cities, would follow any proposition . . . if it offered a prospect of a solution even though it may be very remote.

With this construction of superblocks [high-rise, low-income housing] . . . , maintaining minimal conditions of sanitation . . . was extremely difficult. It was a problem of education. They were not used to community living, having someone above and below, and that if the stairway was clean it was clean for all. . . . They used to throw garbage down it and then they had to go up a dirty staircase.[26]

Paradoxically, as has been remarked earlier, this tendency to view BURDEN problems as both critical and perhaps insurmountable goes with considerable complacency with respect to present levels of effort and investment rather than calls for intensification of action.

The obstacle is the money that is needed for all these things. But every day new foundations are being developed by people who have been successful in business. I know of one foundation that has donated a house, resources for the blind. . . . I believe good work is going on, but this cannot be achieved in a day. The people of means in Venezuela, or the rich, however one wants to call them, are becoming aware that something has to be done for the old, the blind, and the ill. . . . But all this takes time. This is new in Venezuela, these forms of charity in an organized way.

Nothing more can be demanded of the government. Recently I read that in the last five years in Venezuela more has been done than in the last twenty or twenty-four years. . . . The government is doing things, private indi-

[25] Interview 075233, pp. 16–20.
[26] Interview 067202, Part A, pp. 39, 59, 70.

viduals are acting. I believe we are all helping to solve this general problem the country has.[27]

Various strands of the emergent criollo version of an ideology of business-class social action are present in the final extended citation that follows. Prominent are the central concern with education and the rehabilitation of the family, the admixture of moralizing and sociological interpretations, the very tentative acceptance of technical-professional approaches, the reliance on human relations therapies, the detachment of the analysis of problems of individual socialization from the economic context of family breakdown and educational failure.

I would say the number one problem is educational. . . . From this all the rest derive, because from it derives the family problem. I believe that one of the most serious situations we have in Venezuela is the lack of an organized family structure which produces what cannot be considered anything less than a catastrophe or tragedy . . . , the abandonment of children. . . . If we had had an education, a culture that was better structured, we wouldn't have such weakness in family structure . . . and we would not have abandoned children on the scale that we do.

[The abandonment of children] is a consequence. . . . It will in turn produce a series of harmful results, but it is not a cause. It is an effect of a problem which is the lack of education.

The problem of education in all its phases . . . moral education, religious education . . . , seems to me to require conformity in man's behavior to a set of norms that exist in even the most primitive cultures and that I deduce are not being satisfied among us judging by the number of abandoned children.

I believe the violence is one of the more or less acute manifestations of this fundamental thing which is the lack of organized family structure. . . . They are all young people who have not or ought not to have . . . left the family environment. Many of them are still or ought to be under the jurisdiction of the *pater familiae*.

I would like to be enough of a historian and a sociologist to be able to give an intelligent answer. I perceive only the fact. I believe it is the fruit of our years of civil war, of anarchy, of the juxtaposition of groups of very different origins that have not integrated . . . culturally. On the contrary, the shock of these very cultures caused them to abandon their own cultures in the absence of anything to grasp.

What is absurd is the abandonment of the child . . . of the family. That is what does not exist, I believe, not even in Africa nor among our indigenous people. It exists rather within this somewhat cosmopolitan and absurd society that we have been creating. . . . For this reason we have to give them

[27] Interview 010031, p. 77.

back values through an educational process containing ethical, moral, and religious aspects.

This means, first, the impossibility of transmitting what one does not have. That is, if the child does not receive that family culture, he cannot transmit it. Second, not having anything on which to anchor a scale of values, not feeling protected by a family circle even in the weakest moments a human being has, must create in the individual an attitude . . . of defense and rejection of the society that has not defended him and has rejected him. Third, the very fact that he has lacked that initial protection of the family means that he has not had anyone to induce him to enter through the normal channels that incorporate an individual into society, which are a series of human relations within the group.

The first step toward a solution is to have the problem recognized and to have it receive the importance it merits. I think these two things have been achieved. From that point on the technicians, the experts in education, the sociologists . . . will start finding solutions. I find it difficult to propose concrete solutions different from the social worker. I see it almost like . . . a national crusade . . . in behalf of man . . . of human solidarity.

I don't believe it will be through an institution or a state organism that the problem will be solved. . . . I am not going to say that those organisms are not necessary. They are very much needed. They are efficacious, though one might hope they were much more. But . . . they have the coldness of professionalism and it seems difficult to me that a problem of this nature and dimensions . . . could be resolved on the basis of professionals pure and simply.

I, who am part of the directorate of Fé y Alegría [Faith and Joy] . . . , contribute the possibility of the participation of persons without institutional responsibility . . . that permits immediate contact and not mediated awareness on the basis of cold statistics . . . on the percentage of children not in schools.

I don't believe the family can be created in months. . . . But I believe the education of the child is one of the most interesting paths for the education of the family . . . through the pride the family may take in the fact that any of its children is acquiring an education.[28]

The connection of BURDEN problems to economics is not made here as a starting point or cause as among the VICTIM theorizers. Moral and cultural dilemmas overshadow economics until the very end, when it is revealed that the resurrection of man by man at this extreme of the ideological spectrum also means the resurrection of markets, consumption, and production. The mystique of community development as the road to a happy economy is another keystone of the social action theories of the new, involved entrepreneur.

[28] Interview 004013, pp. 53–59, 63, 70–72, 77, 78.

Everything that a man receives as a gift he fails to appreciate, whereas everything the community by uniting its forces achieves for itself is invaluable. In my view . . . the only true solution in the long run is to promote community development. This is all incalculable, above all the chain reaction that is produced on certain occasions by raising educational levels in this integral fashion of which I have spoken. Small industries begin to be born, artisanry develops. . . . I would regard as the golden seal, as the final point of this solution, the cooperative. . . . In this sense it is not only the individual who feels himself master of his destiny, who values his human dignity because he knows he is skilled and can produce and values, moreover, the united effort of the community, which is no less than the resurrection of man by man. Moreover it is an immediate influence on the progress of the whole country . . . new markets, new consumption, more production. That is, all economic levels are raised. That is the path.[29]

Ideologies of the Mass

The bodies of thought that have been described display many of the characteristics of ideologies in content, organization, and style. The analytical framework (see pages 251 and 258 in this chapter) guiding this effort in "perceptual clarification" seems to have been successful in eliciting revealing expressions of points of view with an internal order and coherence that justifies talking about them as ideological.[30] These elements of coherence and order are not all to be associated with correctness or elegance of style. Bias, oversimplification, emotive language, adaptation to prejudice — all contribute recognizably to the patternings of thought and value that have been reviewed. Close attention to the forms of analogy and metaphor invoked has been especially rewarding.[31]

Perhaps the most impressive feature of the totality of the materials on elite perspectives of the mass is the marked absence in them of the mass as main actor in any kind of role, and especially as an independent agent of anything. All allusions to mass action are hypothetical and contingent on events few leaders seem prepared to predict. The mass is expected to break into action either when its patience finally runs out, when the feared demagogue arrives to mobilize it, or when it is galvanized by the revolutionary or reformist leader yet to come. Alternatively, the mass will come

[29] Interview 031089, Part A, pp. 62, 63.

[30] William E. Connolly, *Political Science and Ideology*, offers the term "perceptual clarification" for the much needed effort to study how ideologies can be formulated, presented, and criticized in responsible ways.

[31] Clifford Geertz, "Ideology as a Cultural System," in David E. Apter, ed., *Ideology and Discontent* (New York: Free Press, 1964) discusses engagingly these stylistic features of ideological formulations.

into its own by a long process of re-education, by in effect ceasing to be a mass and merging into the middle-class norm of education, work, and propriety. No sense is obtained here that any elite sector reached feels itself directly under mass pressures even though its own social theories or mere instinct tell it to act to forestall such pressures or prepare to meet them because they are inevitably coming. To this extent both the VICTIM and BURDEN perspectives are theoretical formulations only minimally tested in action by the men who state them. Sustained contacts with the mass are rare among respondents, and even among the politicians, who have more direct ties and experiences of this kind, encounters between mass followings and leaders by all accounts conform more to traditional, personalistic patterns than to the idealized formulations of left and right that have been examined.[32] We have not been talking in this chapter about how mass and elites interact but about elite ideas of what the mass is like and how it should be approached.

The two generalized perspectives on social change as it relates to mass populations that emerge here parallel but also overlap more formalized party ideologies. They also cross-cut institutional sectors, though one of the two views has been appropriated and elaborated by the business sector and its growing political and social action arms. Surface agreement on needs, goals, and modalities of action masks radically different levels of commitment as regards the pacing of reforms, the volume of investment in the redressing of inequalities, in root beliefs about causes and responsibility as well as about the capacity of people to change or continue to endure deprivation and inferior status. Though this patterning is clear, it is also complex and does not imply a clearly demarcated array of opposed forces. Each of these ideological subsets operates as well under different forms of constraint, internal change, and political capabilities. The compulsion to act of VICTIM ideologists exposes them to greater risks of visibility, failure, and accountability than the more elusive countergroup whose byword is caution. Surface signs of consensus imply impasse rather than a promise of action, as groups range themselves on both sides of too many issues. If the most dangerous future for Venezuela is the continuation of the status quo, almost any resolution of this conflict may be preferable to continued accommodation and deadlock at the top.[33]

[32] Some formalized evidence on leadership patterns at the local level in rural party and syndical units is presented by John R. Mathiason in "Political Organization and Attitudes among Venezuelan Campesinos," unpublished Ph.D. dissertation, Massachusetts Institute of Technology, 1968.

[33] Refer to Volume 3, Chapter 9.

9   THE "INVISIBLE" ELITES

Taking multiple perspectives on elite behavior is one response to the obvious limitations on studying the workings of power, influence, and the making of decisions through the scrutiny of the lives of a restricted number of notables, however selected. Each of the foregoing chapters has brought into view part of the field of elite thought and action. But what if this searching sequence of observations has simply by-passed critical actors or failed to uncover or correctly interpret the nature of connections among elite individuals, elite subsectors, and the realization of national goals? [1]

Elite studies are routinely expected to reveal latent or concealed networks of power. Elite research unsuccessful in this respect is likely to encounter the suspicion that it has only skimmed the surface of power relations. In the present case the grounds for such concern are compounded by several circumstances. Some patently key figures (chiefly military officers and the top officeholders in proscribed parties) were not reached by interviewers. Supplementary studies of United States businessmen and diplomats, initially visualized as an integral part of the research, were realized only partially. Obviously these are not random losses. Therefore, much more is at stake than rounding out a slightly incomplete picture or shoring up the reliability of study statistics. Sectors widely alleged to be exercising veto power over government action and explicitly perceived by many elite informants as the source of decisive constraint on national options eluded open confrontation with the study team. As will be seen, the significance

[1] Some interesting suggestions in this connection, very much in line with the open approach taken in this research, are offered by Charles Kadushin, "Power, Influence, and Social Circles: A New Methodology for Studying Opinion-Makers," *American Sociological Review*, vol. 33, no. 5 (October 1968).

of this information loss and the availability of compensating sources varies substantially from one to another of the groups not reached.

It should come as no surprise that the inaccessible and the reticent are concentrated among those elite actors whose behavior needs most to be understood in order to arrive at some sense of the relative autonomy of national decisions. Clearly this autonomy is seriously compromised if effective control over many decisions is external to the nation or is very narrowly concentrated within it (that is, is responsive only to the desires of a very restricted segment of those articulating collective aspirations). In short, the questions of the possible degree of military dominance, of the presence of clandestine armed opposition, and of dependency on the United States must be dealt with here, however impressionistically. Such questions have become extremely complex and need to be pressed well beyond the simple uncovering of improprieties or acts of prepotency in the political conduct of military men or United States officials or business interests.[2] The matter of dependency in particular has taken on altogether new dimensions and promises to become the critical issue of the 1970's in Latin America as the realization grows that, although older forms of external domination have been superseded more subtle forms of penetration are rapidly taking hold. It is by no means clear, in addition, that those who have the greatest stake in consolidating new forms of dependency fully grasp the process they are promoting in a piecemeal fashion.[3]

Whatever the real weight of the direct action of the military, terrorists, or the United States may be on specific events, there are additional subjective factors to be assessed. Major political actors measure their own

[2] A recent study of the *golpe* that ousted Pérez Jiménez in 1958 states blandly in the introduction: "There is no useful evidence to suggest that the United States played *any* role concerning Pérez Jiménez in 1957 and 1958, and none worthy of credence that private American interests did so, either." (Italics in the original.) It is hard to know just what such a statement means or how political analysis is advanced by writing central actors out of the script in advance. If it is meant merely to absolve the United States of conspiratorial complicity, it may be relevant, but is still not a substitute for more realistic analysis of the U.S. presence. See Philip B. Taylor, Jr., *The Venezuelan Golpe de Estado of 1958: The Fall of Marcos Pérez Jiménez* (Washington, D.C.: Institute for the Comparative Study of Political Systems (ICOPS), 1968), p. 2.

[3] Refer to Helio Jaguaribe, "Dependência e autonomia na América Latina," paper presented to the Second General Assembly, Latin American Social Science Council (CLACSO), Lima, October 1968. A particularly lucid exposition of the dependency issue in the light of the early exhaustion of import substitution and integration as viable roads to national autonomy can be found in Luciano Martins, *Industrialização, burguesia nacional e desenvolvimento* (Rio de Janeiro: Editora Saga, 1968). See also the several essays in *La dominación de América Latina* (Lima: Francisco Moncloa Editores, 1968).

conduct and are perceived to be doing so in terms of appraisals of the capacity and disposition to act of these "veto" groups. During the period studied, the governing party (AD) in particular offered rationales for its own policies couched in these terms. The party was widely pictured as pursuing a course of action that was little more than a desperate struggle for survival in the face of contrary pressures from all these fronts.[4]

Whether such adaptation is taken as indicative of a mature pragmatism and political adroitness or merely as evidence of political exhaustion and cowardice, the fact of ostensive deference to power blocs lying outside the legally constituted machinery of decision making compounds the elements of subjectivity in political choices. Guesses about the limits of tolerance of the military or of Washington are bound to vary as widely as the motivation to test these limits. Misreadings of intent and unity of purpose among self-designated and marginally legitimate monitors of the political process may lead to the self-imposition of unnecessary constraints on political initiatives. Once such constraints are accepted, it does not take long for the conditions that objectively validate them to materialize. The defection of youth and intellectuals from AD and its loss of mass support in the cities have been largely explained in these terms.

The pages that follow, then, are not just an effort to track down and unmask hidden power wielders who eluded the net of interviewers. A considerable amount of information about these more inaccessible groups — the armed forces, the U.S. "community," and the insurgent left — was obtained in the course of interviews with respondents in the formal sample as well as with special informants within or close to each sector. All respondents gave appraisals of the military and of the impact on Venezuela of foreign influences. The matter of terrorism as a public issue has been treated elsewhere.[5] Although some of the top leadership of these groups may be reluctant to open themselves to the probing interrogation of social scientists, this does not mean that they do not seek other ways to manifest political preferences and intentions. Much of their action is by no means hidden from view. Nevertheless, the analysis that follows is a necessary venture into areas where the data and adequate guides to their interpretation begin to dwindle. Still, the depiction of Venezuelan elite action pieced together thus far would be gapingly incomplete without some

---

[4] See the section on government leaders in Chapter 7. Some of the ideas on subjective constraints elaborated here were first spelled out by Julio Cotler in an internal memorandum on Acción Democrática.

[5] *SRSP*, Chapter 7.

attention to the overshadowing presence of external and domestic power blocs not formally within the political arena.

The Armed Forces

In 1963 there were approximately 33,000 men in the Venezuelan armed forces (army, 16,000; navy, 5,000; air force, 3,000; and national guards 9,000). Three additional bodies of national police (Digepol, a political police; PTJ (Policía Técnico Judicial), a technical, investigative corps similar to the U.S. Federal Bureau of Investigation; and a traffic police) shared the mission of maintaining order and countering armed opposition to the government. Four national ministries were thus involved in the government's efforts to control insurgency in the countryside and terrorism in urban centers — Defense, Communications, Interior, and Justice.[6]

The police bodies were all relatively new (post-1958), inexperienced, untrained, poorly paid, and precariously equipped. Elite respondents tended to deprecate police efficiency when they were not outright pitying in tone. Barely literate recruits were pictured as unfairly pitted against terrorists with college diplomas in a political struggle beyond the comprehension of its most frequent victims. Twenty-six policemen were killed and fifty-five wounded in Caracas alone during 1962. Alternatively, incidents of police brutality and arbitrariness were explained in terms of the difficulty of managing undisciplined men inured to cruelty and driven by fear. USAID teams and police missions from other countries were striving to improve police organization and investigative techniques along with equipment in order to beef up the effectiveness of these forces against the urban tactical units of the Communist and MIR parties. Thus, behind the overlay of international ideological contention and modern technologies of insurrection and repression, the protagonists were acting out a drama familiar in Venezuela's past — one in which dissident sons of the bourgeoisie were brought into deadly confrontation with the very men whose liberation they claimed to desire. Police organization in Venezuela had by the early 1960's still not come very far in human terms beyond its primitive models established in the framework of nineteenth-century *caudillismo*.

The brunt of casualties in the government's defense were thus being borne by newly created police forces with low morale, limited resources, no

---

[6] Much of the factual material on the national security apparatus given here is taken from the *U.S. Army Area Handbook for Venezuela* prepared by the Special Operations Research Office.

visible political weight, and ambiguous political support. At the same time the traditional armed forces, especially the army and national guard (Fuerzas Armadas de Cooperación) were gaining public prestige, material rewards, and professional self-respect as the true guarantors of the security of the regime and nation. Despite the fact that officers in both these services as well as the small navy had been implicated in attempts from both the right and left to overthrow the Junta Patriótica and depose Betancourt, the regime's survival was insistently, and apparently with persuasive effect, interpreted by the government and military spokesmen as evidence of a new professionalism, "institutionalism," and dedication to democratic values within the several officer corps. This dramatic change in relations with the armed forces between the first and second AD governments is attributed by an informant who was very close to events in both periods to a wise change in Betancourt's tactics in dealing with the military.

> Instead of treating them like enemies, he has sought to draw them to him. The military policy of Betancourt has the following features: flattery, giving them homes, better salaries, giving national prominence to military ceremonies, introducing technology into the armed forces, and surrounding himself with military men who were slighted for being against Pérez Jiménez or pro-AD and promoting these men rapidly.[7]

Although these measures may have circumvented threats from within the armed forces against the present government and thereby also won applause for the military for their civic responsibility, such techniques do not seem realistically to encourage the kind of withdrawal of the military from politics that would put power securely in the hands of civilian politicians. It is, of course, those who are politically active and not in uniform who would most like to see the military disappear from the political arena. But clearly large sectors of the public continue to approve a role in politics for the military; many others will go along depending on the ideological coloration of the military group reaching openly for power, and many who on the surface lament the prepotency of the armed services nevertheless see them as a bulwark against greater evils.[8] The most common mark of elite comment on the military is the combination of mild reproach with the openness to the possibility that the armed forces may independently exercise wholesome political functions given the right circumstances.

[7] Interview 424315, p. 31. These aspects of AD military policy in its second ascent to power are documented in the *U.S. Army Area Handbook for Venezuela,* especially pp. 531 ff. and 547. Here and in the following quotations, six-digit numbers indicate interviews with Venezuelans. Three-digit numbers identify U.S. respondents.

[8] CONVEN results on this point are given in Volume 3

[My evaluation of the armed forces is] positive, but I don't see why we need as large an army as we have nor why we need such expensive equipment. For example, why do we need submarines? It's something beyond my understanding, and I have many other ideas about the military. But basically I believe that in the Venezuelan milieu and the Latin American milieu in general they serve an extremely useful function, though it may be just a necessary evil to balance certain political tendencies of the extreme left.[9]

The military who have seized power by force in many cases were not oligarchs nor bourgeois and for that reason . . . they should have had the notion that what was needed in Venezuela was the application of social change. Unfortunately, we lacked a Nasser in Venezuela. It is not that I am at all a Nasserist, but I observe that Nasser being a soldier realized that his country needed social change and is bringing it about.[10]

The armed forces have always had great influence and one never knows when they will have it again. So this is a public that also needs to be kept informed. Moreover, it is a public at the present time infiltrated by an almost sickly nationalism. This then is another thing I believe we need to fight over and discuss and not be afraid to say — that nationalism is fine up to a certain point but that there are harmful forms of nationalism.[11]

The range of appeals and demands on the military thus covers the full political spectrum, and in the years since the fall of Pérez Jiménez vigorous moves from within the armed forces have come from both extremes.[12] Although the country may congratulate itself on having avoided a regression to the raw militarism of the past despite the pressures of a combative insurgent challenge, it seems premature to talk of a new institutional equilibrium in which a stable and nonpolitical role for armed groups has been established.

Of the twenty officers who were nominated for interview within the formal elite sample (none of them was reached), eleven were lieutenant colonels and five were colonels. Only three were generals.[13] This would be consistent with the tactic attributed to Betancourt of assigning younger staff officers in his confidence to strategic command posts. These men were in their middle forties at the time; practically all had had some U.S. training. Although these men did not provide information on themselves,

[9] Interview 408306, p. 37.

[10] Interview 409313, p. 91.

[11] Interview 407305, p. 49.

[12] Edward W. Gude reviews attempted *golpes* from right and left in "Political Violence in Venezuela, 1958–1964," paper presented at the Annual Meeting of the American Political Science Association, Chicago, September 1967.

[13] Efforts to obtain authorization to interview the selected officers ground to a halt at a high level in the Ministry of Defense. No individual approaches were made.

some idea of their relative isolation from other elite sectors can be gained from the sociometric tests in which other elite informants had a chance to indicate degree of friendship, frequency of communication, activities in common, and kinship with the military figures reputed among knowledgeable civilians to be among the most influential. The proportion of sociometrical choices directed toward these military officers from other elite sectors was notably lower than that among other sectors. The figures suggest practically no communication between top officers and the cultural sector and very selective contacts with businessmen and politicians.

Nor is there any suggestion in the data of gradual incorporation of military men into the business sphere as they move toward the end of their careers. In part this may be a matter of training and experience, for the group now at the peak of their careers represents the first cohort with technical and managerial skills that might be transferable to the business world. Whatever the case may be, the over-all impression remains one of relative impermeability and aloofness even vis-à-vis highly placed civilians.

Cleavages within the military are by all accounts more significantly linked to factors of age, training, and regional origin than to ideology as such, though older officers are invariably reputed to be steadfast conservatives. The generational break overlaps considerably with the regional factor of Andean influence still markedly present within the middle and upper military ranks. The control over key command posts, recruitment, and advancement as well as political influence by Andeans within the military was momentarily broken in 1945 but reimposed with the ascent to power of Pérez Jiménez. The much vaunted "institutionalization" of the armed forces after 1958 consisted basically of the displacement or marginalization of this conservative, antiparty Andean circle and the insertion into command positions of a new group loyal to AD. The operation is described in the following terms by one informant:

> Pérez Jiménez put them in prison, others he deported or retired from the armed forces so that they lost their chance for promotions and salaries. When Rómulo Betancourt came to power, his policy consisted in returning these men to service, giving them an opportunity to take accelerated courses so they could reach the rank they would have had save for the earlier interruption and giving them all their back pay. The group was given the responsibility of managing the armed forces by Rómulo Betancourt so that they would find themselves committed to him and by extension to AD. Now these officers face the opposition of those whose military careers were not interrupted and who continued to study and to be promoted regularly. They object that these offi-

cers installed at the last moment have the advantage of special courses, salary payments, accelerated promotions, and party connections.[14]

To round out the picture of the generational-ideological configuration emerging within the armed forces the informant goes on to state,

> By contrast, at the lower ranks one observes an ideological penetration of a leftist nature. But I don't believe very much in the ideological factor in the movements of Carúpano and Puerto Cabello. I think rather that the more ambitious have raised the flag of *fidelismo* to advance their personal interests.[15]

Thus new generational and ideological tensions take shape while the measures intended to breach older cleavages produce only incomplete and sometimes contrary results. The formalizing of selection procedures for the several academies and the effort to democratize recruitment and disperse choices throughout the nation may finally break the regional hold on armed power, but that struggle is not yet decided. In addition, interservice rivalries, especially between the navy and other forces, continue to smolder; the involvement of marines in the 1962 uprisings is symptomatic of persisting tensions. The national guard (Fuerzas Armadas de Cooperación) and the air force are offshoots of the army and cordial relations reportedly reign at the upper command levels. Not so with the navy.

> The navy always sought to raise its head and to become independent, but it was never able to do so. On the contrary, during the time of Pérez Jiménez ways were sought to subjugate it even more. In an effort to smooth over these conflicts, Pérez Jiménez created the Basic Military School, a two-year course for all cadets after which each went on to the school of his own service. This affected the navy greatly, on the one hand because it lowered the quality of training and on the other because it blocked the creation of that spirit of pride that each service tries to develop in its members. When Larrazabal became president of the Junta de Gobierno, one of his first acts was to create the Joint Staff, in which each arm had a representative, and the separate commands that administer their organizations autonomously. This reorganization makes possible the existence of a permanent rivalry between army and navy . . . that can lead to serious difficulties.[16]

The armed forces, then, are in the throes of a struggle to find a new identity and unity. Interestingly, as this process of redefinition advances and the prospects that a truly national fighting force may emerge increase,

[14] Interview 426315, Appendix A, pp. 4–5.

[15] Ibid., p. 5. The reference is to leftist uprisings in May and June 1962, involving chiefly marines and some national guardsmen.

[16] Ibid., p. 6.

the armed services have become more accepting than ever of foreign influence. The extent of United States influence is difficult to assess but is suggested by the two following statements from the U.S. Army publication cited earlier.

> The United States Army mission is the largest in Latin America and assists both the army and the national guard. The navy depends almost entirely on the United States Navy mission for advice and assistance on current procedures. The United States Air Force mission members are stationed with each tactical unit, in all schools except the cadet school, as well as at air force headquarters.
> Large numbers of officers of all services have attended service schools in the United States, and many officers and noncommissioned officers receive specialized training at military schools in the Canal Zone.
> The armed forces maintain an extensive training establishment for officer aspirants, for recruits and for officer, noncommissioned officer, and specialist training. The system is modeled on that of the United States, and members of the United States military missions assist in the program at all schools and in many units. Much of the instructional material has been translated directly from manuals used in the United States military school system.[17]

Given the United States stake in ensuring the defeat of insurgency in Venezuela and its commitment to the survival of the Betancourt regime, it seems safe to surmise that this massive takeover of training and advisory functions within the armed forces represents only a fraction of the supporting actions that were undertaken by the United States at the time. However, the matter clearly goes well beyond gauging the magnitude or internal impact of an effort mounted from abroad to help a friendly regime meet a particular crisis. A national institution, still imperfectly formed and unintegrated yet vital to the nation's security and internal stability, passes into unequal symbiosis with another of its kind abroad. It is this patent denationalization of pivotal institutions at the moment when they seem close to acquiring the capacity effectively to serve national aspirations that has set off fresh debate on the changing character of Latin American dependency on the United States.[18] More is involved than an immediate frustration of nationalist aims, nor is the fear merely that the region will be frozen by military compact into a given mold of slow-paced meliorism.[19]

[17] *U.S. Army Area Handbook for Venezuela,* pp. 544, 546.
[18] Refer to Helio Jaguaribe, "Dependência e autonomia," pp. 10–13.
[19] John Saxe Fernández, in "The Central American Defense Council and Pax Americana," a paper presented at a Latin American Spring Colloquium at Brandeis University in 1967, spells out details of current U.S. military policy in the region and traces some of its implications in terms of political controls and future change.

Such concerns go well beyond the scope of this research except as they touch on Venezuela. The implications of the partial fusion of security functions (with those of the U.S.) taking shape in that country are by no means clear and have not been seriously examined on either side except in terms of the simple canons of immediate effectiveness in a given police operation and of an emerging doctrine promoting the internationalization of internal security operations under the aegis of the United States armed forces. Keeping in view similar relationships crystallizing in other spheres of the society, there seem to be grounds for challenging official optimism about the significance for political development of present trends within the armed forces. The military may well be on the path to an even more regressive and antinational role than they have had in the past.

The United States Presence

It is a commonplace device to capsule the basic facts of the U.S. presence in Venezuela in a few statistics that almost any literate Venezuelan can recite. Oil accounts for about 90 percent of the country's exports and about 60 percent of the government's tax income. More than 90 percent of the investment in oil as well as iron deposits is controlled by U.S. interests. If a Venezuelan has been attentive to the public relations efforts of the oil companies, he will also know that the government is sharing in oil exploitation profits in a ratio of about 67 to 33 (the two thirds going to Venezuela), a substantially better arrangement than any other oil-producing nation has managed to wrest from foreign investors. A few Venezuelans may be able to add that the oil industry employs less than 3 percent of the labor force, who, however, take home close to half of the wages and salaries paid in the nation.

These figures in themselves, though they point to grave imbalances in the economy and in the distribution of income and employment, convey little of the quality of relations clearly in play among the several human elements — the oil companies, government, oil workers, and the mass of outsiders looking in on the most technologically advanced and productive sector of the economy. Nor do these numbers provide useful guidance as to which of numerous versions of the quality of such relations merit credence. A U.S. historian writing about midway through the period of the last dictatorship gives the oil companies few points on citizenship.

> The history of company policy clearly shows that what cooperation there was came mainly through fear and where resistance could hope to succeed, a policy of resistance was found.

The industry had resisted the claims and demands of labor with all the force that the respective Venezuelan governments would allow them to exert.[20]

A present-day Venezuelan spokesman for the oil companies forcefully argues a decidedly contrary view.

Our purpose is to talk with them [government officials] so that they can know that we are honest men, that we don't wish to hoodwink the country [*echarle vaina al pais*], that we don't wish to ruin the country, that we don't want to overthrow the government, that we are not interested in bringing back Pérez Jiménez.

The major difficulty is that the political leaders who are the ones who write, the ones who get on the public platform, have clung to an image of the oil companies dating back to the beginning of the century, and they don't want to admit or can't realize that things are not the same, that there has been some progress.[21]

Study data do not in fact provide much foundation for judgment about the motives or morality of oilmen, past or present. Nor is that matter at issue here. More significant to the purpose at hand are the operations of the oil companies and others in the U.S. community as producers of leaders — as a socializing agent for Venezuelans who take their places in the local management of U.S. firms and as political activists and statesmen within the larger business community.

It is probably too early to judge the outcome of the takeover by United States cadres of socializing functions within the armed forces and the police. As has been seen, these operations remain shrouded in a reserve not easily penetrated by research of the present kind. The socializing action of U.S. corporations, particularly the oil companies who have been at it for some time, is more visible, as are the present extensions of that influence into social and political efforts financed and ideologically oriented by corporate philosophies formulated within and propagated from that sector. The diversification of the United States community with the inflow of new industries and the concentration of U.S. aid and advisory missions has also amplified the range of such influences and the guises in which they are brought to bear. It is in this sense that it is necessary to treat the problem in terms of a United States or American *community* rather than simply one of oil company influences.

The American community in Venezuela according to an estimate of the North American Association numbered some 30,000 in 1962. This number

---

[20] Edwin Lieuwen, *Petroleum in Venezuela* (New York: Russell and Russell, 1967), p. 118.

[21] Interview 407305, pp. 13, 44.

was believed to have declined somewhat as a result of a recession and the uncertain political climate. A slowdown in oil company investment and exploration activities as a consequence of the announced policy of no further oil concessions by the government was believed to have contributed to that decline. No breakdown by numbers of the diverse groups making up this total is possible but at least four should be distinguished, for each responded in a different way to the appeal to participate in this research and has a perspective of its own on its experience in Venezuela.[22]

We do not pretend that a detailed study of these subcommunities has been made, but their presence is worth noting. They include American oil executives, the corporate heads of more recently established manufacturing concerns and business services, the American "criollos" (a group of older men, long-time residents in Venezuela, and generally in business on their own or in association with Venezuelans), and the embassy staff (numbering officially about 250 with an additional Peace Corps contingent of 98). Apart from the embassy and its services, the visible representational apparatus of this community constituted the North American Association, the American Chamber of Commerce, a daily newspaper (*The Caracas Journal*) and, more marginally, the Venezuelan-American Institute. It should be emphasized at once that the connections among persons and organizations in this network of activities are extremely informal, predominantly voluntary, and involve a relatively minor fraction of American residents. Programs are underwritten both by public subscription (a very successful annual raffle and dance) but also directly by corporate contributions of monies, facilities, and especially executive time.

The preceding figures should not be taken to mean that Americans as a physical presence weigh obtrusively in the ranks of local company staff, especially in the oil industry. In Venezuela the number of foreigners in employment at any level within a firm cannot by law exceed 25 percent. None of the thirty or so major corporations reached by study interviewers came anywhere near that proportion in number of U.S. employees. Total foreign employees, including notably refugee Cubans but also other Latin

---

[22] Though response within the oil industry varied, the tendency was to delegate interviews to Venezuelans in top management positions. Numerous such individuals, both within the formal sample and as special informants, freely gave much useful information about themselves, their own firms, and the industry. The U.S. corporate heads of firms other than oil also proved readily accessible to two American members of the study team, Paula Lawton Bevington and Tamara Z. Bonilla. The American "criollos" were the most open and proved influential in securing cooperation from the North American Association and the American Chamber of Commerce. The embassy restricted interviewing to one extended conversation with the First Minister.

Americans and Europeans, ranged generally between 10 and 15 percent. Americans rarely came to 5 percent of the total work force though, of course, they clustered heavily in the very top positions. Competition for capable or promising Venezuelans is vigorous. Thus the process of "Venezuelanization" of foreign enterprise, which might be more accurately called the Americanization of selected Venezuelans for corporate duty, is already well advanced and continues to be intensively implemented.

Oil company recruitment of young Venezuelan professionals goes back to the late 1920's and has gravitated naturally toward geologists, engineers, and lawyers. Men of that generation now hold important positions at the highest corporate levels in major oil companies and many others are being groomed for these functions. Useful family and political connections have never hurt a candidate, and some personnel men are today frank to say that families are investigated before serious investment is made in prospective executive trainees. Some typical corporate careers have been discussed in the chapter on paths to elitehood. The entry into the recruitment arena of new oil companies and of many new enterprises has sharpened competition and produced some impatience with the carefully paced process of corporate ascent, with consequent attrition among executive trainees in the more conservative companies. Still the select group involved is very much aware of its privileged status.

> I want to say on the basis of my own experience that the [company name] oil corporation is a very selective company as regards its management. It is a company that spares no expense when a person shows a hint of administrative talent in order to give that person all the knowledge necessary to do a good job. . . . The company goes to the extreme of giving every facility to its employees. And another factor in that success is not only that it is selective but that [company name] spares no expense also in paying well when it believes a person does or can do a good job in the company.[23]

Some sense of the scale of such recruitment operations can be obtained from the remarks that follow. The second company concerned, by no means the largest of its kind, had 32 persons in undergraduate training at the time of the interview, 28 of them in the United States.

> Each year the executives of the department of industrial relations . . . do a study of students who are about to graduate in the different categories or levels of education — engineers of all kinds, physicians, economists, etc. — . . . in the universities of Venezuela and of Venezuelans studying in the U.S. universities. Then a selection is made of a fairly large number of such students

[23] Interview 404317, Part B, pp. 95–96.

according to their grades. . . . This is later submitted to management and distributed to all department heads so that they can indicate the needs they may have in the immediate future when these students will graduate.[24]

When we began testing actively . . . the program was almost completely unknown and almost all of the people at the time at the university were receiving scholarships from someone so that we couldn't draw on existing university students as a set of candidates. We recruited from the senior classes of the local high schools and made quite a campaign out of it. . . . Now then, since that time our recruiting efforts have tapered off. We still do some of it but nowhere near the extent we did ten years ago. The program has become better known among high school students and university students and we get a sufficient number of fairly well qualified candidates coming in off the street. . . .[25]

Understandably, the less glamorous industries that require more prosaic duties of executive trainees have a difficult time attracting young talent.

We're trying to hire people all the time. We have an objective of replacing the non-Venezuelans with locally trained Venezuelan personnel. We can't find them. We certainly are looking all the time. We have a hard time coming up with good people and the ones we do get are the fortunate few who've been educated abroad. . . . The average Venezuelan that you hire out of the university, he doesn't want to work. He wants a big desk and wants to be an executive in ten minutes' time.[26]

If some of the young Venezuelans beginning business careers are in a hurry, foreign corporate management is not. One of the things that all Americans doing business in Venezuela have in common is the belief that the country has an enormous potential as a continuing base for high profit ventures; they understandably have a strong desire to keep it that way, and their eye is on the long-run future. It could hardly be otherwise with an accumulated U.S. investment of more than four billion dollars. In these circumstances training management obviously means more than imparting technical or administrative skills, and the needs of business go far beyond preparing nationals to take over productive and managerial responsibilities. The recency of the Cuban experience, the presence of insurgency in the country, and the memories of the dramatic outburst of hostility toward the United States on the occasion of the visit to Venezuela of Vice President Nixon created a sense of crisis and need for action in the early 1960's. Thus the mobilization of business forces being cham-

---

[24] Ibid., pp. 9–10.
[25] Interview 428, p. 16.
[26] Interview 413, p. 10.

pioned from within the American community was propelled by a powerful mix of motivations — economic, ideological, patriotic, civic, and religious. Prominent among these was a missionary anti-Communist zeal.

If businessmen in Venezuela generally are apprehensive about the economic role of government, the foreign sector of the business community is even more sensitive on this score, being faced with the additional need to avoid at all costs any action that might be interpreted as disrespectful of national authorities.[27] The permanent sense of pressure and peril emanating from government brings particular tensions into these relationships. The oil companies especially have learned to tread lightly in all public encounters. The prime functions of Venezuelans at the upper levels of management are to mediate relations with government agencies, to negotiate with labor, and to represent company interests in business organizations. Among the sizable array of issues in contention between the oil companies and the government, for example, the most nettlesome to oilmen seems to be the matter of concessions — not, according to oil company spokesmen, because the companies feel they must have new concessions but because they are unable to plan ahead without a definition of policy. That issue has come to symbolize the government's capacity to keep the industry off balance with respect to the future.

> What means of defense does the company have? Too few in my view because with the spirit that prevails it is very difficult to go and simply say what we think. So one has to do this in a very diplomatic way and try to convince with solid arguments those persons who influence public opinion, explain our point of view to all kinds of persons as well as the press, politicians, government officials. . . . We do not insist at all that the nation continue giving concessions. . . . We are perfectly willing to consider any other arrangement that commercially is sufficiently attractive, that we can live with. . . . As regards the general atmosphere, it would be much more desirable to have all principles clarified for the long-run future. Our exploration is not made for the bread we are going to eat tomorrow . . . but for what we are going to produce ten, twenty, or thirty years from now. The bases of an agreement in my view would be a definition of conditions by the state of what they want and more security than we have had in recent years that conditions will not change continuously.[28]

The underlying fear, of course, is that the dream of expropriation or some new form of socialization may not be dead and that politicians may be in secret plotting new incursions on the industry.

[27] See *SRSP,* Chapter 7.
[28] Interview 408306, pp. 54, 70, 71.

So these gentlemen who had been saying since '28 that the oil industry has to be nationalized reach a point at which they realize this can't be done. Then they feel defrauded. What to do? What shall we do with this monster that we have in here? Then they begin to invent formulas and to study ways in which to improve the nation's take without ruining the oil companies, much to their sorrow for what they would really like to do is to expropriate them.[29]

Such fears touch industries other than oil far less directly. They find considerable freedom of operation; their complaints center more on bureaucratic inefficiencies and delays in their dealing with government agencies. Nevertheless, all feel in some degree subject to the arbitrariness of government and exposed to nationalistic backlash for any defensive maneuver attempted.[30] Suspicion of government runs deep among these men and is by no means reserved for that of Venezuela alone.

As the publicly announced primary target of terrorists, United States businessmen were also understandably less complacent about terrorism and less generous in analyzing its sources than the main body of Venezuelan elites. Numbers among them had direct experience of armed attacks and sabotage of installations; all were forcibly involved in mounting expensive security operations and lived under the prolonged strain of anticipating unpredictable violence. Telephone campaigns threatening firms, individuals, and their families added to the anxiety and frustration, though few attacks on persons materialized. Protecting citizens against violence, a relatively low priority reform measure for most in the main elite sample, was almost invariably chosen as the most urgent of reforms by the U.S. businessmen questioned.[31] Of significance here is the extent to which this resentment and hostility had come to focus on the university. The problem of terrorism had fused in people's minds with that of the university; nothing short of wiping out that institution's autonomy would bring terrorism to a halt.

I certainly would reform their school system upward to where this so-called independence and so-called autonomy . . . cease to exist. Isn't it silly to have an army standing outside trying to catch a bunch of criminals and there's no way for them . . . to go into the university and drag them out. I saw that here just about a year ago. They had the university surrounded and inside were a bunch of young punks that are shooting policemen, shooting soldiers.[32]

[29] Interview 407305, p. 15.
[30] Government was credited, however, with being helpful on security (making national guardsmen available to private firms) and with holding the line on labor unrest.
[31] See Table 8.2.
[32] Interview 404, pp. 19–20.

The great problem in Venezuela has been this tendency to confuse autonomy with sovereignty. Any autonomy that an institution has been granted by a sovereign state can by no means infringe upon the sovereign power of that state and, unfortunately, I don't believe that the present administration has driven this point home not only to the students but to the general population. By remaining quiet they permit the growth of the theory that the autonomy of the institute grants them sovereign powers within their own territorial limits, which is just not a fact. And of course the absurd situation of watching students using the university as an armed fortress to fire guns outside and killing citizens and even military personnel and then trying to claim the protection of their autonomy is a complete mockery of the entire theory behind it.[33]

The one thing that strikes one as being a glaring defect is this question of autonomy, the carrying over from European universities that the university is a law unto itself. This has a very unfortunate effect on students, their outlook. . . . In the paper this morning there's an article about the big protest . . . on the fact that in the engineering school if the students fail they should be put out just like in the States. . . . But they feel that there's some sort of special right that they have to continue on indefinitely. There's no discipline in their life or in their mental approach.[34]

Now the first thing I think they should do in the university is withdraw their autonomy — you might call it an immunity from police action there. I think that's ridiculous when it's known to be a source of trouble, known to be a source of agitation and a nest for extremists. They should withdraw their autonomy and permit the police not only to go in there but they should arrange it so that police come through there regularly. By taking their weapons away from them that's one thing — at least they can do less damage. But follow up the same process of weeding through the professors in the university that I mentioned; they should do [the same thing] to the high schools and later to the public schools. If the professors are encouraging these pupils to carry on what they are doing or teaching them Communist doctrine, well that's one source of the problem. It's very important to get to that source. Weed them out. . . .[35]

These views have been documented in some detail because they reveal an important third strand in the preoccupations of this group. Next to the control of violence, these men assign the highest priority among needed social reforms to improving the quality of education. The main body of economic leaders mean, by improvement in quality, not only that the educational system should deliver individuals well motivated and technically prepared for productive work but that these individuals should be ideologically unspoiled. As a matter of fact, the companies are well

[33] Interview 410, p. 39.
[34] Interview 413, pp. 36–37.
[35] Interview 415, pp. 32–33.

set up to take care of training for their own manpower needs at every level. It is undoing or preventing the ideological damage that they believe is taking place in the schools that presents grave challenges and risks.

The American business response to felt pressures on these multiple fronts has been mounted in three main ways — through the business organizations directly (especially by way of the Cámara del Petróleo with its extensions into Fedecamaras), through the American organizations that have been mentioned, and through the support of newly formed social action groups sponsored by a combination of Venezuelan business interests and Church groups. Some of these organizations are reputedly part of an international network set up to ensure the long-term survival of free enterprise in Latin America.[36]

The Cámara del Petróleo is a recent (1958) and highly successful venture into which the oil companies entered with some trepidation. The industry, reluctant to appear openly as a pressure group or to provide exposed targets for its opponents, had never sought formal representation in the various business chambers. The new Cámara operates as a forum and an informational organ for the industry but carefully avoids anything that might be construed as promotion of narrow industry interests. On important issues on which the chamber board cannot get unanimity, decision reverts to a committee of company presidents and managers, a nonstatutory, informal sort of security council. The importance of the Cámara is that it has given the industry direct access to the board of the national confederation (Fedecamaras), where its representatives have been active in totally transforming that body.

> After the creation of the Cámara del Petróleo and the introduction of certain members . . . into the directing council of the Federation of Chambers it went through a complete turnabout in philosophy, more profound, much more orienting. Today, after the last four years, the Federation has acquired enormous prestige. I believe that the Cámara del Petróleo has had great influence on this; we have worked intensely. It hasn't been possible to eliminate altogether all those trivial requests — such and such town wants x. . . . This still exists. The requests for special credits for someone who wants to plant olives in the Andes also exists. But this has been relegated to a second plane with matters of the philosophy of private enterprise and managerial awareness coming into first place.
>
> It is true that we put into the mouth of Fedecamaras our propositions as regards oil problems because Fedecamaras doesn't know anything about oil. Then we put in the mouth of Fedecamaras our points of view, always taking care

[36] Refer to footnote 150 in Chapter 7.

to dilute them and to avoid a direct identification of our Cámara or the industry with these positions. It is a form of lobbying. We simply reason that this is what we believe should be the oil policy of the nation, and we put it in the hands of an association of businessmen who analyze it. It is not that they accept it verbatim or parrot it, but that they analyze it. Because it is reasonable, they take it up as their own.[37]

Success has been such that the oil company representatives have had to step in to curb the aggressiveness in their behalf of their new champions.

The Association . . . got an economist to write them a position paper on petroleum. That paper was incendiary, it was materially worse than anything that could have been written by the most reactionary company in the country. Then we got into the Hydrocarbons Committee to study that document and came out with a much more temperate, elevated document. . . .[38]

In earlier conventions we often had to defend ourselves vigorously against the officials of the Ministry [of Mines] . . . who used to arrive in great force and with considerable support of certain sectors. We have slowly dominated that situation to the extreme that things like the following occur in Fedecamaras. . . . At the last convention when the oil position paper was being discussed [name of ministry official] arrived late and when he sought to speak at the end he was not allowed to do so. Fearing that the representative of the Ministry of Mines might not get to speak and that it might be construed as an action on our part [name of oil executive] rose to request that he be allowed to speak.[39]

The success in Fedecamaras has been accompanied by the proliferation of social-action-oriented business organizations under the guidance of elder statesmen of the Venezuelan economic sector but sparked by younger men, including energetic Venezuelan oil company executives. The group promoting the new image of the socially responsible and politically aware (and perhaps even politically engaged) executive has not, however, been able completely to convert the indifference, timidity, and cynicism of some business leaders (see Chapter 7, pages 221 to 227). But in general their entry into the arena of social action has been hailed as a step forward in the political and social modernization of the country (through a presumed diversification and institutionalization of pressure groups and the establishment of organized philanthropy).

The second front of action, via the mobilization of U.S. residents, capitalizes on the patriotism of Americans, their sense of community concern, and their desire to strike back in some effective way at the Com-

---

[37] Interview 407305, pp. 22, 38.
[38] Ibid., p. 39.
[39] Interview 426315, p. 80.

munist enemy. The North American Association, revived after the Nixon incident by concerned businessmen, by 1963 had an annual budget of a million bolivares and several very active committees. The Association is in theory broadly based (all resident Americans are automatically members) but is actually run by a small number of dedicated men with long standing in the community. Committee work is more open to newcomers. At the time of the study about a third of the Association's budget (some $75,000) was being contributed by corporations operating in Venezuela, with substantial support coming from the oil companies.

I think that there is a certain domination by the oil companies particularly in certain committees. However, that is not as bad as it sounds because the oil companies in the first place have public relations groups of so much size that they can devote a great deal of time to the homework involved in getting these people moving. We can use the brains of other people, in fact of all people on the committee, but when it comes time to sitting down with the Venezuelan government and preparing the arrangements for the local seminar, you have to have people who have a lot of time available, and the oil companies always seem to be able to shake loose people to do these things. That happens, of course, not only in the public relations committee. I think it happens in several of the other committees also. The oil companies are also, I might say, the biggest provider of funds for the North American Association, so it is not at all illogical that they should assume a very major role.[40]

Reports on the involvement of the embassy in the Association's work are somewhat conflicting but suggest a natural close contact and effort at coordination.

The embassy cooperates very closely with the North American Association. The ambassador is on call for the various social events, but the embassy people take no part in the deliberations of the Association, nor do they hold any positions on committees or in the leadership of the organizations.[41]

The ambassador attends these meetings. . . . He participates and he and his right-hand fellows sit down and listen to what's happening. That's an interesting thing in the American community in Venezuela, it works together pretty much. And there is some criticism of these various American organizations, that they're in the bag and they're run by an oligarchy, but by and large you don't have the competition here that you would normally find in a foreign community — criticism of the embassy, criticism of this group. The Americans here are inclined to work together pretty well.[42]

[40] Interview 423, p. 42.
[41] Ibid., p. 36.
[42] Interview 400, p. 8.

Individual motives for involvement in the Association's work as well as that of the American Chamber of Commerce (which includes Venezuelans doing business with the United States as well as Americans) vary widely but tend to hark back to anticommunism and the defense of the profit motive.

Well, there's no question that Americans have obligations that don't exist in the States because they are on their best behavior here and they should realize it. And they have another job to do since there is a certain amount of anti-Americanism here as elsewhere in South America. . . . The progress they're supposed to have made [in education] still leaves a terrific amount to be desired. That is, bringing the average Venezuelan up to a level where he won't be a dupe of Communists, for example, and where he'll be able to read and listen as an adult and so forth. And that requires a certain reform in the entire educational system which probably takes years and years and millions and millions of bolivars or dollars.[43]

The North American Association developed a very definite philosophy which was interpreted through four committees: the public relations, the sports, the friendship, and the educational committee, trying to do things among the Venezuelans which would, one, return their hospitality for . . . having quite a good life here and, secondly, to show how Americans are generally and that they are outgoing, friendly, helpful, and considerate, charitable people, and really, sincerely interested in the people around them. . . . While I'm not an experienced statesman, to me it was strictly an ostrich with its head stuck in the sand attitude that we had. . . . The net result was that we lost Cuba, we lost 800 million, and now we have a cancer inside of the Western hemisphere where communism is being embedded and terrorists are being trained to make our job harder. Had we had an active North American Association, had we had all these different things that we're starting to do today in Venezuela, Cuba wouldn't be Cuba today.[44]

[Americans] should join in communal activities more than they do. . . . It goes back to the old isolationism that I was talking about the other day. It's one form of mingling with the Venezuelans, becoming part of the communal life. . . . First of all, there's business contacts, that sort of thing, and secondly, it helps promote the American viewpoint. American thinking gets to the Venezuelan better. . . . If you're going to combat communism you've got to be able to expound your reasons and have an audience by being members of an organization.[45]

We all believe that Junior Achievement has a very definite purpose in Venezuela, especially to train younger people that the *imperialistas* don't come by

[43] Interview 408, pp. 33, 38.
[44] Interview 405, pp. 25, 33.
[45] Interview 404, p. 24.

their lot without a lot of hard work. We hope that, if this program is successful, to finally get down to the underprivileged children — those who are subject to a lot of wrong kind of propaganda, and who can learn that there's a good deal of hard work and honor involved in running a company and that there's no disease involved in making a profit. . . .[46]

The focus on education and anticommunism has produced an extraordinary accommodation between the largely Protestant American community and numerous programs administered by Catholics that have in fact been mounted by a combination of resources and leadership representing both the U.S. business sector and a small but influential Venezuelan group. Many North American contacts with Venezuelans are limited almost exclusively to this small circle, who are the single source of interpretation of Venezuela; it is one that is both readily available and persuasive, for it largely echoes their own propaganda. Because in practical terms the Church is considered the only ideologically trustworthy educator in sight, the marriage of free enterprise and social concern is made effective in Venezuela almost exclusively through the agency of Church-centered groups.

In the American colony some of the most prominent people are Catholics. . . . And they're very close with the Church. But I think most of the Americans, my mother for instance is very violently anti-Catholic. But I don't think that's made much difference because I think that down here the Catholics are obviously — this is a Catholic country, and the Catholics are obviously on our side. So I haven't seen any problem.[47]

There is no question about it. Every priest is outright anticommunist. The Church as such is one of the bulwarks, I would say, against Communist infiltration in these Catholic countries. And I think we should give them all the support we can.[48]

It should be plain here that no effort has been made to expose some presumed conspiratorial, imperialistic design. Analyzed in those terms, the material cited has as many ingenuous as sinister tonalities. The data obtained on the United States community, although extensive, are fragmentary; the study team was by no means equipped to carry out the kind of probing investigation required to uncover facts that subjects might conspire to conceal. The embassy staff was explicitly placed off-limits to researchers. It is self-evident that there was more rather than

[46] Interview 425, p. 7.
[47] Interview 400, pp. 51, 52.
[48] Interview 415, p. 52.

less to the United States presence in Venezuela than can be adumbrated in these pages.

No more is required for this analysis than to think of the American community in Venezuela as a concentration of several thousand high-powered individuals — well trained, self-confident, affluent, representing a major world power, securely linked to organizations of the first rank, facing specific threats and challenges, and thoroughly convinced that the best service they can do the host country is to effect a rapid transfer there of home institutions. Most are just Americans being themselves, meeting problems much as they would in their home communities. It happens, however, that although they speak and act in the name of the United States, they represent a very select albeit relatively powerful segment of U.S. life. Moreover, they plainly are in communication with, or have as allies, an equally select segment of the host society they are seeking to transform. Few among them are likely to believe that they are having enough effect to seriously alarm anyone; certainly few Venezuelans seem to perceive the actual and potential impact of the spreading web of socializing influence being deployed from the business sector.[49] As the following citation demonstrates, the new Venezuelan executive cast in the U.S. mold is already a reality. One may wonder what aims he will eventually share with the new Venezuelan soldier made in the United States.

> The young executive is doing an enormous amount. He is getting into everything. He has tremendous activity. I know about my friends. All my friends of my age are involved in social activities that need leadership. I personally am involved in the boards of directors of four organizations. [Mentions four organizations — one youth group, one community action association, one support group for a presidential candidate, and a semisecret Catholic reaffirmation movement.] . . . In addition my wife is working in several neighborhood projects. I confess that I would not have thought about this five years ago. I wouldn't have thought of it but I have such faith and great pride in my country that I am doing it because I know that the entire future of Venezuela depends on us young executives. I say this with very firm conviction.[50]

The Proscribed Parties

The top leaders of the Venezuelan Communist Party (PCV) and the Revolutionary Movement of the Left (MIR) who figured within the

---

[49] No mention has been made here of the very extensive training and public relations activities among employees below the management level. In the armed services as well, troop information programs modeled on the U.S. prototype were being initiated at this time.

[50] Interview 410325, pp. 21, 22.

main sample of political leaders were almost all in prison or in hiding during the months of field work. Most of them refused to participate in research they saw as a bourgeois exercise incongruent with the prevailing semirevolutionary situation of armed struggle and repression. Some interviews were obtained with lesser party figures and with younger militants, including a commander of urban tactical units of the Armed Forces of Liberation (FALN). A psychological study of the political involvement of a young Communist Party activist has also been included in *SRSP*. In 1962 tensions and disillusionment were already present between the younger leadership and the elder statesmen of these parties. Most of the latter were seasoned politicians and elected legislators inclined to seek negotiation, amnesty, and tactical alliance with sympathetic political groups not ready to take up arms.[51] In this sense the interviews with the younger men may be more important to an understanding of revolutionary action in Venezuela than the conversations not realized with the formal party leadership.

Party intellectuals clearly perceived the emerging accommodation and articulation of forces between government, the military, the oil industry, and the United States as leading to an effective containment of opposition and consequently to a blocking of all change not arbitrated by these selected actors.

> Oil investments in our country . . . maintain a series of mechanisms which bring the Venezuelan state to promote a so-called salutary climate for this kind of investment, what the oil company ideologues call a wholesome climate, a propitious climate. . . . This is nothing less than the political security, and one could even go a little further, the police security required for their own activities in the country. This implies that there exists no spoken or written opposition to their interests, and that they may have the liberty to proceed to increase their profits . . . even through devices arbitrated in secret without public opinion, especially opposed opinion, reacting.[52]

This internal combination of forces is seen as ultimately backed by the armed power of the United States.

> Venezuela produces oil which is a strategic material of first importance for any powerful nation. It is particularly so for the Western world and very

---

[51] An informative overview of the situation during the time this research was under way can be found in Timothy S. Harding and Saul Landau, "Terrorism, Guerrilla Warfare, and the Democratic Left in Venezuela," *Studies on the Left*, vol. 4, no. 4 (Fall 1964). See also James Cockcroft, "Venezuela's Fidelistas: Two Generations," mimeo (National Student Association, 1963).

[52] Interview 402311, p. 35.

concretely for the United States. If a movement similar to that of Fidel Castro were successfully mounted here, it is almost certain that the United States Marines would intervene, and would drown that movement in blood as well as all our people who would have to rise to fight the invader, supposing that this was a genuinely national movement. . . . To defend . . . the petroleum, the United States, without any concern for policy or how it will be judged, will surely intervene to smash that movement in Venezuela.[53]

At the same time awareness of the potential cultural impact of the combined educational, ideological, and public relations apparatus visibly being modeled under U.S. guidance was growing more acute.

A series of maneuvers is already evident in our country . . . procedures of the social classes opposed to the realization of [revolutionary] objectives. In this sense we speak of cultural colonialism which implies the deformation of Venezuelan reality, the mystification of our historical reality, and the distortion of the national personality through an externally imposed subservient mentality.[54]

This diagnosis of the situation was widely shared in Venezuela; the strategic inferences drawn were varied. A small core of young PCV-MIR militants with small contingents from other parties (their number has never been put at more than a few hundred at any given moment) decided to fight.

Practically all the study's information on insurgency as experienced from the inside comes from a single MIR commander of urban units. The history of his involvement may be taken as typical of young MIR leadership — early militancy in AD, experience of clandestine activity in close association with Communist youth during the Pérez Jiménez regime, conflict with returned AD heads at first over organizational issues, a subsequent disillusion and revolt against AD policies of accommodation and scaling down of revolutionary goals. In this process the gradual escalation of confrontations and hostilities, particularly in the months following the open break with AD, make it difficult to define the moment at which violence is taken up as the main practical instrument of contention. In a sense the individual feels that *he* has not chosen violence, yet he must affirm categorically his commitment to the violent road.

Well, the move toward armed struggle was certainly not sought by . . . MIR. That is, the theory that we took up violence is entirely mistaken. . . . We did not turn to violence because we like violence. No one likes violence. No one likes war. Everyone, whether he is a Communist or anything else, likes

[53] Interview 405321, pp. 72, 73.
[54] Interview 402311, p. 89.

peace, unless he is mentally unsound. There are concrete reasons that determine that one has to leave his tranquility, his wife, a comfortable job in order
to dedicate oneself to this. . . . What brings them to this concrete position is
the deliberate and growing repression of the rest. . . . Violence rises as the
self-defense of the masses.

Force will always be decisive in the end. Thus having seen this in the first
analysis one concludes that there exists here a single apparatus of force
which is the army and whose mechanisms and controls are in the hands of
the class opposed to our liberation. The only way to confront this is by creating a military apparatus of our own, which may be incipient, may have grave
defects, but which may develop as the struggle goes forward.[55]

Though the MIR break with AD came in mid-1960, the first critical
tests of the newly structured revolutionary forces came in 1962 and
1963.[56] The failure of the leftist military uprisings in Carúpano and
Puerto Cabello in May and June of 1962 closed the door on fantasies of
quick victory through *golpes* from within the armed forces. It also provided the impetus and some resources for a more formal organization of
the armed opposition and for a more realistic appraisal of the possible
duration and nature of the struggle ahead.

Now, when does the structural organic birth [of the FALN] take place?
When the nuclei of this party and the nuclei of this other party, these honest
soldiers of the armed forces and other people [*pueblo*] unite to rise up in
Carúpano. Then FALN rises as an amalgamated incipient structure. There
the need becomes clear to establish an organization, to analyze the political
situation of the country. The conclusion is reached that a final solution to the
political problem of this country will never be obtained in a peaceful
way. . . .[57]

During 1962 and 1963 FALN forces in the cities were able to mount
an impressive number of incidents and do considerable property damage.
A number of imaginative and daring operations were carried off along
with a great many lesser harassing actions. By their own appraisal in
early 1964, the FALN found themselves guilty of "exhibitionism, lack
of security and discipline, romanticism, lack of tactical imagination, over-
confidence and underestimation of the well-equipped forces arrayed against
them." [58] The defensive combination of forces that the police and armed

[55] Interview 416320, pp. 14, 17.
[56] Edward G. Gude, "Political Violence in Venezuela," records a jump from 33 to
120 incidents of leftist political violence from 1961 to 1962. His figure for 1963 is 181.
[57] Interview 416320, p. 16.
[58] Harding and Landau, "Terrorism, Guerrilla Warfare, and the Democratic Left,"
p. 125.

services under the guidance of their foreign advisers were able to set up to guarantee the 1963 election made plain the great difficulty of carrying out sustained actions requiring a strong hold over any part of the city for more than minutes.

> All of Caracas was divided into zones with their respective commands, dependent on a central command which operated in the Simón Bolívar Center. With this distribution, they mobilized thousands of soldiers, police, traffic cops, and secret agents of the Digepol, PTJ, and SIFA (Servício de Inteligencia de Las Fuerzas), who worked in a synchronized way in the capital. All the hills were taken militarily 72 hours before the elections, military and police effectives being placed in strategic positions with machine guns and observation posts guarded by tanks. Likewise all the sites outside the hills were taken so that any commotion could be observed and the information flashed by radio to the posts on each hill. Where they could not do this, they undertook encircling maneuvers, with extreme caution and slowness, against the focal points hostile to the government.[59]

In the aftermath of this serious setback came a lull in operations that, however, led to no effective negotiations.

> During the month that our halt on operations has lasted, conditions remain the same. No prisoners have been freed, there is no talk of rehabilitation. . . . We therefore can't say . . . we mean to suspend operations, especially because we are convinced, as reality demonstrates, that we can get nothing from them. This confirms our idea that we make gains only to the degree that we strengthen our instrument of power. And if we say that we move closer to liberation only through strengthening our instrument of power, we help to make the long war shorter. Thus our basic tasks in this new phase, unless political conditions point in other directions . . . must lie in the strengthening of our army, in finding new perspectives for the struggle, in fortifying our rural outposts, in devising new modes of operation for urban units. That is, to continue to spread among the people the idea that only armed struggle will bring them peace.[60]

Even as youthful FALN leaders girded themselves for the grim prospect of a prolonged struggle with few victories and many dangers in sight, older Communist leaders, always skeptical of the viability of terrorism as the road to power in Venezuela, became increasingly open in their criticism.

> Illusions have grown about the possibility of producing profound changes through the action of elites, of minorities. That is, goals and objectives remain the same, the welfare of the mass is desired, but there is variation in that some forget that it is the action of the masses that can make that transformation possible, and that the problem is one of mobilizing human groups and not a

[59] FALN, "Our Errors," *Studies on the Left,* vol. 4, no. 4 (1964), pp. 130, 131.
[60] Interview 416320, p. 68.

select minority different from the mass because it is cultivated, has social consciousness, because it has a higher ideological level. . . . The minorities may
provoke transformations, but these minorities can also degenerate into adventurers, into false movements that through lack of consistency in their social
base do not achieve changes.[61]

Efforts to sustain and expand guerrilla action in the countryside and
cities over the next few years became increasingly anarchic, fragmented,
and costly to those involved. The devastating attack on the Venezuelan
Communist Party by Fidel Castro as he closed the 1967 OLAS conference
(Organization of Latin American Solidarity) was a harsh catalogue of
revolutionary errors in the Venezuelan movement.[62] Some of these Castro
went so far as to label criminal. In the movement that sought to find some
structural form while testing itself in action during 1962 and 1963 in
Venezuela, many of the problems later thrown into doctrinal dispute by
Castro were already very apparent.

It was Castro's thesis that political and military command must be
fused in order to maintain a single direction and the absolute priority of
military demands in the phase of armed struggle. Yet in Venezuela the
relations of the parties to their armed wings and of the political command of the liberation movement (FLN) to the fighting units (FALN)
was cumbersome and made even more chaotic by the uncertainties and
difficulties of communication during actual operations, especially as police
efficiency improved. Running guerrillas from the city was to Castro a
crime and an absurdity; in Venezuela the idea of the urban focus of
operations had been elevated almost to a point of national honor as a
distinctive, local revolutionary innovation.

What we have developed most . . . is the urban struggle, even though the
classicists and technicians in guerrilla action insist that it is impossible to
develop the struggle in cities. . . . Many people don't understand how here
one can go out of the city, take a rural place, and return to the city, when the
normal pattern is to descend from a rural place, take the city, and return to
the countryside.[63]

Most disastrous of all in Castro's view were the efforts to carry on
military operations and seek political accommodations simultaneously,
especially when political and military action was not under a single command. Throughout the present period of insurgency in Venezuela and

[61] Interview 425328, p. 25.
[62] Speech by Major Fidel Castro at the closing of the first conference of OLAS, Aug-
ust 1967 (Instituto del Libro).
[63] Interview 416320, p. 20.

especially during electoral periods the temptation to reach for power through participation in some voting front has been a present and divisive issue for the PCV and MIR.

The PCV and similar parties around the hemisphere have, of course, not failed to reply in kind to the criticism from Havana. They argue for the authority of parties over insurgent armies, against the premature militarization of the political struggle, against messianic leadership and for democratic centralism, against an overemphasis on youth and physical prowess, for the importance of the city and the worker as against the peasant.

For thousands in Venezuela these arguments are not theoretical, for they have in one way or another put their lives on the line to test their belief in some form of revolutionary action. As this is written news of moves toward pacification, wholesale amnesty, relegalization of the Marxist parties, and reconciliation fills the headlines. The left in Venezuela emerges from this period of insurgency debilitated, confused, and divided. Its own press shows no signs of jubilation; its headlines pose dark questions: "Why is the left silent?" "Reflections on the rout of the left." [64] A third recent and vital experience of socialization among Venezuelans within the circle of potential elitehood has gone largely unstudied and uncomprehended.

The left, with its penchant for self-doubt and self-laceration, continues to brood on its failure to elicit a mass response to the message of revolution. But whether competing voices — those of the Church, military civic-action groups, agents of the government, or young executives — will have better fortune remains uncertain. In the final analysis it is the vast gulf between the mass and all those in contention at the top that seems most difficult to bridge. Who will do it and how? Early in 1964, when things looked no less bleak for revolution than in early 1969, the writer put a sociologist's question to the FALN commander whose words have been cited before in this section: "How does it feel to be a revolutionary in a country that doesn't want revolution?"

> Perhaps if I were a revolutionary . . . of 1810 when independence was declared, when we began to struggle against Spain, and you were interviewing me . . . you might make the same observation. You would see the Venezuelan people, the *conuqueros* peacefully on their haciendas and a few visionaries, among whom I might number, trying to win independence from Spain. But how? . . . Yet history shows the result. It was a just cause and it was a

[64] Headlines from *Cambio,* Caracas, February–March 1969 (nos. 8–9).

struggle that caught up the mass and opened perspectives for victory to the people, who then made these perspectives their own and were led to political emancipation.[65]

This is a fine statement of revolutionary faith, but it is less impressive now that the research has come some distance. Elites of all persuasions will need to reflect carefully on the significance of the attitudinal configurations uncovered by the CONVEN studies among the mass of Venezuelans. More importantly: They will need to re-examine the cumulative political effect of successive abdications of socializing functions within important sectors as well as their own incapacity to establish meaningful connections with those they would lead.

[65] Interview 416320, p. 110.

10 ELITES AND NATIONAL CAPACITY

The closing pages of each of the three volumes in the present series contain a variety of approaches to partial synthesis of the vast amount of information and analytical description that fills each of them. In these final stocktakings the writers have sought to remain true to the spirit of the total enterprise. That is, they seek to continue to do justice to the full range and complexity of the data and analysis without side-stepping the need to point out some acceptable ways of moving toward a higher order integration of research findings and operations.

In Volume 3 Silva presents the most formalized efforts at such synthesis. One of these builds on a primarily analytical tool (ADMINS), which also permits a systematic search for configurations of relations and facilitates inferences concerning the implications of such configurations for global states or capacities of the system studied. The second synthesis, based on a computer-operated sociopolitical model (VENUTOPIA) lays down explicit rules for calculating system parameters departing from configurations in the original data as well as changes in them also produced according to specified rules (laws or hypotheses).[1]

Neither of the formal approaches taken by Silva is practicable at this writing for the elite data, though the main lines of immediately open experimentation in this direction are clear. A genuinely comprehensive integration of all results thus remains beyond reach. The partial successes of the surveys in this difficult area nevertheless provide useful guidelines for the present effort to place elite findings in context. The Silva syntheses are particularly suggestive in this connection because several of

[1] See especially his Chapter 9. Some basic facts about ADMINS and the VENUTOPIA model are given in the first chapter of the present volume. Refer also to *SRSP*, Chapter 12, and the Appendix to Volume 3.

the sample groups he treats (for example, business executives, government officials, and university professors) represent the very occupational sectors within which most of those in our more narrowly selected elite samplings operate.

The systems perspective taken throughout has focused attention on macroguidance and self-steering capacity, on the contribution of subgroups and individual actors to enhancing or undercutting the collective potential for the realization of desired goals. The balancing or constraining norm on this adaptive capacity has been stated in terms of the social cost of maintaining given states or achieving desired new ones. In VENUTOPIA such social costs appear in the form of measures of antagonism, conflict levels, the presence of official repression, and other indicators of social tension and individual deprivation. Later versions of the model include more varied indicators of the social cost dimension and quite complex hypotheses concerning the interaction of such variables and their meaning for system capacity.[2] The present analysis cannot strike for the level of rigor and elegance of the models. Moreover, some of the precision in the models is, of course, won at the price of considerable loss of empirical connection with the reality represented. Nevertheless the exposition that follows is disciplined and enriched by the experience gained in those exercises.

The principal blockages to effective action on broad social issues as revealed in the survey findings are depicted in broad strokes by Silva: a structurally rooted conservative drift in the society, unyielding contention among the groups who have benefited most from recent change and are most firmly ensconced within the modern sector of the nation, a disconnection of these groups from the mass of the citizenry. Past change has produced substantial social gains across the board. Despite this the end product has been greater inequality and an accentuation of social distances. However, satisfaction and optimism prevail not only among those who are getting the most out of ongoing change but among low status groups whose relative share in expanding benefits seems to be shrinking.

The low political capacity, passivity, and bullish mood of the mass might be seen as endowing the system with a resiliency and flexibility that a dynamic leadership could put to good purpose. Two facts cast doubt on such a comforting interpretation. In part because they are quite mod-

[2] Carlos Domingo, "VENSEP," mimeo (CENDES, 1968).

est, mass aspirations continue to focus on immediate consumption goals and look directly to government and the political sector generally as the primary provider of such improvements. Any sharp setback or interruption of the modest flow of economic gains could provoke a radical shift of mood. Middle- and upper-status groups incline much more toward the BURDEN than VICTIM perspective on the mass (refer to Chapter 8) and are content to take quite a long-range view of solutions as long as they perceive political pressures as emanating principally from within their own circle. Infighting is found to be fiercest among the most committed to national aims and structural solutions to social inequality. A warning is sounded that the leadership may not only be losing contact with the mass but may be losing contact as well with national problems insofar as present elites fail to perceive new constellations of issues that make still current ideologies and strategies of national development less relevant as the decade of the sixties closes.

Silva's VENUTOPIA numerical experiments go a step beyond this kind of synthesis to a tentative form of projection. However, these experiments remain of greater interest in terms of the mechanisms for representing sociopolitical processes they essay than in their predictive power. Probably they are too shortly tethered to facts and to the poverty of our knowledge about change to prove useful in the latter regard for some time to come. Still, at this point again, the experiments force into explicit terms the elements of projection inevitably smuggled into summaries such as that in the foregoing paragraph.

Two "results" or patterns in the experimental sequences worked through in Volume 3 are of particular interest here. The first of these has to do with the notion of a high-cost status quo. Allowing the system to continue to operate without intervention for a given time span constitutes a political solution higher in social cost than modifications over an equivalent time span representing either conservative reforms or more progressive attempts at structural change short of revolution. In the experiment, progressive policy emphasizes broad political mobilization, expansion of education with a high priority for the incorporation of popular sectors, a diminution in the repressive use of police and armed forces on the mass, and economic measures favoring popular groups. The conservative policies include a strengthening of police and army, elitist education, censorship and information control, economic policies favorable to the national bourgeoisie and foreign investors, and a centralization of political action limiting mass participation. Conflict levels spiral rapidly both with respect to the performance of key roles and key institutions when no endogenous change (that is, corrective policy) is posited. Conservative policies bring pressures to bear on particular roles (government, army, police) whereas the progressive options center conflict on important subsystems (foreign relations, the economy, and political institutions).[3] The high price of immobility or impasse demands attention, for the elite materials indicate a similar high social cost for deadlocks in intraelite interactions. Further reference to this suggestive result will be made in the pages that follow.

A second pattern or recurrent event in the VENUTOPIA experiments suggests one underlying dynamic in the prolongation of this high-cost status quo. This cycle repeats itself within experiments that attempt to represent both progressive and conservative lines of action designed to break the existing stalemate. In these sequences professors and students are chronically in the opposition, shearing off from other upper-status groups to enter into coalition with sectors of the mass early in the game. However, this coalition of intellectuals and mass elements proves unstable. Conflict escalates and takes a direction that the mass is unwilling to accompany. A reapproximation between the mass and other leadership sectors occurs, and the intellectual opposition is left in isolation. Deprived of its mass support, this group moves gradually to a reconciliation or accommodation with the existing power configuration until a new crisis which sensitizes the mass provides a fresh opportunity to test the readiness of the system for more profound change.

This experimentally produced sequence is a plausible schematization of recent events in Venezuela. One question raised, of course, is how long Venezuela and other nations like it can remain locked in cycles like this without losing in some definitive way the historical options of development and autonomy in whose name the national leadership of the 1950's and 1960's has sought legitimation.[4] More alarming perhaps is the growing intuition that those options may never have been open in quite the terms envisioned. In that event the present crisis is one not only of unremitting conflict at the top and a disconnection of elites from the mass but also of disconnection from the root problems of national self-realization that now loom over the final decades of the century.

---

[3] Volume 3, Table 9.5.
[4] Helio Jaguaribe, "Dependência e autonomia na América Latina" (paper presented at the Lima conference of the Latin American Social Science Council [CLACSO], 1958).

The Ascendance of Middle-Sector Elites

The surveys and the VENUTOPIA experiments yield a sense of the global structure of conflict, the shifting coalitions, and the constraints on solutions to national problems. The more narrowly focused elite research brings out details concerning the nature of differentiation, lack of consensus, and noncommunication at the very top and thus points to the sources of elite inefficacy or impotence with respect to particular issues. It is important in this connection not to equate the idea of issue inefficacy with lack of defensive capacity among elites. The international, military, economic, and political substructures that undergird and guarantee the privileged position of incumbent elites have been explored in considerable detail at various points. However, the greater part of the research effort has sought to bring into view connections between these basic constituents of power and interest and the superstructure of values, ideologies, and concrete issues that constitute the substantive content of day-to-day political contention.

As has been shown chiefly in Chapters 3 and 4, contemporary Venezuelan elites, except for a fraction of the entrepreneurial class, are the vanguard of rising middle sectors. Only among a select group within the economic elite is any evidence to be found of stability, continuity, and the transmission of status across generations. Major blocs within the political and cultural elites are of modest, provincial, middle-class origins. That background, for early experience of politics, means immersion in the milieu of violence, arbitrariness, and clientelism that permeated political life at all levels in Venezuela from the turn of the century until at least the death of Gómez in 1936. In the social context of everyday life, this background means the continued immersion in a world of limited intellectual perspectives and petty bourgeois sentiments and values. Practically all male kin of elite informants (fathers, brothers, brothers-in-law) are in occupations and positions a substantial cut in status below that of respondents and have fewer years of education. The limitations of this intimate cultural milieu are even more starkly delineated with respect to female kin — the mothers, wives, and sisters of this elite have extremely modest schooling. Whatever moral and affective qualities these women bring into the lives of elite individuals, their own perspectives on public affairs must be quite limited. It is difficult to estimate the political consequences of this restrictive private experience, but in view of the central importance to these men of family commitments, values, and sentiments (see Chapter 5), it is a feature of elite life that bears elucidation. In short, as a group, elite individuals in their public life are ostensibly dedicated to rationalizing, reforming, and modernizing functions whereas in private they remain steeped (apparently quite by choice) in a family- and class-rooted traditionalism heavily freighted with idealized sentimentality in personal relations and preoccupation with external formalism, decorum, and propriety as certification of family status and individual worth. The Silva volume documents in considerable detail variant configurations of middle-sector psychological states, value orientations, and political dispositions. The elite data reveal the extent to which action and decisions at the top in Venezuela represent projections of these heterogeneous and often conflicting middle-sector interests, aspirations, and fears. Apart from a shallow overlay of technical expertise and ideological sensibility, there is very little in the elite interviews that differentiates them in thought or value patterns from the main body of respondents within the social sectors in which elites originate. Without question these middle sectors have benefited disproportionately from the nation's partial development. But the issue here is not whether these groups have appropriated more than an equitable share of the social values (economic, political, and cultural) generated over the last few decades, largely under the aegis and persistent pressure of this elite vanguard. The issue has rather to do with the further potential of this group as a dynamizing and liberating force, given the new array of tasks they face.

Some of the peculiarities and inefficiencies of the structure of command and control thrown up by the struggle for self-affirmation and power of middle-sector groups derive, of course, from the differential recruitment from these sectors to the several elite spheres as well as the class mix particular to each sphere. Details here again are to be found chiefly in Chapters 4 and 5. At this level there is a fusion or cross-cutting of class and occupational or institutionally grounded values that is perhaps impossible to unscramble. What is clear is the contrast or distance between the economic and other spheres, especially the political. The economic sector as an elite arena holds out the promise of stability, continuity, regularity, material success, and social distinction. It is also a sector of well-controlled access, regularized and carefully paced patterns of ascent, and one in which foreigners participate directly in the early identification and grooming of individuals for high position. Stepping out of line or being too aggressive while on the way up can prove fatal here, whether or not short-run gains are made. Signs of some generational conflict and tension over the pace of ascent, style of operation, political venturesomeness, and so on are present but muted still by a distaste for open conflicts in which visible material gains for the contenders are not clearly in evidence. In all these respects the economic sector is akin to the military and out of tune with the world of politicians.

Obviously the class mix of the individuals in each elite sphere does not by itself account for the prominence of sphere (occupational and institutional) differences in elite orientation and behavior.[5] Class, institutional, and organizational factors are all visibly in play and have been explored in some detail at various points. But it is of some interest that the most permeable sphere, and that with the largest component of individuals of modest social beginnings, the political, should be most characterized by continuous struggle, risk, precariousness of achievement, and sudden turns of fortune. Conflict, schism, mésalliance, fear of outside power blocs (rival parties, the economic sector, the military, the United States) are constant shadows over the activity of the politician. There is no instance of a successful transfer of political leadership within an organized party from one generation to another. The barriers to an easy transmuting of political power into social acceptability and status seem more rigid than those faced by money or cultural achievement as social currencies.

On all class-related variables the men in the cultural sphere lie between those in the economic and political, though generally closer to the latter. If businessmen still cultivate an ostensive detachment from politics, intellectuals viscerally resist narrow organizational or sectarian loyalties. The intellectuals' perennial concern with the relevance and authenticity of cultural institutions and activity throws them into frustrating conflict with what they experience as the lack of vision and mental rigidities in other elite spheres. From the perspectives of the business and political worlds it is, of course, the intellectuals who are seen as destructively committed to untried ideas and disloyally critical of existing social arrangements. The resentful dependency of intellectuals and their institutions on the largesse of business and government reveals nonetheless how exposed the cultural sphere remains to hostile monitoring from other sectors. Thus, whatever affinities based on common or relatively close status origins may bring elements of such an elite together, a second major internal cleavage

[5] For a more generalized commentary on this theme, see the author's "Occupation as a Unit of Cross-National Political Analysis" (Center for International Studies, Massachusetts Institute of Technology, 1968).

is marked by the main sphere of activity to which elite actors have gravitated.

Yet the problem of intraelite cleavage is by no means to be viewed simply in terms of lack of communication across institutional spheres. Relatively high densities of within-sphere communication have in fact been observed (see especially Chapter 6) but such high intraset densities are also observed when the informants are grouped by relative power standing and the number of high status antecedents they possess. Communications bonds are most concentrated at the higher levels of the power hierarchy and in general seem to be directed upward. However, many of the natural clusterings or cliques uncovered reach across institutional spheres. Rather than a tightly compartmentalized structure with three or four independent power pyramids, the findings suggest multiple pyramids of an interinstitutional kind, each identified primarily by its political component. Though it may be selective, communication across spheres seems appreciable. Of course, no sure canons are at hand for hard judgments about just how much communication such a complex system requires in order to meet policy demands adequately. Over-all communication densities within the elite sampling are in fact not impressive. As noted earlier, just under one in ten of the possible communication links among informants is mutually reported to be frequently active. But probing into the interconnections among strategically located individuals in the various spheres does not generate the impression of an elite rendered impotent by lack of intercommunication.

The notion of the upward drift of intraelite communication drawn from the examination of acknowledged communication links among informants (also in Chapter 6) helps to explain and further qualify the nature of noncommunication within this circle. The fact that power initiatives are generally directed upward or toward peers means that intraelite interactions are much more often framed in terms of persuasion and conciliation than in terms of authoritative command or decisive power in a clear-cut pecking order (Chapter 7). Behind the overlay of conflict and aggressiveness there is more often great caution, timidity, accommodation, self-imposed limits on action, and fear of exceeding imagined restrictions. In short, what is most apparent is the operation of subjective constraints on action and acknowledged deference to power blocs with a marginally legitimated political role — the army, economic pressure groups, oil companies, the United States. The resultant prolonged deadlocks in many power or influence attempts lead more often to the rupture of social ties among elites than do the failures that have been examined.

Nowhere is the disposition to inaction or trivial actions more in evidence than with respect to problems affecting the mass of Venezuelans. The contradictions and complacency in this respect strain credibility (Chapter 8). A very generalized position can be stated in only mild caricature in the following terms: "Unless something serious is done about the situation of the mass of the poor in Venezuela, disaster will surely overtake us. Probably little or nothing will be done. Everything will come out all right."

This form of reconciling felt impotence with a certain social awareness is as common among reformists and moderates as among those who believe only structural transformations will free most Venezuelans from the deforming grip of oppression and inequality. Common to those two groups as well is a frank detachment in speech and action from the mass. Neither group sees any clear role for the mass itself in its own liberation; few report more than sporadic contacts with poor Venezuelans, and these tend to occur in very stereotyped contexts. The image of the nation as a sensate nucleus ringed by a chaotic, unassimilable horde continues to be evoked despite the extensive renewal of leadership at the top along with considerable movement and dynamism at all social levels.

What the millions of words poured out by elite informants make patent is the rapid exhaustion and loss of direction of the reformist impulse that brought this vanguard of middle-sector individuals to power. The present crisis of the middle-sector establishment can thus be seen in the Venezuelan case along three dimensions:[6] (1) the inability to formulate a project capable of holding together a decisive proportion of the middle-sector elements now in power; the inability to break the present impasse or to use conflict productively; (2) the persistence of an image and approach to the mass that justifies inaction or only limited actions in their behalf; loss of contact with the mass; (3) the very slow recognition that the legitimating national goals of the 1940's and 1950's may no longer be relevant or realizable in the terms then defined; loss of connection with national problems. A few additional comments concerning the first and third dimensions are worth making.

[6] Espártaco, in *La dominación de América Latina* (Lima: Francisco Moncloa, 1968) pictures this establishment as hedged in by pressures from right and left, the threat of populism (urban and rural masses with electoral freedom), conservatism in the army, and leftism in the Church.

Intraelite Conflict

Pointing out the nature of the impasse within the middle-sector establishment, its origins, modalities, and some of the substantive issues on which it centers, only begins to explain its peculiar persistence. Despite the extensive discussion in Chapter 7 some additional features of conflict in intraelite relations bear mention in this connection.[7] In the first place much of this conflict is intrainstitutional and intraorganizational. This means, as has been seen in almost all the discussion of issue orientations and power interactions, that there is considerable agreement on superordinate goals and sharp dissidence with respect to means, agents, allocation of resources, or the pacing of action. That is, people are at odds over things in which all have a stake, with respect to which some antecedent bond of unity exists, and in which some overarching loyalty or interest is in play. Groups in conflict are temporary, shifting in composition, not recognized as part of any formal structure, and may even be denied to exist by those acting in vague accord on a particular issue. The difficulty of pinpointing just who is in conflict and with respect to what makes solutions elusive and most forms of negotiation impossible. The idea of surplus conflict mentioned in *SRSP* — that is, conflict that is unregulated, exceeds the expectations or intent of parties to a controversy, and interferes in unforeseen ways with the subset of goals still shared by those involved — is pertinent here. The ambivalence and incompleteness of open schisms, the nostalgic desire for reconnection, for the reconstitution of former associations, further charges these situations emotionally, obstructing rather than facilitating resolution and a pragmatic advance on new problems.

The fact that such conflict surges and diffuses throughout the interstices of a society, having no readily identifiable organized locus, beginning or end, has made it easy to treat as symptomatic of aberrant individualism, a proneness to anarchy, or a transitory immaturity on the way to a well-institutionalized pluralism. The present research and other studies have found this type of conflict to be most acute among the most politically aware, the most progressive or radical, the most firmly committed to nationalist goals. Another facile inference has been that neurotics gravitate to the left. These brief comments are intended to make clear that in the

---

[7] This discussion draws substantially on an unusually insightful essay by P. N. Rastogi, "Anatomy of Factional Conflict," *Sociological Bulletin, Indian Sociological Society,* vol. 16, no. 1 (March 1969).

present work such conflict is seen as an integral feature of the full system of relations brought into view. It is no surprise here to find among those who most identify with national aspirations visible effects of felt dependency or powerlessness, of a dogged casting about for alternative designs or paths toward desired futures that remain always just beyond reach — not merely beyond the reach of action but beyond the grasp of a convincing frame of ideas. What has been called in earlier pages the loss of connection with national problems among incumbent elites points directly to the present absence of such a design or paradigm. Neither political action nor ideology nor social science can move forward more than fragmentarily or fitfully until such a paradigm takes form.

The Collapse of the Development Paradigm

The exhaustion of the development paradigm as a design for the emancipation of nations like Venezuela becomes more and more evident as the decade of the sixties closes. Aspects of the new dependency now taking shape and compounding the effects of earlier constraints on self-affirmative actions have been described in Chapter 9. The capacity of the middle-sector elites studied can thus no longer be measured only against the national development goals they articulated and partly realized during the 1950's and 1960's. At issue is the realism, self-awareness, and energy with which they may respond to new opportunities for social diagnosis, self-analysis, and action.

Stated most simply, the critical discovery of the present decade is that as national institutions in Latin America begin to acquire the capacity to operate as instruments of national affirmation, they are taken over or absorbed in new ways by agents of the metropolitan or developed center. This new dependency or process of denationalization is widely in evidence though still only sketchily analyzed and perhaps only dimly apprehended by many who are its active promoters. Some aspects of the takeover of socializing functions by the United States and Americans within the military and within the business sector have been documented in earlier pages. Recent pronouncements in the United States make clear that the policy of import substitution, linchpin of nationalist development strategies of the last two decades, has been appropriated at the center and turned against the development aspirations of poor nations.[8] In 1965 the United States was already producing four times as much abroad as it exports.

[8] *NACLA Newsletter,* vol. 2, no. 7 (November 1968).

According to the president of a major U.S. corporation with extensive operations overseas, substituting other people's imports by producing for them in their own markets is far more profitable than trade. Between 1950 and 1960, he reports, twenty billion dollars in excess of all investment outflows of this kind were returned to the United States. The actual return, as he affirms is known to all businessmen, is really much larger. The rational policy for the United States in the coming years is to replace trade with direct investment (that is, *export* substitution). The efforts by the United States government to control or influence the investment policy of multinational corporations with U.S. headquarters (at that time a reduction in overseas investments was sought) are therefore rejected by this spokesman as "a radical extraterritorial claim." Plainly a wholly new framework of economic domination is emerging, and the thinking of politicians, ideologues, and academics is running well behind that of international entrepreneurs in coming to grips with the new situation.

As the realization grows that the battle as earlier defined has been lost on other institutional fronts, pressures and hopes shift to new areas. National armies, national parties, national bourgeoisies all have fallen short of the immediate challenge. The present crisis of the universities signals the transfer of expectations to the cultural sphere as well as the apprehension of new dangers within it. In none of these areas did Venezuelan middle-sector elites, speaking in the mid-1960's, display any manifest sensibility. The most articulate among them were still beginning to assimilate and manipulate the rudimentary ideas of development, planning, and social reform. Enlightened leadership and the long-term effects of education and increasing participation continued to be viewed as main levers of long-term change. From this perspective the mesocratic vanguard hardly seems relevant to the Venezuela that would be.

INDEX